Blender for Digital Artists

Sham Tickoo
Professor
Purdue University Northwest
Hammond, Indiana, USA

Contributing Authors
Arti Deshpande
Sr. Digital Artist
Tickoo Institute of Emerging Technologies(TIET)

CADCIM Technologies, USA

Tickoo Institute of Emerging Technologies (TIET), India

BPB PUBLICATIONS

ISBN: 978-93-88176-26-2
(For distribution in SAARC countries only)

Limits of Liability and Disclaimer of Warranty

Distributors

BPB PUBLICATIONS
20, Ansari Road, Darya Ganj
New Delhi-110002
Ph: 23254990/23254991

DECCAN AGENCIES
4-3-329, Bank Street
HYDERABAD-500195
Ph: 24756967/24756400

MICRO MEDIA
Shop No. 5, Mahendra Chambers
150 DN Rd. Next to Capital Cinema
V.T (C.S.T.) Station
MUMBAI-400001
Ph: 22078296/22078297

BPB BOOK CENTRE
376 Old Lajpat Rai Market
DELHI-110006
Ph: 23861747

COMPUTER BOOK CENTRE
12, Shrungar Shopping Centre
M.G. Road
BENGALURU–560001
Ph: 25587923/25584641

Published by Manish Jain for BPB Publications, 20 Ansari Road, Darya Ganj
New Delhi-110002 and Printed by Repro India Pvt. Ltd, Mumbai

DEDICATION

To teachers, who make it possible to disseminate knowledge to enlighten the young and curious minds of our future generations

To students, who are dedicated to learning new technologies and making the world a better place to live in

THANKS

To employees of CADCIM Technologies and Tickoo Institute of Emerging Technologies (TIET) for their valuable help

Note

If you are a faculty member, you can register by clicking on the following link to access the teaching resources: ***https://www.cadcim.com/Registration.aspx***. The student resources are available at ***https://www.cadcim.com***. We also provide ***Live Virtual Online Training*** on various software packages. For more information, write us at ***sales@cadcim.com***.

Table of Contents

Chapter 8: Lights and Cameras

Chapter 9: Basics of Rigging and Animation

Chapter 10: Rigid Body Dynamics

Chapter 11: Working with Particles

This page is intentionally left blank

Preface

Blender

Blender is a powerful, free open-source 3D computer graphics software used for 3D modeling, sculpting, texturing, and animation. It is also used to composite and edit video and image sequences and in motion graphics. In addition, it has an integrated game engine to set up and edit game logic. This enables game developers, visual effect artists, architects, designers, and visualization specialists to create stunning artwork.

Blender for Digital Artists textbook covers major features of Blender 2.79 in a simple, lucid, and comprehensive manner. Keeping in view the varied requirements of the users, the textbook introduces the basic features of Blender 2.79 and then gradually progresses to cover the advanced features.

This book will help you unleash your creativity, thus helping you create stunning 3D models. The textbook will help the learners transform their imagination into reality with ease. Also, it takes the users through progressive tutorials, numerous illustrations, and ample exercises.

The main features of this textbook are as follows:

- **Tutorial Approach**
  The author has adopted the tutorial point-of-view and the learn-by-doing theme throughout the textbook. About 20 real-world projects have been used as tutorials in the textbook. This enables the readers to relate these tutorials to the real-world models. In addition, there are about 20 exercises based on the real-world projects.

- **Tips and Notes**
  Additional information related to various topics is provided to the users in the form of tips and notes.

- **Learning Objectives**
  The first page of every chapter summarizes the topics that will be covered in that chapter. This will help the users to easily refer to a topic.

- **Self-Evaluation Test, Review Questions, and Exercises**
  Every chapter ends with a Self-Evaluation Test so that the users can assess their knowledge of the chapter. The answers to Self-Evaluation Test are given at the end of the chapter. Also,

the Review Questions and Exercises are given at the end of the chapters and they can be used by the Instructors as test questions and exercises.

- **Heavily Illustrated Text**
  The text in this book is heavily illustrated with about 250 diagrams and screen captures.

Symbols Used in the Textbook

Note
The author has provided additional information to the users about the topic being discussed in the form of notes.

Tip
Special information and techniques are provided in the form of tips that helps in increasing the efficiency of the users.

Formatting Conventions Used in the Textbook

Please refer to the following list for the formatting conventions used in this textbook.

- Names of tools, buttons, panels, and tabs are written in boldface. — Example: The **Translate** tool, the **Object Data** button, the **Transform** panel, the **Tools** tab, and so on.
- Names of dialog boxes, drop-downs, sliders, areas, edit boxes, and check boxes, are written in boldface. — Example: The **Blender User Preferences** dialog box, the **Mode** drop-down, the **Radius** slider, the **Mesh** area, the **Opacity** edit box, **Cyclic** check box, and so on.
- Values entered in sliders are written in boldface. — Example: Enter **10** in the **Radius** slider.
- Names of the files are italicized. — Example: *c02_tut1.blend*

Naming Conventions Used in the Textbook

Tool

If you click on an item in a panel, a command is invoked to create/edit an object or perform some action, then that item is termed as **tool**.

For example:
Translate tool, **Rotate** tool, **Cube** tool
Scale tool, **Bezier** tool, **Armature** tool

Flyout

A flyout is a menu that contains options with similar type of functions. Figure 1 shows the flyout displayed on choosing the Dot button next to the **Color** swatch in the **Surface** panel of **Properties Editor**.

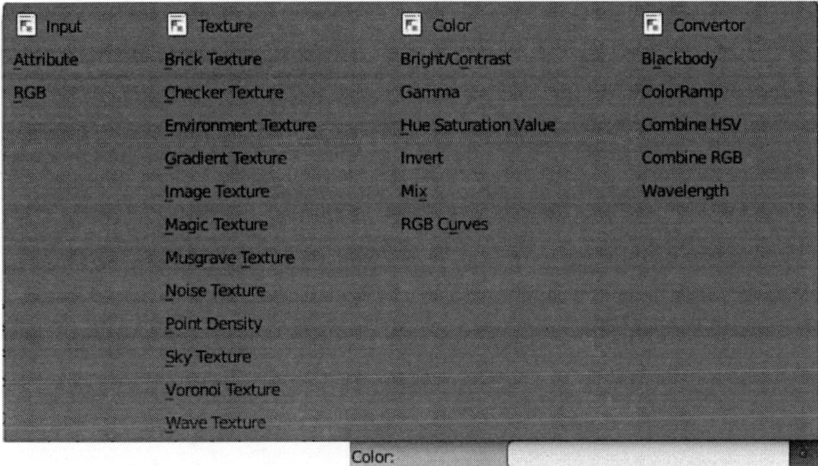

Figure 1 The flyout displayed

Menus

In Blender, the menus provide quick access to the commonly used commands that are related to the current selection of an object. When you hover a cursor in 3D view or Node area and use specific key combinations; a menu will be displayed. Figure 2 shows the menu displayed when you hover the cursor in 3D view and press SHIFT+A. Some of the options in the menu have an arrow on their right side. If you move the mouse on these options, a cascading menu will be displayed, refer to Figure 3.

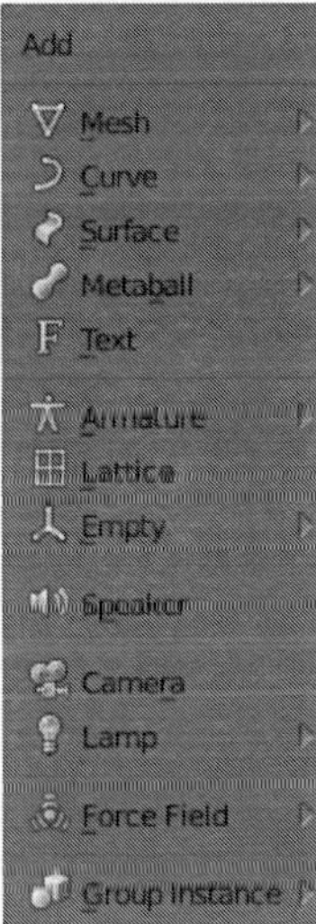

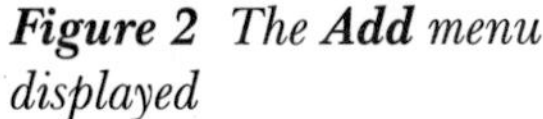

*Figure 2 The **Add** menu displayed*

Figure 3 The cascading menu displayed

Button

The item that has a 3D shape is termed as **Button**. For example, **Object Data** button, **New** button, **Fluid** button, and so on, refer to Figure 4.

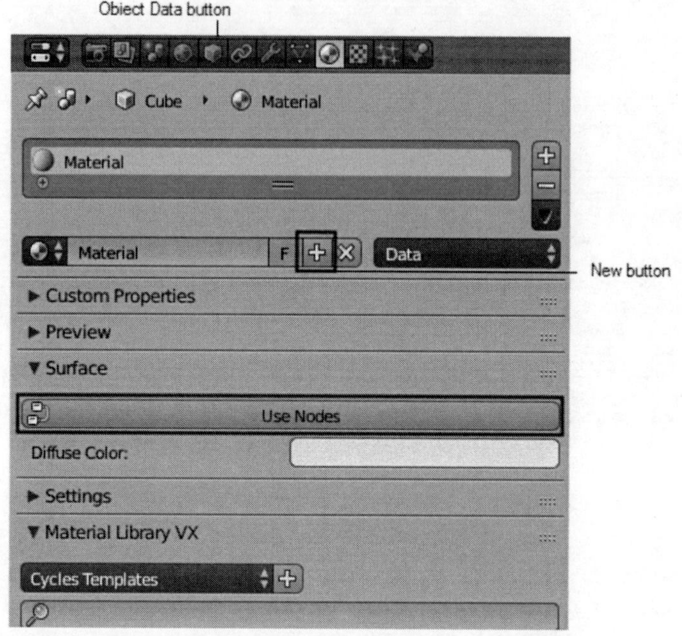

Figure 4** Various buttons in **Properties Editor

Drop-down

A drop-down is the one in which a set of options are grouped together. You can identify a drop-down with two arrows at its right. For example, **Mode** drop-down, **Viewport Shading** drop-down, and so on; refer to Figure 5.

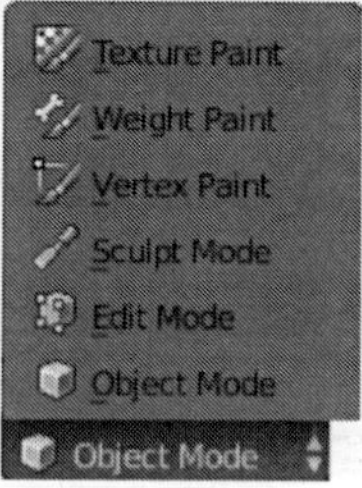

***Figure 5** Choosing an option from the **Mode** drop-down*

Dialog Box

In this textbook, different terms are used for referring to the components of a dialog box. Refer to Figure 6 for the terminology used.

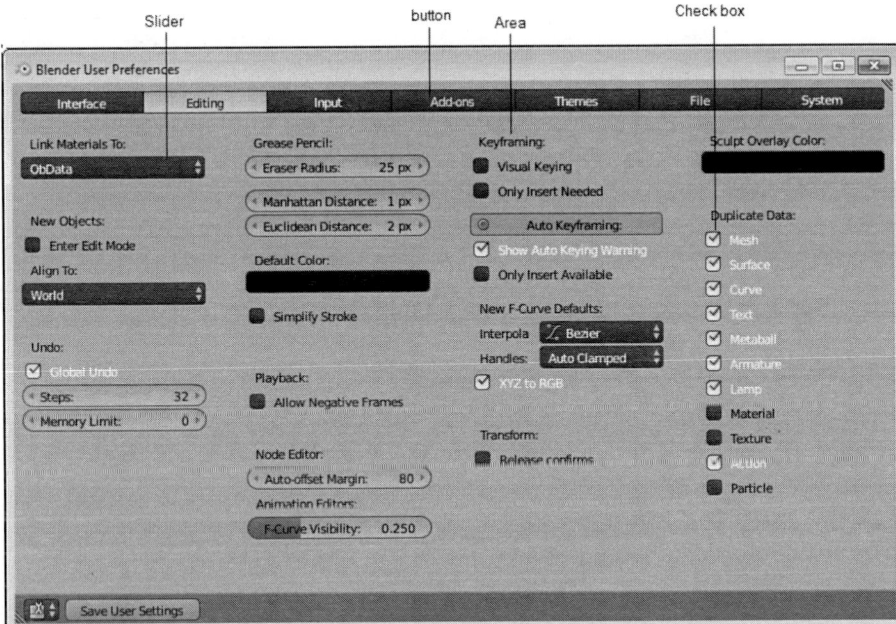

Figure 6 Different components used in a dialog box

Free Companion Website

It has been our constant endeavor to provide you the best textbooks and services at affordable price. In this endeavor, we have come out with a Free Companion Website that will facilitate the process of teaching and learning of Blender 2.79. If you purchase this textbook, you will get access to the files on the Companion website. The following resources are available for faculty and students in this website:

Faculty Resources

- **Technical Support**
  You can get online technical support by contacting *techsupport@cadcim.com.*

- **Instructor Guide**
  Solutions to all the review questions and exercises in the textbook are provided to help the faculty members test the skills of the students.

- **PowerPoint Presentations**
  The contents of the book are arranged in PowerPoint slides that can be used by the faculty for their lectures.

- **Blender Files**
  The Blender files used in illustration, tutorials, and exercises are available for free download.

- **Rendered Images**
  If you do an exercise or tutorial, you can compare your rendered output with the one provided in the CADCIM website.

- **Colored Images**
  You can download the PDF file containing color images of the screenshots used in this textbook from CADCIM website.

Student Resources

- **Technical Support**
  You can get online technical support by contacting *techsupport@cadcim.com.*

- **Blender Files**
  The Blender files used in illustrations and tutorials are available for free download.

- **Rendered Images**
  If you do an exercise or tutorial, you can compare your rendered output with the one provided in the CADCIM website.

- **Colored Images**
  You can download the PDF file containing color images of the screenshots used in this textbook from CADCIM website.

If you face any problem in accessing these files, please contact the publisher at ***sales@cadcim.com*** or the author at ***stickoo@pnw.edu*** or ***tickoo525@gmail.com***.

Stay Connected

You can now stay connected with us through Facebook and Twitter to get the latest information about our textbooks, videos, and teaching/learning resources. To stay informed of such updates, follow us on Facebook ***(www.facebook.com/cadcim)*** and Twitter (***@cadcimtech***). You can also subscribe to our YouTube channel ***(www.youtube.com/cadcimtech)*** to get the information about our latest video tutorials.

Chapter 1

Introduction to Blender Interface

Learning Objectives

After completing this chapter, you will be able to:

- *Understand the Blender interface components*
- *Use controls for creating or modifying objects*
- *Use hotkeys in Blender*
- *Customize the Blender layout*
- *Customize the colors of the scene components*

INTRODUCTION

Blender, developed by Blender Foundation - a Dutch non-profit public benefit corporation, is a free and open source application that is used to create still or animated 3D scenes. This application helps you to create realistic scenes by creating and modifying objects, applying textures and materials to a scene, adding lights and cameras, creating animation, and so on. You can composite and edit video sequence and image sequences as well as set up and edit game logic in Blender. Before working with Blender, you should have the basic knowledge of various tools and commands available in this software. In this chapter, you will learn the basic features of Blender.

GETTING STARTED With Blender 2.79

First, install Blender 2.79 on your system. Next, start Blender 2.79 from the taskbar. To do so, choose **Start > All Programs > Blender > blender** from the taskbar, refer to Figure 1-1.

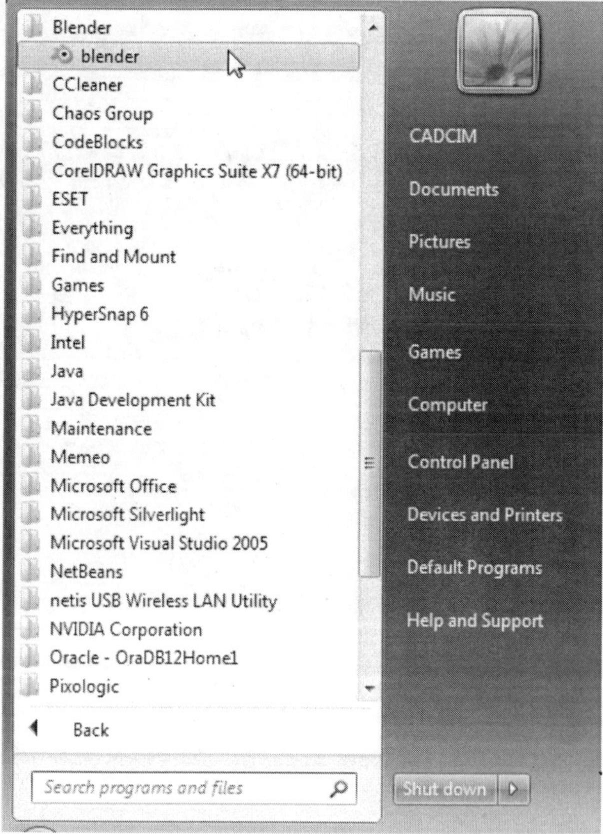

Figure 1-1 *Starting Blender 2.79 using the taskbar*

The system will prepare to start Blender 2.79 by loading all the required files. Once Blender 2.79 starts, the **Blender 2.79** splash screen will be displayed, as shown in Figure 1-2. This splash screen has various links to blender websites and a list of recent files. You can also recover the last session using this splash screen and change the type of interaction mode using the **Interaction** drop-down which has three types of interaction modes: **Blender**, **3ds Max**, and **Maya**. By default,

Blender is chosen in this drop-down. Click anywhere outside the splash screen or press ESC; the splash screen disappears. Now, you can start working in Blender. To display the splash screen again, choose **Help > Splash Screen** from the **Info Editor** menu bar.

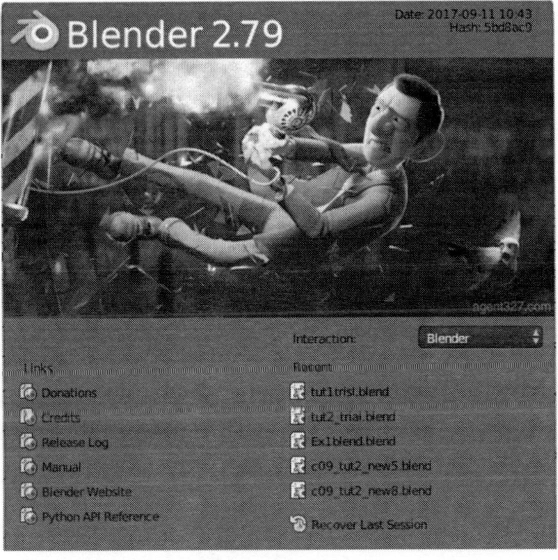

***Figure 1-2** The **Blender 2.79** splash screen*

STARTUP FILE IN Blender 2.79

When you install Blender 2.79, a default startup file is included in it. This default startup file displays a cube on the screen along with a 3D Cursor, Grid Floor, a camera, and a lamp.

To load the startup file, press CTRL+N or choose **File > New** from the **Info Editor** menu bar; a menu will be displayed, as shown in Figure 1-3. Choose **Reload Start-Up File**; the menu will disappear and the startup file will be loaded. You can customize a startup file as per your requirement and save it by choosing **File > Save Startup File** from the **Info Editor** menu bar. Alternatively, you can press CTRL+U to save the customized startup file.

***Figure 1-3** The menu displayed*

Note

*When you choose the **Reload Start-Up File** option from the menu, the current scene is not saved and you will loose all the unsaved work.*

BLENDER INTERFACE COMPONENTS

The Blender interface mainly consists of five components: **Info Editor**, **3D View Editor**, **Outliner**, **Properties Editor**, and **Timeline**, as shown in Figure 1-4. These components are discussed next.

Info Editor

Info Editor is located below the title bar of the Blender interface, refer to Figure 1-4. It consists of components: the **Editor Type** drop-down, the **Info Editor** menu bar, the **Screen Layout**

drop-down, the **Scene** drop-down, the **Engine** drop-down, and version information, refer to Figure 1-5. The components of **Info Editor** are discussed next.

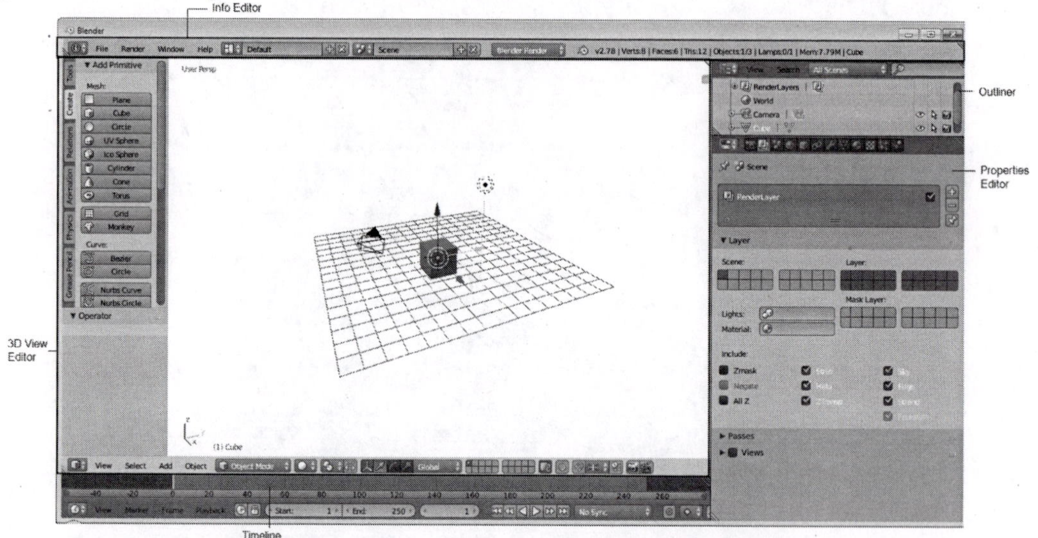

***Figure 1-4** Five different components of Blender interface*

Figure 1-5** The **Info Editor

Editor Type Drop-down

The **Editor Type** drop-down is available for all editors in Blender. It consists of a list of all the editors, as shown in Figure 1-6. You can switch to any of the editors by choosing an option from the **Editor Type** drop-down. You can also open the same editor multiple times in the interface.

Info Editor Menu Bar

The **Info Editor** menu bar consists of the **File**, **Render**, **Window**, and **Help** menus. The options in the **File** menu are used to create a new file, open and save existing file, save the customized startup file, and recover the last session. It also contains options for importing and exporting files, linking other Blender files, working with external data, and so on.

Screen Layout Drop-down

The **Screen Layout** drop-down is located next to the **Info Editor** menu bar. Click on the icon of the drop-down to view the available layouts, refer to Figure 1-7. To add a customized screen layout, adjust the Blender interface as desired. Next, click on the **+** sign in the drop-down and enter a desired name for the layout in the drop-down field. To remove any of the layouts, choose the layout from the drop-down and click on the **X** sign on the drop-down. To switch between different layouts, place the cursor on the drop-down and press CTRL+RIGHT ARROW key or CTRL+LEFT ARROW key.

Note

Once you switch over to a different layout, the last scene saved for that layout will be displayed in the view.

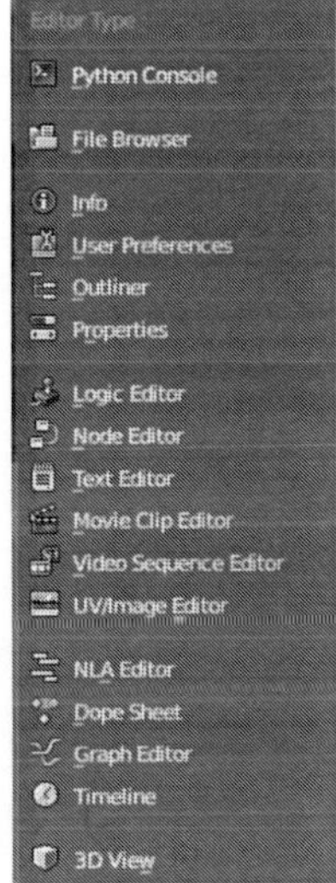

Figure 1-6 *The **Editor Type** drop-down*

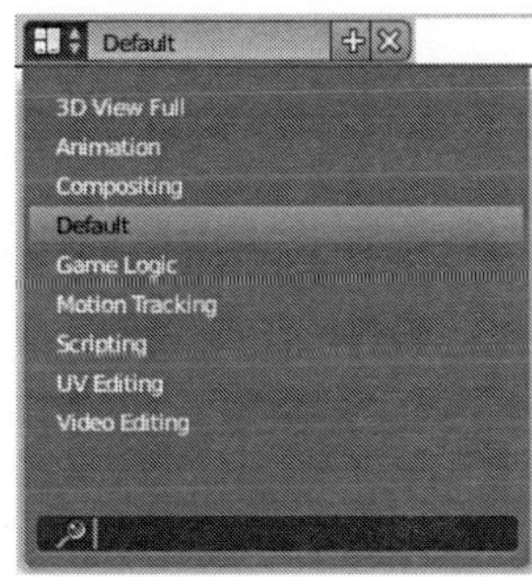

Figure 1-7 *The **Screen Layout** drop-down*

Scene Drop-down

The **Scene** drop-down is used to save and use different scenes. By default, only default startup scene is loaded when you launch Blender. To add a scene to the drop-down, create a new scene and then click on the **+** sign on the drop-down and enter a desired name for the scene in the drop-down field. To remove any of the layouts, choose the scene from the drop-down and click on the **X** sign of the drop-down. To choose a scene from the drop-down, click on the icon to view the saved scenes and then choose the desired scene.

Engine Drop-down

The **Engine** drop-down is used to choose the Blender engine for rendering, refer to Figure 1-8.

Figure 1-8 *The **Engine** drop-down*

3D View Editor

3D View Editor consumes most of the space in the default Blender interface, refer to Figure 1-4. It consists of the following components: the **Editor Type** drop-down, the **3D View Editor** menu bar, view, **Toolshelf**, the **Mode** drop-down, **Properties Region**, and other miscellaneous tools, as shown in Figure 1-9. The components of **3D View Editor** are discussed next.

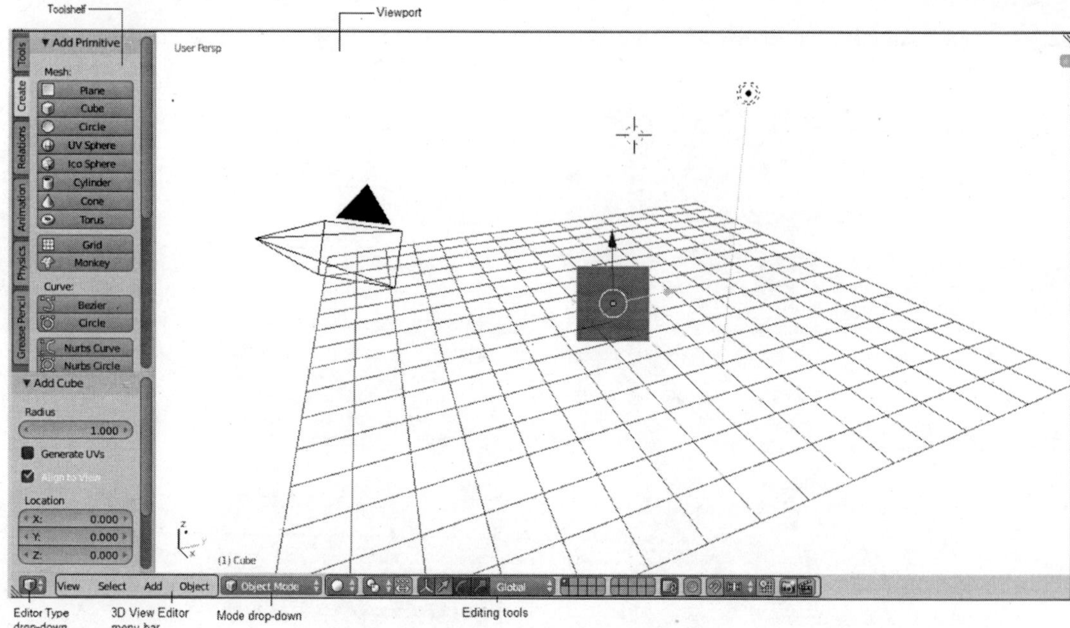

Figure 1-9 The 3D View Editor

3D View Editor Menu Bar

The default menus in the **3D View Editor** menu bar are **View**, **Select**, **Add**, and **Object**, refer to Figure 1-9. These menus vary depending on the mode chosen from the **Mode** drop-down. The options in these menus are used to create or modify the objects as per the mode chosen from the **Mode** drop-down.

Toolshelf

It consists of six tabs: **Tools**, **Create**, **Relations**, **Animation**, **Physics**, and **Grease Pencil**. When you choose a tab, corresponding panels are displayed on the right of these tabs. For example, if you choose the **Tools** tab, the panels displayed are **Transform**, **Edit**, and **History**. You can collapse and expand these panels by clicking on the arrow on the left of these panels. The tools in these panels are used to create and modify the objects in the scene.

Properties Region

Properties Region of **3D View Editor** is not displayed by default in the Blender interface. To display it, press N or place the cursor on the square with a + sign located at the upper right corner of the view and drag the cursor to the left.

It consists of various panels such as **Grease Pencil**, **3D Cursor**, **Display**, **Shading**, **Background Images**, and so on, refer to Figure 1-10. All these panels comprise of parameters to change the properties of the selected object and **3D View Editor**.

Note

Properties Region *is also available for some other editors such as the* ***Graph Editor***, ***UV/Image Editor***, ***Movie Clip Editor***, *and so on.*

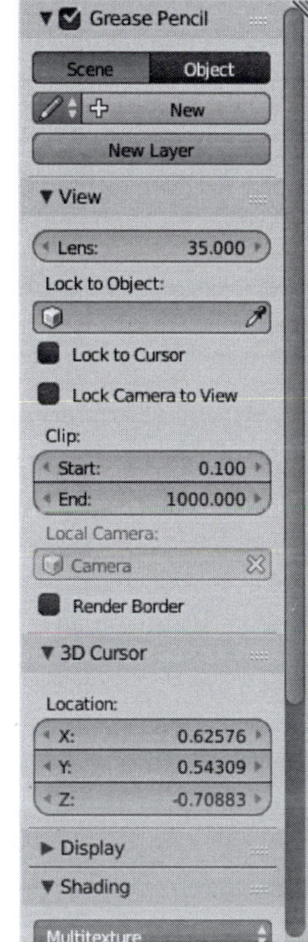

Figure 1-10 The ***Properties*** *Region*

View

The default Blender interface consists of a view at the center. This view is labeled as User Persp. By default, view consists of a cube at the origin, 3D Cursor, camera, lamp, axes tripod, and a grid floor, as shown in Figure 1-11. The axes tripod has three axes, X, Y, and Z which are displayed in red, green, and blue colors, respectively. The view is used to create 3D scenes. Also, it enables you to view a scene from different angles.

You can split the view into a number of small views as per your requirement, refer to Figure 1-12. The procedure to split the view is explained in the **Customizing the Blender layout** section later in the chapter. You can modify the size of the view by dragging the border of the view. After splitting the 3D view, you can change split views to Top Persp, Front Persp, Right Persp, Top Ortho, and so on. You can do so by choosing an option from the **View** menu of the **3D View Editor** menu bar, as shown in Figure 1-13. You can also use hot keys to change the views. These keys are mentioned in the **Hot Keys** section later in the chapter.

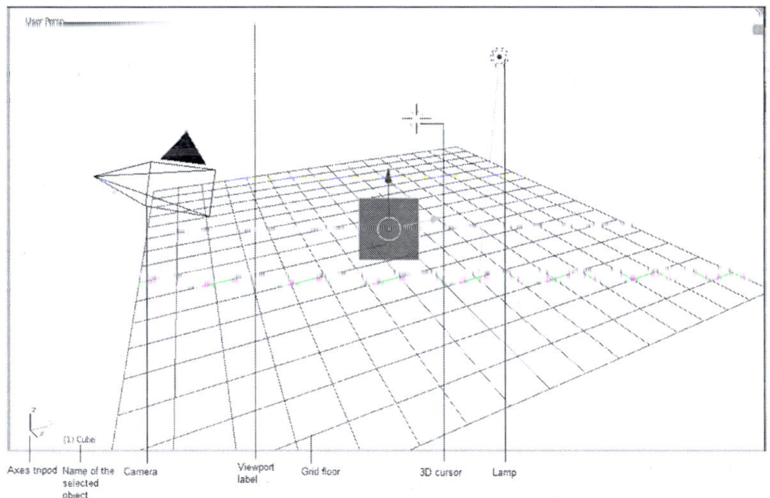

Figure 1-11 The view components

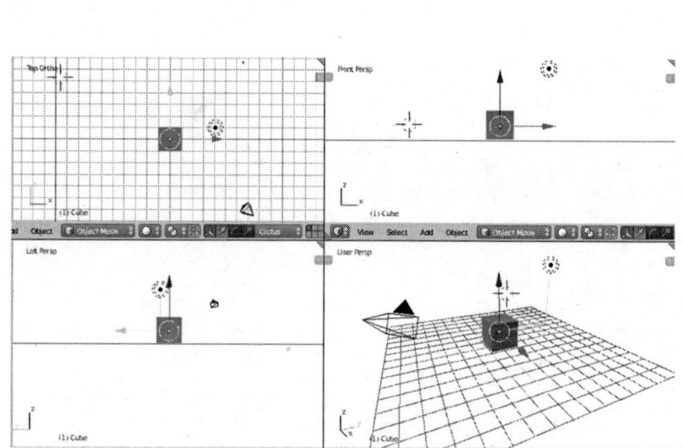

Figure 1-12 The four views

Figure 1-13 *The **View** menu*

Note

*Each view in Blender has its own **ToolShelf**. To save the screen space, you can collapse the shelves. To do so, drag the boundary of the shelf towards left until the shelf disappears and a **+** sign appears on the view. To expand the shelf, click on the **+** sign.*

You can also change 3D View to a quad view. To do so, choose **Toggle Quad View** from the **View** menu or hover the cursor in the view and press CTRL+ALT+Q. To maximize the displayed view area, press Alt+F10. In this mode, only views are displayed and no corresponding shelf, header, or panels are available. Press ALT+F10 again to restore.

Note

*If you want to toggle minimized view area with **ToolShelf**, press CTRL+UP ARROW.*

3D Cursor

3D Cursor is a point on the view, refer to Figure 1-11. When you create a new object, it will always be at the location of the 3D cursor. To place the 3D cursor at a specific point, you need to left-click at that point or change the values in the **Location** area of the **3D Cursor** panel in **Properties Region**, refer to Figure 1-10. By default, 3D Cursor is located at the center of the grid.

To snap the 3D cursor to the selected object, to the center of the grid, or to the nearest point on the grid, choose **Object > Snap** from the **3D View Editor** menu bar and then choose the desired option from the cascading menu displayed. To restore 3D Cursor to the center of the grid, press SHIFT+C.

Mode Drop-down

The **Mode** drop-down is located next to the **3D View Editor** menu bar, refer to Figure 1-9. This is the most frequently used drop-down of the Blender interface. The modes in this drop-down are shown in Figure 1-14 and are discussed next.

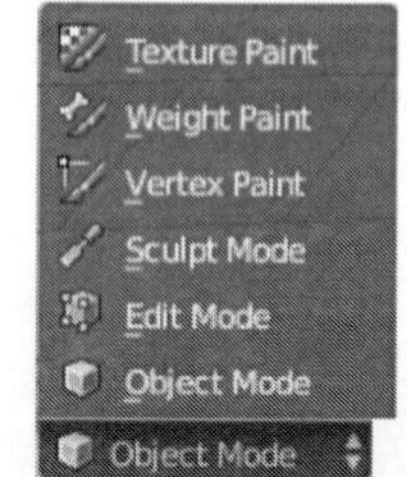

***Figure 1-14** The **Mode** drop-down*

Object Mode
The **Object Mode** option is the default mode chosen in the **Mode** drop-down. This mode is used to create various types of objects such as primitives, curves, surfaces, and so on in the scene. This mode should be active if you intend to select objects in the scene.

Edit Mode
The **Edit Mode** option is used to modify the objects in the scene. If **Object Mode** is chosen, place the cursor at any place in the view and press the TAB key to choose **Edit Mode**. On choosing **Edit Mode**, the menus in the **3D View Editor** menu bar, tabs and panels in **Toolshelf**, and some miscellaneous tools in **3D View Editor** change. Various tools and options in this mode are used to modify the objects in the scene.

Sculpt Mode
The **Sculpt Mode** option is used to modify the object using brush. Once you choose this option, a red circle is attached along with the cursor. This circle specifies the size of the brush. You can change the properties of the brush such as size, strength, smoothness, and so on using the panels in **Toolshelf**.

Vertex Paint Mode
The **Vertex Paint** option is used to paint vertices of an object using brush. On choosing this option, a red circle is attached along with the cursor. To paint the vertices, drag the cursor on the specific area of the object. On doing so, a single color stroke is applied. You can use different colors to mark different vertex groups.

Weight Paint Mode
The **Weight Paint** option is mainly useful in rigging. This mode is similar to the **Vertex Paint** option with the only difference that the weight brush is used in the **Weight Paint** mode. On choosing the **Weight Paint** option, a red circle is attached along with the cursor. You can change the properties of the brush such as size, weight, strength, blending mode, stroke, and so on using the panels in **ToolShelf**.

To apply weight, paint the strokes on the object. On doing so, color gradient will appear on the surface of the object which visualizes the strength of the weight applied. The color range appears from blue to red. The blue color represents 0 weighted area whereas the red color represents fully weighted area.

Note

To customize the color gradient, choose ***File > User Preferences*** *from the* ***Info Editor*** *menu bar; the* ***Blender User Preferences*** *dialog box will be displayed. In this dialog box, select the* ***Custom Weight Paint Range*** *check box from the* ***Color Picker Type*** *area in the* ***Systems*** *tab. Click on the* + *icon to create a new color stop for the gradient and then click on the color swatch to assign a color to the color stop. If you want to remove a stop, first select it and then click the* - *icon.*

Texture Paint Mode
The **Texture Paint** option is used to edit UV textures and images in **3D View Editor** or the **UV/Image Editor**. In this mode, you need to unwrap the mesh first to paint on a mesh. If you are using the **UV/Image Editor** to texture paint the mesh, you need to choose the **Paint** option from the **Mode** drop-down of **UV/Image Editor**.

Outliner

Outliner is located at the top right corner of the interface, refer to Figure 1-4. It consists of the following components: the **Editor Type** drop-down, the **Outliner** menu bar, the **Display** drop-down, the **Search** field, and a list of objects in the current scene, refer to Figure 1-15. The components of **Outliner** are discussed next.

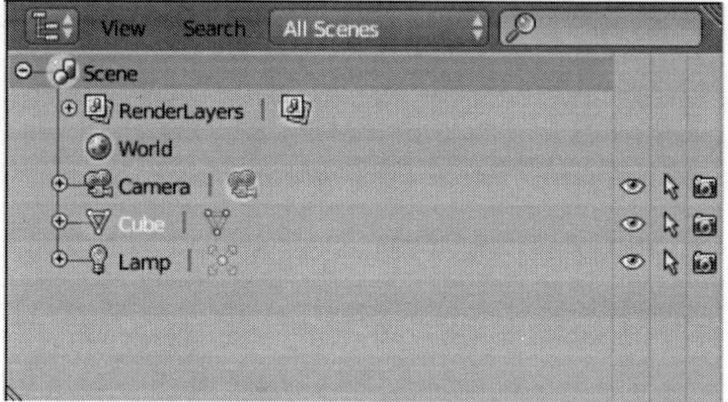

Figure 1-15 *The* ***Outliner***

Outliner Menu Bar

There are two menus in the **Outliner** menu bar: **View** and **Search**. The options in the **View** menu are used to perform various operations, such as alphabetical sorting or showing of active object on the objects listed in **Outliner**. You can also change the size of **Outliner** using the options in this menu. The options in the **Search** menu allow you to set criteria for search results. You can perform a case-sensitive search or complete match search.

Display Drop-down

The **Display** drop-down is used to filter the objects listed in **Outliner**. The options in the **Display** drop-down are shown in Figure 1-16. By default, **All Scenes** is chosen in this drop-down. As a result, the objects in all the scenes are visible in **Outliner**. Similarly, if you choose **Selected** from this drop-down, the objects selected in the scene will only be listed in **Outliner**.

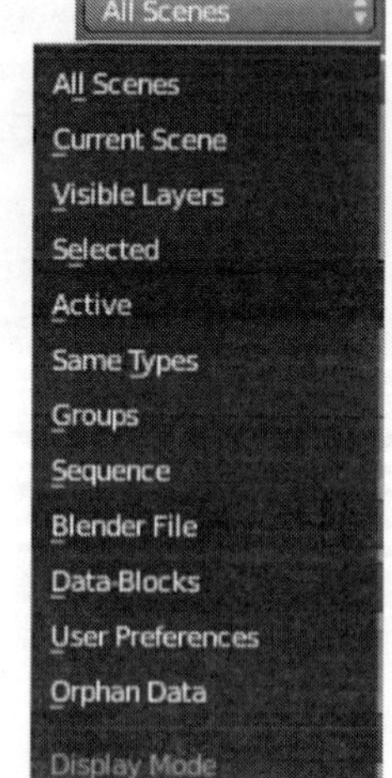

Figure 1-16 *The* ***Display*** *drop-down*

Search Field

The **Search** field is used to find an object from the list in **Outliner**. This field is helpful when there are large number of objects in a complex scene. Enter whole or partial name of the object to find it in **Outliner**.

Properties Editor

Properties Editor is located below **Outliner** in the interface, refer to Figure 1-4. It consists of the **Editor Type** drop-down, various buttons such as **Render**, **Render layers**, **Object Constraints** as well as **Object Modifiers**, **Material**, **Physics**, and so on, refer to Figure 1-17. When you choose any of these buttons, related panels are displayed below these buttons in **Properties Editor**. These panels consist of various parameters to change the properties of the selected object.

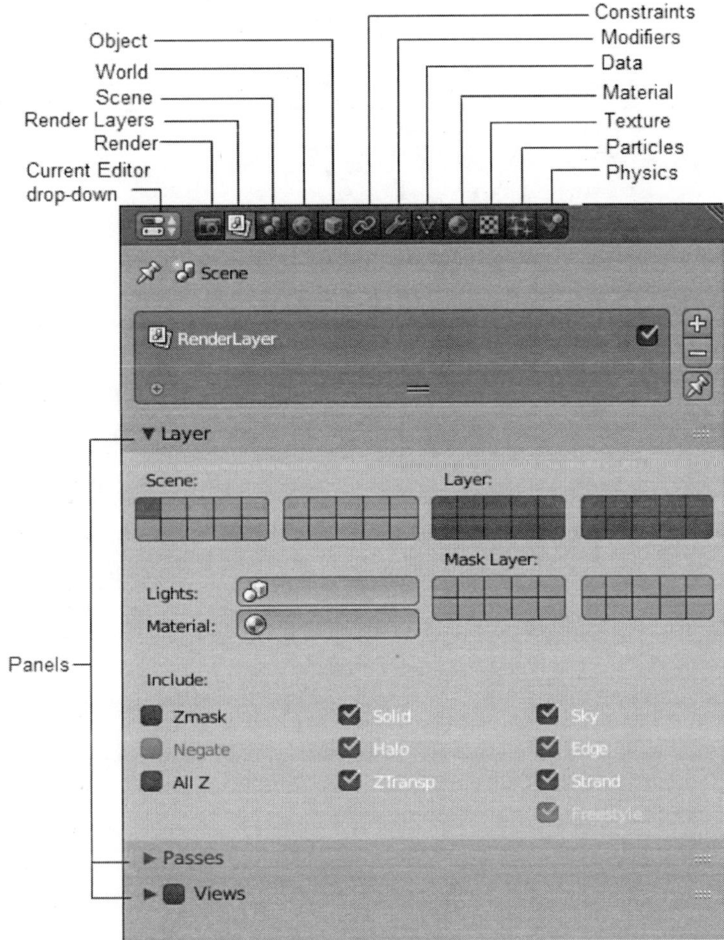

*Figure 1-17 The **Properties Editor***

Timeline

Timeline is located at the bottom in the interface. It consists of the following components: **Editor Type** drop-down, track bar, time slider, the **Timeline** menu bar, the **Sync** drop-down, and various buttons to setup animation in the scene, refer to Figure 1-18.

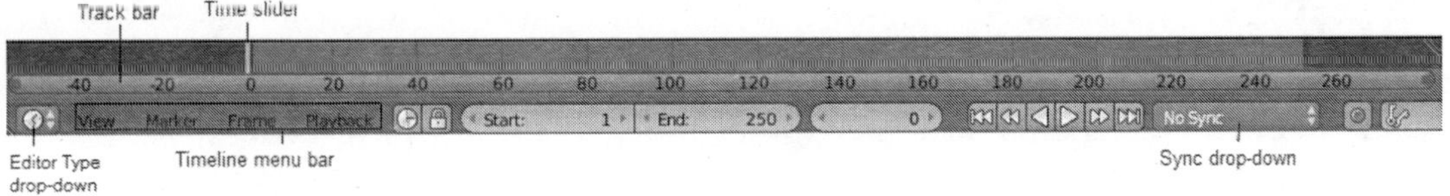

*Figure 1-18 The **Timeline***

File Browser

The **File Browser** is one of the unique features of Blender. You can open the **File Browser** by choosing **File > Open** from the **Info Editor** menu bar. Alternatively, press CTRL+O or F1 to open the **File Browser**. To switch back to the main interface, choose the **Back to Previous** button available on the right of the **Info Editor** menu bar, refer to Figure 1-19.

Figure 1-19** The **File Browser

It consists of various components such as the **Editor Type** drop-down, the **File Browser** menu bar, and the **File Browser** toolbar. Below the toolbar, there are two panes. The left pane comprises of various panels that are used to select drives, manage system bookmarks, create custom bookmarks, and so on. The right pane shows the folder structure of the drive.

The **File Browser** toolbar has various types of buttons that are used to navigate to various folders and files, sort the files, display specific types of files, search files in the right pane, and so on.

Other Editors

Blender has a number of other editors such as **Text Editor**, **Node Editor**, **Video Sequence Editor**, and so on. By default, these editors are not displayed in Blender interface. To display any of these editors, click on the **Editor Type** drop-down of any editor and then choose the desired editor from the list displayed. These editors are discussed next.

Text Editor

Text Editor is used to write and execute the script. It is also used to add text to the scene, load text from the external file to the scene, and to edit the existing text in the scene. You can open **Text Editor** by choosing the **Text Editor** option from the **Editor Type** drop-down of any of the main editors discussed above. Alternatively, press SHIFT + F11 to open **Text Editor**. It consists of the following components: the **Text** area, the **Editor Type** drop-down, the **Text Editor** menu bar, the **Text link** drop-down, the **Create Text Block** button, the **Open Text Block** button, the **Run Script** button, and text editing features, refer to Figure 1-20.

When you choose the **Create Text Block** button to add text to the scene for the first time, the **Create Text Block** button changes to the **Text Block** drop-down. The **Register** check box, the **Run Script** button, and two menus: **Edit** and **Format** are also added to the **Text Editor** menu bar.

As you enter text to create a new text block or select a text block from the external file using the **Open Text Block** button, the text appears in the **Text** area. You can then edit the whole or partial text by selecting it from the **Text** area. You can enter the name for the newly created text block in the **Text Block** drop-down. To add a new text block, click on the **+** sign. Similarly, to remove the existing text block, choose the text block from the **Text Block** drop-down and then click on the **X** sign available on the left of the **Text Block** drop-down.

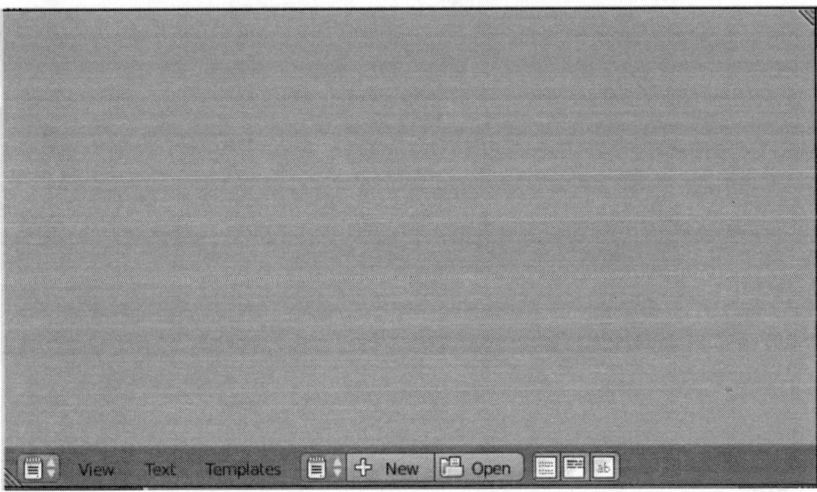

Figure 1-20** The **Text Editor

Graph Editor

Graph Editor is an animation editor. It consists of the **Editor Type** drop-down, the **Graph Editor** menu bar, the **Curve Editor** area, and some miscellaneous tools for modifying the animation in the scene, refer to Figure 1-21.

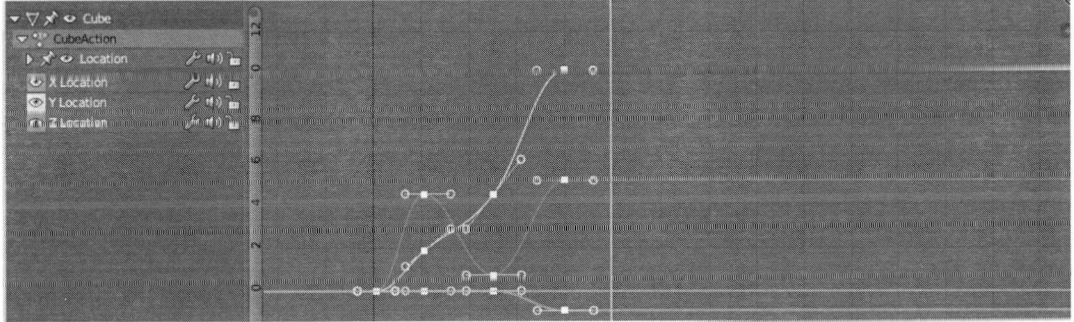

Figure 1-21** The **Graph Editor

Video Sequence Editor

Video Sequence Editor is one of the unique editors in Blender, refer to Figure 1-22. As the name suggests, this editor is used to combine and edit multiple video clips, add transition effects in between them, add audio, and synchronize the timing of the video sequence.

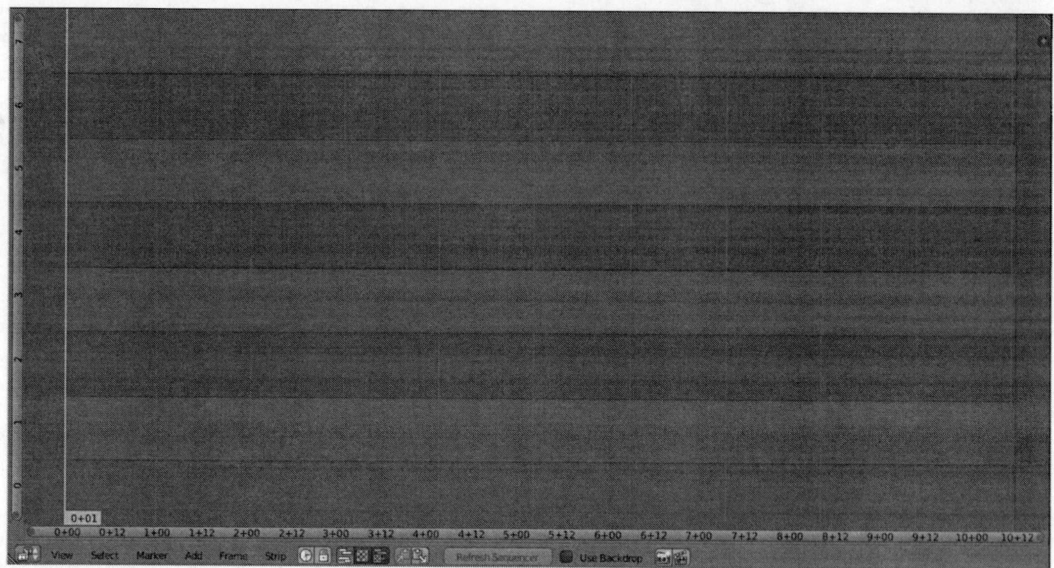

Figure 1-22 The Video Sequence Editor

Movie Clip Editor

Movie Clip Editor is used to track and mask the movies. You can also track and mask image sequences using the **Movie Clip Editor**, provided the names of the images are sequential. As you open a clip, some panels such as **Objects**, **Track**, **Plane Track**, and so on are added to this editor. Figure 1-23 shows **Movie Clip Editor**.

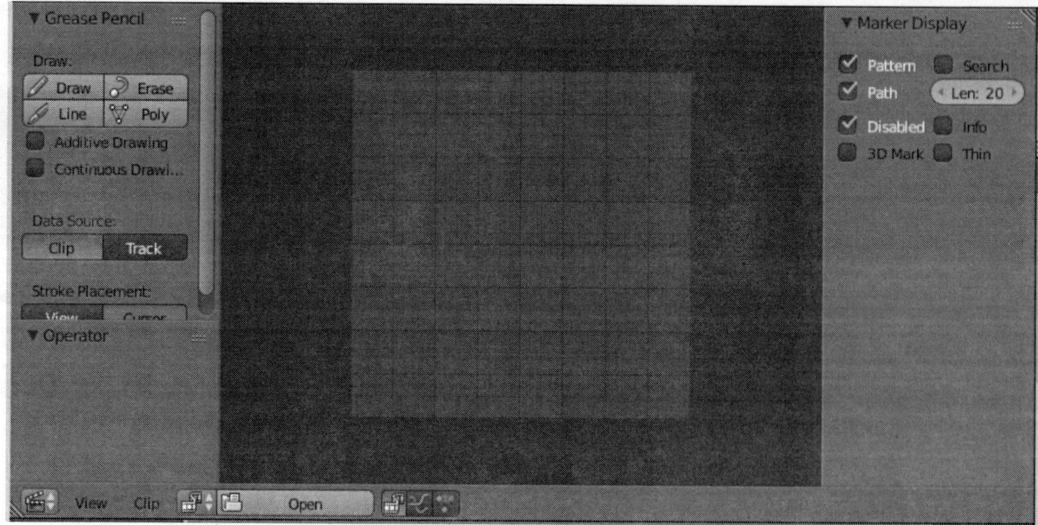

Figure 1-23 The Movie Clip Editor

Dope Sheet

Dope Sheet is also an animation editor. This editor uses four modes: **Dope Sheet, Action Editor, Shape Key Editor**, and **Grease Pencil**. The **Dope Sheet** mode is used to simultaneously edit multiple actions. The **Action Editor** mode is used to define new action and control existing actions. The **Grease Pencil** mode is used to edit keyframes of grease pencil tool. Figure 1-24 shows **Dope Sheet**.

*Figure 1-24 The **Dope Sheet***

NLA EDITOR

NLA (Non-Linear Animation) **Editor** is used to change actions without keyframe manipulation, refer to Figure 1-25. You can use it to make broad changes in the animation with relative ease as it supports layered actions.

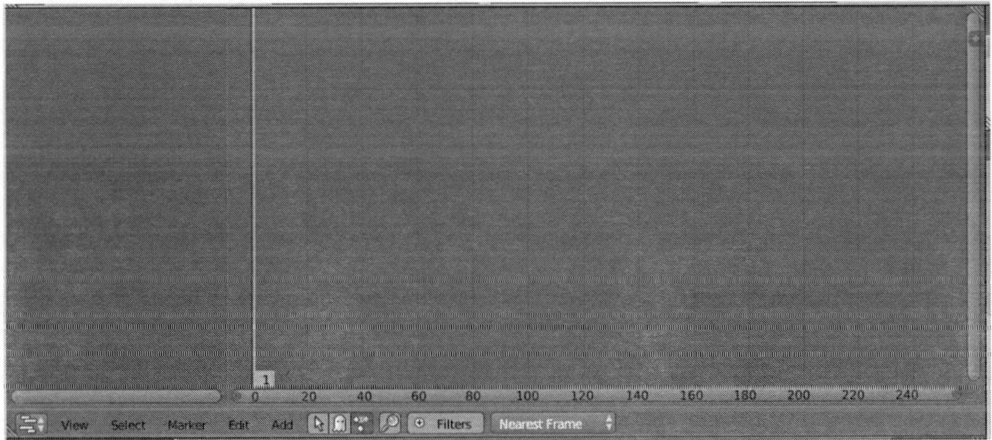

*Figure 1-25 The **NLA Editor***

Logic Editor

Logic Editor is used to set up a game logic and edit the same for objects in the scene, refer to Figure 1-26.

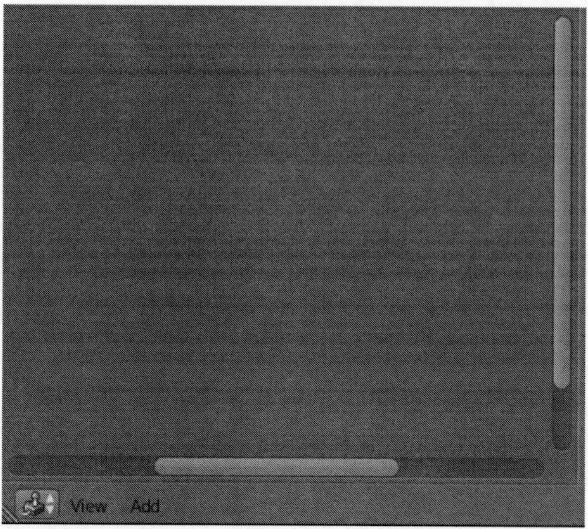

Figure 1-26 The ***Logic Editor***

Node Editor

In Blender, you can use various types of node trees such as material node tree, texture node tree, and composite node tree to modify materials, textures, and to composite scenes. **Node Editor** is used to work with all these node trees, refer to Figure 1-27.

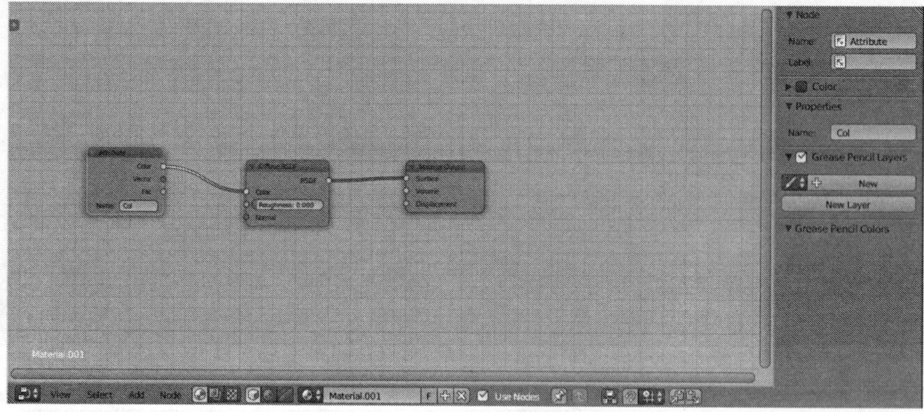

Figure 1-27 The ***Node Editor***

UV/Image Editor

UV/Image Editor is used to edit textures of an object, external images used for texturing the object, and the UVs. You can also use **UV/Image Editor** to texture paint the mesh in the **Texture Paint** mode. Figure 1-28 shows **UV/Image Editor**.

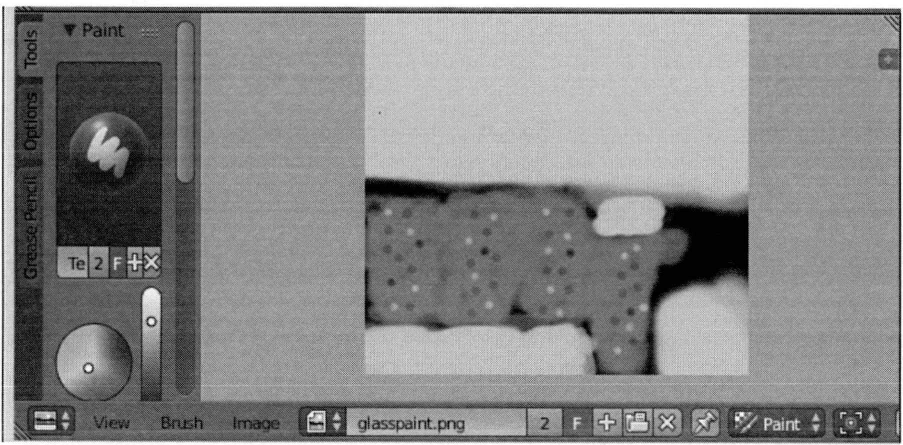

Figure 1-28 The ***UV/Image Editor***

CUSTOMIZING THE BLENDER LAYOUT

You can customize the Blender layout as per your requirement in the following ways:

1. Place the cursor on the boundary of any of the editors or its components. On doing so, a cursor changes into a double headed arrow. Drag the cursor to resize the editors or its components, refer to Figure 1-29.

2. Hover the cursor on the splitter widget, refer to Figure 1-30. When the double headed arrow appears, right-click on it; a menu will be displayed, as shown in Figure 1-31.

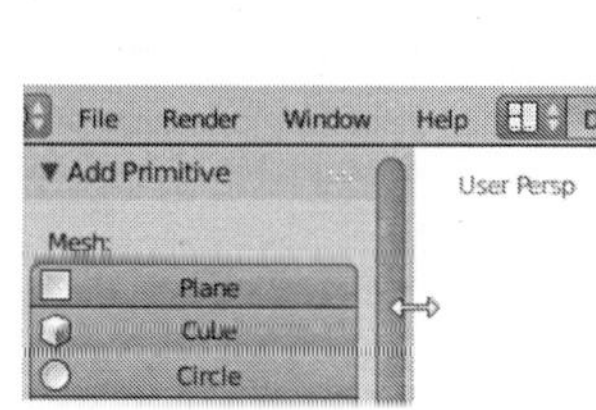

Figure 1-29 Resizing the editors

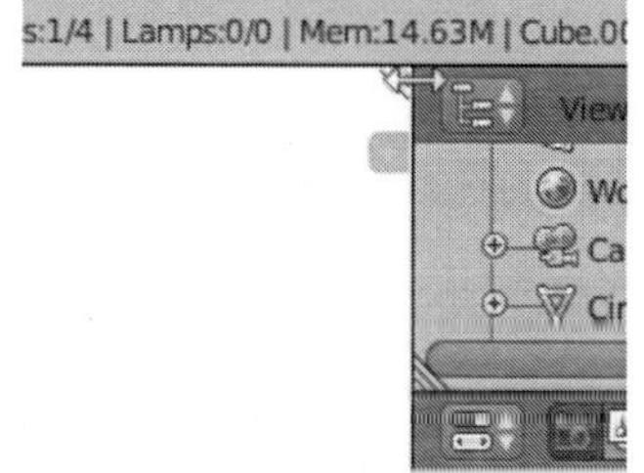

Figure 1-30 Double-headed arrow on the splitter widget

3. To split the editor, choose **Split Area** from the menu; a line will be attached with the double headed arrow. Move the double headed arrow with the attached line to a point where you want to split the editor, refer to Figure 1-32 and then click.

Figure 1-31 The menu displayed

Note

If the double headed arrow is horizontal, the editor will split horizontally and if the double headed arrow is vertical, the editor will split vertically.

4. To join the two split editors, right-click on the common border of the editors to be joined; a menu will be displayed, as shown in Figure 1-31. Choose **Join Area** from this menu and hover the cursor on one of the editors; an arrow will be displayed at the center of that editor and its color turns grey, as shown in Figure 1-33. Now, click on this editor to join it with the other editor.

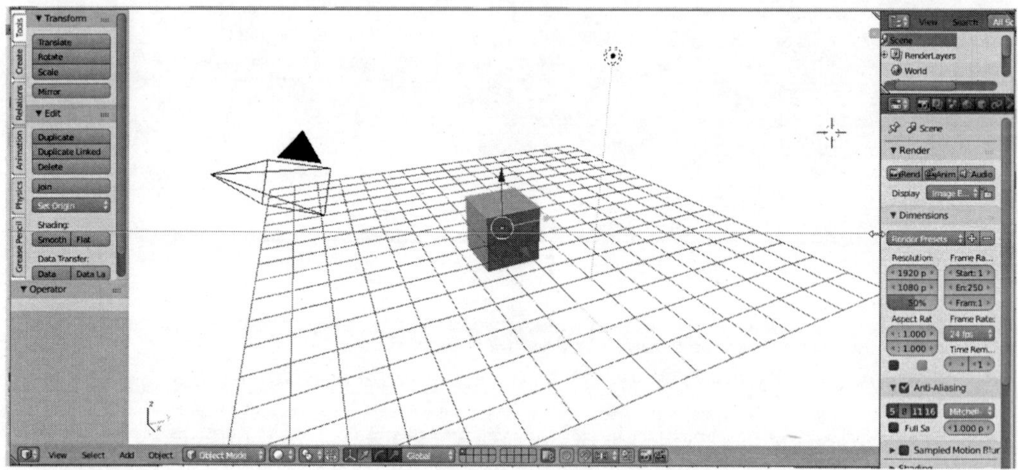

Figure 1-32 *Splitting the editor*

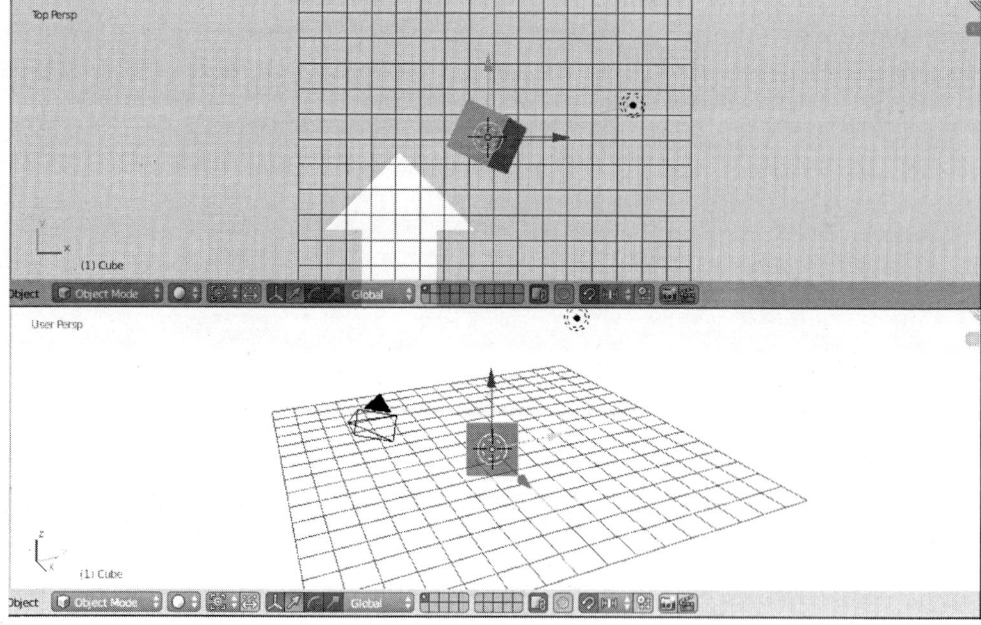

Figure 1-33 *Joining the editors*

UNDO AND REDO TOOLS

To undo an action, press CTRL+Z. You need to press CTRL+Z repeatedly till all the previously performed actions are reversed. By default, you can reverse your actions up to 32 times. If you want to change this number, choose **File > User Preferences** from the **Info Editor** menu bar;

the **Blender User Preferences** dialog box will be displayed. Choose the **Editing** button in this dialog box. In the **Undo** area, set the new value in the **Steps** slider, refer to Figure 1-34.

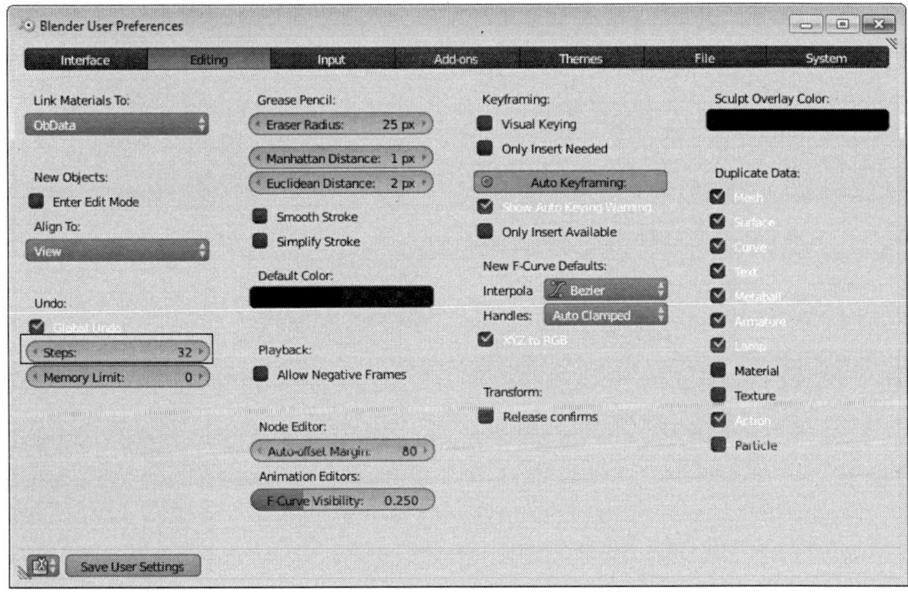

***Figure 1-34** The **Blender User Preferences** dialog box*

To reverse back the last undo action, press CTRL+SHIFT+Z. Similarly, to repeat the last action, press SHIFT+R.

To access the history of the commands, press CTRL+ALT+Z; the **Undo History** menu will be displayed. Figure 1-35 shows a scene and Figure 1-36 shows the **Undo History** menu for this scene. This menu displays the actions performed in the scene.

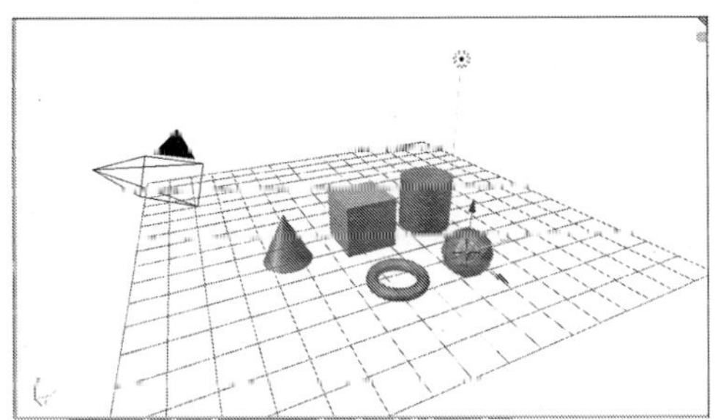

***Figure 1-35** The scene displayed*

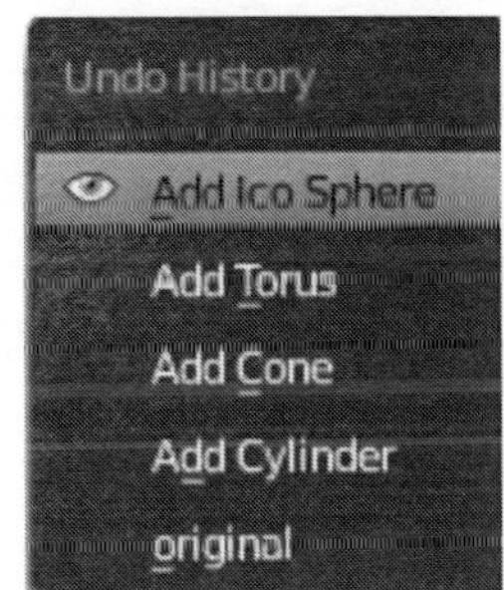

***Figure 1-36** The **Undo History** menu*

For example, if you choose **Add Cone** from this menu, the actions performed after the **Add Cone** in the menu will be reversed back and a modified scene will be displayed, as shown in Figure 1-37. Also, an eye icon will be shifted prior to **Add Cone** in the menu. Now, when you perform a new action in the scene, the actions performed after **Add Cone** will be deleted from the menu, as shown in Figure 1-38.

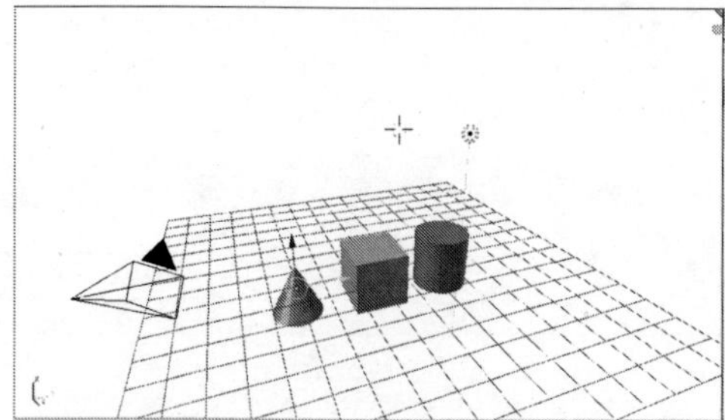

Figure 1-37 The modified scene

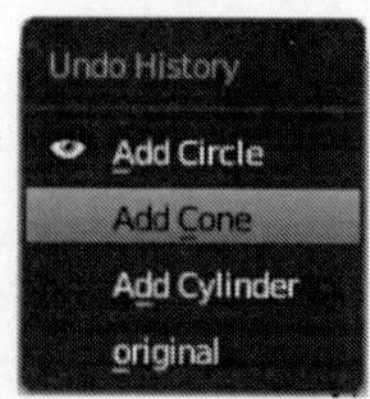

Figure 1-38 The modified menu

To repeat history, press F3; the **Repeat History** menu will be displayed, refer to Figure 1-39. You can select an action to repeat by choosing it from this menu.

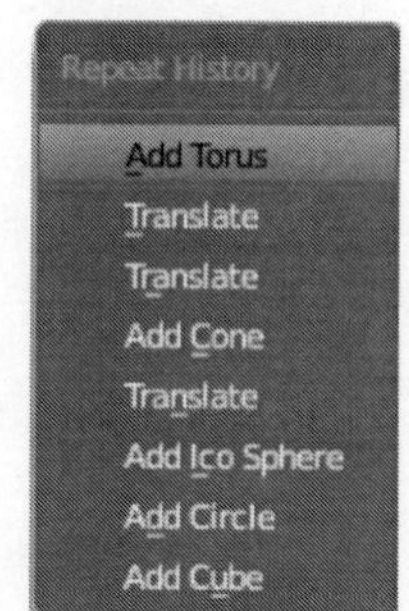

*Figure 1-39 The **Repeat History** menu*

Note

*1. There will be two separate **Undo History** menus for **Object Mode** and **Edit Mode** in the current session of Blender scene.*

*2. If you quit the Blender even after saving the Blender file, the list of actions in **Undo History** and **Repeat History** will be lost.*

HOT KEYS

You can use the hot keys to choose some of the commonly used tools and commands. These keys are known as the hot keys. You can work faster and more efficiently using the hot keys. The major hot keys and their functions are listed next.

Table 1-1 A list of hot keys and commands

Numpad 1	Invokes Front view
Numpad 3	Invokes Right view
Numpad 4	Invokes Perspective view
Numpad 7	Invokes Top view
CTRL + Numpad 3	Invokes Left view
CTRL + Numpad 7	Invokes Bottom view
Numpad 0	Invokes Camera view
Middle mouse button	Orbits in a view
SHIFT + middle mouse button	To pan in the view
CTRL+middle mouse button/ Scroll the middle mouse button	Zooms in and zooms out in the view
T	To enlarge the view by removing **Toolshelf**

Numpad 5	Toggles the Orthographic/Perspective view
CTRL+ALT+Q	Toggles the quad view
ALT +F10	Toggles full screen area
CTRL + Spacebar	Invokes the **Transform** tool
R	Invokes the **Rotate** tool
S	Invokes the **Scale** tool
S and then X	Scales the object in X direction
S and then Y	Scales the object in Y direction
S and then Z	Scales the object in Z direction
Right-click on the object	Selects the object
SHIFT + Right mouse button	Selects multiple objects
H	Hides the object
Alt + H	Unhides the object
X	Invokes the menu to delete the selected object
F12	Invokes the **Render** tool
I	Inserts a keyframe
ALT + I	Clears a keyframe
ALT + SHIFT + I	Clears all keyframes
ALT + A	Toggles Play animation
Down arrow	Go to previous frame
Up arrow	Go to next frame
CTRL+J	Combines the selected meshes
N	Opens **Properties Region**
Home key	To zoom in
. key on numpad	To zoom out

CUSTOMIZING THE COLORS OF THE USER INTERFACE

You can customize the colors of the user interface by choosing **File > User Preferences** from the **Info Editor** menu bar. Alternatively, press CTRL+ALT+U. On doing so, the **Blender User Preferences** dialog box will be displayed. In this dialog box, choose the **Themes** button. You will notice that all the editors of Blender user interface are available in the left pane of this dialog box. Figure 1-40 shows the **Blender User Preferences** dialog box with **Outliner** selected in the left pane and the corresponding color parameters displayed in the right pane. To change the color theme of the editors of Blender, select the editor from the left pane of the dialog box; the color parameters for the components of that editor will be available in the right pane of the dialog box. You can customize the colors of these components one by one as per your requirement.

After customizing the colors, choose the **Save User Settings** button from this dialog box to reflect the color changes done. If you want to restore the default settings, choose the **Reset to**

Default Theme button. To install already saved theme, choose the **Install Theme** button; the **File Browser** will be displayed. Navigate to the installed theme.

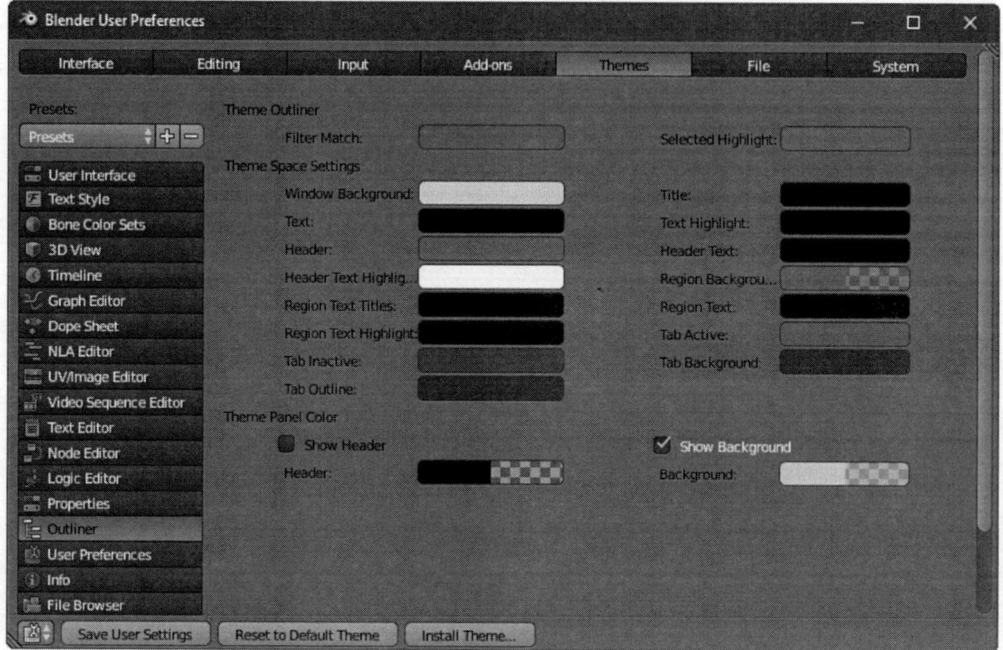

***Figure 1-40** The **Blender User Preferences** dialog box*

PIE MENU

A pie menu is a special type of menu in which options are available radially around the cursor. Pie menus are not activated by default. To activate the pie menus, choose **File > User Preferences** from the **3D View Editor** menu bar; the **Blender User Preferences** dialog box will be displayed. Choose the **Add-ons** button and then select the **Pie menu: UI Pie menu Official** check box.

Figures 1-41 through 1-44 show various types of pie menus. Press TAB to display **Mode** pie menu, Z to display **Shading** pie menu, Q to display **View** pie menu, . to display **Pivot** pie menu, SHIFT+CTRL and then TAB to display **Snapping** pie menu, and so on.

Pie menus are easy to use menus. To choose any option from a pie menu, move the cursor on the wheel in the pie menu; the option located near the cursor will be highlighted. Click in the vicinity of the option to choose it. As you choose the option, pie menu will disappear. Press ESC to remove the pie menu from the screen without choosing an option from it. You can also choose an option from a pie menu by pressing the shortcut key mentioned next to the required option in the pie menu.

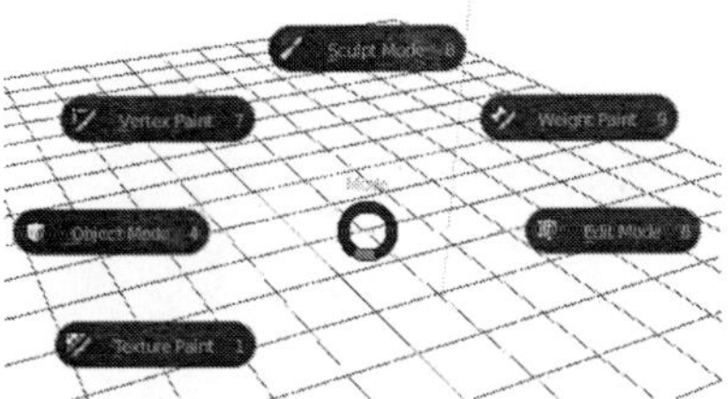

*Figure 1-41 The **Mode** pie menu*

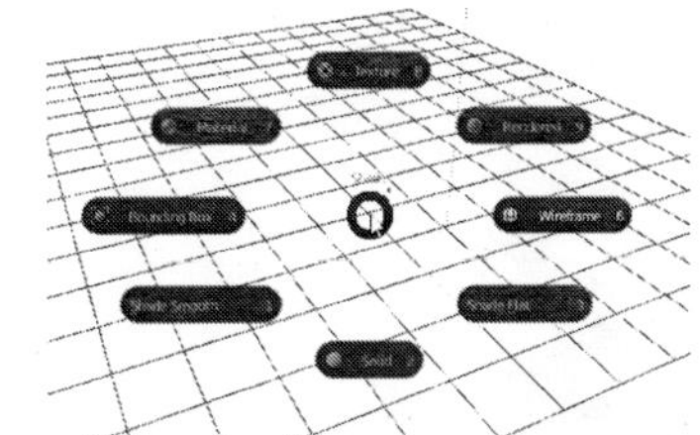

*Figure 1-42 The **Shading** pie menu*

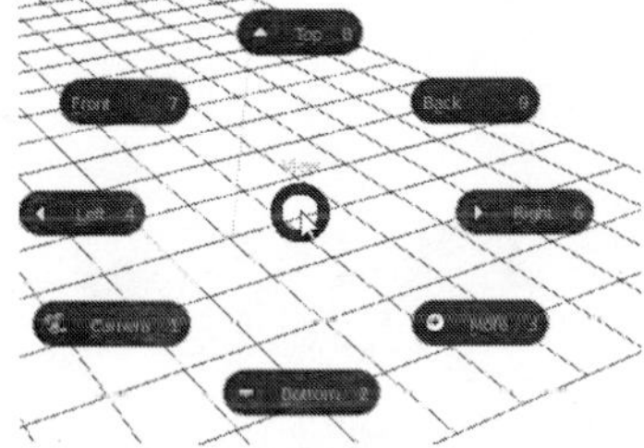

*Figure 1-43 The **View** pie menu*

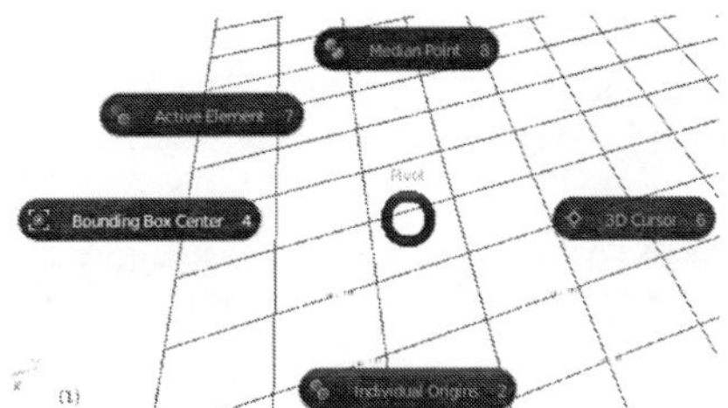

*Figure 1-44 The **Pivot** pie menu*

BLENDER HELP

You can get online help and documentation about the working of Blender 2.79 commands from the **Help** menu in the **Info Editor** menu bar, refer to Figure 1-45. The options in this menu are used to open various Blender websites such as **Blender Reference Manual**, **Blender 2.79 Release Notes**, **Support**, **Get Involved**, and so on.

*Figure 1-45 The options in the **Help** menu*

To access the main Blender reference manual, choose **Help > Manual** from the **Info Editor** menu bar; the **Blender Reference Manual** window will be displayed, as shown in Figure 1-46.

You can use this window to access help on different topics and commands. Left side of the window displays different sections such as Getting Started, User Interface, Editors, and so on. Click on a section on the left side; the list of topics covered under the section will be displayed below it. Also, the content of the selected section will be displayed on the right side in the **Blender Reference Manual** window. You can select a specific topic from this window to get help on that topic.

The Search Field is also available at the top left corner of the window. When you type any word in the Search Field and press ENTER, a list of topics related to the typed word will be displayed on the right side in the window. You can select the desired topic from the list; the information related to that topic will be displayed in the **Blender Reference Manual** window.

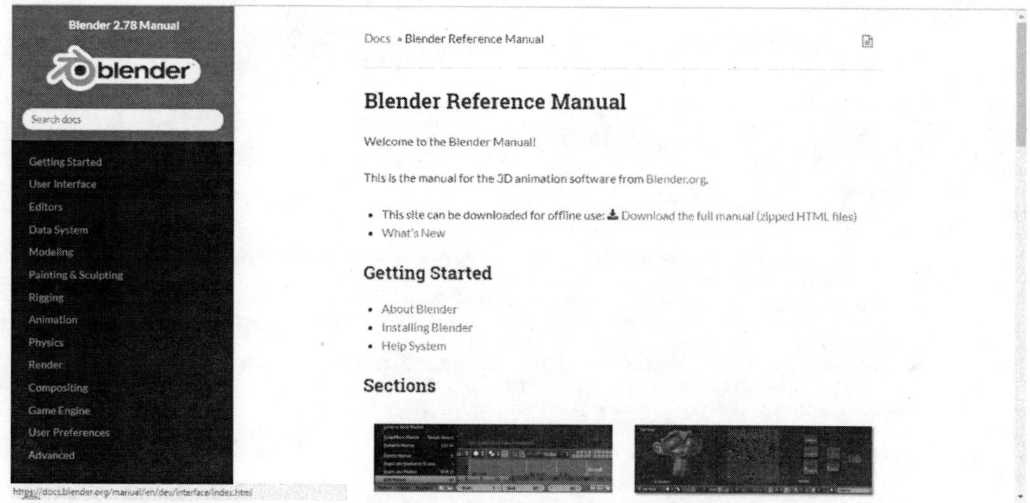

Figure 1-46 *The* ***Blender Reference Manual*** *window*

Note

In Blender, you can interactively open the help documentation for a tool. To do so, hover the mouse pointer on the required tool and then press ALT+F1; a page related to the tool will be displayed under the cursor. Note that this feature is not available for all tools. Alternatively, you can right-click on a tool and then choose ***Online Manual*** *from the menu displayed.*

Self-Evaluation Test

Answer the following questions and then compare them to those given at the end of this chapter:

1. Which of the following editors is used to write and execute the script?

   (a) **NLA Editor** (b) **Text editor**
   (c) **Logic Editor** (d) None of these

2. Which of the following combinations of shortcut keys is used to save the customized startup file?

   (a) CTRL+N (b) CTRL+W
   (c) CTRL+U (d) CTRL+Z

3. The __________ key is used to display the **Mode** pie menu if pie menus are activated.

4. The __________ drop-down in **3D View Editor** is used to save and use different scenes.

5. The __________ mode is used to paint vertices of an object using brush.

6. The __________ drop-down in **Info Editor** is used to add customized screen layout.

7. The __________ is used to track and mask the movies.

8. The **Weight Paint** mode is used to edit UV textures and images in **3D View Editor** or **UV/Image Editor**. (T/F)

9. You need to press the Z key to display the **Shading** pie menu. (T/F)

Review Questions

Answer the following questions:

1. Which of the following combinations of keys is used to change a 3D view to a quad view?

    (a) CTRL+ALT+Q (b) CTRL+ALT+W
    (c) CTRL+SHIFT+Q (d) SHIFT+ALT+Q

2. The __________ drop-down is used to filter the list of objects visible in **Outliner**.

3. The __________ is used to display the **View** pie menu.

4. You need to press the / key to display the **Pivot** pie menu. (T/F)

5. There are two separate **Undo History** menus for **Object Mode** and **Edit Mode** in the current session of Blender scene. (T/F)

6. You can split a view into a number of small views as per your requirement. (T/F)

7. The numpad 6 key is used to toggle the orthographic and perspective views. (T/F)

Answers to Self-Evaluation Test

1. b, **2.** c, **3.** TAB, **4. Scene Layout**, **5. Vertex Paint**, **6. Screen Layout**, **7. Movie Clip Editor**, **8.** F, **9.** T

Chapter 2

Working with Mesh Primitives

Learning Objectives

After completing this chapter, you will be able to:

- *Understand viewport navigation controls*
- *Understand selection techniques*
- *Understand the Object and Edit modes*
- *Create and edit mesh primitives*
- *Understand the proportional editing*
- *Change the object color and the background color of a scene*
- *Render a still image*

INTRODUCTION

Mesh Primitives are polygonal shapes comprising of sub-objects: vertices, edges, and faces. In this chapter, you will first create simple 3D objects using mesh primitives and then edit these primitives by modifying vertices, edges, and faces to create complex 3D objects. You will also learn to change the background color of the scene and render still image.

VIEWPORT NAVIGATION CONTROLS

To adjust the view of an object in a viewport, you need to be familiar with the viewport navigation control tools. To navigate the viewport using these tools, choose **View > Navigation** from the **3D View Editor** menu bar. On doing so, a cascading menu will be displayed, as shown in Figure 2-1.

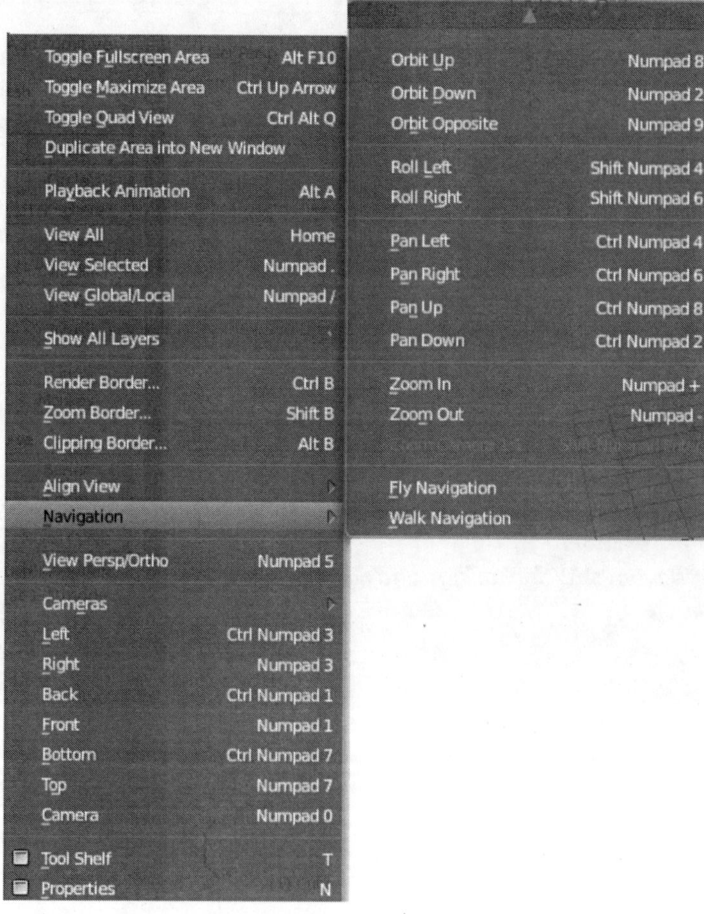

Figure 2-1 *The cascading menu displayed*

You can also navigate the viewport using the middle mouse button. To zoom the viewport, scroll the middle mouse button. Alternatively, press the CTRL key and hold the middle mouse button and drag the cursor to zoom in and zoom out the viewport. To orbit the viewport, hold down the middle mouse button and move in any direction. To pan the viewport, press the SHIFT key and hold down the middle mouse button and move in a desired direction. Note that here onwards the viewport is referred to as view in this book.

UNDERSTANDING OBJECT MODE

Object Mode is the default mode chosen in the **Mode** drop-down of **3D View Editor**. Figure 2-2 displays various parameters that will be available in **3D view Editor** when **Object Mode** is chosen from the **Mode** drop-down, refer to Figure 2-2.

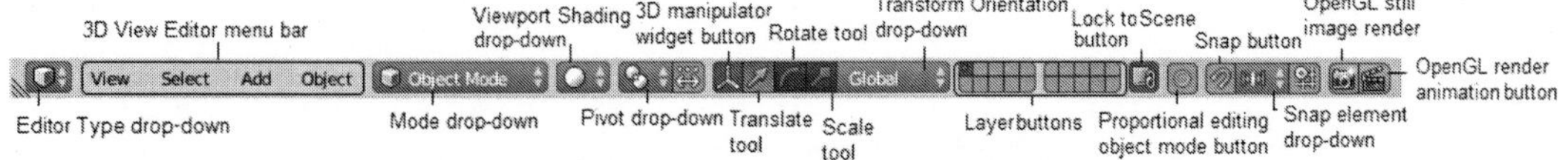

*Figure 2-2 Various parameters in **3D View Editor***

In this mode, you can create various types of primitives, curves, surfaces, and so on in the scene. Also, you can duplicate object(s), group the objects, as well as create new layers, add objects to existing layers, and select the objects in the scene using different selection techniques. The functioning of this mode is discussed next.

Selection Techniques

In Blender, there are various selection techniques to select the objects in the view. When you select multiple objects, the last selected object is termed as active object and will have yellow border around it whereas other selected objects will have orange border around them. Various selection techniques are discussed next.

1. Point Selection - Right-click on an object to select it. If more than one objects is to be selected, then press SHIFT and right-click on the objects one by one to add them to the selection.

2. Border Selection - Press B; dotted cross lines will be attached to the cursor. Click at a point in the view and then drag the cursor to form a dotted rectangle. The objects lying fully and partially within the dotted rectangle will be selected. Note that object(s) previously selected will also get added to this selection.

3. Lasso Selection - Press CTRL+LMB and then drag around the objects to be selected; dotted region is formed around the objects. The objects whose pivot points fall under this dotted region get selected. Note that object(s) previously selected will also be added to the selection.

4. Circle Selection - Press C; the circle will be attached to the cursor. Scroll the middle mouse button to change the size of the circle and then click; the objects fully and partially covered in the circle will be selected. Note that object(s) previously selected will also be added to the selection.

   The other selection techniques are available in the **Select** menu of the **3D View Editor** menu bar, as shown in Figure 2-3.

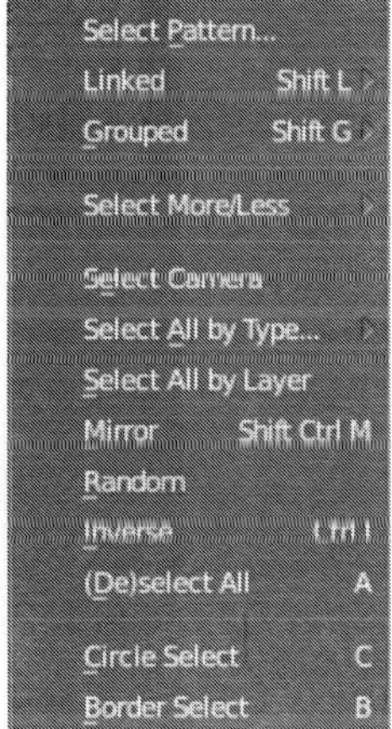

***Figure 2-3** The **Select** menu*

Note

To isolate the object(s) from the scene, select the object(s) and press / from the numpad; the objects other than the selected object(s) will be hidden.

Snapping

Snapping restricts the movement of the cursor to an active or selected object, its sub-objects, 3D Cursor, or grid floor.

You can snap the cursor to the nearest point on the grid, selected object, active object, or to the center of the grid. Also, you can snap the selected object (in **Object Mode**) or its sub-object(s) (in **Edit Mode**) to grid and cursor. To do so, choose **Object > Snap** from the **3D View Editor** menu bar; a cascading menu will be displayed, as shown in Figure 2-4. Alternatively, press SHIFT+S to display the **Snap** menu, as shown in Figure 2-5.

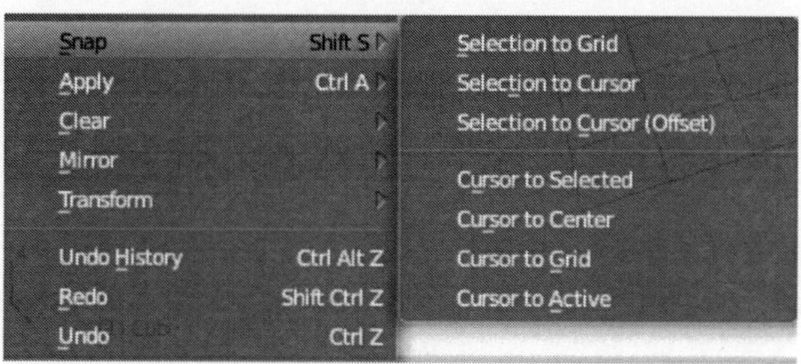

***Figure 2-4** The cascading menu displayed*

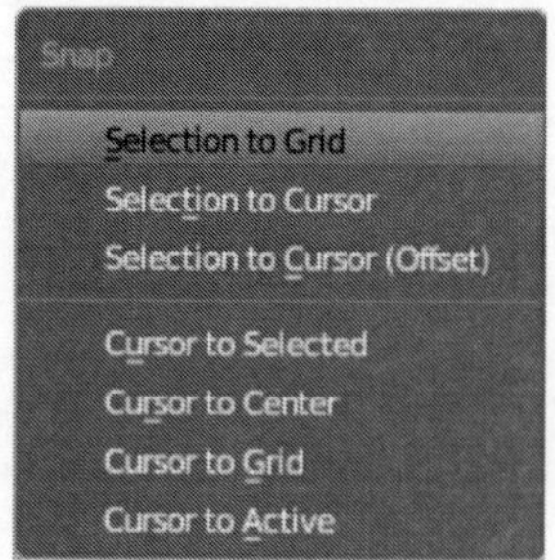

***Figure 2-5** The **Snap** menu*

You can snap the object(s) and its sub-object(s) during transformation in **Object Mode** as well as in **Edit Mode**. The transform snapping for these modes is discussed next.

The **Snap** button in **3D view Editor** is used to toggle the snap mode. The **Snap Element** drop-down located next to the **Snap** button is used to specify the element of the selected object that has to be snapped to the target object. Figure 2-6 displays the options in this drop-down. If you select the option other than **Increment** from this drop-down, the **Snap Target** drop-down will be added next to the **Snap Element** drop-down and the **Increment** button will be replaced by different button(s) for rest of the four options in the **Snap Element** drop-down, refer to Figure 2-7. The options in the **Snap Target** drop-down are used to specify the placement point of the target object to which the selected object will be snapped. The options in this drop-down are displayed in Figure 2-8.

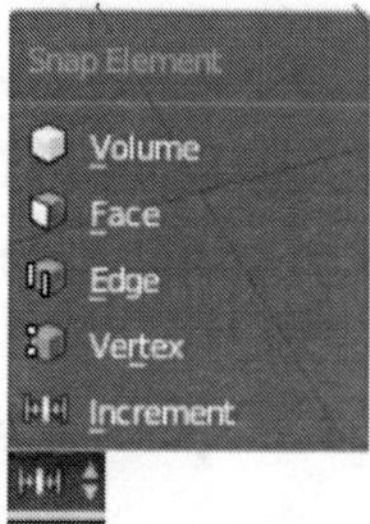

***Figure 2-6** The **Snap Element** drop-down*

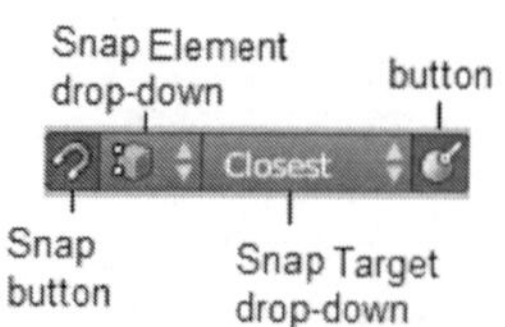

***Figure 2-7** The **Snap Target** drop-down and a button added*

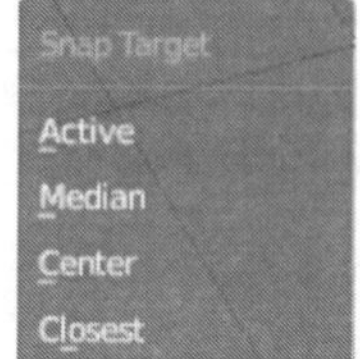

***Figure 2-8** The **Snap Target** drop-down*

Creating Objects Using Mesh Primitives

To create an object using the mesh primitive, choose the **Create** tab in **Toolshelf** of **3D View Editor**. The primitives will be listed in the **Mesh** area of the **Add Primitive** panel. Choose the desired primitive from this area to create an object in the view. Note that the object will be created at a position where 3D cursor is located in the view. Figure 2-9 shows all the mesh primitives available in Blender.

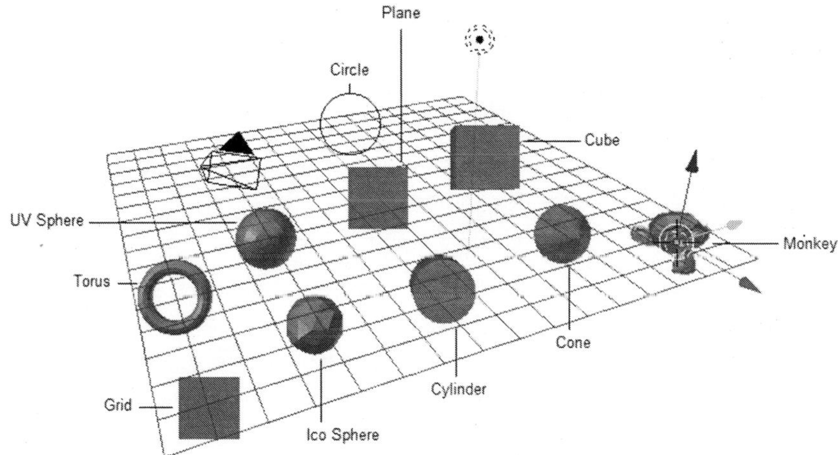

Figure 2-9 *The mesh primitives available in Blender*

As you create the object using a primitive, the **Add XXX** panel will be added to **Toolshelf** where **XXX** stands for the name of the primitive chosen. The parameters in this panel are used to change the dimensions, position and rotation coordinates of the object. The **Generate UVs** and the **Align to View** check boxes available in this panel are used to generate UVs and to align the object to view, respectively. Figure 2-10 shows the **Add UV Sphere** panel.

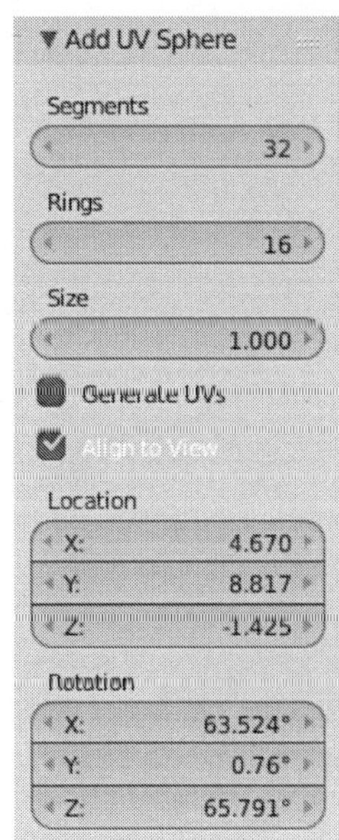

Figure 2-10 *The* ***Add UV Sphere*** *panel*

As you transform the object in the view, the **Add XXX** panel will disappear and the **Translate** panel will be displayed at the same place. The options in this panel are used to constrain the transformation of object along specific axes, change the orientation of the object, enable proportional editing, and so on. To change the other properties of the object, choose the **Object** button from the **Properties Editor**. On doing so, various panels such as **Transform**, **Delta Transform**, **Groups**, **Display**, and so on will be displayed in the **Properties Editor**.

To move, rotate, and scale the object manually in the view, select the object and choose the **Translate**, **Rotate**, and **Scale** tools, respectively from **3D View Editor**, refer to Figure 2-2 and then transform the object accordingly. Alternatively, choose **Object > Transform** from the **3D View Editor** menu bar and then choose the respective option from the cascading menu displayed. When you choose the **Grab/Move** option in the cascading menu, the object gets attached to the cursor and moves along with the cursor. Next, you need to click at a point in the view to place the object in the view. You can also use the G key, R key, and the S key to Grab/move, rotate, and scale the object, respectively.

Duplicating Objects

In Blender, you can duplicate an object using the **Duplicate** tool. In duplication, a copy of the object is created and it is not linked to the original object. It means the modifications made in the copy do not affect the original object. Also, you can create an instance of an object by using the **Duplicate Linked** tool. The instances are linked to the original object, implying that the modifications made in the instances are reflected in the original object and vise-versa.

To duplicate the object(s) as a copy, select the object(s) in the view. Next, choose the **Tools** tab from **Toolshelf** in **3D View Editor**. Now, choose the **Duplicate** tool from the **Edit** panel in **Toolshelf**. Alternatively, press SHIFT+D. On doing so, the duplicated object(s) will be attached to the cursor as in the **Grab/Move** option discussed earlier. Next, click at a point in the view to position it. The **Duplicate** tool works in both **Object Mode** and **Edit Mode**.

To duplicate the object(s) as an instance, select the object(s) in the view. Next, choose the **Tools** tab from **Toolshelf** in **3D View Editor**. Now, choose the **Duplicate Linked** tool from the **Edit** panel in **Toolshelf**. Alternatively, press ALT+D. On doing so, the duplicated object(s) will be attached to the cursor as in the **Grab/Move** option discussed earlier. Next, click at a point in the view to position it. The **Duplicate Linked** tool works only in the **Object Mode**.

Figure 2-11 shows the object copied using the **Duplicate** and **Duplicate Linked** tools.

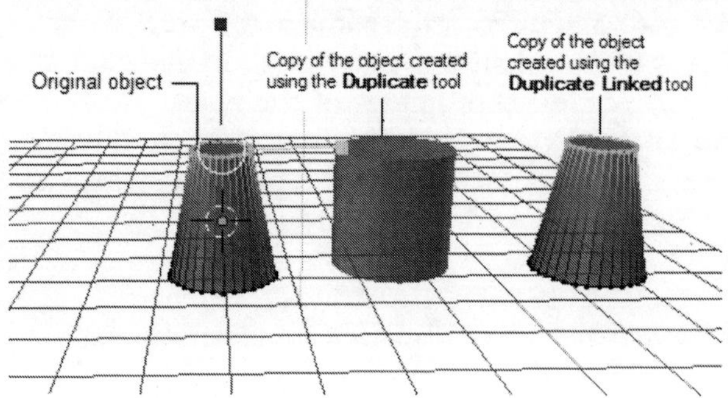

***Figure 2-11** The objects copied using the **Duplicate** and **Duplicate Linked** tools*

Note

If you press ENTER after pressing SHIFT+D, the duplicated object(s) will be created at the same place as that of original object(s).

Grouping Objects

To create a new group for specific type of objects, select the objects in the view or in **Outliner**. Next, choose **Object > Group** from the **3D View Editor** menu bar; a cascading menu will be displayed, as shown in Figure 2-12. Choose the **Create New Group** option from the cascading menu or press CTRL+G. Note that the grouped objects are shown in the view with the green border when selected.

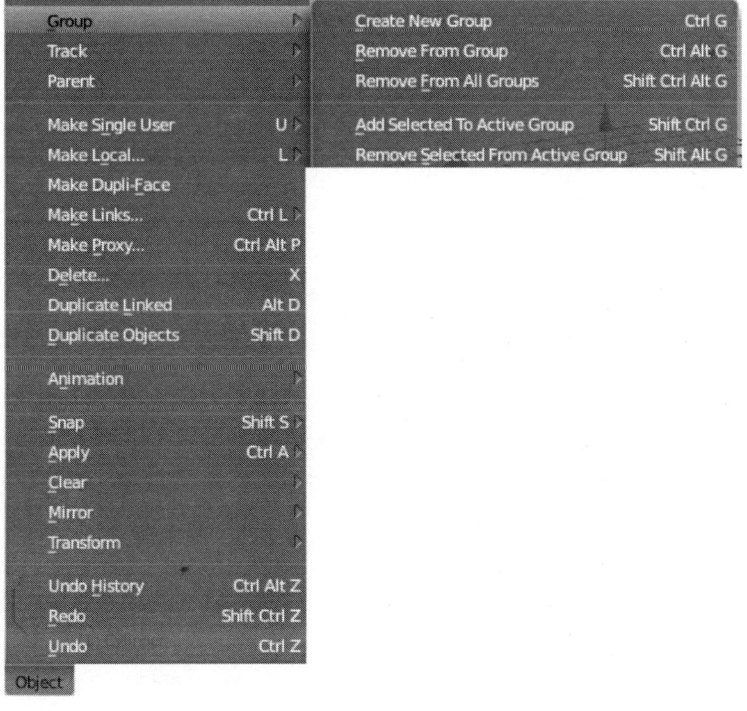

__Figure 2-12__ The cascading menu displayed

Similarly, you can use other options from this cascading menu to add or remove selected objects from the group(s). To select all the objects from the group, you need to first select an object from the group and then choose **Select > Grouped** from the **3D View Editor** menu bar; a cascading menu will be displayed. Choose **Group** from the cascading menu, as shown in Figure 2-13.

Some of the options discussed above are also available in the **Group** panel of **Properties Editor** when the **Object** button is chosen.

Note
In Blender, you can individually transform the objects in the group without affecting other objects in the group.

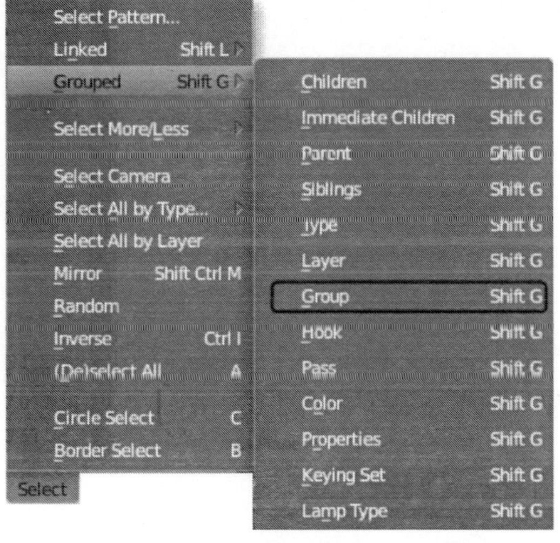

__Figure 2-13__ Choosing __Group__ from the cascading menu displayed

Creating Layers

Layers are used to organize complex scenes. There are 20 layers available in Blender. For each of these layers twenty small light grey colored buttons are available in **3D View Editor**, refer to

Figure 2-2. When you select a layer button, it turns dark grey and the respective layer is selected. As you add objects in a layer, a small circle appears on that layer. By default, layer 1 button is chosen and the objects created in the scene are added to layer 1, refer to Figure 2-14.

Small orange colored circle on a layer button indicates that the layer is selected and there are objects in that layer. Small grey colored circle on a layer button indicates that there are objects in the layer but the layer is not selected, refer to Figure 2-14.

To move any object from one layer to another, select the object(s) and press M; the **Move to Layer** menu will be displayed, refer to Figure 2-15. All the layer buttons are available in this menu. Choose the desired layer button from this menu to move the selected object to that layer. Similarly, to keep an object on multiple layers, select the object(s) and press M. Next, press SHIFT and then choose the desired layer button(s). To select multiple layers, press and hold SHIFT and click on the desired layers one by one. Press ` to select all the layers in the scene.

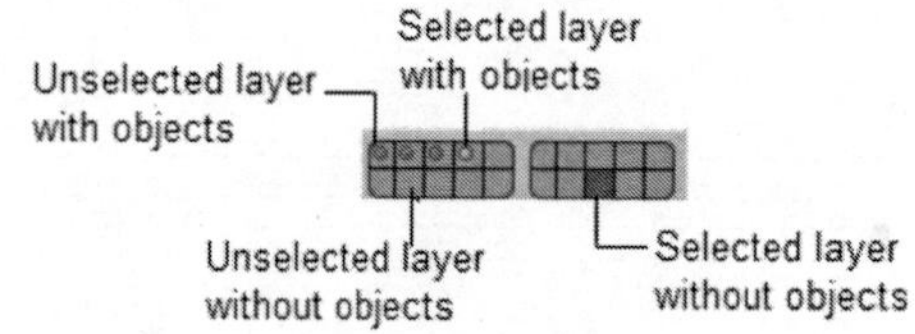

Figure 2-14 *Various layer buttons*

Figure 2-15 *The* ***Move to Layer*** menu

Note

To select layers 1 to 10, press 1 to 0, respectively and to select layers from 11 to 20, press ALT+1 to ALT+0, respectively.

UNDERSTANDING EDIT MODE

Edit Mode is used to modify the objects created using primitives, curves, surfaces, and so on to create complex objects. You need to hover the cursor in the view and press TAB to switch from **Object Mode** to **Edit Mode**. As you change from **Object Mode** to **Edit Mode**, the **Object** menu will be changed to the **Mesh** menu in the **3D View Editor** menu bar. The **Mesh** menu has various options to modify the sub-objects (vertices, edges, and faces) such as **Extrude**, **Inset Faces**, **Subdivide**, **Bevel**, and so on. These options are also available in the **Tools** tab of **Toolshelf**. Most commonly used options of the **Mesh** menu are discussed next.

Note

*If you have activated pie menus, the **Mode** pie menu will be displayed on pressing the TAB key. You need to choose **Edit Mode** from this pie menu or press 6 to switch to **Edit Mode**. The procedure to activate the pie menus is discussed in Chapter 1.*

Extrude

The **Extrude** option is available for all the three sub-object levels: Vertex, Edge, and Face. It is used to extrude the sub-objects either by dragging the cursor or by entering the value in the sliders available in the panels of **Toolshelf**. To extrude an object, select the object in the view and switch to **Edit Mode**. Next, choose the **Face Select**, **Edge Select**, or **Vertex Select** button depending on the sub-object to be extruded and then select the sub-object(s) from the view. Next, choose **Mesh > Extrude** from the **3D View Editor** menu bar or press ALT+E; various options will be displayed in the cascading menu depending on the sub-object selected, refer to Figure 2-16. Choose the desired option from the cascading menu to extrude the sub-object.

Figure 2-17 shows the faces extruded using the **Region** and **Individual Faces** options. To change the amount, set the number of segments, constrain the extrusion to specific axis, and so on, you need to set the parameters in the panel displayed at the bottom in **Toolshelf**.

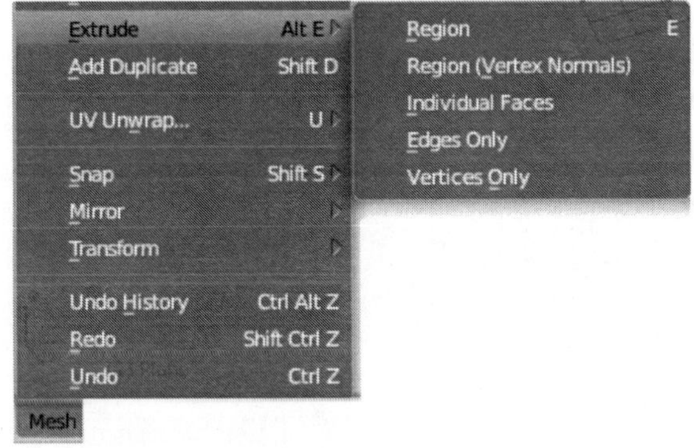

Figure 2-16 Various extrude options in the cascading menu

*Figure 2-17 Faces extruded using the **Individual Faces** and the **Region** option*

Bevel

The **Bevel** option is available for all the three sub-object levels: Vertex, Edge, and Face. It is used to bevel the sub-objects either by dragging the cursor or by entering the value in the sliders available in the panels of **Toolshelf**. To do so, make sure **Edit Mode** is activated. To bevel face of an object, choose the **Face Select** button and then select face(s) from the view. Next, choose **Mesh > Faces > Bevel** from the **3D View Editor** menu bar or press CTRL+B; a dotted line will be attached to the cursor. Drag and move the cursor in the view and click at a point; the **Bevel** panel will be added to **Toolshelf**. To change the bevel amount, amount type, number of segments, profile, and so on, you need to set the parameters in the **Bevel** panel of **Toolshelf**.

You can also interactively change the profile of the beveled part of the object by using the P key. To do so, press P and then either change the profile moving the mouse or specifying a numerical value using Numpad on the keyboard. Release the P key to exit the interactive mode.

Similarly, you can change the number of segments in the beveled area by using the S key.

You can also bevel edges and vertices of the object. Figure 2-18 shows upper face of a cylinder with various bevel amount types applied.

Subdivide

The **Subdivide** option is available for edge sub-object level. It is used to subdivide the selected edges. To do so, make sure **Edit Mode** is activated. Next, choose the **Edge Select** button and then choose **Mesh > Edges > Subdivide** from the **3D View Editor** menu bar; the selected edges will be divided with a single cut by default. To change the number of cuts, smoothness, type of cut, and so on, you need to set the parameters in the **Subdivide** panel of **Toolshelf**. Figures 2-19 and 2-20 show the subdivision of edges with **Smoothness = 0** and **Smoothness = 0.5**, respectively.

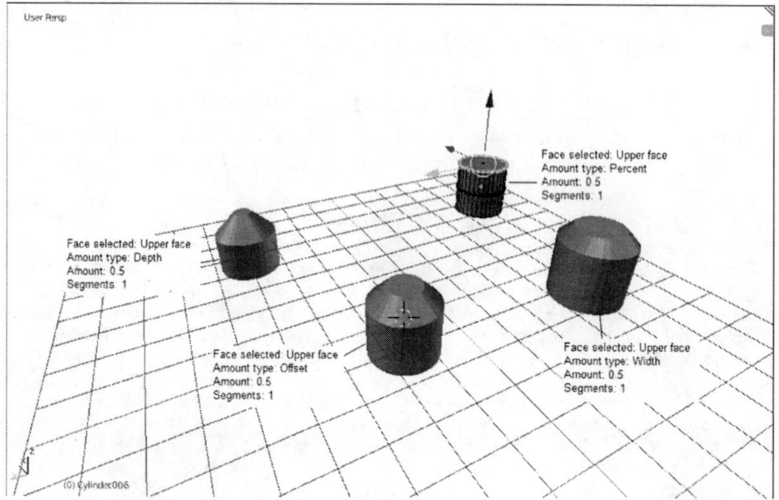

***Figure 2-18** Upper face of a cylinder with various bevel amount types*

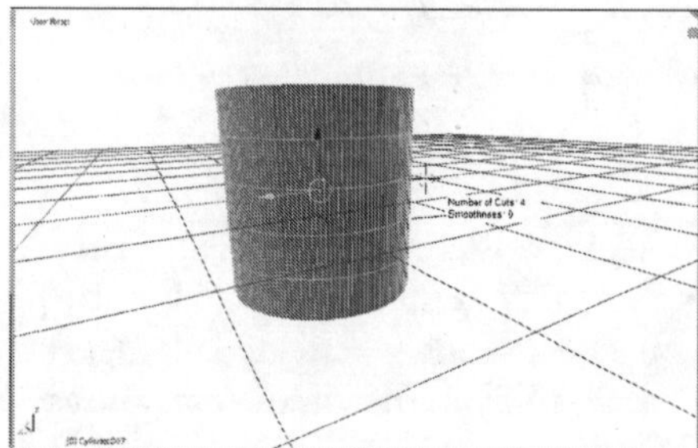

Figure 2-19** The subdivision of edges with **Smoothness = 0

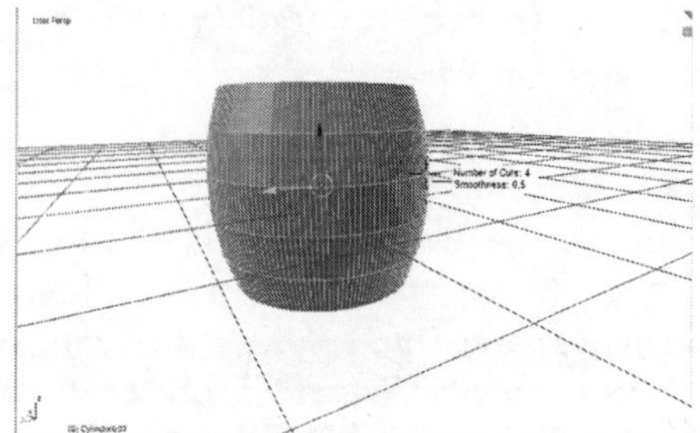

Figure 2-20** The subdivision of edges with **Smoothness = 0.5

Proportional Editing

Proportional editing is useful for smooth deformation of the object in the **Object Mode** or its sub-objects in **Edit Mode**. The proportional editing in these modes is discussed next.

To activate proportional editing in the **Object Mode**, choose the **Proportional editing object mode** button from the **3D View Editor** menu bar or hover the cursor in the view and press O; the **Falloff** drop-down will be added next to the **Proportional editing object mode** button, refer to Figure 2-21 and a circle will be attached to the cursor. Now, select the object(s) in the view and then transform the object(s) as desired; selected object(s) will transform along with unselected objects around the selected object(s) within a area covered by the circle attached to the cursor. You can change the radius of this circle by scrolling the middle mouse button and holding the left mouse button. You can also use the PAGE UP and PAGE DOWN keys instead of scrolling the middle mouse button. The transformation of unselected objects within the circle will be inversely proportional to their distance with the selected object(s). The objects which are closer to the selected ones will transform more than those which are farther from the selected objects. The options in the **Falloff** drop-down are used to specify the falloff of the transformation.

Proportional editing in **Edit Mode** is similar to that in **Object Mode** with the difference that in **Edit Mode**, the **Proportional editing object mode** button will be replaced by the **Proportional editing mode** drop-down, refer to Figure 2-22 and the proportional editing is carried out on the sub-objects. Also, the type of transformation depends on the option chosen from the **Proportional editing mode** and **Falloff** drop-downs. The options in the **Proportional editing mode** drop-down are discussed next.

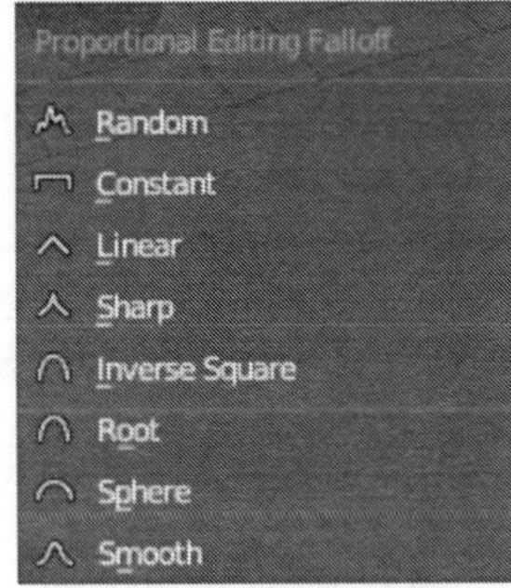

*Figure 2-21 The **Proportional Editing Falloff** drop-down*

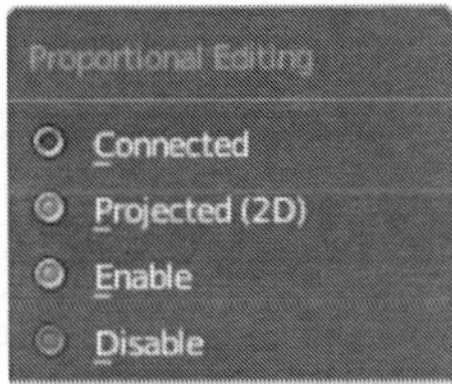

*Figure 2-22 The **Proportional editing mode** drop-down*

The **Enable** and **Disable** options in the **Proportional editing mode** drop-down are self explanatory.

When the **Connected** option is chosen, the unselected sub-objects which are connected to the selected sub-objects will only be affected.

When the **Projected 2D** option is chosen, the depth along the view is ignored.

RENDERING A STILL IMAGE

Rendering is a process of generating a 2D image from a 3D scene. It shows the lighting effects, materials applied, background, and other settings that you have applied to the scene. There are two types of render engines in Blender: **Blender Render** and **Cycles Render**. You can choose the desired render engine from the **Engine** drop-down in **3D View Editor**. By default, **Blender Render** is chosen in this drop-down. The basic rendering for a still scene is discussed next.

By default, the **Render** button is chosen in **Properties Editor**. There are various panels such as **Render**, **Dimensions**, **Shading**, **Output**, and so on in **Properties Editor** when the **Render** button is chosen. The options in the **Render** panel are discussed next.

Choose the **Render** button or press F12 to render a still image in **UV/Image Editor**. To render an animation sequence in the **UV/Image Editor**, choose the **Animation** button. Similarly, choose the **Audio** button to mix audio in the rendering process. The options in the **Display** drop-down are used to choose the type of window/editor used for rendering. By default, **UV/Image Editor** is chosen in this drop-down. As a result, the rendered image/sequence will be displayed in **UV/Image Editor**. To display rendered image/sequence in a separate window, choose **New Window** from this drop-down. To display rendered image/sequence on a full screen, choose **Full Screen** from this drop-down. If you choose **Keep UI**, current user interface will not change and you need to open the **UV/Image Editor** to see the rendered image/animation sequence.

To return to the Blender layout, press the ESC key. To save the rendered image, choose **Image > Save As Image** from the **UV/Image Editor** menu bar; the **File Browser** will be displayed. Now, select the type of image format from the drop-down in the **Save as Image** panel and type the name of the image in the **File name** text box. Next, browse to the folder where you want to save the scene and choose the **Save As Image** button; the image file will be saved at the selected location.

Note

*To see the quick render without light effects, choose the **Open GL still image render** button from **3D View Editor**.*

Changing the Color of the Object

To change the color of the object without applying material to it, you need to first choose the **Material** button from the **Properties Editor**. Next, click on the **New** button located next to the **Material** drop-down; a material will be added along with some panels. Next, select the **Object Color** check box from the **Options** panel, as shown in Figure 2-23.

Now, choose the **Object** button from the **Properties Editor** and then click on the **Object Color** swatch in the **Display** panel; the Color Picker window will be displayed, as shown in Figure 2-24. Select the desired color from this window; color of the selected object will be changed in the view.

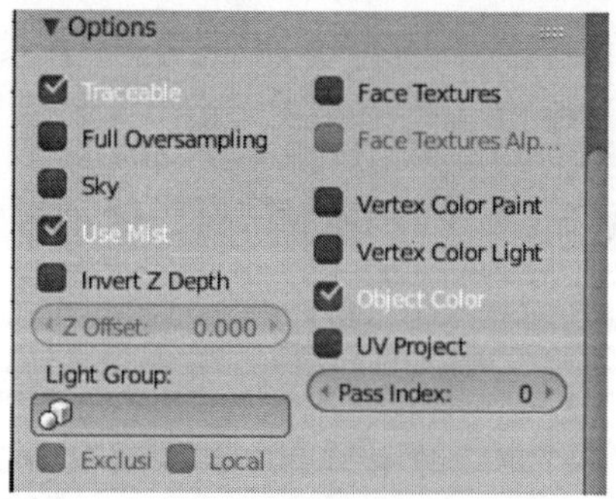

***Figure 2-23** The **Object Color** check box selected*

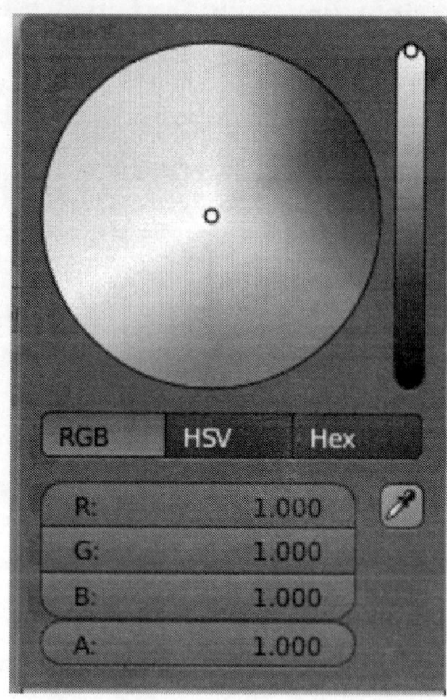

***Figure 2-24** The Color Picker window*

Changing the Background Color of the Scene

By default, the background color of the final output is grey at the time of rendering. To change the background color, choose the **World** button from the **Properties Editor**. Next, click on the **Horizon Color** color swatch in the **World** panel, refer to Figure 2-25; the Color Picker window will be displayed. Select a new color in this window; the background will display the new color in the background on rendering.

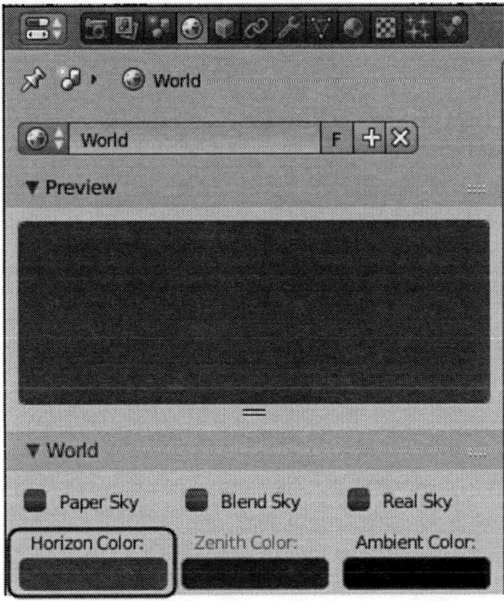

***Figure 2-25** The **Horizon Color** swatch*

TUTORIALS

Before you start tutorials of this chapter, you need to create a folder in which you will save all the files created and used in this book. To do so, navigate to the *\Documents* folder and create a new folder with the name *blender2.79*.

Tutorial 1

In this tutorial, you will create 3D model of a TV unit, as shown in Figure 2-26, using **Object Mode**. **(Expected time: 20 min)**

The following steps are required to complete this tutorial:

a. Create the folder.
b. Create the back portion of the TV unit.
c. Create the base of the TV unit.
d. Create the drawers.
e. Create shelves of the TV unit.
f. Save and render the scene.

Figure 2-26 The model of a TV unit

Creating the Folder

1. Navigate to *\Documents\blender2.79*. Create a new folder with the name *c02*. Next, create a folder with the name *c02_tut1* in the *c02* folder.

2. Press CTRL+N or choose **File > New** from the **Info Editor** menu bar; a menu is displayed. Choose **Reload Start-Up File**; the menu disappears and the startup file is loaded.

3. Choose **File > Save** from the **Info Editor** menu bar; the **File Browser** is displayed

4. Navigate to *\Documents\blender2.79\c02\c02_tut1* and enter **TV unit** in the **File Name** edit box. Next, choose the **Save Blender File** button to save the file at the specified location.

Note

It is recommended that you frequently save the files while you are working on them by pressing the CTRL+S keys.

Creating the Back Portion of the TV Unit

In this section, you will create the back portion of the TV unit by using the **Cube** tool. You will also change the color of the back of the TV unit.

1. Choose **View > Toggle Quad View** from the **3D View Editor** menu bar or Press CTRL+ALT+Q; the quad view is displayed.

Note

If you left-click at any point other than the center on the view, the 3D Cursor shifts to that point. The new object is created at the current position of the 3D Cursor. To bring back the 3D Cursor to the center of the grid, press SHIFT+C.

2. Make sure the **Cube** is selected in the views. Choose the **Object** button from the **Properties Editor**. Click on the **Transform** panel to expand it.

3. Enter the following values in the **Scale** area of the **Transform** panel in the **Properties Editor**.

   X: **6** Y: **0.15** Z: **6**

4. Double-click on *Cube* in **Outliner** and enter **back** to rename it.

   Next, you will change the color of *back*.

5. Choose the **Material** button from the **Properties Editor**. Next, choose the **New** button located next to the **Material** drop-down, refer to Figure 2-27; a new material is added to the **Material** drop-down along with various panels below it. Now, select the **Object Color** check box from the **Options** panel, refer to Figure 2-28.

*Figure 2-27 Choosing the **New** button*

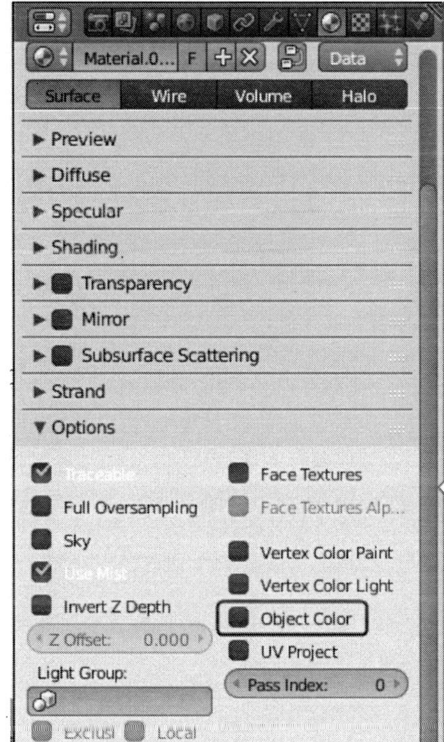

*Figure 2-28 The **Object Color** check box in the **Options** Panel*

6. Choose the **Object** button from the **Properties Editor**. Next, choose the **Object Color** swatch from the **Display** panel; a Color Picker window is displayed. Enter the following values in the Color Picker window:

   R: **0.115** G: **0.005** B: **0.008**

   Figure 2-29 shows *back* in the quad view.

   Next, you will create TV and a part above TV.

7. Choose the **Cube** tool from the **Add Primitive** panel in **Toolshelf**; a cube is created at the center of the view. Next, double-click on *Cube* in **Outliner** and enter **TV1** to rename it.

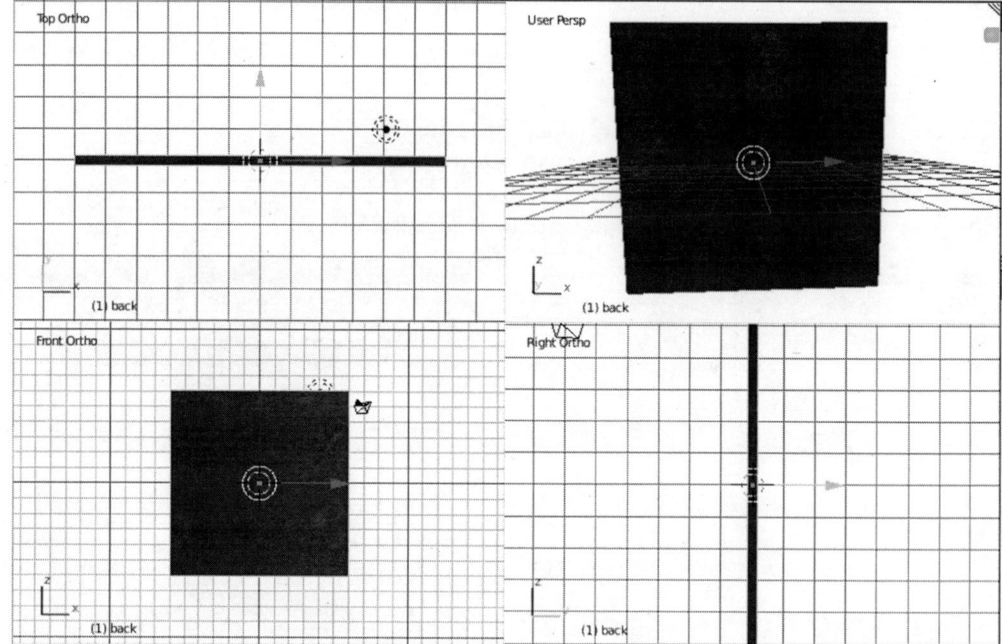

Figure 2-29 *The back of the TV unit*

8. Make sure the **Object** button is chosen in the **Properties Editor** and enter the following values in the **Scale** area of the **Transform** panel in the **Properties Editor.**

   X: **4** Y: **0.065** Z: **2.3**

   Next, you will change the color of *TV1*.

9. Choose the **Material** button from the **Properties Editor**. Next, choose the **Material001** option from the **Material** drop-down.

10. Choose the **Object** button from the **Properties Editor** and then choose the **Object Color** swatch; the Color Picker window is displayed. Enter the following values in the **Object Color** swatch:

    R: **0.099** G: **0.099** B: **0.099**

    TV1 turns dark grey.

11. Align *TV1* in all the views using the **Translate** tool from **3D View Editor**, as shown in Figure 2-30.

12. Choose the **Plane** tool from the **Add Primitive** panel in **Toolshelf**; a plane is created at the center of the view. Next, double-click on *Plane* in **Outliner** and enter **TV Screen** to rename it.

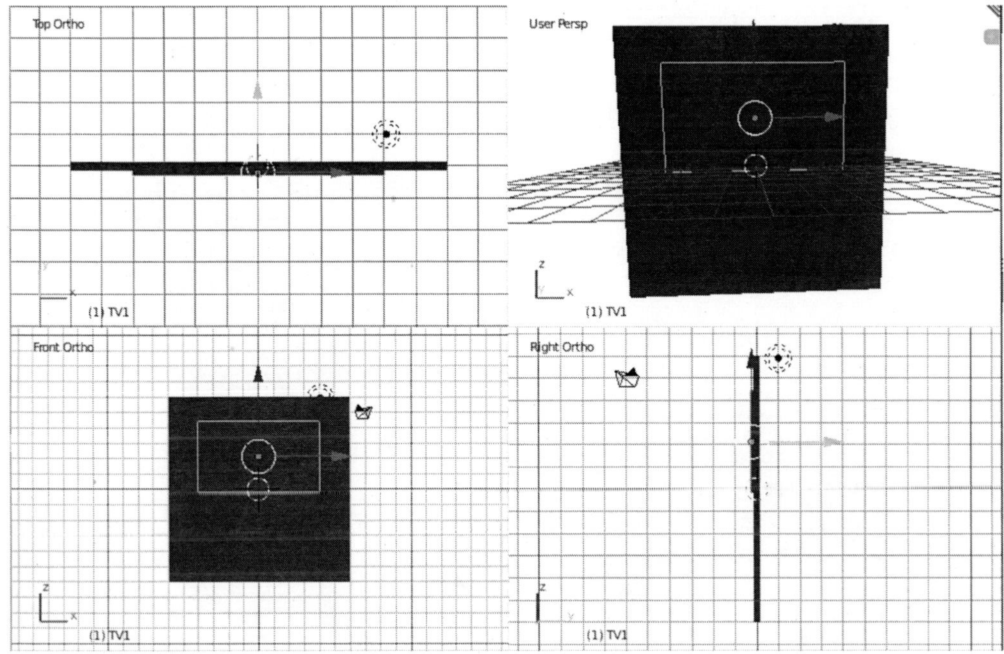

Figure 2-30 *The TV1 aligned*

13. Make sure the **Object** button is chosen in the **Properties Editor**. Next, enter the following values in the **Transform** panel of the **Properties Editor**.

    Scale area:
    X: **3.75** Y: **2.1**

    Rotation area:
    x: **90**

    TV Screen is scaled and oriented. Now, align it in all the views, as shown in Figure 2-31.

    Next, you will create a part above *TV Screen* using the **Cube** tool.

14. Choose the **Cube** tool from the **Add Primitive** panel in **Toolshelf**; a cube is created at the center of the view. Next, double-click on *Cube* in **Outliner** and enter **Top1** to rename it.

15. Make sure the **Object** button is chosen in the **Properties Editor**. Next, enter the following values in the **Scale** area of the **Transform** panel in the **Properties Editor**.

    X: **4** Y: **0.150** Z: **0.08**

16. Change the color of *Top1* as done for *back*.

17. Ailgn *Top1* on the upper side of *back,* as shown in Figure 2-32.

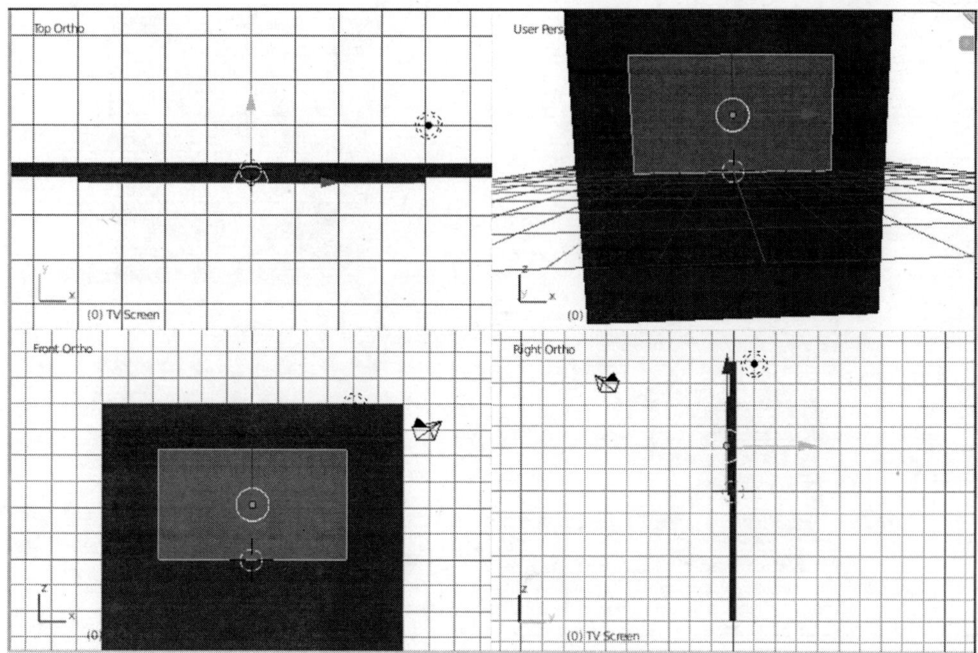

Figure 2-31 *The TV Screen aligned*

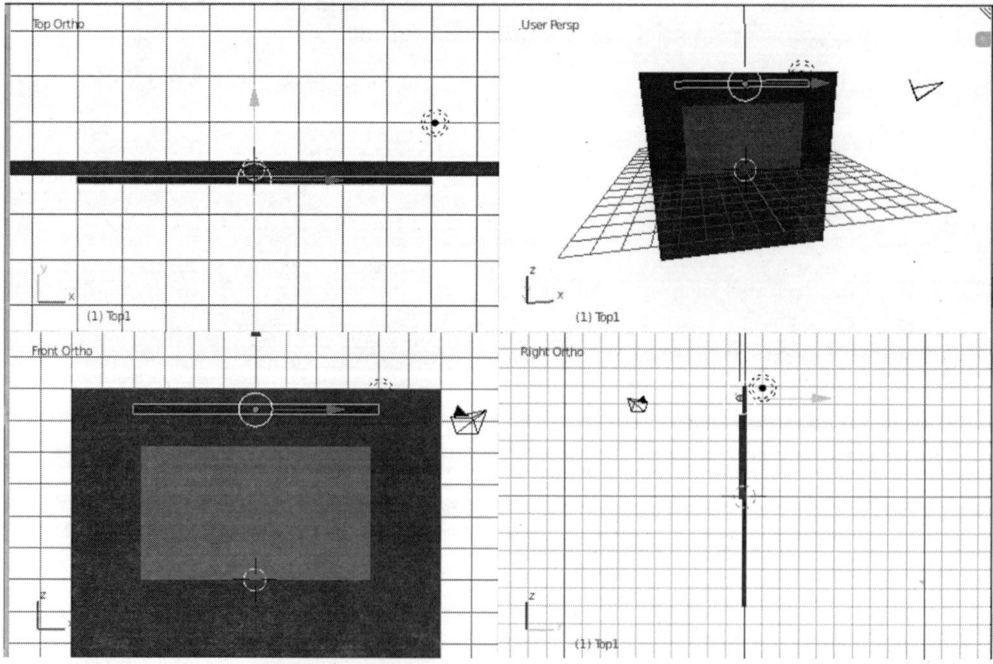

Figure 2-32 *The Top1 aligned*

Next, you will group all parts created so far as *back portion*.

18. Select all parts created so far with border selection technique. Make sure you do not select *lamp* and *camera*.

19. Choose **Object > Group > Create New Group** from the **3D View Editor** menu bar; A group of all selected objects is created with the name *Group*.

20. Make sure the **Object** button is chosen in the **Properties Editor**. Enter **back portion** in the edit box of the **Groups** panel, refer to Figure 2-33; the name of the group is changed to *back portion*.

Tip

*1. You can also rename a group using **Outliner**. To do so, choose **Groups** from the **Display** drop-down of **Outliner**. The list of all the groups in the scene is displayed in **Outliner**. Double-click on a group and enter its name in the edit box created.*

2. The green border around the object in the scene indicates that the object belongs to one or more groups.

Creating the Base of the TV Unit

1. Choose the **Cube** tool from the **Add Primitive** panel in **Toolshelf**; a cube is created at the center of the view. Next, double-click on *Cube* in **Outliner** and enter **base** to rename it.

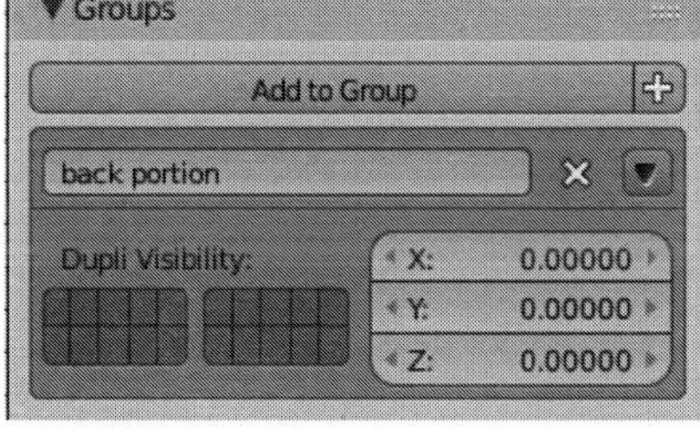

***Figure 2-33** The **Groups** panel*

2. Make sure the **Object** button is chosen in the **Properties Editor**. Next, enter the following values in the **Transform** panel of the **Properties Editor**.

   Scale area:
   X: **2** Y: **0.1** Z: **6**

   Rotation area:
   x: **90** Z: **90**

3. Change the color of *base* as done for *back*.

4. Align *base* in all the views, as shown in Figure 2-34.

   Next, you will create supports for *base*.

5. Choose the **Cylinder** tool from the **Add Primitive** panel in **Toolshelf**; a cylinder is created with the name *Cylinder* at the center of the view.

6. Change the color of *Cylinder* to dull white, as discussed earlier.

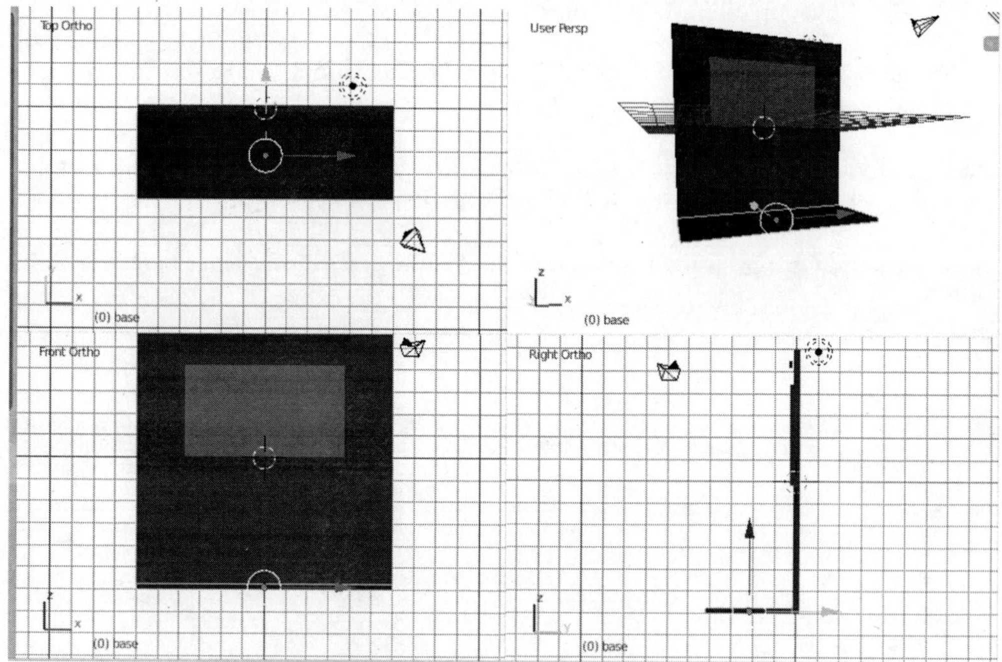

Figure 2-34 The base aligned

7. Enter the following values in the **Add Cylinder** panel of **Toolshelf**.

   Vertices: **64** Radius: **0.15** Depth: **0.6**

8. Align *Cylinder* with *base* in all the views, as shown in Figure 2-35.

9. Choose the **Cylinder** tool from the **Add Primitive** panel in **Toolshelf**; a cylinder is created with the name *Cylinder.001* at the center of the view.

10. Enter the following values in the **Add Cylinder** panel of **Toolshelf.**

    Vertices: **64** Radius: **0.25** Depth: **0.15**

11. Select *Cylinder* from any of the views. Next, press SHIFT+S; the **Snap** menu is displayed.

12. Choose **Cursor to Selected** from this menu. You will notice that 3D cursor moves from the center of the grid to the center of *Cylinder.*

13. Select *Cylinder.001* from any of the views. Next, press SHIFT + S again and select **Selection to Cursor** from the **Snap** menu displayed; center of *Cylinder.001* is aligned with the center of *Cylinder*. Now, move *Cylinder.001* to the bottom of *Cylinder,* as shown in Figure 2-36.

14. Make sure *Cylinder001* is selected. Next, press SHIFT and select *Cylinder.* Choose **Object > Group > Create New Group** from the **3D View Editor** menu bar. Next, rename the newly created group as *basesupport*.

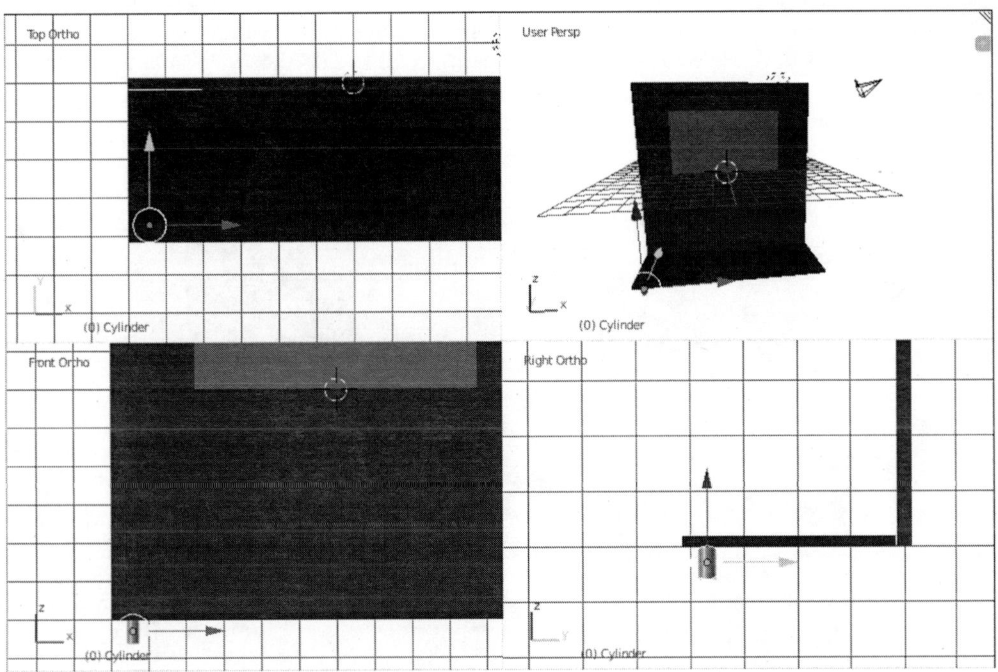

Figure 2-35 *The cylinder aligned*

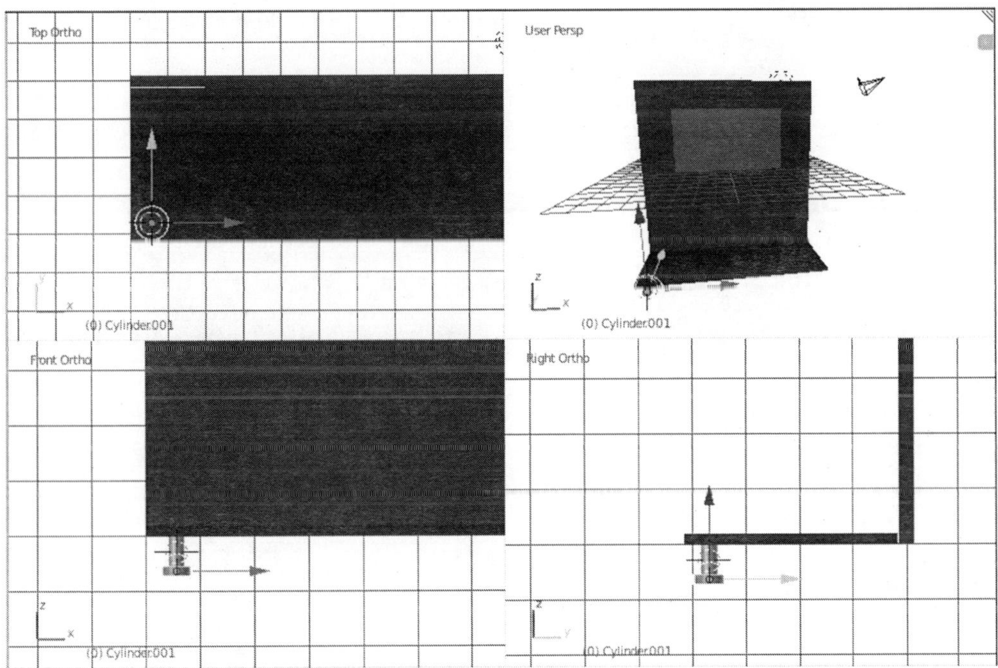

Figure 2-36 *The Cylinder001 moved*

15. Press SHIFT+D and then press ENTER; a copy of *cylinder* and *cylinder001* is created. Create two more copies of these two cylinders. Next, align all the copies of *cylinder* and *cylinder001*, as shown in Figure 2-37. You will notice that all the copies are automatically added to the *basesupport* group.

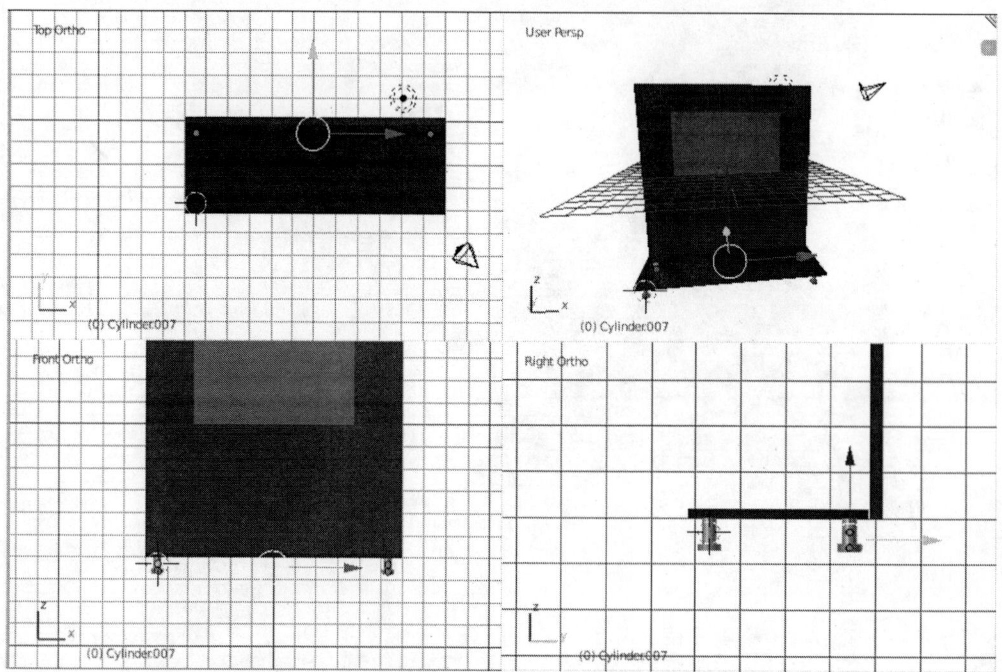

Figure 2-37 *All the copies of cylinder aligned*

16. Press SHIFT + C to place the 3D Cursor at the center of the view.

Creating the Drawers of the TV Unit

1. Choose the **Cube** tool from the **Add Primitive** panel in **Toolshelf**; a cube is created at the center of the view. Next, double-click on *Cube* in **Outliner** and enter **side** to rename it.

2. Make sure the **Object** button is chosen in the **Properties Editor**. Next, enter the following values in the **Scale** area of the **Transform** panel in the **Properties Editor**.

   X: **0.08** Y: **2.0**

3. Change the color of *side* to black as discussed earlier. Align *side* in all the views, as shown in Figure 2-38.

   Next, you will create a drawer of the TV unit.

4. Choose the **Cube** tool from the **Add Primitive** panel in **Toolshelf**; a cube is created at the center of the view. Next, double-click on *Cube* in **Outliner** and enter **drawer** to rename it.

5. Make sure the **Object** button is chosen in the **Properties Editor**. Next, enter the following values in the **Scale** area of the **Transform** panel in the **Properties Editor**.

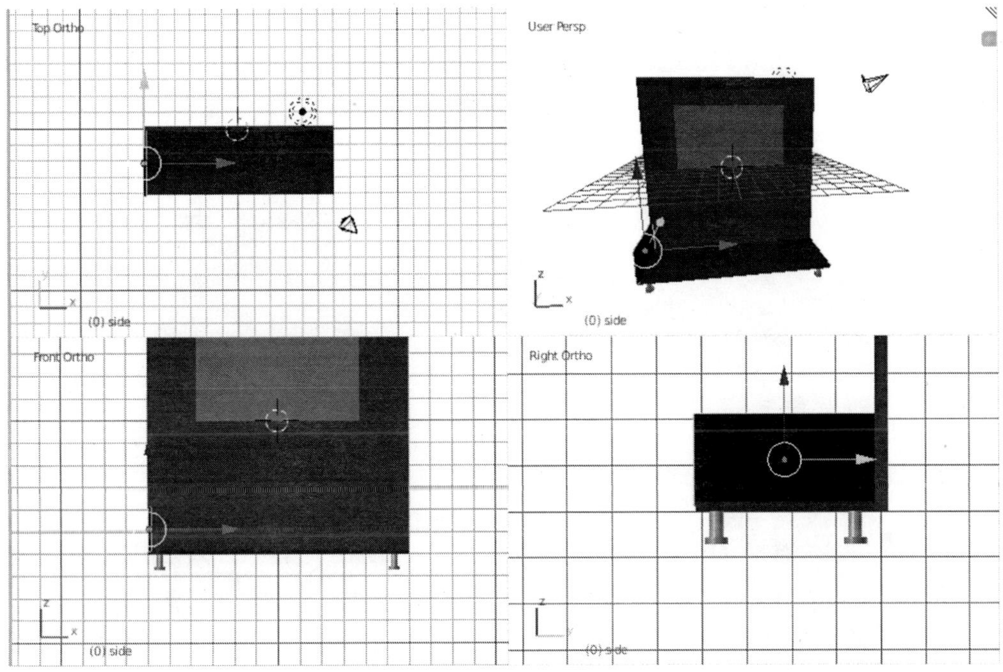

Figure 2-38 *The side aligned*

6. Align *drawer* in all the views, as shown in Figure 2-39.

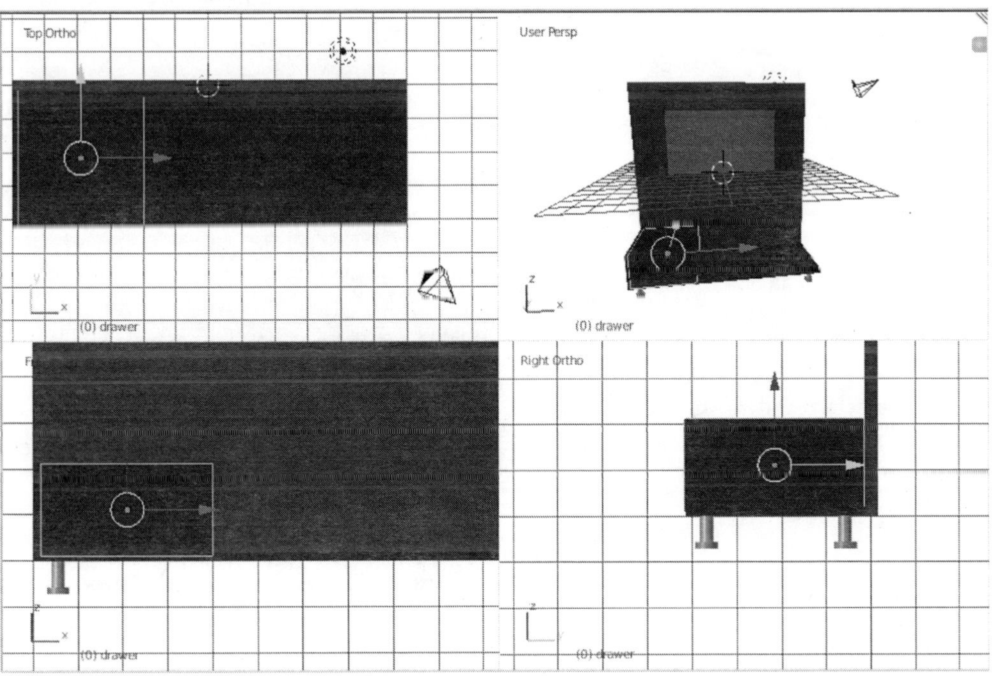

Figure 2-39 *The drawer aligned*

7. Select *drawer* and *side*. Press SHIFT +D and ENTER; a copy of *drawer* and *side* is created. Create one more copy of *drawer* and *side*. Also, make one more separate copy of *side*. Next, align all the copies of *drawer* and *side* in all the views, as shown in Figure 2- 40.

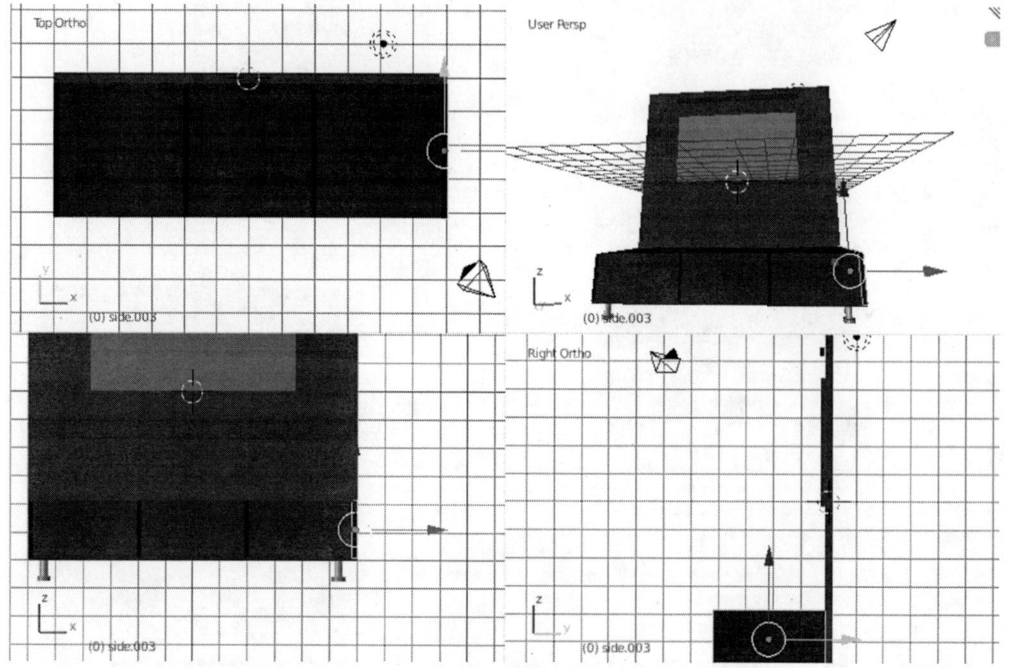

***Figure 2-40** All the copies of side and drawer aligned*

Next, you will create handles for the drawers.

8. Choose the **Torus** tool from the **Add Primitive** panel in **Toolshelf**; a torus is created at the center of the view. Rename it as *handle*, as discussed earlier.

9. Enter the following values in the **Add Torus** panel of **Toolshelf**.

   Major Segments: **96** Major radius : **0.5** Minor radius: **0.05**

10. Press SHIFT+D and ENTER; a copy of *handle* is created with the name *handle001*. Next, create one more copy of *handle* and then align *handle* and its copies, as shown in Figure 2-41.

Creating Shelves of the TV Unit

1. Select *base* in the view. Press SHIFT+D and ENTER; the copy of *base* with the name *base.001* is created. Rename it as *shelfbottom* in **Outliner**, as discussed earlier. Next, align *shelfbottom* above the drawers, as shown in Figure 2-42.

2. Select *side* in the view. Press SHIFT+D and ENTER; a copy of *side* is created. Rename it as *shelfside* in **Outliner**, as discussed earlier.

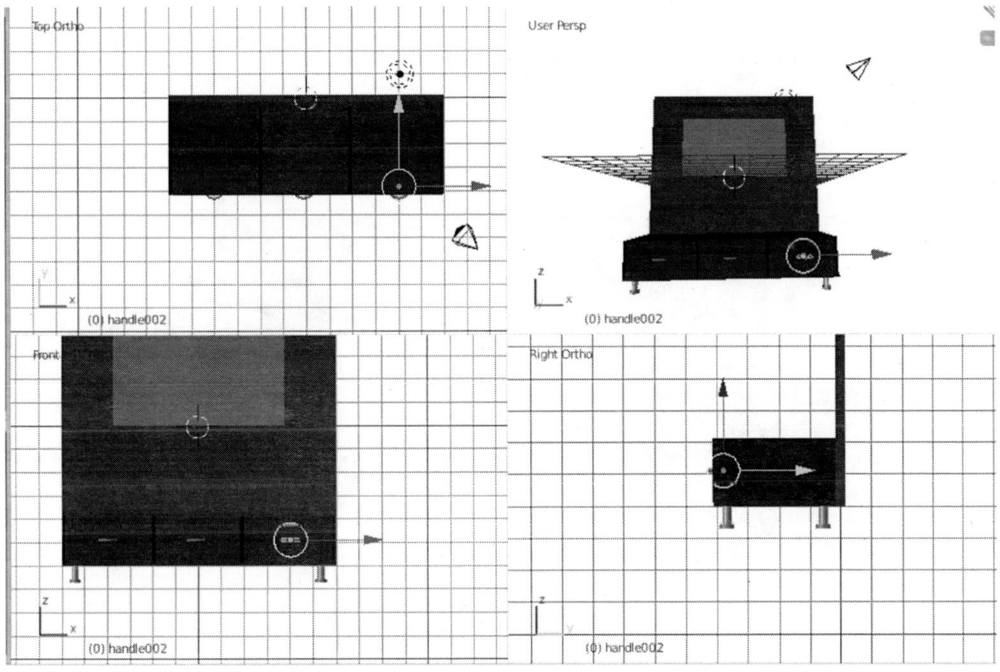

Figure 2-41 The handle and its copies aligned

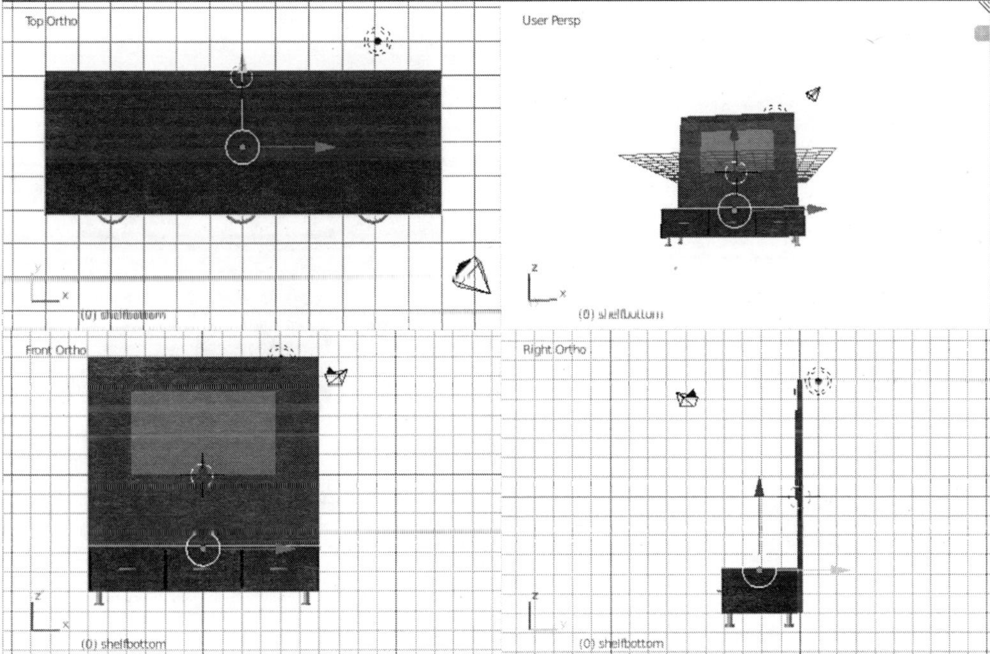

Figure 2-42 The shelfbottom aligned

3. Make sure the **Object** button is chosen in the **Properties Editor**. Next, enter the following values in the **Scale** area of the **Transform** panel in the **Properties Editor**.

Y: **1.25** Z: **0.75**

4. Align *shelfside* in all the views, as shown in Figure 2-43.

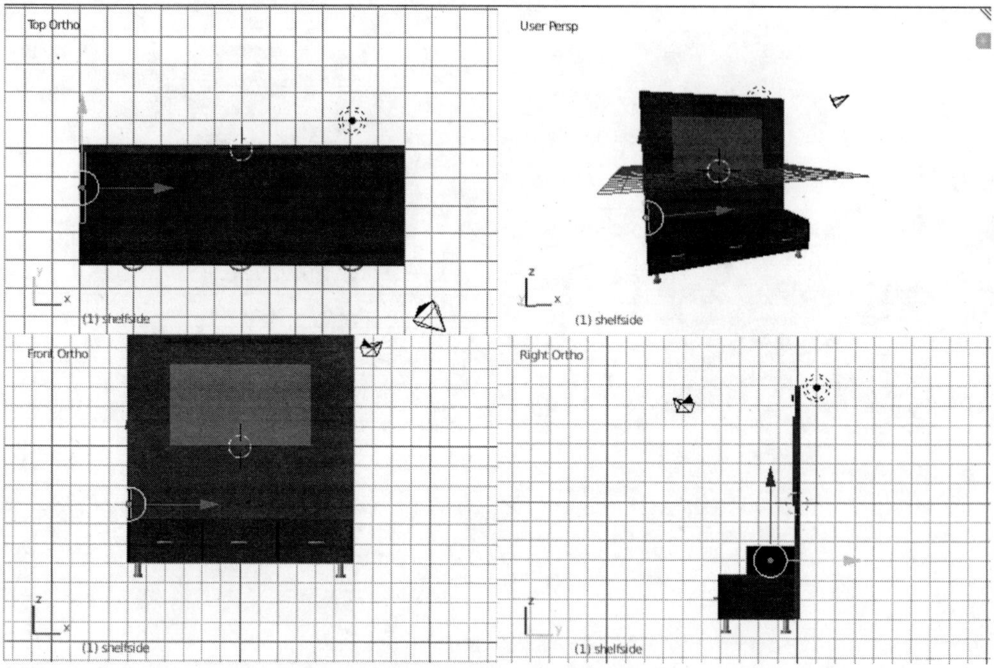

Figure 2-43 *The shelfside aligned*

5. Press SHIFT+D; the copy of *shelfside* with the name *shelfside.001* is created. Create three more copies of *shelfside*. Next, align all the copies in the views, as shown in Figure 2-44.

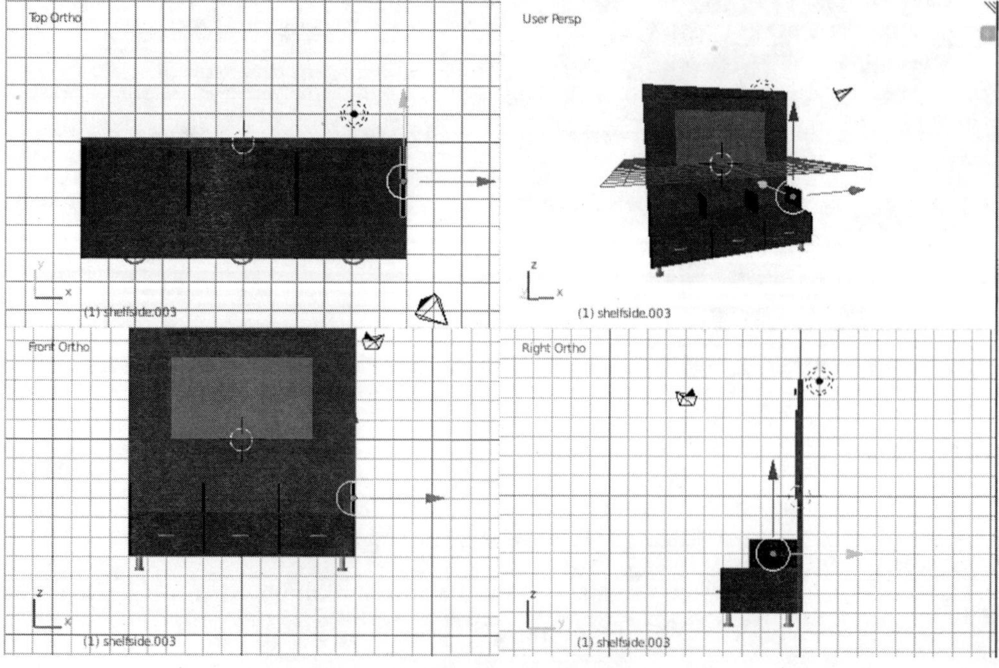

Figure 2-44 *The copies of shelfside aligned*

6. Select *shelfbottom* in the view. Press SHIFT +D and ENTER; a copy of *shelfbottom* is created. Next, rename it as *shelftop* and align it in all the views, as shown in Figure 2-45.

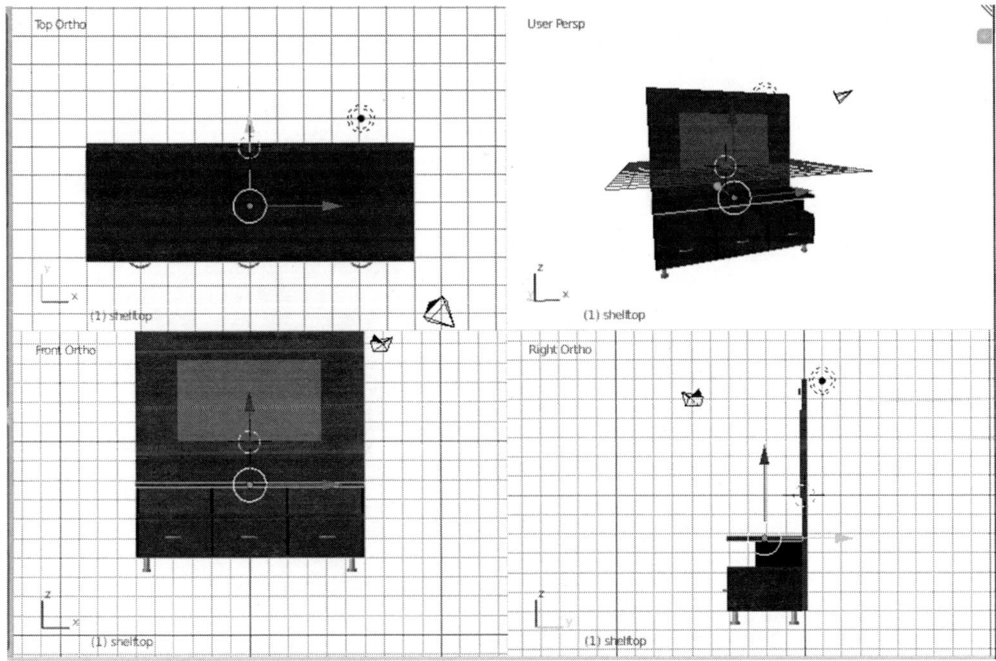

***Figure 2-45** The shelftop aligned*

Changing the Background Color of the Scene

In this section, you will change the background color of the scene.

1. Choose the **World** button from the **Properties Editor**. Next, click on the **Horizon Color** swatch in the **World** panel, refer to Figure 2-46, the Color Picker window is displayed.

2. Select white color in this window; the background will display the white color on rendering.

***Figure 2-46** The Horizon Color swatch*

Saving and Rendering the Scene

In this section, you will save the scene that you have created and then render it. You can also view the final rendered image of this model by downloading the *c02_blender_2.79_rndr.zip* file from *www.cadcim.com*. The path of the file is as follows: *Textbooks > Animation and Visual Effects > Blender > Blender 2.79 for Digital Artists*

1. Choose **File > Save** from the **Info Editor** menu bar.

2. Adjust the view in the User Persp view. Next, choose the **Open GL still image render** button from **3D View Editor**; the rendered image is displayed in the **UV/Image Editor**; refer to Figure 2-26.

Tutorial 2

In this tutorial, you will create 3D model of a dining table set, as shown in Figure 2-47, by using **Edit Mode**. **(Expected time: 30 min)**

Figure 2-47 *The dining table set*

The following steps are required to complete this tutorial:

a. Create the folder.
b. Create top of the table.
c. Create legs of the table.
d. Create base and legs of the chair.
e. Create back of the chair.
f. Save and render the scene.

Creating the Folder

1. Navigate to *\Documents\blender2.79\ c02* and create a new folder with the name *c02_tut2.*

2. Press CTRL+N or choose **File > New** from the **Info Editor** menu bar; a menu is displayed. Choose **Reload Start-Up File**; the menu disappears and the startup file is loaded.

3. Choose **File > Save** from the **Info Editor** menu bar; the **File Browser** is displayed

4. Navigate to *\Documents\blender2.79\c02\c02_tut2* and enter **Dining table set** in the **File Name** edit box. Next, choose the **Save Blender File** button to save the file at the specified location.

Creating Top of the Table

In this section, you will create top of the table using the **Cube** tool.

1. Press CTRL+ALT+Q; the quad view is displayed.

2. Choose the **Cube** tool from the **Add Primitive** panel in **Toolshelf**; a cube is created at the center of the view. Next, double-click on *Cube* in **Outliner** and enter **tabletop** to rename it.

3. Enter the following values in the **Scale** area of the **Transform** panel in **Properties Editor**:

   X: **12** Y: **20** Z: **0.2**

   The cube is modified, refer to Figure 2-48.

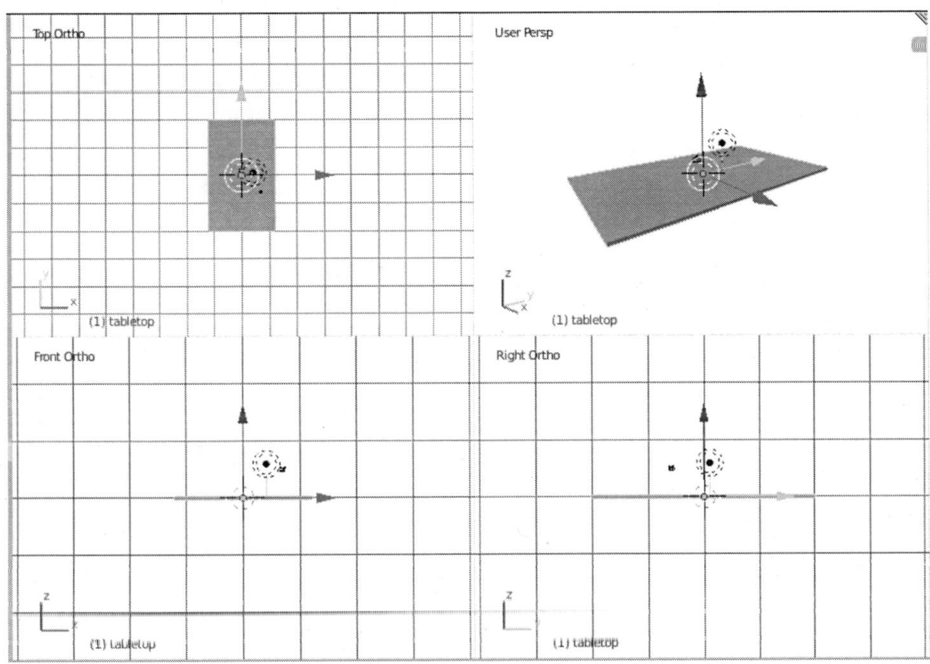

Figure 2-48 The modified cube displayed

4. Press the TAB key and choose **Edit Mode** from the pie menu displayed. Next, choose the **Edge Select** button from **3D View Editor**; all the edges of *tabletop* are highlighted.

5. Press and hold the SHIFT key and select all the vertical edges of *tabletop* to deselect them, refer to Figure 2-49.

6. Choose **Mesh > Edges > Subdivide** from the **3D View Editor** menu bar; two edges (one horizontal and one vertical) passing through the center of tabletop and dividing it into four parts get added.

7. Enter **16** in the **Number of Cuts** slider of the **Subdivide** panel in **Toolshelf**; *tabletop* is subdivided, as shown in Figure 2-50.

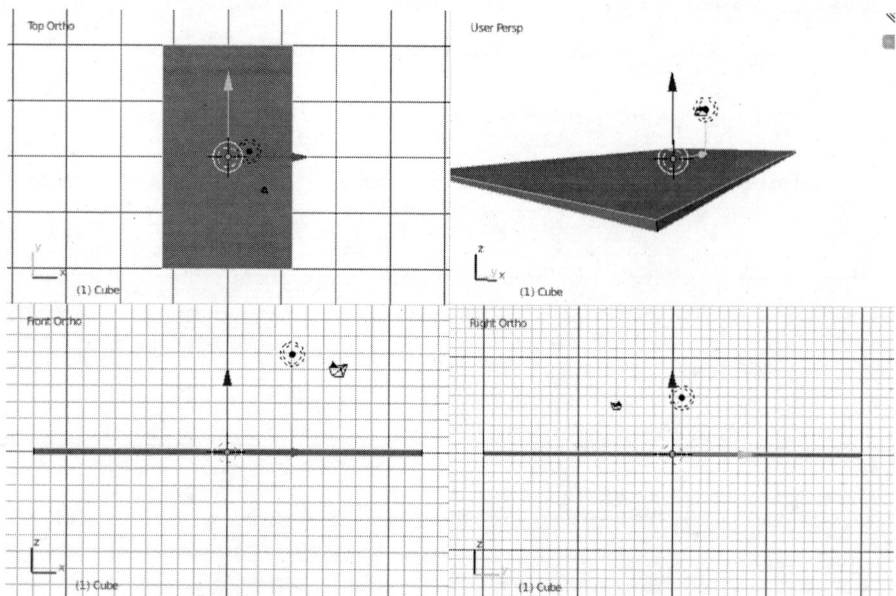

Figure 2-49 *All the corner edges deselected*

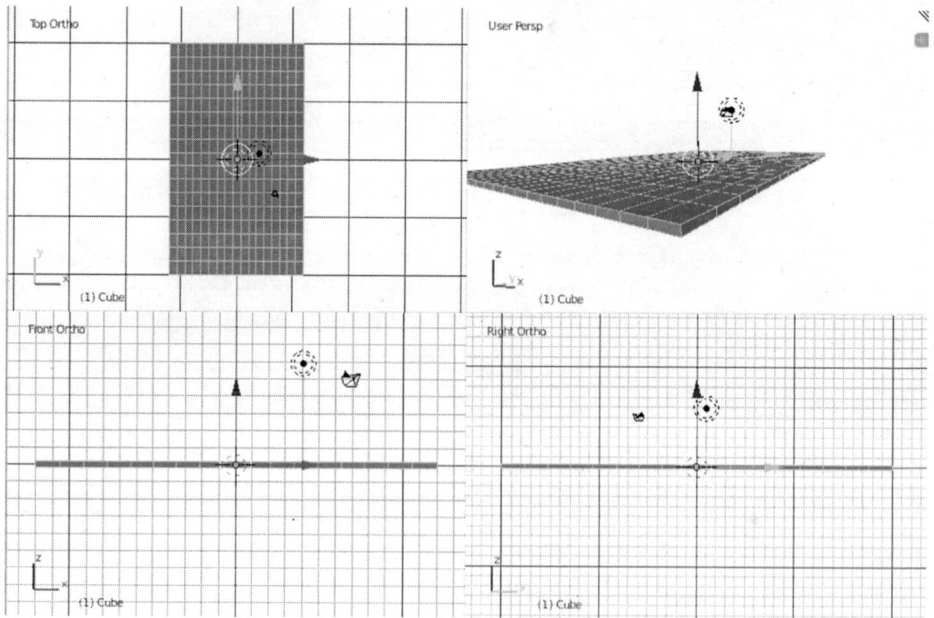

Figure 2-50 *The tabletop subdivided*

Next, you will make the corners of *tabletop* smooth. To achieve this, you need to use the **Bevel** tool on the corner edges.

8. Select all the four vertical edges in the User Persp view, as shown in Figure 2-51.

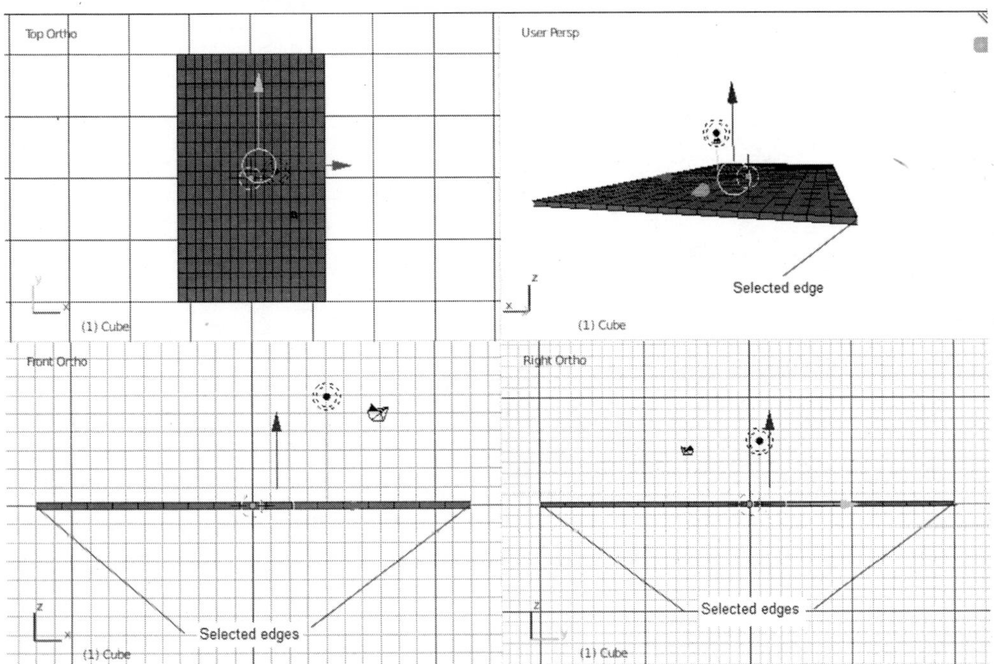

Figure 2-51 *Four corner edges selected*

9. Choose **Mesh > Edges > Bevel** from the **3D View Editor** menu bar or press CTRL+B; a dotted line is attached to the cursor. Next, drag and move the cursor in the view and click at a point; the **Bevel** panel is added to **Toolshelf**. Set the parameters in the **Bevel** panel as follows:

   Amount Type: **Depth** Amount: **0.05** Segments: **4**

   tabletop is smoothened at the corners, refer to Figure 2-52.

Creating Legs of the Table

In this section, you will create legs of the table using the **Cylinder** tool.

1. Choose the **Cylinder** tool from the **Add Primitive** panel in **Toolshelf**; a cylinder is created at the center of the view. Next, double-click on *Cylinder* in **Outliner** and enter **leg** to rename it.

2. Enter the following values in the **Add Cylinder** panel of **Toolshelf**.

   Vertices: **64** Radius: **0.5** Depth: 2

3. Press / on numpad; *tabletop* gets hidden and *leg* becomes isolated and you get more room to modify *leg*, refer to Figure 2-53.

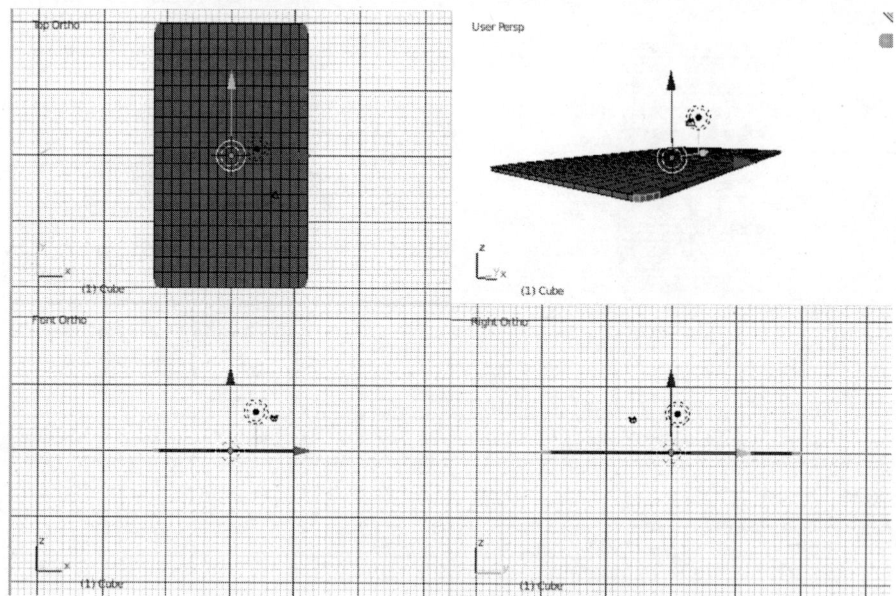

***Figure 2-52** The tabletop smoothened at the corners*

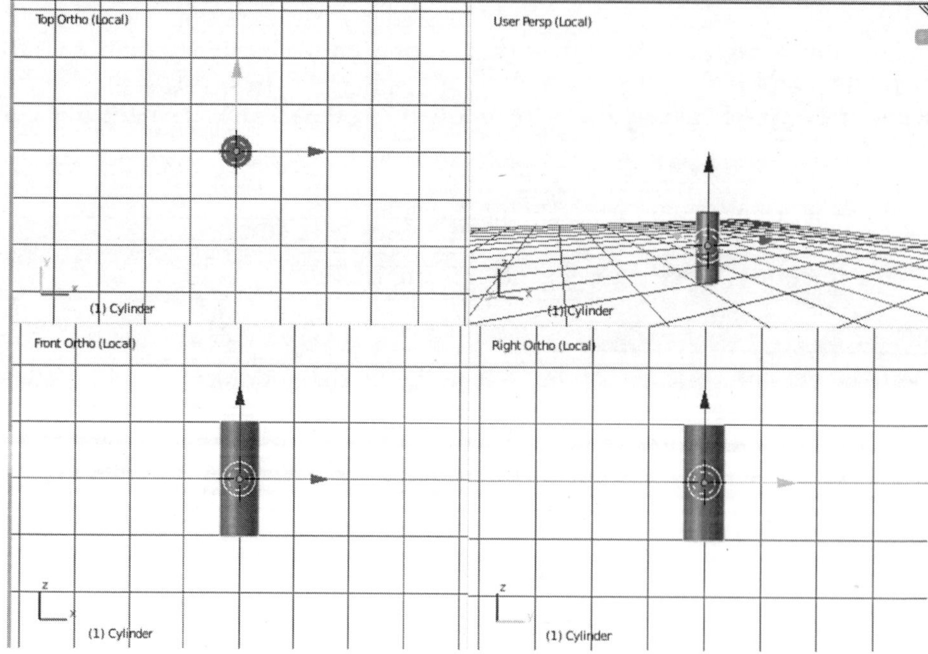

***Figure 2-53** The leg displayed*

4. Press the TAB key and choose **Edit Mode** from the pie menu displayed. Next, choose the **Face Select** button from **3D View Editor**; all the faces of *leg* are highlighted.

5. Choose the **Tools** tab from **Toolshelf**. Select the bottom face of *leg* and then vertical edges

of *cylinder* and then choose **Mesh > Faces > Bevel** from the **3D View Editor** menu bar or press CTRL+ B and then click at a point in the view; the **Bevel** panel is added to **Toolshelf.**

6. Enter **0.150** in the **Amount** slider and choose **Width** from the **Amount Type** drop-down of the **Bevel** panel; face of *leg* is beveled, as shown in Figure 2-54.

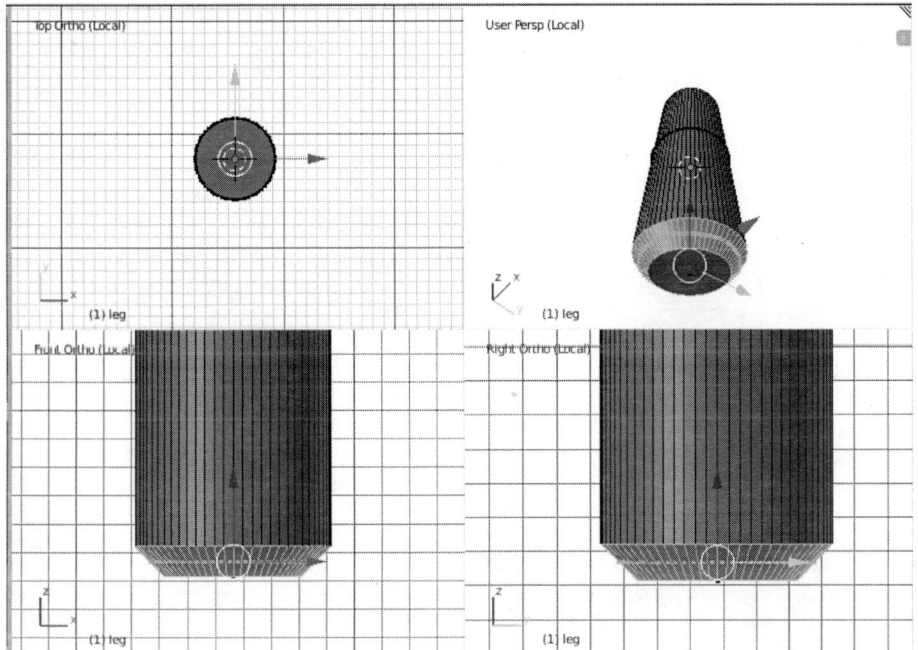

Figure 2-54 *The face of leg beveled*

7. Select the bottommost face of *leg* again. Next, choose **Extrude Region** from the **Add** area of the **Mesh Tools** panel in **Toolshelf** and then click at a point in the view; the **Extrude Region and Move** panel is displayed at the bottom in **Toolshelf.**

8. Enter **0.25** in the **Z** slider of the **Extrude Region and Move** panel; the selected face of *leg* is extruded, as shown in Figure 2-55.

9. Make sure the bottommost face of *leg* is selected. Next, choose **Extrude Region** from the **Add** area of the **Mesh Tools** panel in **Toolshelf** and then click at a point in the view; the **Extrude Region and Move** panel is displayed at the bottom in **Toolshelf.**

10. Enter **0.1** in the **Z** slider of the **Extrude Region and Move** panel; the selected face of *leg* is extruded, as shown in Figure 2-56.

11. Make sure the bottommost face of *leg* is selected. Next, choose the **Scale** tool from **3D View Editor**.

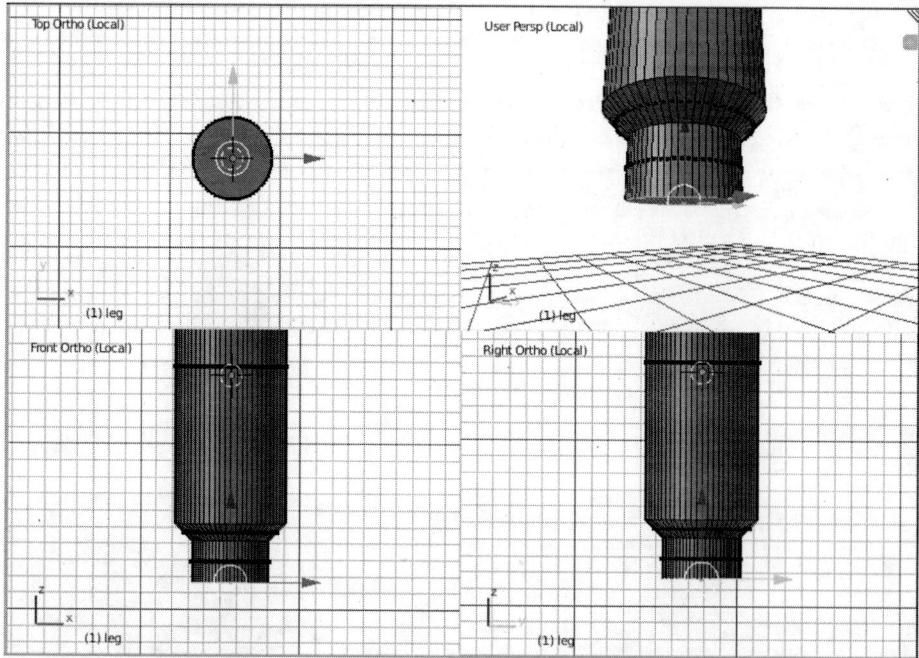

Figure 2-55 The bottommost face extruded

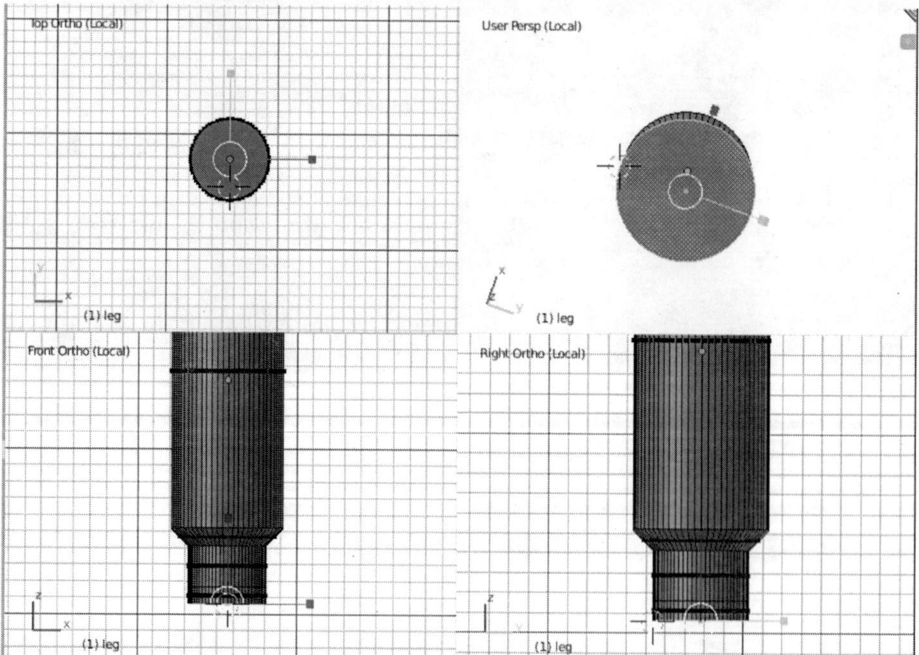

Figure 2-56 The bottommost face extruded

12. Press and hold the left mouse button and move the cursor. Next, click at a point in the view to scale the selected face to some extent manually; the **Resize** panel is added to **Toolshelf**

In this panel, enter **1.5** in the **X**, **Y**, and **Z** sliders and select the **X**, **Y**, and **Z** checkboxes; the selected face is uniformly scaled, as shown in Figure 2-57.

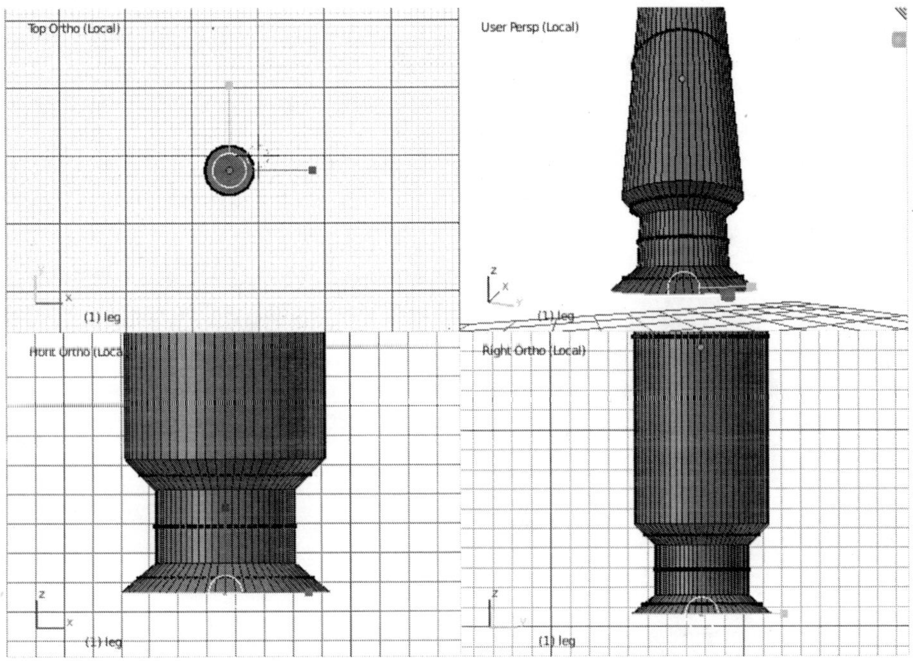

***Figure 2-57** The selected face scaled*

13. Make sure the bottommost face of *leg* is selected. Next, choose **Extrude Region** from the **Add** area of the **Mesh Tools** panel in **Toolshelf** and then click at a point in the view; the **Extrude Region and Move** panel is displayed at the bottom in **Toolshelf**.

14. Enter **10** in the **Z** slider of the **Extrude Region and Move** panel; the selected face of *leg* is extruded, as shown in Figure 2-58.

15. Choose the **Edge Select** tool from **3D View Editor**. Next, choose the **Loop Cut and Slide** tool from the **Add** area in the **Mesh Tools** panel of **Toolshelf** and click on *leg*, refer to Figure 2-59 and then move the edge loop to the lower portion of the leg, as shown in Figure 2-59.

16. Similarly, create four more edge loops using the **Loop Cut and Slide** tool and then place them, as shown in Figure 2-60.

17. Select the edge from *leg*, as shown in Figure 2-61. Next, choose **Mesh > Edges > Edge Rings** from the **3D View Editor** menu bar; all the edges in a ring are selected.

18. Choose the **Scale** tool from **3D View Editor**. Next, press and hold the left mouse button and move the cursor and click at a point in the view; the **Resize** panel is displayed at the bottom in **Toolshelf**.

19. Enter **0.75** in the **X**, **Y**, and **Z** sliders in the **Vector** area of the **Resize** panel. Also, select the **X**, **Y**, and **Z** in this panel; all the edges in the ring are scaled, as shown in Figure 2-62.

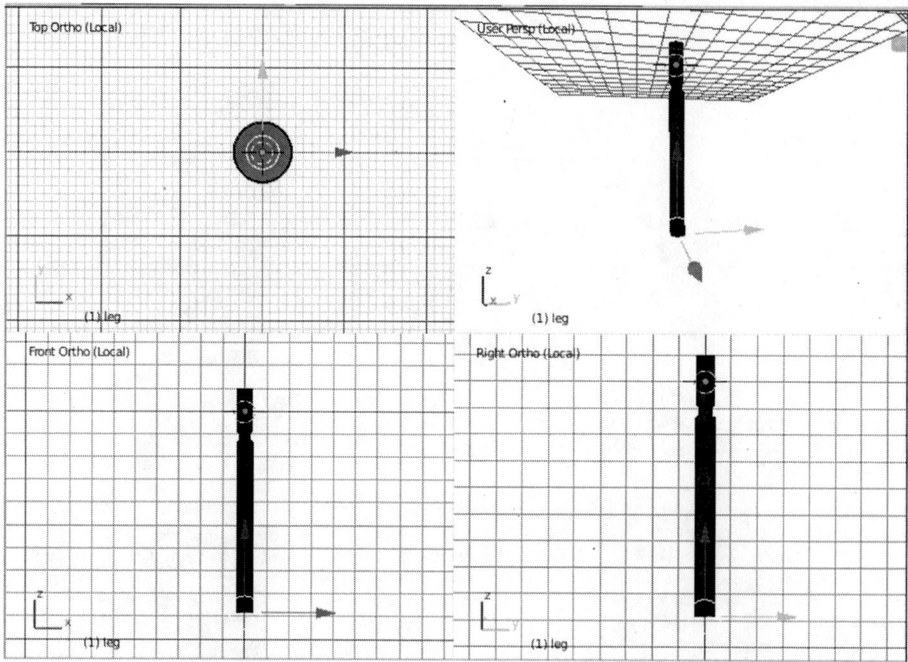

Figure 2-58 *The bottommost face extruded*

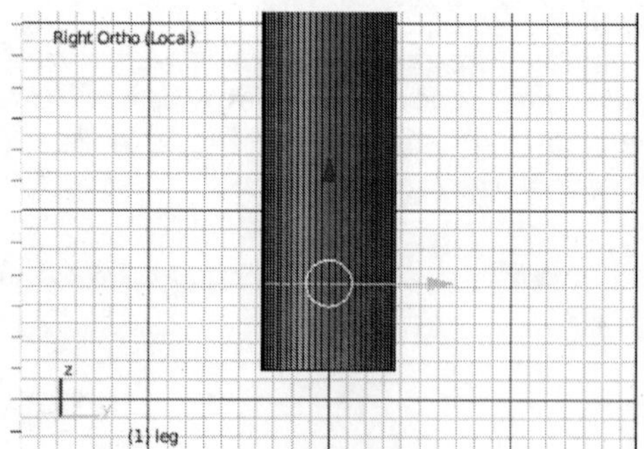

Figure 2-59 *The edge loop created*

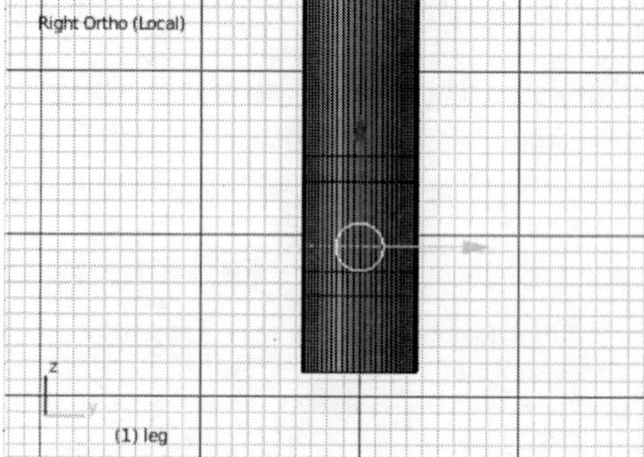

Figure 2-60 *Four edge loops created*

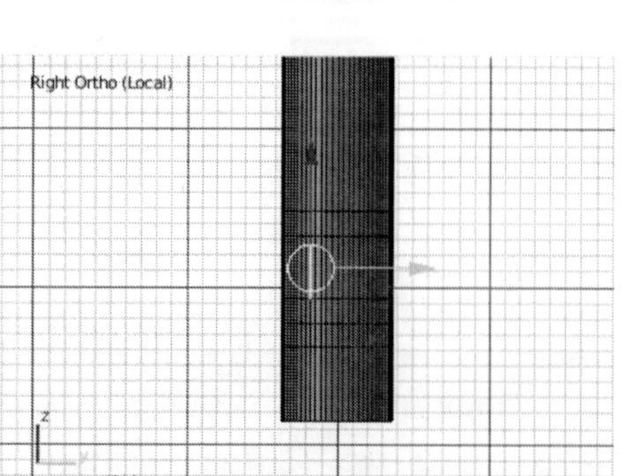

Figure 2-61 *The edge selected*

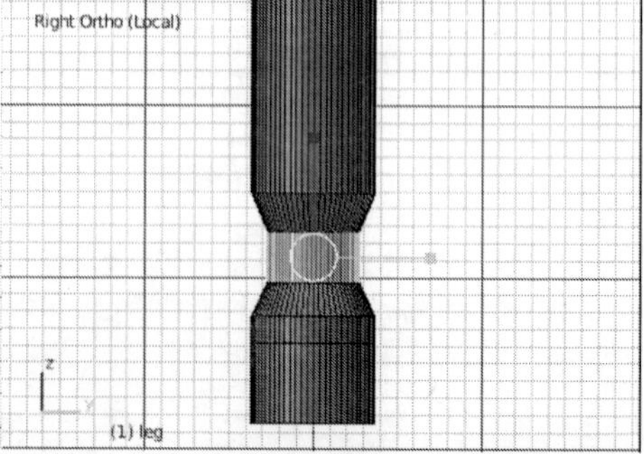

Figure 2-62 *The edges in the ring scaled*

20. Select the edge from the bottommost loop of *leg*, refer to Figure 2-63. Next, choose **Mesh > Edges > Edge Loops** from the **3D View Editor** menu bar; the bottommost edge loop is selected. Now, repeat the steps 18 and 19 to scale this edge loop, refer to Figure 2-63.

21. Press the TAB key and then choose **Object Mode** from the pie menu displayed. Next, press the / key on numpad; *tabletop* is displayed along with *leg*.

22. Select *leg*. Press SHIFT+D and then ENTER; copy of *leg* is created with the name *leg001*. Next, create two more copies of *leg*. Now, align *leg* and all its copies with *tabletop*, as shown in Figure 2-64.

23. Select *tabletop, leg*, and all the copies of *leg* using the SHIFT key. Next, press CTRL+J; all the selected parts are combined to form a single mesh. Note that the combined mesh is automatically renamed with the name of the last selected part. Rename the combined mesh as *table* in **Outliner**, as discussed earlier.

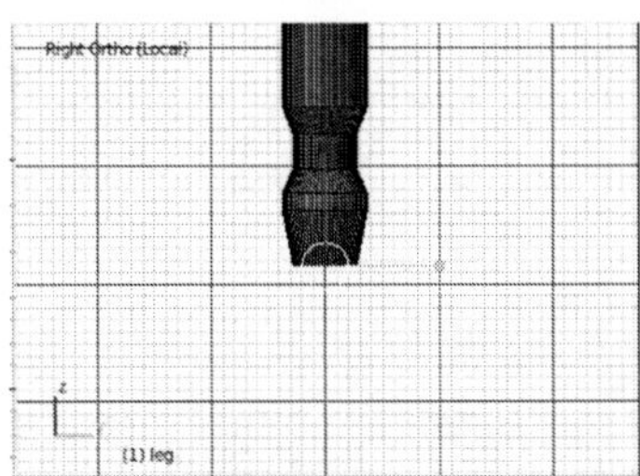

Figure 2-63 *The bottommost edge loop scaled*

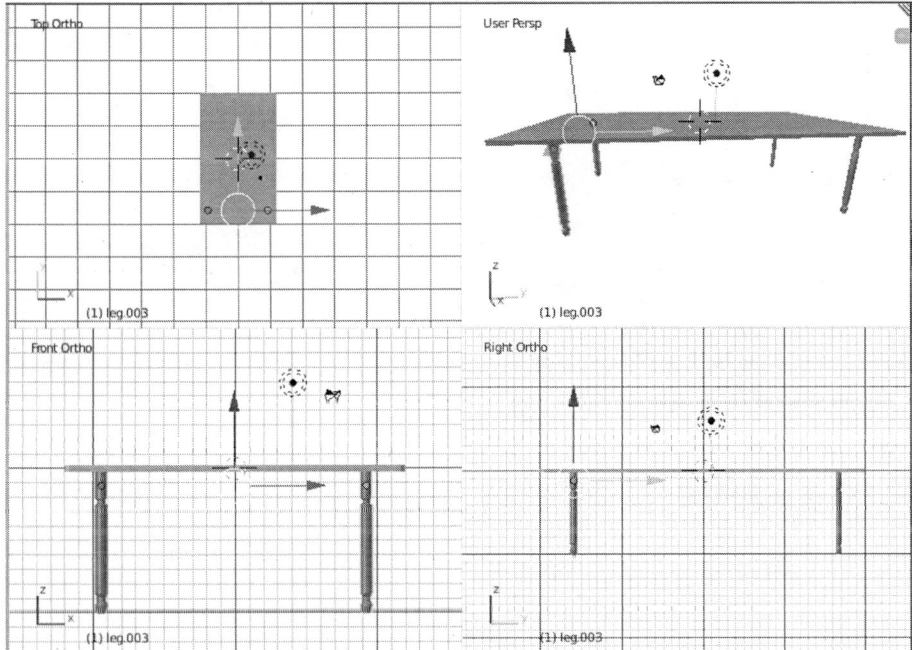

Figure 2-64 *The leg and its copies aligned*

24. Change the color of *table* to color of your choice as discussed in Tutorial 1, refer to Figure 2-65.

Creating Seat of the Chair

In this section, you will create seat of the chair using the **Cube** tool.

1. Choose the **Cube** tool from the **Add Primitive** panel in **Toolshelf**; a cube is created at the center of the view. Next, double-click on *Cube* in **Outliner** and enter **chair** to rename it.

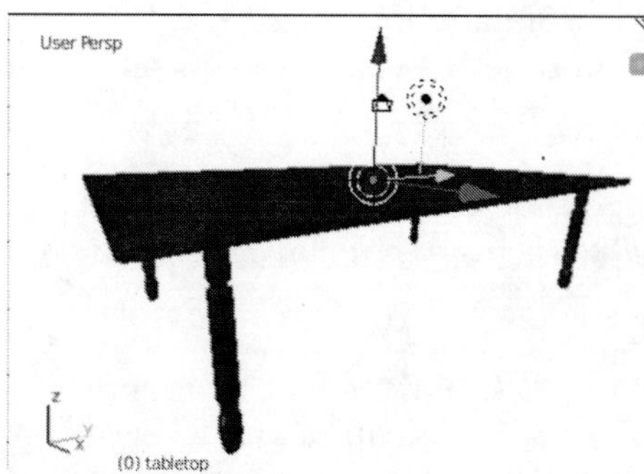

Figure 2-65 The table displayed

2. Move *chair* to one side of *table*. Next, enter the following values in the **Scale** area of the **Transform** panel in the **Properties Editor**:

X: **6** Y: **5** Z: **0.5**

Chair is modified.

3. Press / on numpad; chair becomes isolated and *table* is hidden, refer to Figure 2-66.

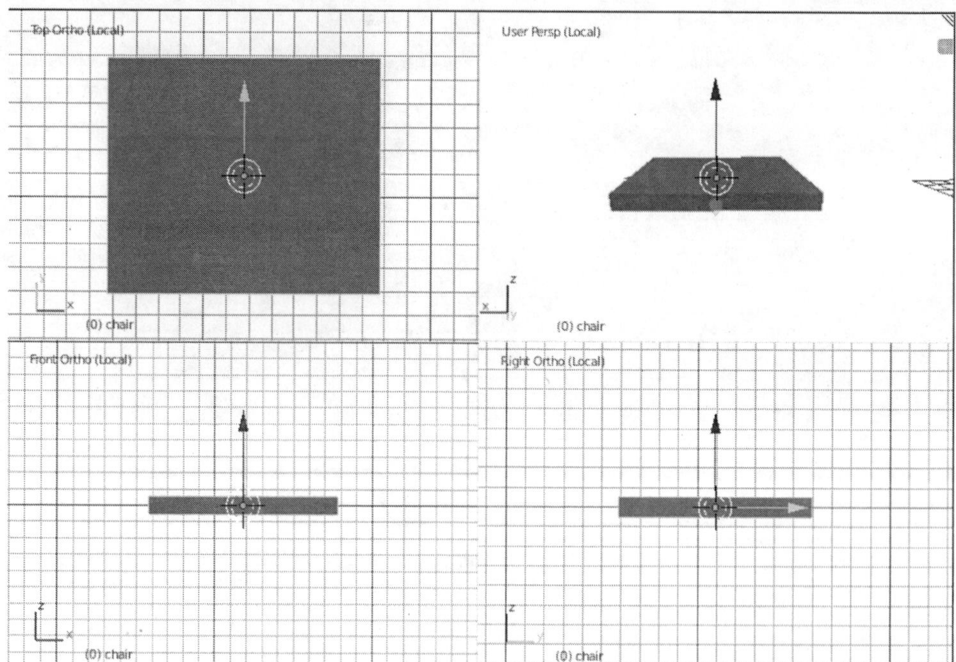

Figure 2-66 The chair modified

4. Press the TAB key and choose **Edit Mode** from the pie menu displayed. Next, choose the **Edge Select** button from **3D View Editor**; all the edges of *chair* are highlighted.

6. Choose the **Loop Cut and Slide** tool from the **Add** area in the **Mesh Tools** panel of **Toolshelf** and click on *chair* in the Top Ortho view; an edge is added to *chair*. Place the newly added edge, as shown in Figure 2-67.

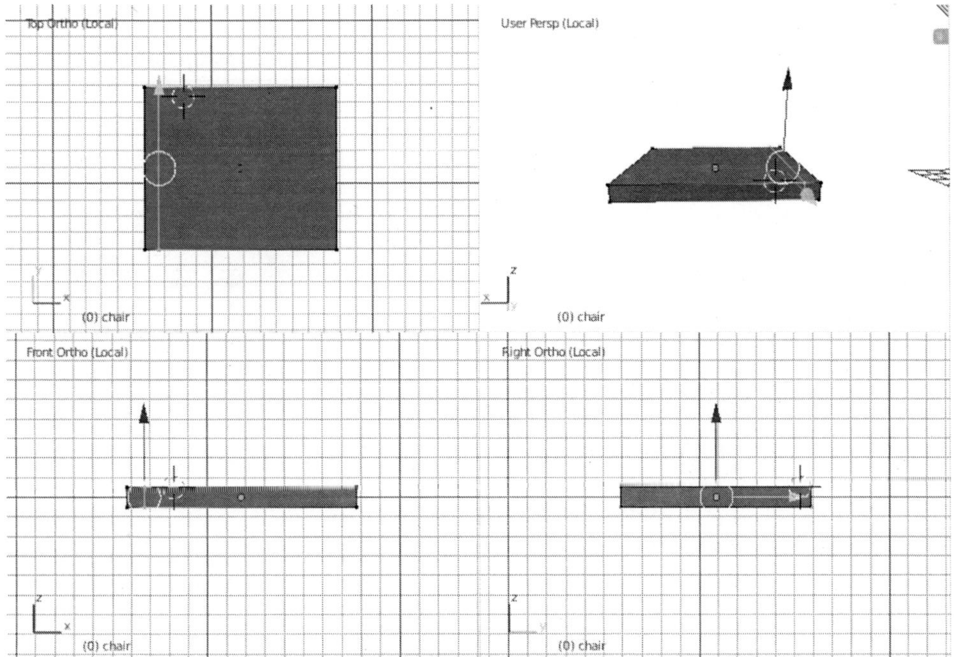

Figure 2-67 *The edge added to chair*

7. Similarly, add three more edges to *chair* using the **Loop Cut and Slide** tool and place them, as shown in Figure 2-68.

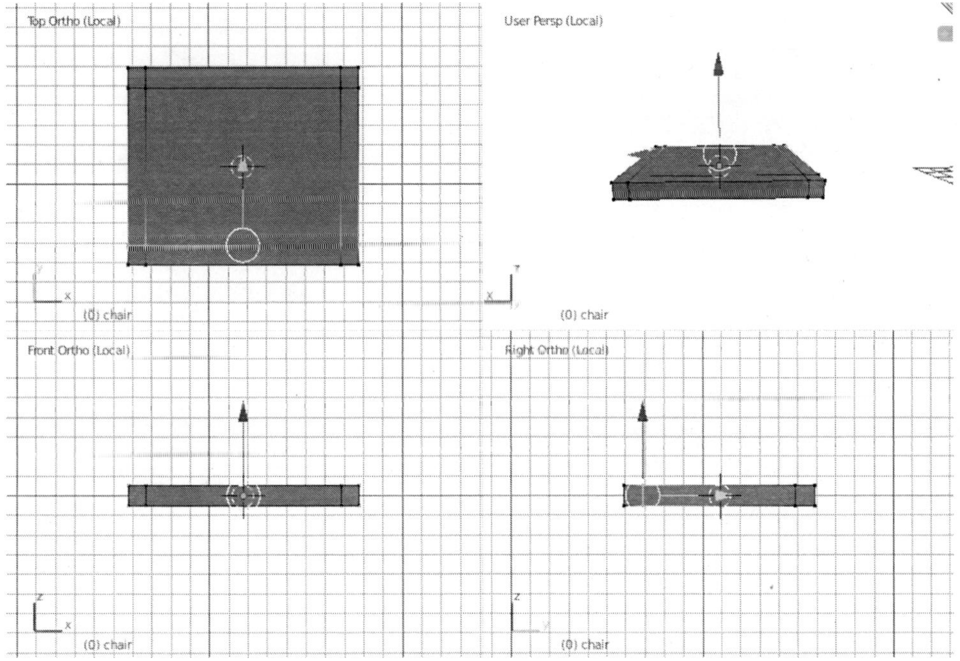

Figure 2-68 *Three more edges added to chair*

Creating Back of the Chair

1. Choose the **Face Select** tool from **3D View Editor**. Next, select the two faces from the Top Ortho(Local) view, as shown in Figure 2-69.

2. Choose the **Tools** tab from **Toolshelf**. Next, choose the **Extrude Individual** from the **Add** area in the **Mesh Tools** panel of **Toolshelf** and move the cursor in the view and click at a point; the **Extrude Individual Faces** panel is displayed at the bottom in **Toolshelf**.

3. Enter **-19** in the **offset** slider in the **Extrude Individual Faces** panel; the selected faces are extruded, as shown in Figure 2-70.

4. Press the **TAB** key and switch to **Object Mode** from the pie menu displayed.

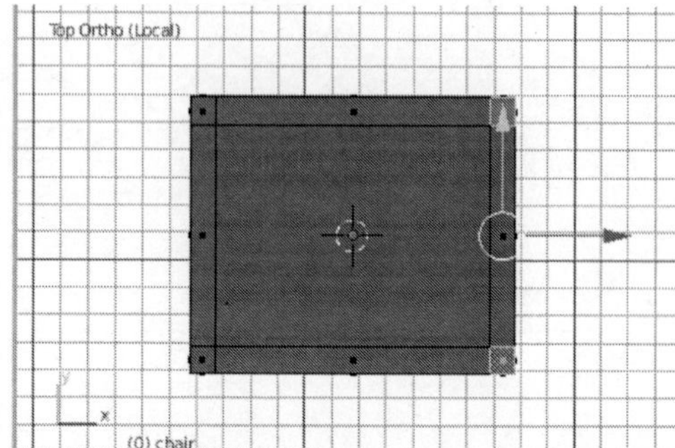

Figure 2-69 *The two faces selected*

5. Choose the **Cube** tool from the **Add Primitive** panel in **Toolshelf**; a cube is created at the center of the view. Next, double-click on *Cube* in **Outliner** and enter **back** to rename it.

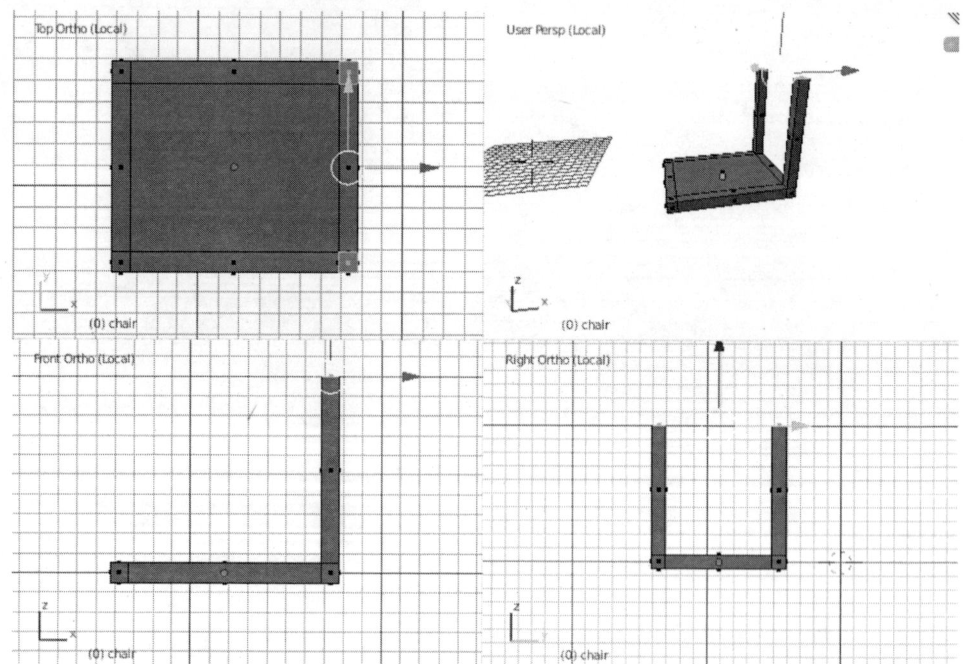

Figure 2-70 *The two faces extruded*

6. Enter the following values in the of the **Transform** panel in the **Properties Editor**:

Scale area:
X: **0.39** Y: **0.5** Z: **4.25**

Rotation area:
X: **90**

back is modified.

Note
You may need to change the value in the **Z** *slider for back depending on the width of the extruded face of chair.*

7. Align *back* with *chair*, as shown in Figure 2-71.

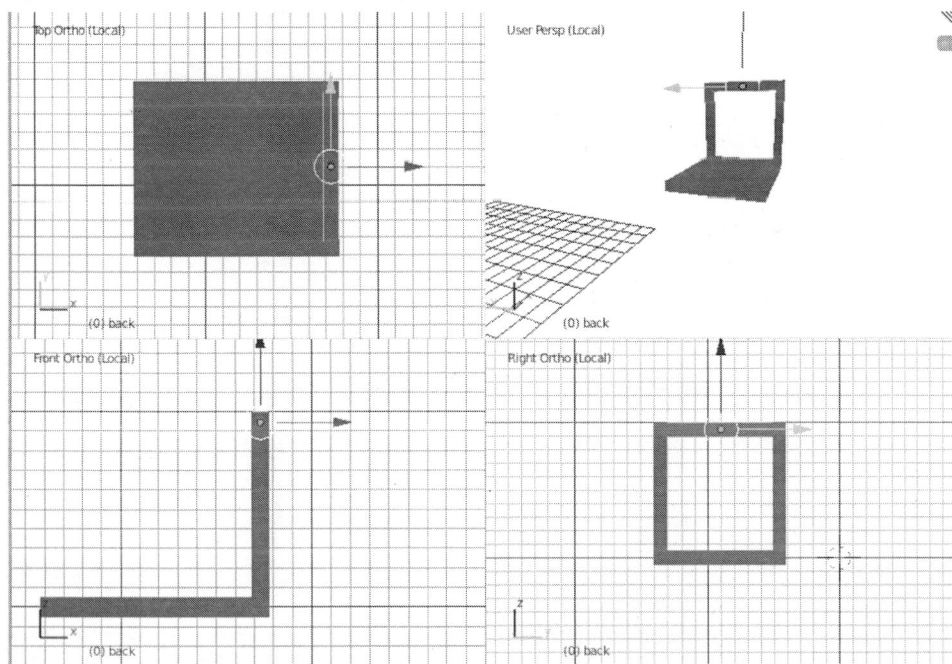

Figure 2-71 *The back aligned*

8. Switch to **Edit Mode** as discussed earlier. Next, choose the **Edge Select** tool and select one of the horizontal edges of *back* in the Right Ortho (Local) view, as shown in Figure 2-72.

9. Choose **Edges > Edge Rings** from the **3D View Editor** menu bar; all the edges in the ring are selected.

10. Choose the **Subdivide** tool from the **Add** area in the **Mesh Tools** panel of **Toolshelf**. Next, enter **12** in the **Number of Cuts** slider of the **Subdivide** panel in **Toolshelf**; *back* is subdivided, as shown in Figure 2-73.

Note
The subdivisions carried out above will help you get a smooth curvature when shape of the chair is modified using proportional editing.

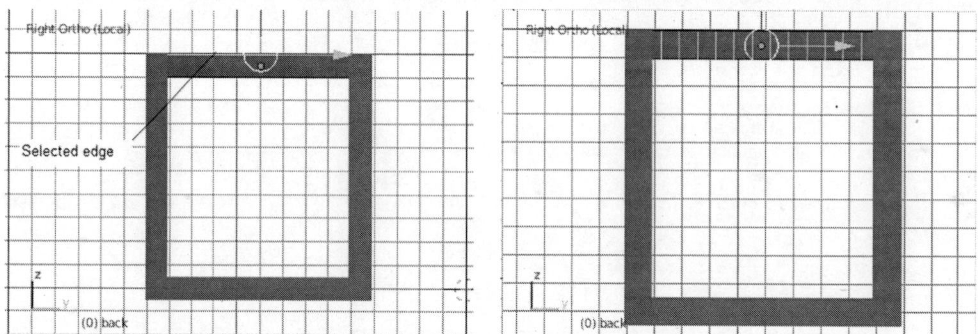

Figure 2-72 The selected edge

Figure 2-73 The back subdivided

11. Switch to **Object Mode** and make sure *back* is selected. Next, press SHIFT+D and ENTER; a copy of *back* is created with the name *back001*. Align it, as shown in Figure 2-74.

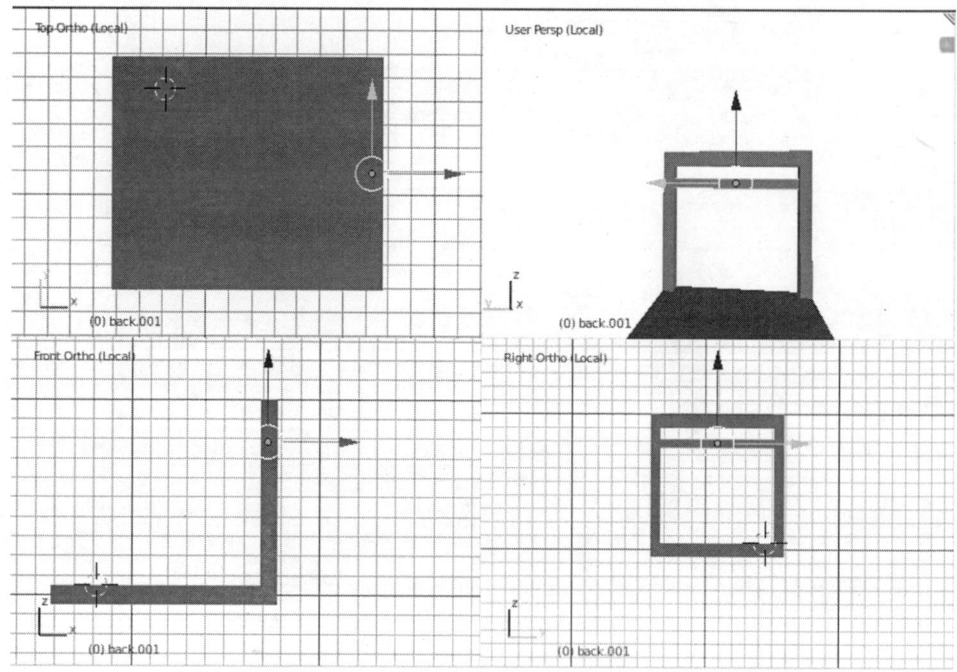

Figure 2-74 The back001 aligned

12. Enter the following values in the **Scale** area of the **Transform** panel in **Properties Editor**:

 X: **0.05** Y: **0.3** Z: **4.25**

 back001 is modified.

13. Create five copies of *back001* as discussed earlier and align them, as shown in Figure 2-75.

14. Create one more copy of *back001*. It is automatically renamed as *back007*. Next, enter **180** in the **X** slider of the **Rotation** area in the **Transform** panel of the **Properties Editor**; *back007* is rotated. Next, align it, as shown in Figure 2-76. Make sure that *back007* is at the front of other back parts.

15. Create five copies of *back007* and align them, as shown in Figure 2-77.

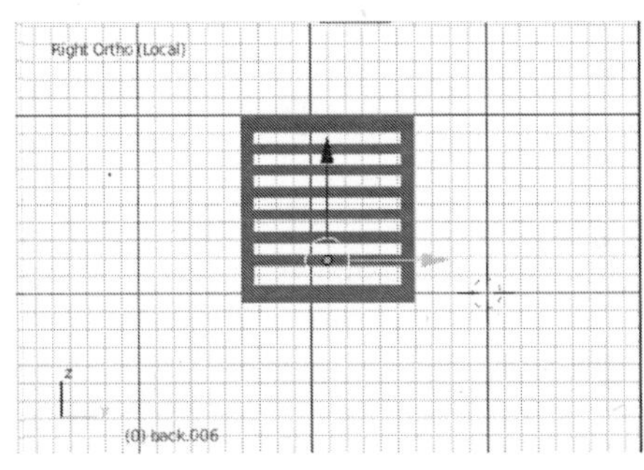

Figure 2-75 *The copies of* back001 aligned

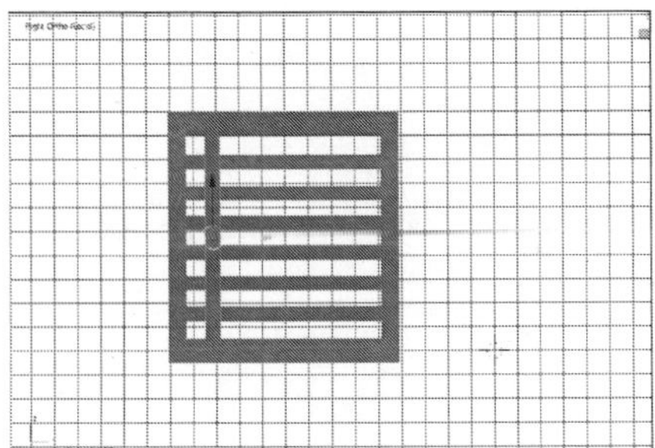

Figure 2-76 *The back007 aligned*

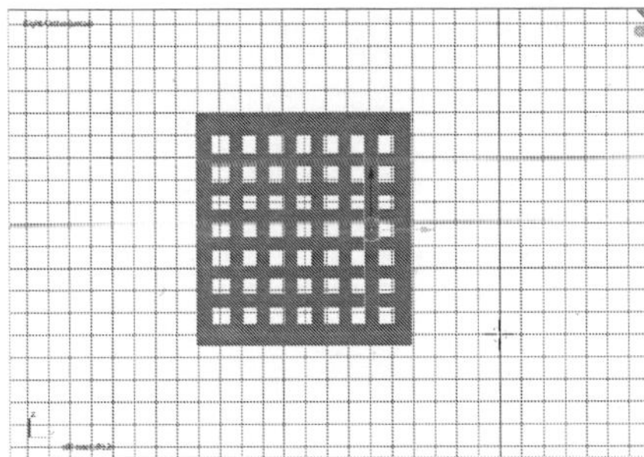

Figure 2-77 *The copies of back007 aligned*

Creating Legs of the Chair

In this section, you will create legs of the chair using the **Extrude Individual** tool.

1. Press CTRL+ALT+Q; User Persp(Local) view is displayed. Next, press CTRL+7 and then press 5; the Bottom Ortho (Local) view is displayed.

2. Select *chair* from **Outliner** and then switch to **Edit Mode**, as discussed earlier. Next, choose the **Face Select** tool from **3D View Editor**. Next, select four faces from the Bottom Ortho(Local) view, as shown in Figure 2-78.

3. Press 4 and then 5, the User Persp (local) view is displayed. Now, adjust the User Persp (local) view to view *chair* properly. Now, press CTRL+ALT+Q to switch over to quad view.

4. Choose the **Tools** tab from **Toolshelf**. Next, choose the **Extrude Individual** from the **Add** area in the **Mesh Tools** panel of **Toolshelf** and move the cursor in the view and click at a point; the **Extrude Individual Faces** panel is displayed at the bottom in **Toolshelf**.

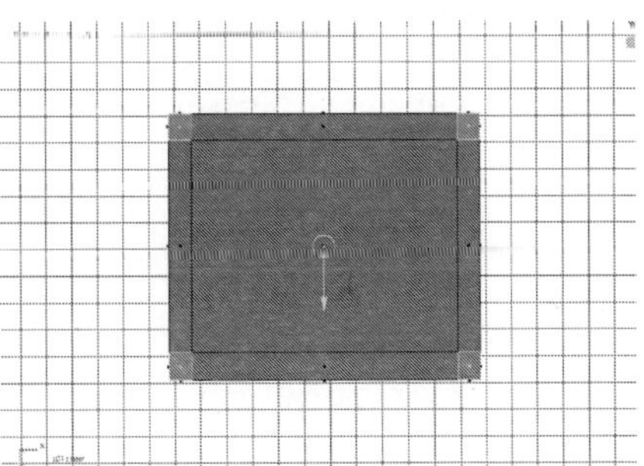

Figure 2-78 *Four faces are selected*

5. Enter **-18** in the **offset** slider of the **Extrude Individual Faces** panel; the selected faces are extruded, as shown in Figure 2-79.

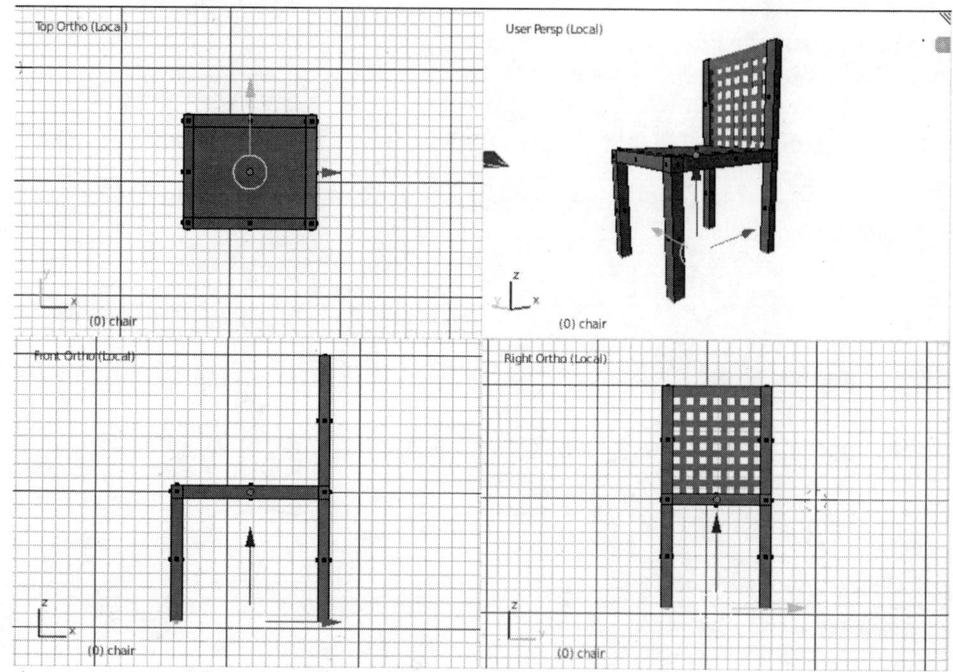

***Figure 2-79** Selected faces extruded*

Next, you need to properly shape the chair using the proportional editing mode.

6. Select *chair*. Next, subdivide parts of *chair* by selecting the respecive edges, as shown in Figure 2-80.

   Next, you need to combine some of the parts of chair before using the proportional editing mode.

7. Select *back* and then *chair*. Next, press CTRL+J; the selected parts are combined to form a single mesh and is automatically named as *chair* as discussed earlier.

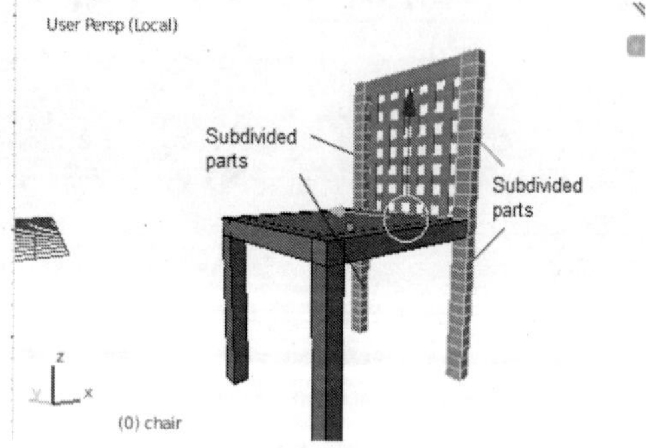

***Figure 2-80** Selected edge rings subdivided*

8. Switch to **Edit Mode**. Select the vertices of *chair*, as shown in Figure 2-81. Adjust the view of UserPersp (local), refer to Figure 2-82. Next, choose **Enable** from the **Proportional Editing mode** drop-down or press O; the proportional editing mode is enabled.

9. Choose the **Translate** tool from **3D View Editor**. Next, press and hold the left mouse button and move the selected vertices in the left direction; a circle is attached to the cursor. Increase the radius of the circle by using the middle mouse button, refer to Figure 2-82. Next, click at a point to get a curve as shown in Figure 2-82.

Note

You can also select faces or edges instead of vertices in proportional editing.

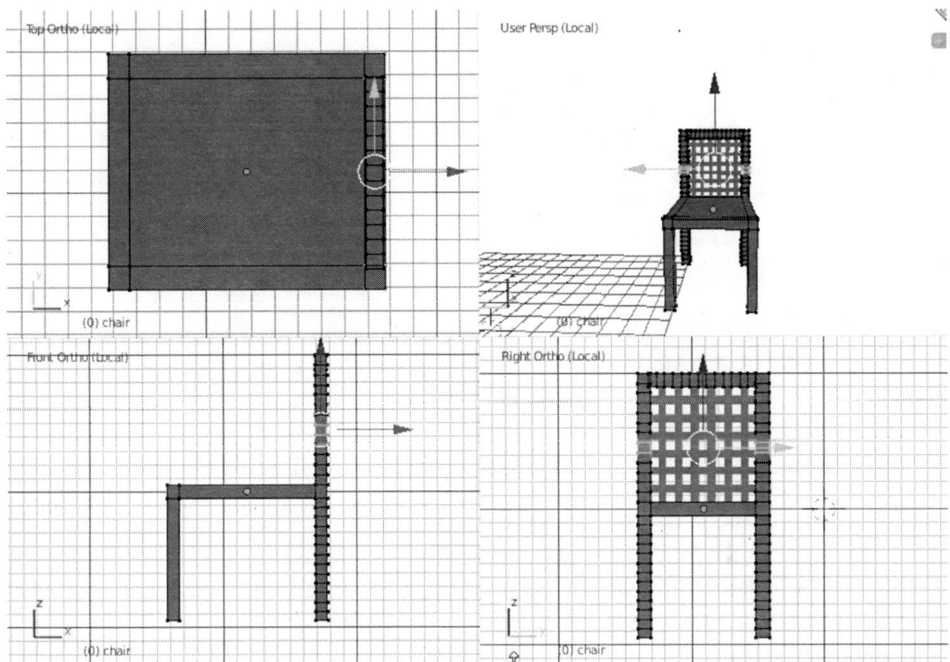

Figure 2-81 *Selected vertices of chair*

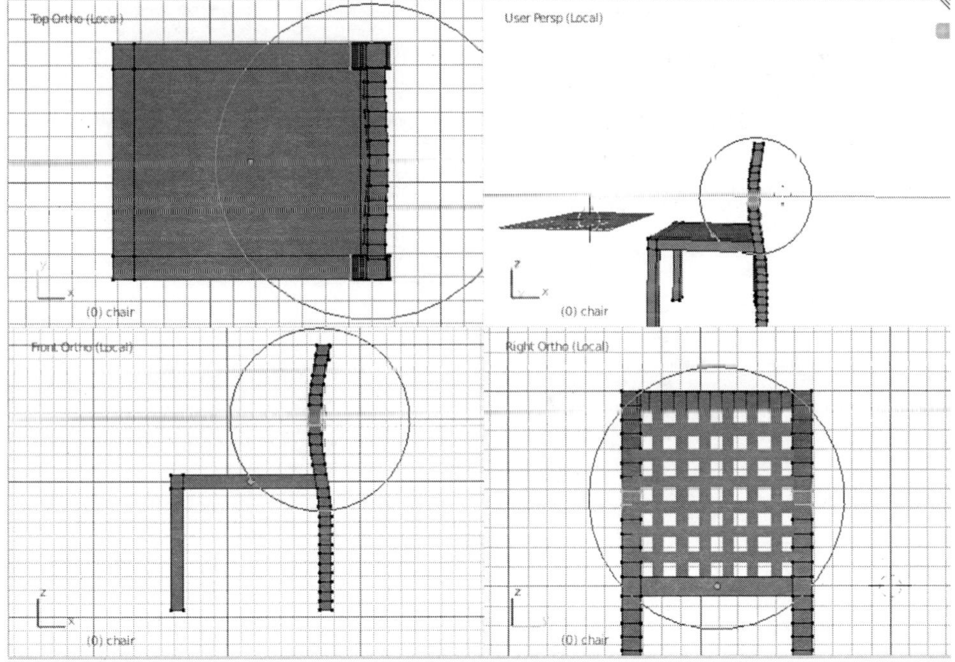

Figure 2-82 *Vertices of chair moved*

10. Similarly, select the center vertices of the top of *chair* and move them to get a curve, as shown in Figure 2-83. Also, select the center vertices of the two legs of *chair* to get a curve, as shown in Figure 2-84.

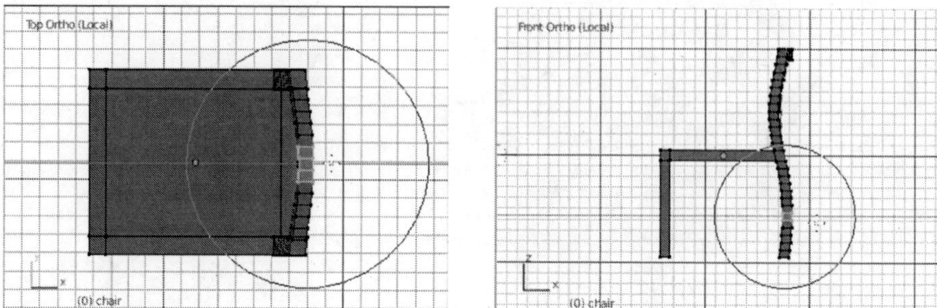

Figure 2-83 *Center vertices of top of chair selected and moved*

Figure 2-84 *Center vertices of two legs selected and moved*

11. Switch to **Object Mode**. Select *back001* to *back012* from **Outliner** using the SHIFT key and then press CTRL+J. Next, rename the combined mesh as *back*.

12. Switch back to **Edit Mode** and select the center vertices from *back*, refer to Figure 2-85. Make sure proportional editing mode is enabled. Next, move the vertices to get a curve, refer to Figure 2-85. Next, move the top vertices of *back* such that the top of *back* fits properly into the top portion of *chair*, refer to Figure 2-86.

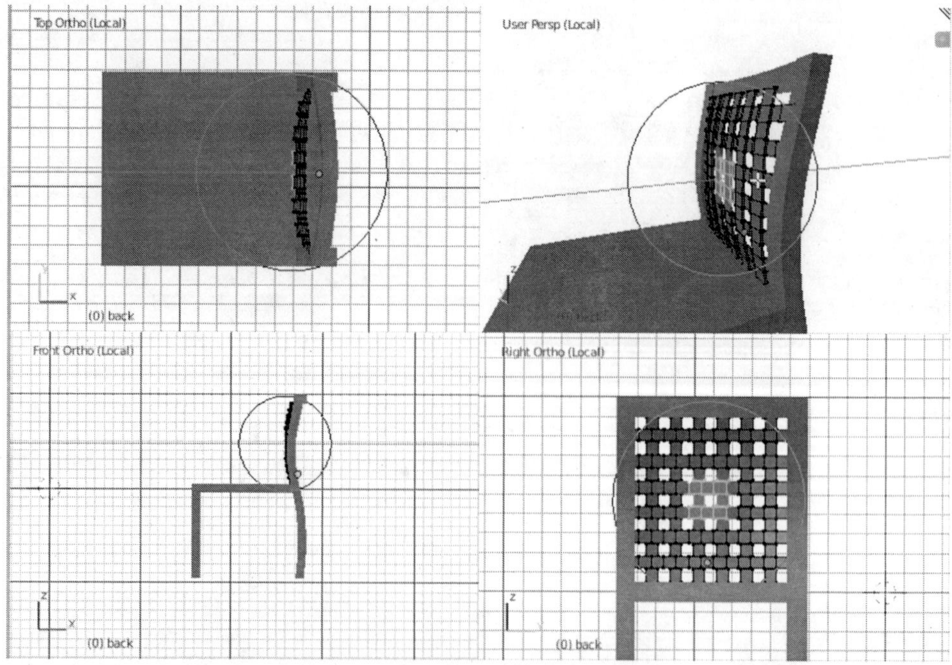

Figure 2-85 *Center vertices of back selected and moved*

13. Select *back* and then *chair*. Next, press CTRL+J; the selected parts are combined to form a single mesh and is automatically named as *chair*.

14. Change the color of *chair* as done for *table*, refer to Figure 2-87.

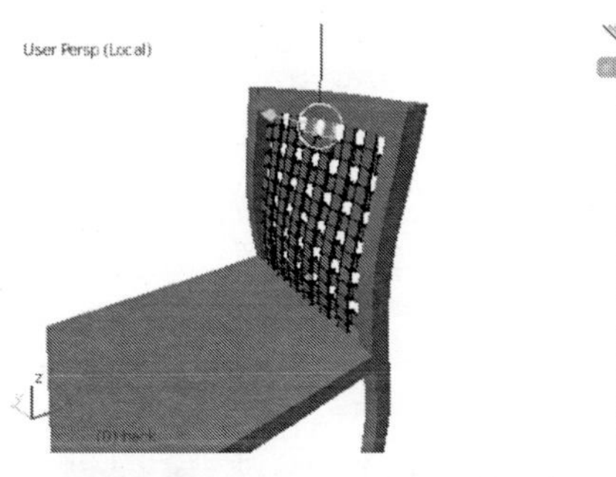

Figure 2-86 *Top vertices of back selected and moved*

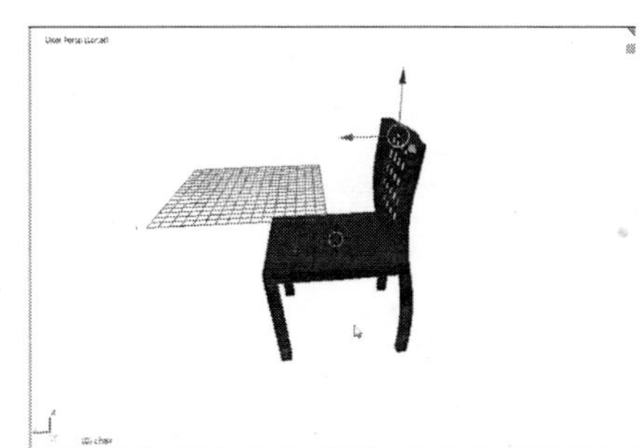

Figure 2-87 *The chair displayed*

Next, you will unhide the hidden table and make five copies of chair.

15. Press the / key on numpad; *table* is displayed. Next, create five copies of *chair* and align them around *table* in all the views. Figure 2-88 shows the dining table set in the User Persp view.

Figure 2-88 *Dining table set*

Saving and Rendering the Scene

In this section, you will save the scene that you have created and then render it. You can also view the final rendered image of this model by downloading the *c02_blender2.79_rndr.zip* file from *www.cadcim.com.* The path of the file is as follows: *Textbooks > Animation and Visual Effects > Blender > Blender 2.79 for Digital Artists*

1. Change the background color of the scene as discussed in Tutorial 1.

2. Choose **File > Save** from the **Info Editor** menu bar.

3. Adjust the view in the User Persp view. Next, choose the **Open GL still image render** button from **3D View Editor**; the rendered image is displayed in the **UV/Image Editor**; refer to Figure 2-47.

Self-Evaluation Test

Answer the following questions and then compare them to those given at the end of this chapter:

1. Which of the following combinations of shortcut keys is used to restore the 3D cursor at the centre of the grid?

   (a) SHIFT+S (b) SHIFT+C
   (c) CTRL+C (d) SHIFT+D

2. The __________ editing mode is used for smooth deformation of object.

3. The __________ tool is used to duplicate an object as an instance of the original object.

4. The __________ border around the selected object indicates that the object is a part of the group.

5. In Blender, you can individually transform the objects in a group without affecting other objects in the group. (T/F)

Review Questions

Answer the following questions:

1. Which of the following combinations of shortcut keys is used to duplicate an object?

   (a) SHIFT+S (b) SHIFT+C
   (c) CTRL+C (d) SHIFT+D

2. Which of the following combinations of shortcut keys is used to select all layers in a scene?

   (a) SHIFT+S (b) SHIFT+~
   (c) CTRL+C (d) SHIFT+D

3. You need to press - key on numpad to isolate the selected object(s) in a scene. (T/F)

4. Selected layer with objects has small orange colored circle on its layer button. (T/F)

5. You need to press CTRL+C to group selected objects. (T/F)

EXERCISES

Exercise 1

Create model of a center table using **Object Mode**, refer to Figure 2-89.

(Expected time: 15 min)

Figure 2-89 The center table

Exercise 2

Create model of a small house using **Edit Mode**, refer to Figure 2-90.

(Expected time: 20 min)

Figure 2-90 The house model

Answers to Self-Evaluation Test

1. b, **2.** proportional, **3.** **Duplicate Linked**, **4.** green, **5.** T

Chapter 3

Working with Curve Primitives

Learning Objectives

After completing this chapter, you will be able to:

- *Use Bezier curve primitives*
- *Use NURBS curve and NURBS surface primitives*
- *Modify Bezier, NURBS curve, and NURBS surface primitives*
- *Create and modify text*
- *Add background image*

INTRODUCTION

Curve primitives are used to create models which consists of complex curves and twists. Models created using curve primitives consume less memory space than those created using the mesh primitives. In this chapter, you will learn various types of curve primitives in detail. In addition, you will learn to create and modify text in the scene. You will also learn to add background image as reference image to create accurate models.

CURVE PRIMITIVES

Curve primitives are representation of a mathematical function compared to the mesh primitives which are defined by vertices, edges, and faces. There are three major types of curve primitives in Blender: Bezier, NURBS, and Draw Curve. All these types are discussed next.

Bezier

Bezier curve primitives are parametric curves which consist of control points, handles, and segments, refer to Figure 3-1. There are two types of Bezier curve primitives: Bezier and Circle. The Bezier is a 2D curve with two control points and Circle is an approximation of a circle with four control points. Figure 3-1 shows Bezier, Circle, and their elements. Each control point has two handles connected to it. You can transform control points and handles to achieve the desired curve.

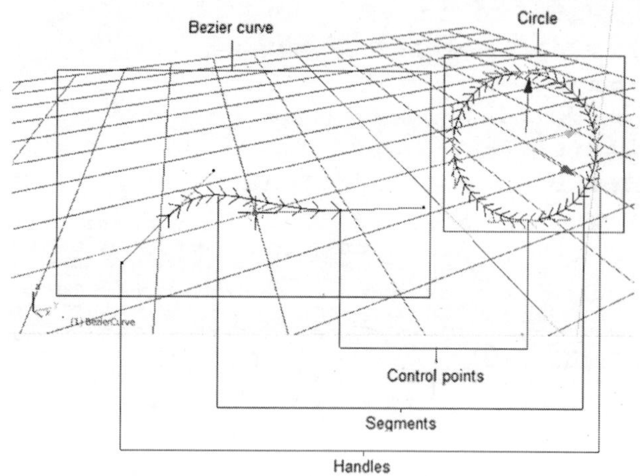

***Figure 3-1** The Bezier and Circle primitives and their elements*

There are four types of handles: **Automatic**, **Vector**, **Aligned**, and **Free**. To change the type of handle, make sure **Edit Mode** is activated and then press V; the **Handle** menu will be displayed, as shown in Figure 3-2. Choose desired option from this menu to change the handle type.

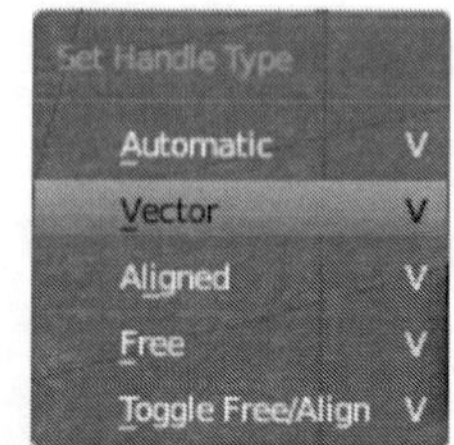

***Figure 3-2** The **Handle** menu displayed*

When you choose the **Automatic** option, handles have automatic length and direction. When you choose the **Vector** option, handles point to the next control point and sharp corners are created in the curve. Similarly, when you choose the **Aligned** option, both the handles lie in a straight line. Also the curve created by moving the Aligned handle have sharp angles. When you choose the **Free** option, both the handles are independent of each other. Note that when you choose the **Automatic** option and move handles, handles get converted into Aligned handle types. Also, when you choose the **Aligned** option and move handles, handles get converted into Free handle types.

Note

To change the handle type of a control point, you need to select the respective control point instead of the handle itself.

Creating and Modifying Bezier Curve Primitives

To create a Bezier curve primitive, choose the **Create** tab from **Toolshelf**. Next, choose the desired tool (**Bezier** or **Circle**) from the **Curve** area in the **Add Primitive** panel; a Bezier curve primitive will be created at the position of the 3D Cursor. Alternatively, press SHIFT+A; the **Add** menu will be displayed. Next, choose **Curve** from the **Add** menu; a cascading menu will be displayed. Choose the desired option (**Bezier** or **Circle**) from the cascading menu, refer to Figure 3-3.

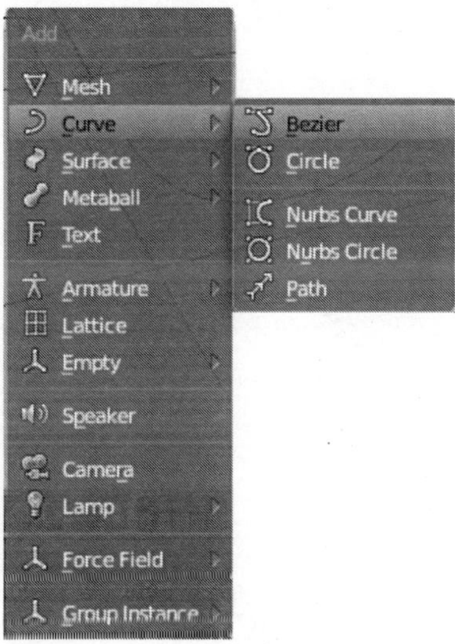

Figure 3-3 *Choosing* ***Bezier*** *from the cascading menu*

To manually modify Bezier curve primitive in the view, select the primitive and switch to **Edit Mode**; control points and handles will be displayed on the Bezier curve primitive along with arrows on the segment of curve. These arrows are called normals. The normals represent the direction and speed of the movement along the curve.

Transform the handles and the control points to achieve specific shape of the curve. Note that you need to right-click on a control point or on a handle to select it. But, at the time of transformation you need to left-click at a point to transform the control point or the handle. If you want to cancel the transformation, right-click to bring back the control point or the handle to its original position. You can also change the handle type to get different types of curvature along the control points as discussed in the earlier section.

To extend the curve, select the last control point and press E; the extension of the curve will be attached to the cursor. Click at a point to place the extension of the cursor in the view.

To subdivide a segment in the curve, select two control points of the segment. Next, press W; the **Specials** menu will be displayed, as shown in Figure 3-4. Choose **Subdivide** from the **Specials** menu; a control point will be added between the selected control points and the **Subdivide** panel will be added to **Toolshelf**. Enter the value in the **Number of Cuts** slider of the **Subdivide** panel, if you need to add more than one control point between the selected control points.

To combine the curve primitives, select them and press CTRL+J; the selected curve primitives will be combined and the name of the last selected curve primitive will be assigned to the resultant curve primitive.

To close the open curve, select the start and end control points of the curve and press F or press ALT+C; the open curve will be closed by a segment joining the selected control points. Similarly, to join two curve primitives, you need to combine these two curve primitives and then follow the same process explained for closing the open curve.

To split the curve primitive into two separate curves, select the two control points of a segment that is to be separated and then press P; a menu will be displayed. Next, choose **Separate** from this menu.

To further modify the Bezier curve primitives, choose the **Object Data** button from **Properties Editor**, refer to Figure 3-5. On doing so, various panels such as **Shape**, **Geometry**, **Path Animation**, **Active Spline**, and so on will be displayed in **Properties Editor**. The options in this panel are used to modify the selected curve primitive.

Non-Uniform Rational B-Splines (NURBS) Curve Primitives

There are three types of NURBS curve primitives: Nurbs Curve, Nurbs Circle, and Path, as shown in Figure 3-6. The Nurbs Curve primitive has four control points and knot vectors whereas Nurbs Circle primitive has eight control points. The Path primitive has five aligned control points and knot vectors. Knot vectors determine the behavior of control points. Nurbs curve primitives are exact shapes compared to Bezier curve primitives.

Creating and Modifying NURBS Curve Primitives

To create a NURBS curve primitive, choose the **Create** tab from **Toolshelf**. Next, choose the desired tool (**Nurbs Curve** or **Nurbs Circle** or **Path**) from the **Curve** area in the **Add Primitive** panel; a NURBS curve primitive will be created at the position of the 3D Cursor. Alternatively, press SHIFT+A; the **Add** menu will be displayed. Next, choose **Curve** from the **Add** menu; a cascading menu will be displayed. Choose the desired tool (**Nurbs Curve** or **Nurbs Circle** or **Path**) from the cascading menu, refer to Figure 3-3.

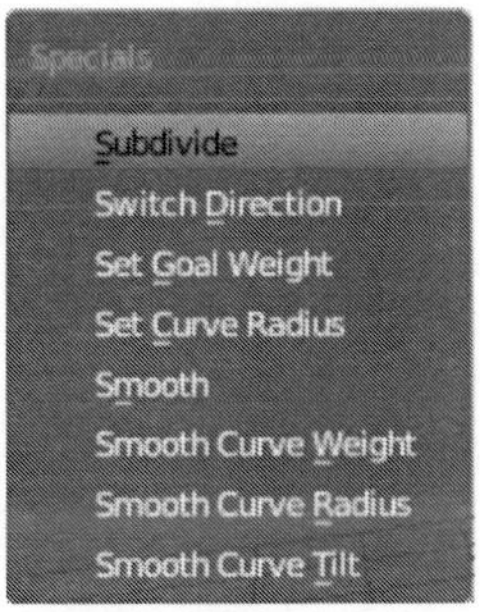

Specials
Subdivide
Switch Direction
Set Goal Weight
Set Curve Radius
Smooth
Smooth Curve Weight
Smooth Curve Radius
Smooth Curve Tilt

Figure 3-4 *The* ***Specials*** *menu displayed*

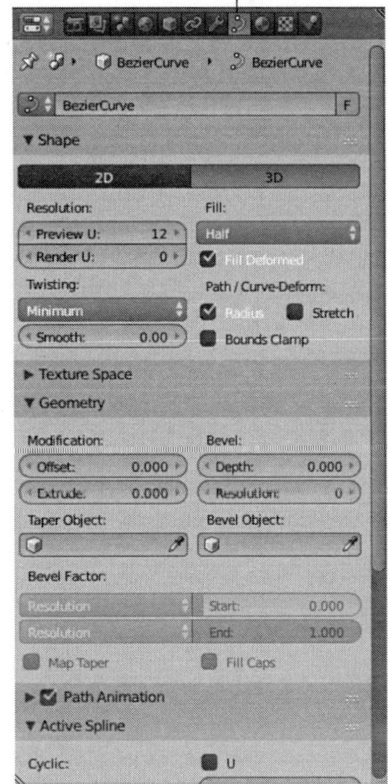

Figure 3-5 *Various panels in the* ***Properties Editor***

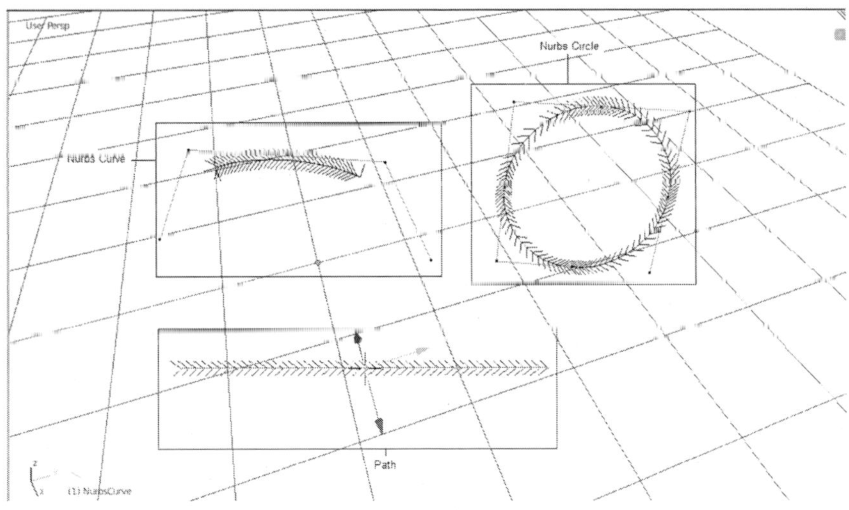

Figure 3-6 *The Nurbs Curve, Nurbs Circle, and Path primitives*

To modify NURBS curve primitives, select it and switch to **Edit Mode**; the control points will be displayed on the NURBS curve primitives along with arrows on the segment of curve.

Transform the control points to provide some specific shape to the curve. Note that you need to right-click the control point to select it and left-click to confirm the transformation. Right-click to bring back the control point at its original position. Rest of the modification techniques such as extending the curve, subdividing segments, and closing the open curve for NURBS curve primitives are same as discussed for Bezier curve primitives.

To further modify the NURBS curve primitives,  choose the **Object Data** button from **Properties Editor**. On doing so, various panels such as **Shape**, **Geometry**, **Path Animation**, **Active Spline**, and so on will be displayed in **Properties Editor**, refer to Figure 3-7. The options in this panel are used to modify the selected curve primitive.

Note
*The check box(es) in the **Curve Display** panel of **Properties Region** are used to show/hide handles and normals of the Bezier curve primitives and normals of NURBS curve primitives in the view.*

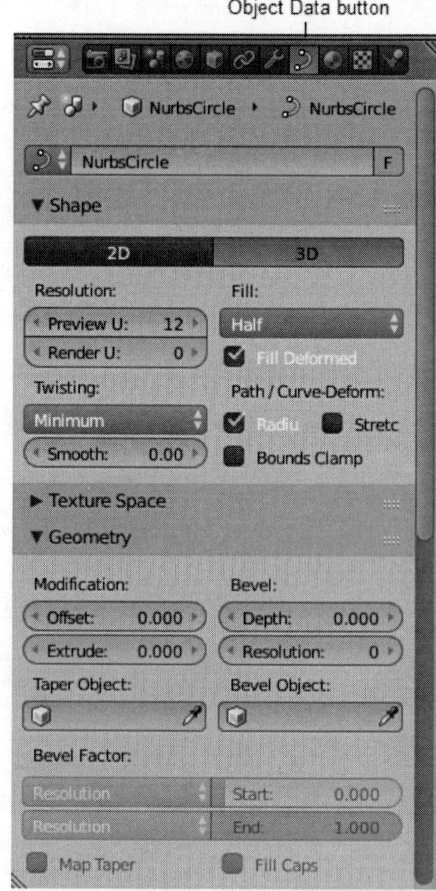

Figure 3-7** Various panels in **Properties Editor

Non-Uniform Rational B-Splines Surfaces

There are four types of NURBS surfaces: Nurbs Surface, Nurbs Cylinder, Nurbs Sphere, and Nurbs Torus, as shown in Figure 3-8. The NURBS surfaces have control points and rows, refer to Figure 3-8. The vertical and horizontal rows of a NURBS surface form a grid. The difference between NURBS curves and NURBS surfaces is that NURBS curves have U axis whereas NURBS surfaces have U and V axes.

Creating and Modifying NURBS Surface Primitives

To create a NURBS surface primitive, press SHIFT+A; the **Add** menu will be displayed. Next, choose **Surface** from the **Add** menu; a cascading menu will be displayed. Choose the desired tool (**Nurbs Surface**, **Nurbs Cylinder**, **Nurbs Sphere** or **Nurbs Torus**) from the cascading menu.

To modify NURBS surface primitive, select the primitive and switch to **Edit Mode**; control points will be displayed on the NURBS surface primitives in the grid. Transform the control points to achieve specific shape of a surface.

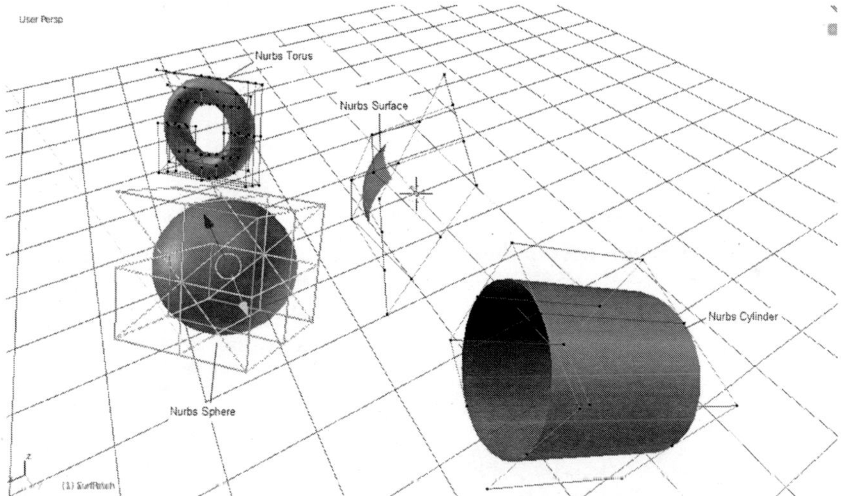

Figure 3-8 All the Nurbs surfaces displayed

The modification techniques such as extending the curve, subdividing segments, closing the open curve, and so on discussed in Bezier curve primitives are same in NURBS surface primitives. The only difference is that you need to select a control point on the NURBS surface primitive and press SHIFT+R to select a row of control points and then use the same shortcut keys explained in Bezier curve primitives. Note that you cannot add control points to a NURBS surface.

To further modify the NURBS surface primitives, choose the **Object Data** button from **Properties Editor**. On doing  so, various panels such as **Shape**, **Texture Shape**, **Active Spline**, and so on will be displayed in **Properties Editor**, refer to Figure 3-9. The options in these panels are used to modify the selected surface primitive.

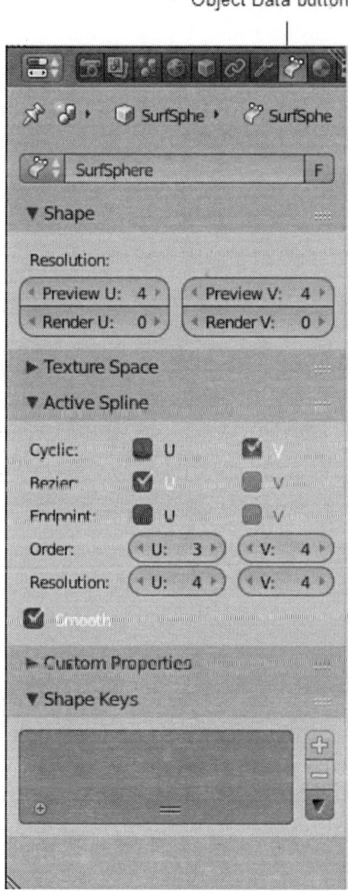

Figure 3-9 Various panels in ***Properties Editor***

Note
NURBS curves can also be converted into 2D and 3D surfaces by using the tools in ***Properties Editor*** *such as* ***Extrude, Depth, Bevel,*** *and so on, refer to Figure 3-7.*

Draw Curve

It is a freehand tool for drawing curves. You need to just drag the mouse in the view to create a curve. Note that the **Draw Curve** tool will be activated only in **Edit Mode** provided you have created and selected a curve primitive.

To draw a curve using the **Draw Curve** tool, create a new curve primitive in the view. Make sure the curve primitive is selected and then switch to **Edit Mode**. Next, choose the **Draw Curve** tool from the **Add Curve** panel in the **Create** tab of **Toolshelf**; the shape of the cursor changes to a pen icon. You can now draw freehand curves in the view, refer to Figure 3-10. Note that the curve primitive selected in **Object Mode** will be part of the freehand curve created using the **Draw Curve** tool. You can retain it or delete its vertices or segments, if it is not required in the freehand curve.

To change the thickness, tapering, corner angle, and so on, set the parameters in the **Options** tab and the **Draw Curve** panel in **Toolshelf**, refer to Figure 3-11. Also, choose the **Object Data** button in **Properties Editor** and set the parameters in the panels displayed to achieve the desired shape as discussed for other curve primitives. Figure 3-12 shows the freehand curve after setting parameters in various panels of **Toolshelf** and **Properties Editor**.

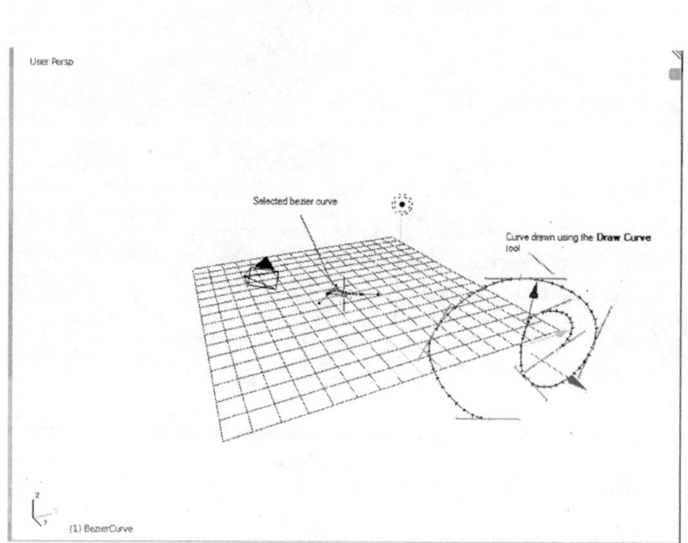

Figure 3-10 The freehand curve drawn

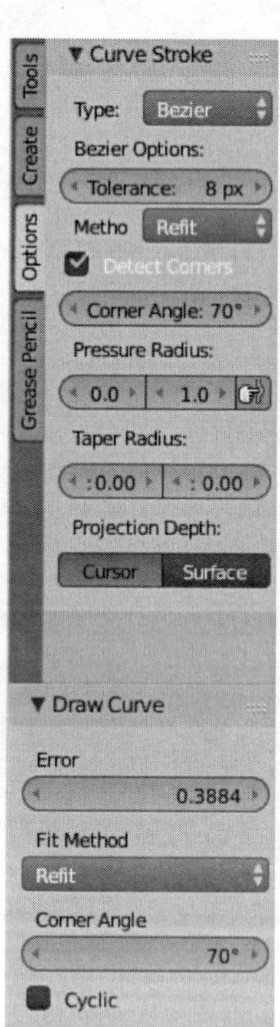

Figure 3-11 The parameters in Toolshelf

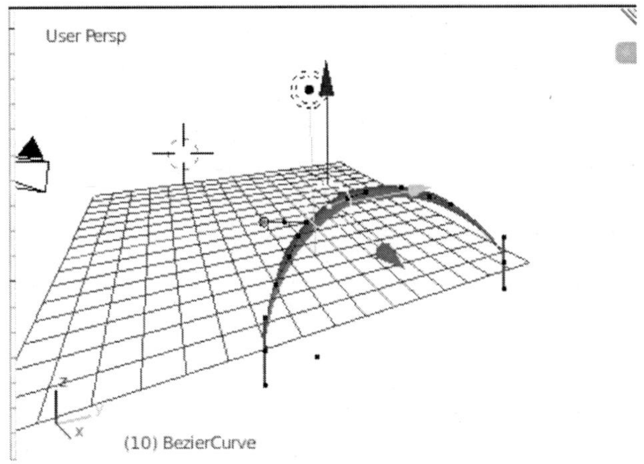

Figure 3-12 Freehand curve drawn after setting the parameters

Creating and Modifying Text

To create text in a scene, choose the **Create** tab from **Toolshelf**. Next, choose the **Text** tool from the **Other** area in the **Add Primitive** panel. '**Text**' will be displayed at the 3D Cursor. To change this text, switch to **Edit Mode**. On doing so, the cursor will be displayed at the end of '**Text**'. Delete '**Text**' by using the BACKSPACE key. Next, enter desired text to replace the existing text. You can use all the transformation tools for text as that of other primitives.

To modify the text, choose the **Object Data** button from **Properties Editor**; various panels such as **Shape**, **Geometry**, **Font**, and so on will be displayed in **Properties Editor**, refer to Figure 3-13. The options in these panels are used to modify the selected text.

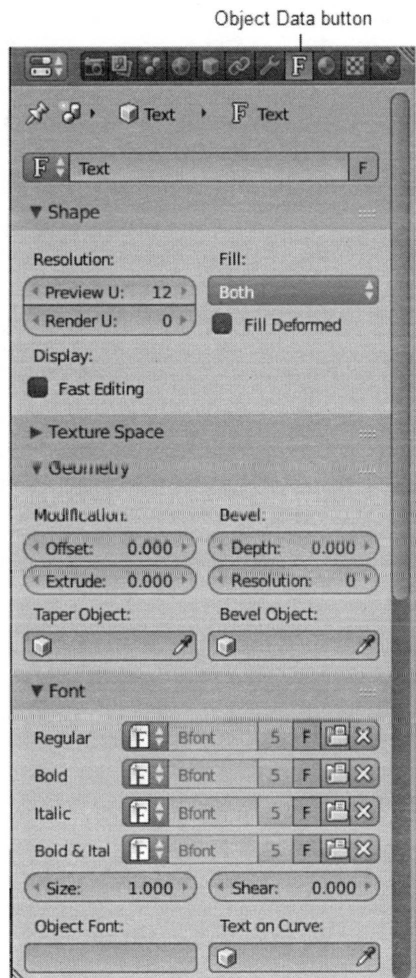

Figure 3-13** Various panels in **Properties Editor

If you want to add text to the scene from external file, create a text 'Text' in **Object Mode**. Next, switch to **Edit Mode** and delete '**Text**'. Now, choose **Edit > Paste File** from the **3D View Editor** menu bar; **File Browser** will be displayed. Navigate to the desired text file and select it. Next, choose **Paste File** from **File Browser**; the content of the text file will be displayed at the cursor.

You can also create and save a text file using **Text Editor** in Blender. To do so, choose **Text Editor** from the **Editor Type** drop-down. Next, choose the **New** button; the **New** button gets converted to a **Text Block** drop-down and the cursor is displayed at the top of **Text Editor**. Enter the desired text at the cursor. Now, choose **Text > Save As** from the **Text Editor** menu bar; **File Browser** is displayed. Navigate to the desired folder and enter the name of the file in the **File Name** text box and choose **Save As**; the text file is saved at the specified location.

To use this text file in the scene, choose **Edit > Paste File** from the **3D View Editor** menu bar; **File Browser** will be displayed. Navigate to the created text file and select it. Next, choose **Paste File** from **File Browser**; the content of the text file will be displayed at the position of cursor in the scene.

Adding Background Image

In Blender, background image is used as a reference image to create accurate models and to paint textures on the model. Similarly, you can also use a video as background video in animation. To use background image or background video, hover the cursor in the view and press N or place the cursor on the square with a + sign located at the upper right corner of the view and drag the cursor to the left; **Properties Region** will be displayed, refer to Figure 3-14. Scroll down and expand the **Background Images** panel. On choosing the **Add Image** button in this panel, the **Not Set** area with various options will be added to the **Background Images** panel, refer to Figure 3-15.

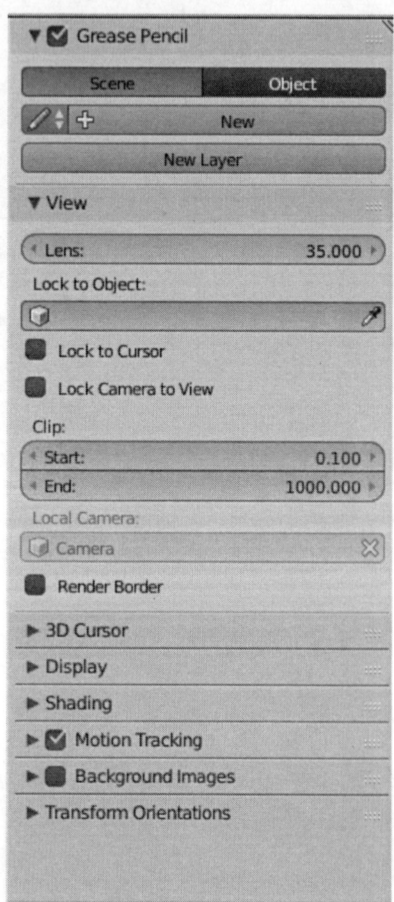

*Figure 3-14 The **Properties Region***

*Figure 3-15 The **Background Images** panel on choosing the **Add Image** button*

To add a background image, make sure the **Image** button is chosen in the **Not Set** area. Next, choose the **Open** button located below it; **File Browser** will be displayed. Navigate to the desired location and select the image to be used as a background image and then choose the **Open Image** button from **File Browser**; the image will be added to all the orthographic views. Also, the **Not Set** area will be renamed with the name of the image selected and some additional options will be added to this area, refer to Figure 3-16. You can change the rotation, opacity, position, and so on of the image in the orthographic views using these options.

To add a background video, choose the **Movie Clip** button from the **Not Set** area. By default, the **Camera Clip** check box is selected. As a result, the clip used for camera tracking will be used as a background video. These clips are added to **Movie Clip Editor** for camera or object tracking. To add a new video clip or a image sequence, clear the **Camera Clip** check box and then choose the **Open** button located below it; **File Browser** will be displayed. Navigate to the desired location and select the video clip or the image sequence to be used as background video and then choose the **Open Clip** button from **File Browser**; the clip will be added to all the orthographic views. Also, the **Not Set** area will now get the name of the clip selected and some additional options will be added to the area, refer to Figure 3-17. You can change the rotation, opacity, position, and so on of the image in the orthographic views using these options.

*Figure 3-16 The **Background Images** panel on adding the image*

*Figure 3-17 The **Background Images** panel on adding the clip*

TUTORIALS

Before you start tutorials of this chapter, you need to download *c03_blender_2.79_tut.zip* file from *www.cadcim.com*. The path of the file is as follows: *Textbooks > Animation and Visual Effects > Blender > Blender 2.79 for Digital Artists*

Browse to *\Documents\blender2.79* and create a folder with the name *c03*. Next, extract the content of the zip file in this folder.

Tutorial 1

In this tutorial, you will create a wallpiece model, as shown in Figure 3-18.

(Expected time: 30 min)

Figure 3-18 *The wallpiece model*

The following steps are required to complete this Tutorial:

a. Create folder.
b. Add reference image.
c. Create the base curve.
d. Create, modify, and align the copies of base curve.
e. Create the center part.
f. Save and render the scene.

Creating Folder

1. Navigate to *\Documents\blender2.79\c03* and create a new folder with the name *c03_tut1*.

2. Press CTRL+N or choose **File > New** from the **Info Editor** menu bar; a menu is displayed. Choose **Reload Start-Up File**; the menu disappears and the startup file is loaded.

3. Choose **File > Save** from the **Info Editor** menu bar; **File Browser** is displayed

4. Navigate to *\Documents\blender2.79\c03\c03_tut1* and enter **Wallpiece** in the **File Name** edit box. Next, choose the **Save Blender File** button to save the file at the specified location.

Adding Reference Image

In this section, you will add a reference image using **Properties Region**.

1. Choose **View > Toggle Quad View** from the **3D View Editor** menu bar or Press CTRL+ALT+Q; the quad view is displayed. Hover the cursor over any of the views and Press N; **Properties Region** is displayed.

2. Expand the **Background Images** panel from **Properties Region**. Next, choose the **Add Image** button from the **Background Images** panel; the **Not Set** area is added to the **Background Images** panel, refer to Figure 3-19. Choose the **Open** button from the **Not Set** area; **File Browser** is displayed.

***Figure 3-19** The **Not Set** area in the **Background Images** panel*

3. Navigate to *\Documents\blender2.79\c03* and select the **design.jpg** image and choose the **Open Image** button; the selected image is displayed in all the three ortho views, as shown in Figure 3-20. Also, the **Not Set** area is replaced by the **design** area in the **Background Images** panel of **Properties Region**. Next, choose **Front** from the **Axis** drop-down to show the image in the Front view only.

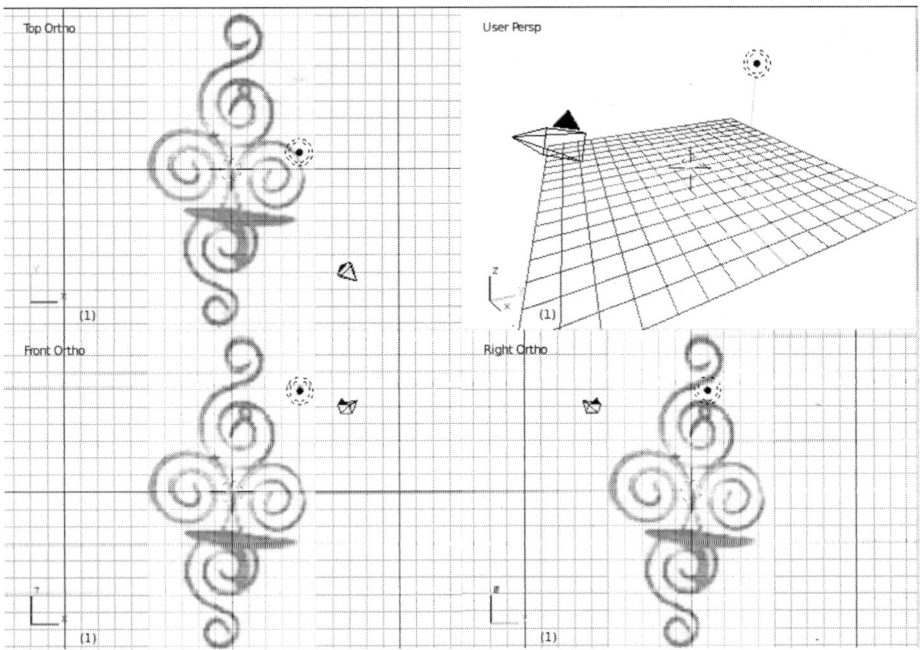

***Figure 3-20** The selected image in ortho views*

4. Enter **0.4** in the **Opacity** edit box in the **Wall Design1** area; the opacity of the reference image is reduced.

Creating the Base Curve

In this section, you will create the base curve of the wall design using the **Bezier** tool.

1. Delete **Cube** from the view. Next, make sure the **Create** tab is chosen in **Toolshelf** and then choose the **Bezier** tool from the **Curve** area in the **Add Primitive** panel; a Bezier curve is created at the center of the grid with the name *BezierCurve*.

2. Move *BezierCurve* towards the top of the image, as shown in Figure 3-21. Switch to **Edit Mode** and zoom in on the top part of the image. Next, move the two control points and their handles to change the curvature of *BezierCurve*, refer to Figure 3-22.

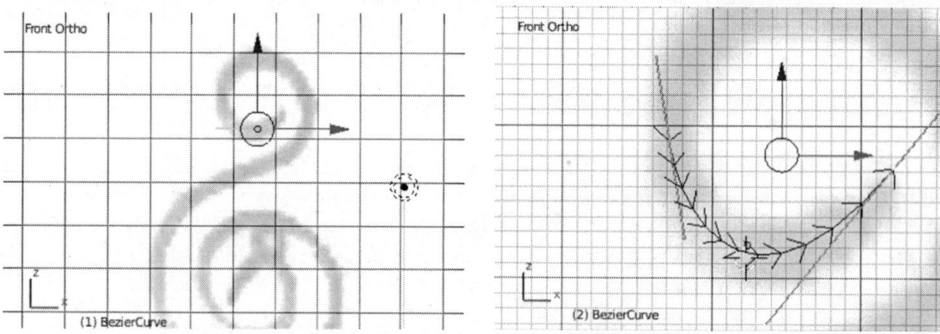

Figure 3-21 *The design moved*

Figure 3-22 *The control points and handles moved*

You will now add a control point between the two control points to make the curvature more precise.

3. Select both the control points using the SHIFT key. Next, press W; the **Specials** menu is displayed, as shown in Figure 3-23. Choose **Subdivide** from the **Specials** menu; a control point is added between the selected points at the center of *BezierCurve*, as shown in Figure 3-24. Now, move this newly added control point and its handles to get the curvature, as shown in Figure 3-25.

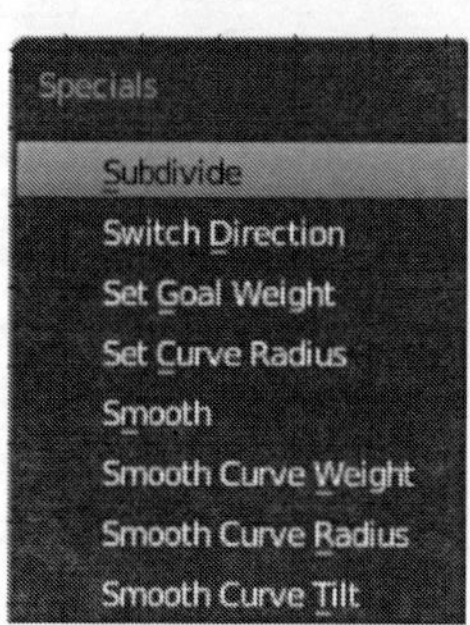

Figure 3-23 *The* ***Specials*** *menu*

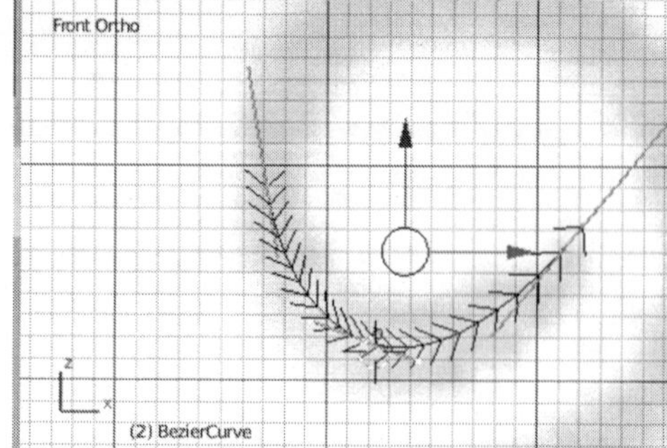

Figure 3-24 *A control point added*

Next, you need to extend the curve to complete the design.

4. Select the end control point of *BezierCurve*, as shown in Figure 3-26. Next, press E and slightly move the cursor. You will notice that the curve is extended with an additional control point, refer to Figure 3-27.

5. Make sure the newly added control point is selected. Next, press V; the **Set Handle Type** menu is displayed. Choose **Automatic** from this menu. Now, move this end control point and its handles to get the curvature, as shown in Figure 3-27.

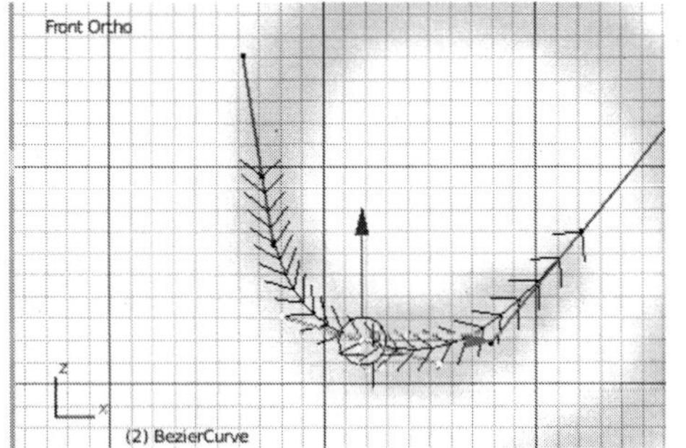

Figure 3-25 *The control point and handles moved*

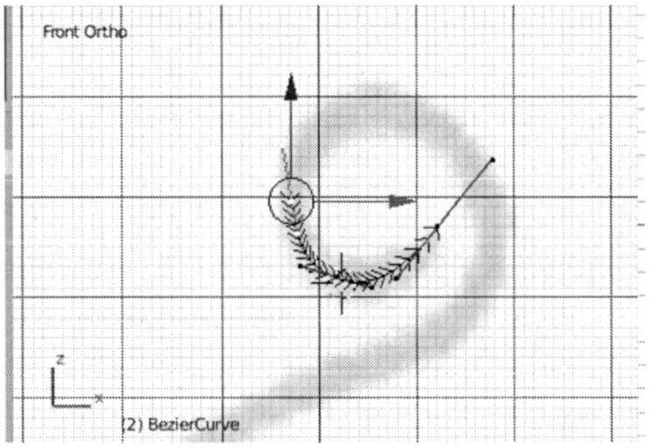

Figure 3-26 *The end control point selected*

6. Similarly, add the control points and move their handles to get the curvature, as shown in Figure 3-28. Rename *BezierCurve* to *design* in **Outliner**.

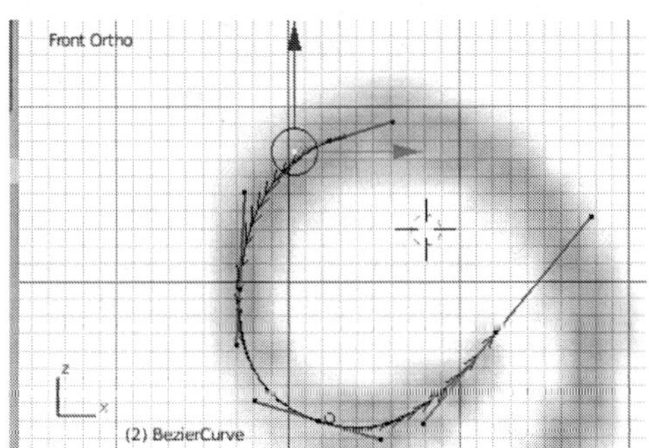

Figure 3-27 *The end control point and handles moved*

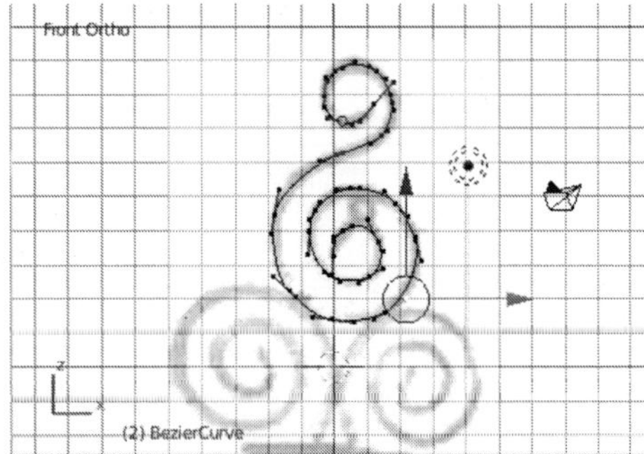

Figure 3-28 *The control points added and handles moved*

Creating, Modifying, and Aligning the Copies of Base Curve

1. Make sure *design* is selected. Switch to **Object Mode**. Next, press SHIFT+D and ENTER; a copy of *design* is created with the name *design.001*. Move it below *design* on the reference image.

2. Choose the **Object** button from **Properties Editor**. In the **Transform** panel, enter **180** in the **Y** and **Z** sliders of the **Rotation** area; *design.001* is rotated vertically. Place it at the bottom on the reference image, refer to Figure 3-29.

3. Switch to **Edit Mode**. Next, change the shape of *design.001* to match the exact shape on the reference image, as shown in Figure 3-30.

4. Switch to **Object Mode**. Next, create a copy of *design.001*. It is automatically renamed as *design.002*. Move *design.002* to the center part of reference image, as shown in Figure 3-31.

5. Delete the bottom control points of *design.002* and position the rest of the control points to get the shape, as shown in Figure 3-32.

Figure 3-29 *The design.001 rotated and moved down*

Figure 3-30 *Control points and handles of design.001 moved*

Figure 3-31 *The design.002 moved*

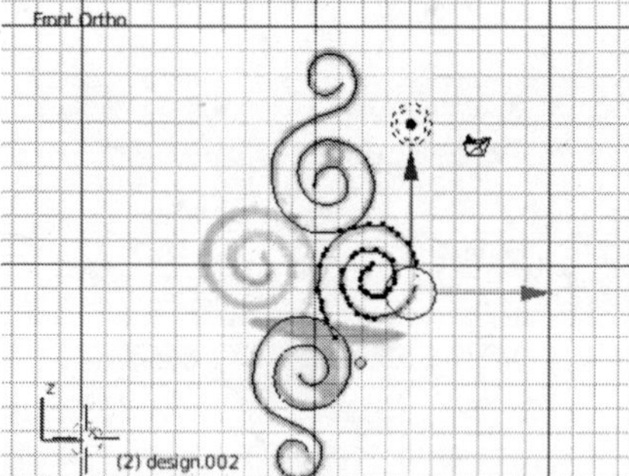

Figure 3-32 *The shape of design.002 changed*

6. Switch to **Object Mode**. Next, create a copy of *design.002*. It is automatically named as *design.003*. Move *design.003* to the left of *design.002*.

7. Make sure the **Object** button is chosen in **Properties Editor**. Enter **0** in the **Z** slider of the **Rotation** area of the **Transform** panel; *design.003* is rotated. Now, place *design.003* on the reference image, as shown in Figure 3-33.

8. Choose the **Nurbs Circle** tool from the **Curve** area in the **Add Primitive** panel; a circle is created at the center of the grid with the name *NurbsCircle*. Also the **Add Nurbs Circle** panel is added to **Toolshelf**. Rename it as *hook*.

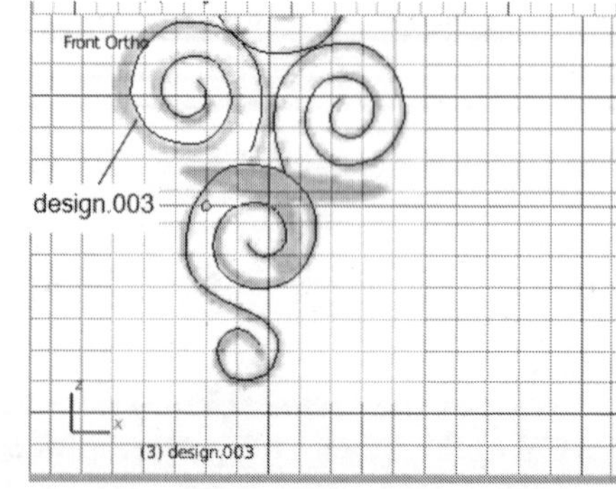

Figure 3-33 *The design003 placed*

9. Enter **0.6** in the **Radius** slider of the **Add Nurbs Circle** panel. Align *hook,* as shown in Figure 3-34.

Note

You may have to change the radius of hook depending on the size of design.

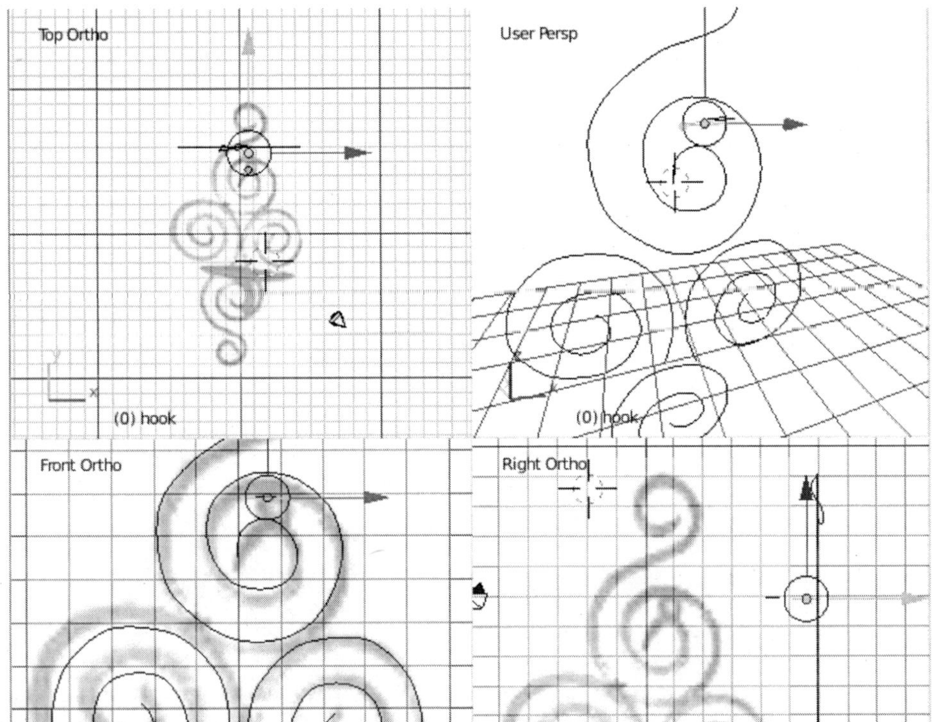

Figure 3-34 *The hook aligned*

Creating the Center Part

In this section, you will create the center part using the **Nurbs Sphere**.

1. Choose **Add > Surface > Nurbs Sphere** from the **3D View Editor** menu bar; a Nurbs sphere is created with the name *SurfSphere*. Also, the **Add Surface Sphere** panel is added to **Toolshelf**. Rename it as *center_part*.

2. Enter **2** in the **Radius** slider of the **Add Surface Sphere** panel of **Toolshelf**. Switch to **Edit Mode**; control points of *center_part* are displayed, as shown in Figure 3-35.

3. Press A to deselect all the control points of *center_part*. Next, press B; and select all the control points of the upper part of *center_part*, as shown in Figure 3-36. Next, move the selected control points downward, as shown in Figure 3-37.

4. Press A to deselect the selected control points of *center_part*. Next, press B and select all the control points of the lower part of *center_part*, as shown in Figure 3-38. Next, move the selected control points upward, as shown in Figure 3-39.

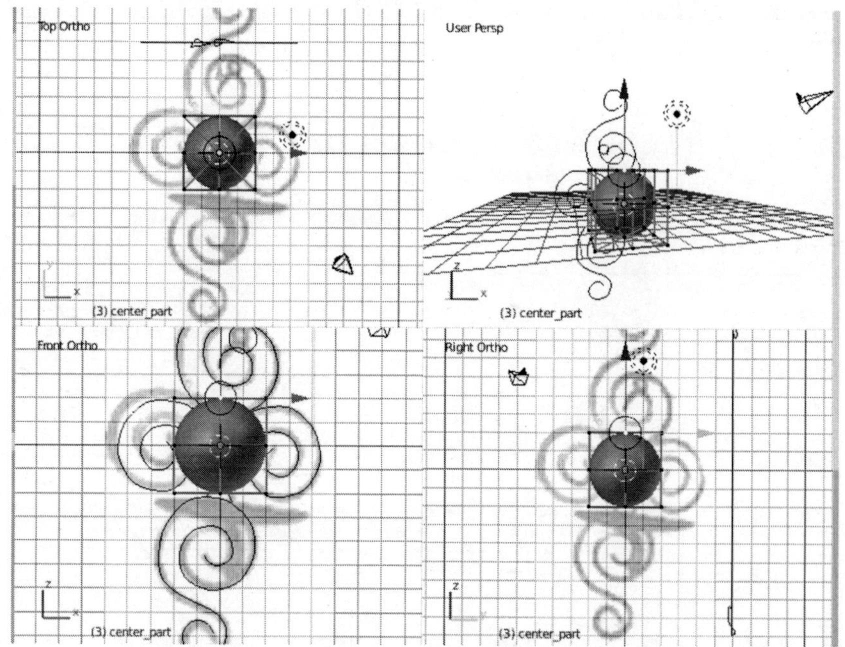

Figure 3-35 *Control points of center_part displayed*

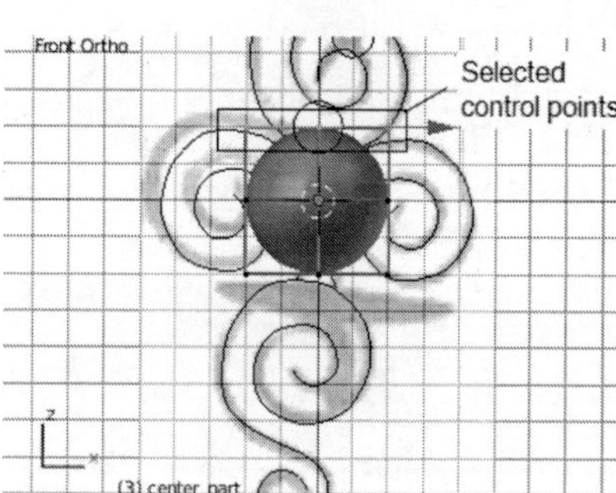

Figure 3-36 *Selected control points of center_part*

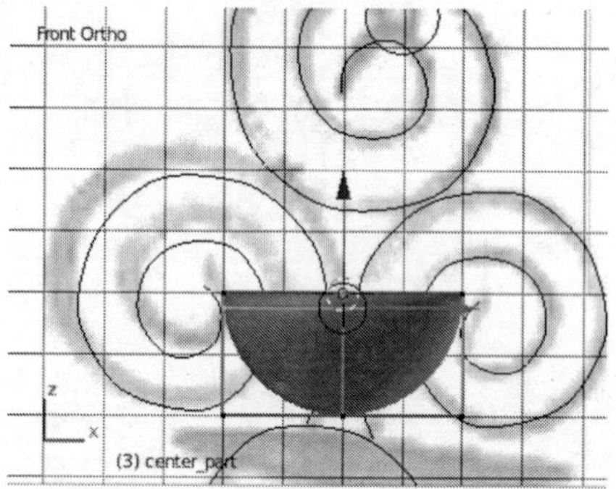

Figure 3-37 *Selected control points of center_part moved down*

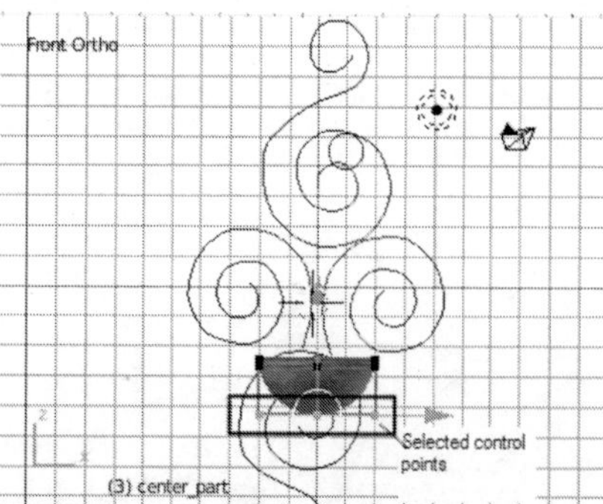

Figure 3-38 *Selected Control points of center_part*

Figure 3-39 *Selected Control points of center_part moved up*

Converting 2D Curves to 3D Shapes

You will now convert all the 2D curves created so far to 3D shapes using the options in **Properties Editor**.

1. Switch to **Object Mode**. Choose the **Nurbs Circle** tool from the **Curve** area in the **Add Primitive** panel; a NURBS circle is created at the center of the grid with the name *NurbsCircle*.

2. Enter **0.25** in the **Radius** slider of the **Add Nurbs Circle** panel of **Toolshelf**; the *NurbsCircle* is resized.

3. Select *design* and switch to **Edit Mode**. Next, choose the **Object Data** button from **Properties Editor**. 

4. Click on the **Bevel Object** edit box; a menu is displayed showing all the curve primitives in the scene. Choose **NurbsCircle** from the menu; *design* is converted into 3D shape, refer to Figure 3-40.

5. Change the color of *design* to black as discussed in Tutorial 1 of Chapter 2. Next, select all the remaining 2D curves and convert them to 3D shapes as discussed above and change the color of these shapes to black, refer to Figure 3-41.

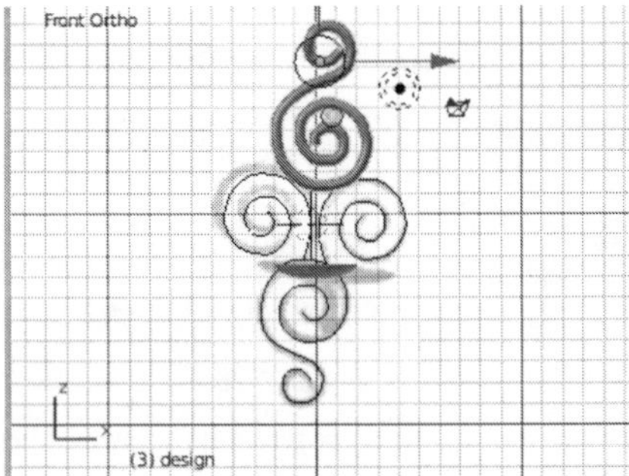

Figure 3-40 *design converted into 3D shape*

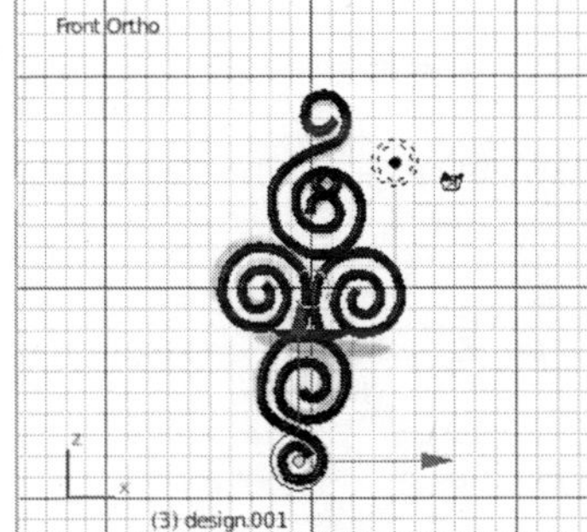

Figure 3-41 *All the 2D curves converted into 3D shape*

Saving and Rendering the Scene

In this section, you will save the scene that you have created and then render it. You can also view the final rendered image of this model by downloading the *c03_blender_2.79_rndr.zip* file from *www.cadcim.com*. The path of the file is as follows: *Textbooks > Animation and Visual Effects > Blender > Blender 2.79 for Digital Artists*

1. Change the background color of the scene as discussed in Tutorial 1 of Chapter 2.

2. Choose **File > Save** from the **Info Editor** menu bar.

3. Adjust the view in the User Persp view. Next, choose the **Open GL still image render** button from **3D View Editor**; the rendered image is displayed in the **UV/Image Editor**; refer to Figure 3-18.

Tutorial 2

In this tutorial, you will create a logo, as shown in Figure 3-42. **(Expected time: 20 min)**

Figure 3-42 *The logo*

The following steps are required to complete this tutorial:

a. Create folder.
b. Add reference image.
c. Create the outer shape.
d. Create the inner shape.
e. Create text.
f. Save and render the scene.

Creating Folder

1. Navigate to *\Documents\blender2.79\c03* and create a new folder with the name *c03_tut2.*

2. Press CTRL+N or choose **File > New** from the **Info Editor** menu bar; a menu is displayed. Choose **Reload Start-Up File**; the menu disappears and the startup file is loaded.

3. Choose **File > Save** from the **Info Editor** menu bar; **File Browser** is displayed.

4. Navigate to *\Documents\blender2.79\c03\c03_tut2* and enter **Logo** in the **File Name** edit box. Next, choose the **Save Blender File** button to save the file at the specified location.

Adding Reference Image

1. Choose **View > Toggle Quad View** from the **3D View Editor menu bar** or Press CTRL+ALT+Q; the quad view is displayed. Hover the cursor over any of the views and Press N; **Properties Region** is displayed.

2. Expand the **Background Images** panel from **Properties Region**. Next, choose the **Add Image** button from the **Background Images** panel; the **Not Set** area is added to the **Background Images** panel. Choose the **Open** button from the **Not Set** area; **File Browser** is displayed. Navigate to *\Documents\blender2.79\c03* and select the **tut2logo** image and choose the **Open Image** button; the selected image is displayed in all the three ortho views. Also the

Not Set area is replaced by the **tut2logo** area in the **Background Images** panel of **Properties Region**. Next, choose **Front** from the **Axis** drop-down to show the image in the Front view only.

3. Enter **0.4** in the **opacity** edit box of the **tut2logo.jpg** area; the opacity of the reference image is reduced, refer to Figure 3-43.

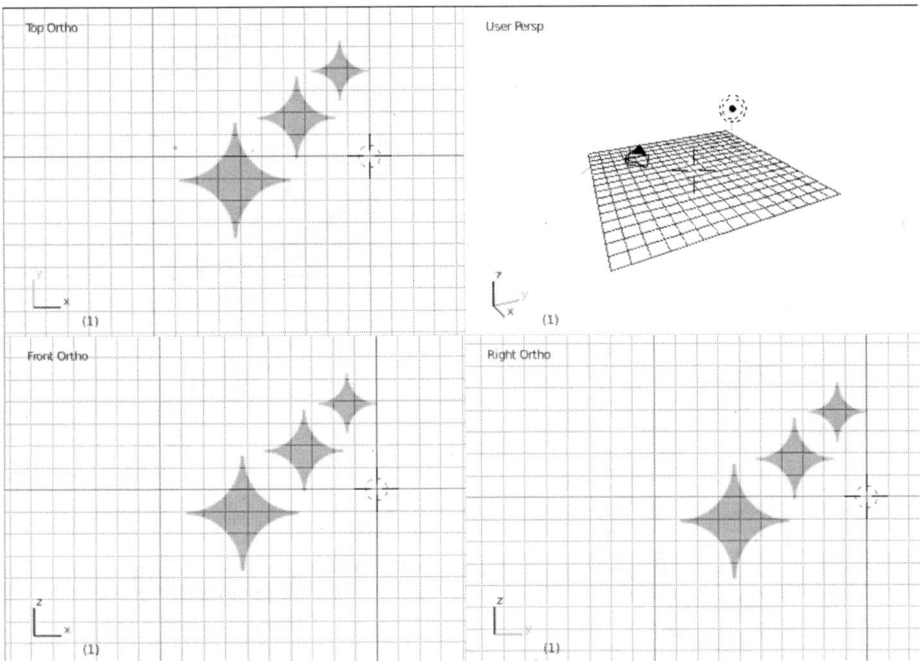

Figure 3-43 *The reference image displayed with reduced opacity*

Creating the Outer Shape

In this section, you will create the outer shape using the **Bezier** tool.

1. Delete **Cube** from the view. Next, choose the **Bezier** tool from the **Curve** area in the **Add Primitive** panel of **Toolshelf**; the Bezier curve is created at the position of the 3D Cursor. Rename it as *outer_curve* in **Outliner**.

2. Position *outer_curve* at the bottom of the outer part of the reference image in the Front Ortho view, as shown in Figure 3-44.

3. Switch to **Edit Mode**. Next, one by one select and move the control points and their handles to change the curvature of *outer_curve* as per the shape of the outer part of the reference image, as shown in Figure 3-45.

   Next, you need to extend *outer_curve* to complete the outer part of the reference image.

4. Select the end control point of *outer_curve* and then press E; *outer_curve* is extended with an additional control point, refer to Figure 3-46.

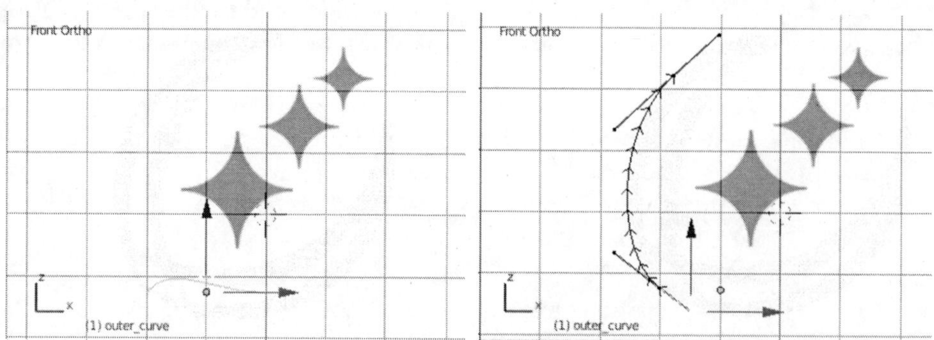

Figure 3-44 *The outer_curve placed*

Figure 3-45 *The control points and handles moved*

Now, you need to change the handle type of the additional control point to achieve the desired curvature.

5. Make sure the additional control point is selected. Next, press V; the **Set handle Type** menu is displayed, as shown in Figure 3-47. Choose the **Free** option from this menu; the handles of the control point are now independent of each other.

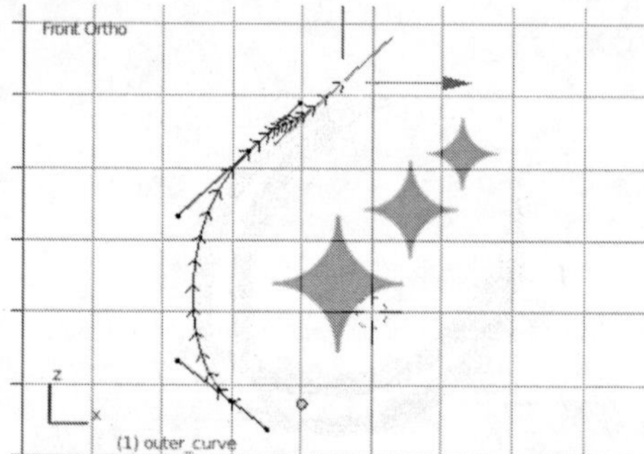

Figure 3-46 *The outer_curve extended*

Figure 3-47 *The* ***Set Handle Type*** *menu*

6. Place this control point at a point and move the handle on its left to get the curvature, as shown in Figure 3-48.

7. Make sure the end control point is selected. Next, press E; *outer_curve* is extended with an additional control point.

8. Make sure the newly added control point is selected. Next, select the control point added before this control point. Next, press W; the **Specials** menu is displayed. Choose **Subdivide** from this menu; a control point is added between the selected control points.

9. Place the two end control points on the outer part of the reference image and then move their handles to get the curvature, as shown in Figure 3-49.

Note

1. You may have to change the handle type of the control points to get the desired curvature.

2. You may have to adjust other control points (already adjusted) of the outer_curve and their handles to get the desired shape.

10. Make sure the end control point is selected. Next, press E; *outer_curve* is extended with an additional control point. Place this last control point near the first control point; refer to Figure 3-50.

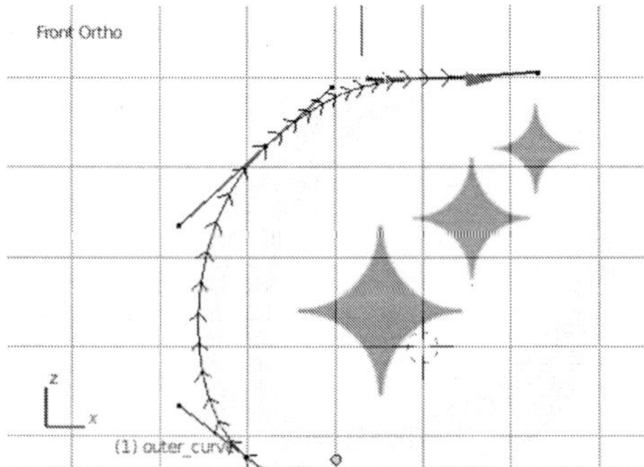

Figure 3-48 *The control point and its handle moved*

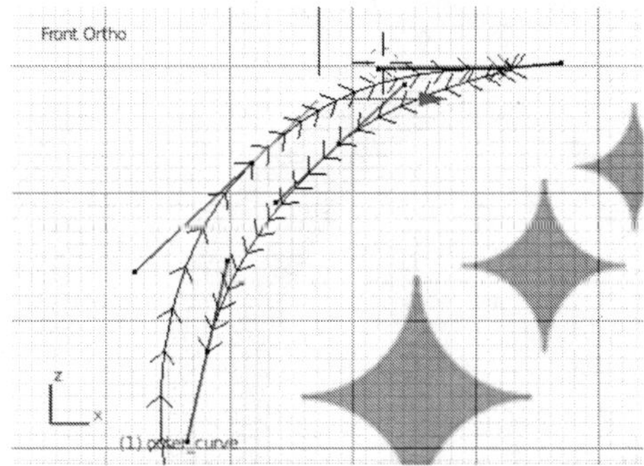

Figure 3-49 *The two end control points and their handles moved*

11. Make sure the last control point is selected. Next, press the SHIFT key and select the first control point; the first and the last control points get selected.

12. Choose the **Object Data** button from **Properties Editor**, refer to Figure 3-51. Scroll down in **Properties Editor** and then select the **Cyclic** check box from the **Active Spline** panel, as shown in Figure 3-51; the two control points are joined, as shown in Figure 3-52.

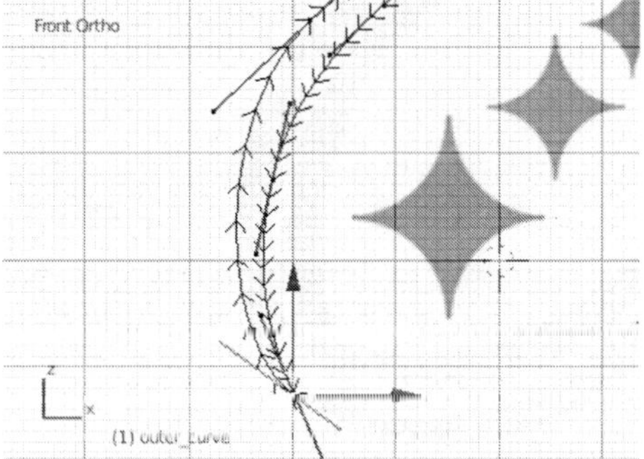

Figure 3-50 *The last control point placed near to the first control point*

13. Change the handle type of both these control points to **Free**, as discussed earlier. Now, place the handles of these two control points to achieve the curvature, as shown in Figure 3-53.

    Next, you need to fill the curve with a solid color.

14. Make sure the **Object Data** button is chosen in **Properties Editor**. Next, choose the **2D** button from the **Shape** panel in **Properties Editor**, refer to Figure 3-51; *outer_curve* is filled with grey color, as shown in Figure 3-54.

15. Change the color of *outer_curve* to the color of your choice, as discussed in Tutorial 1 of Chapter 2. Figure 3-55 shows *outer_curve* with color changed.

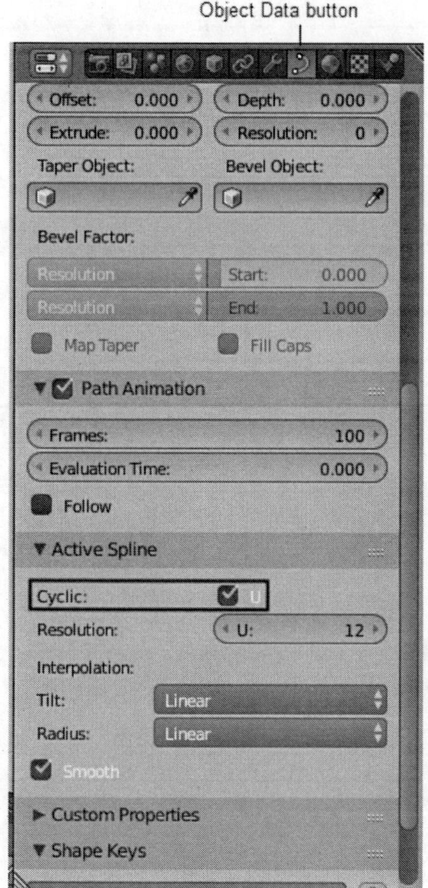

***Figure 3-51** The **Cyclic** check box selected in the **Active Spline** panel*

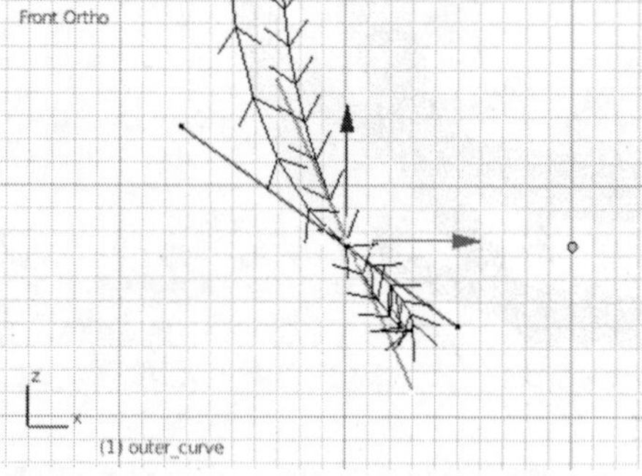

***Figure 3-52** The last control point and first control point joined*

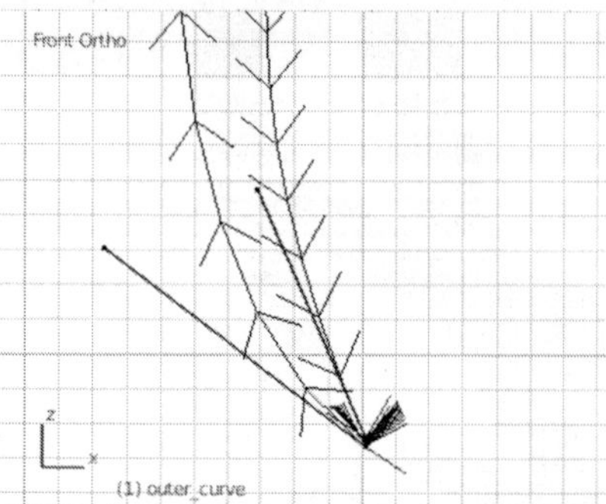

***Figure 3-53** The last and the first control points and handles placed*

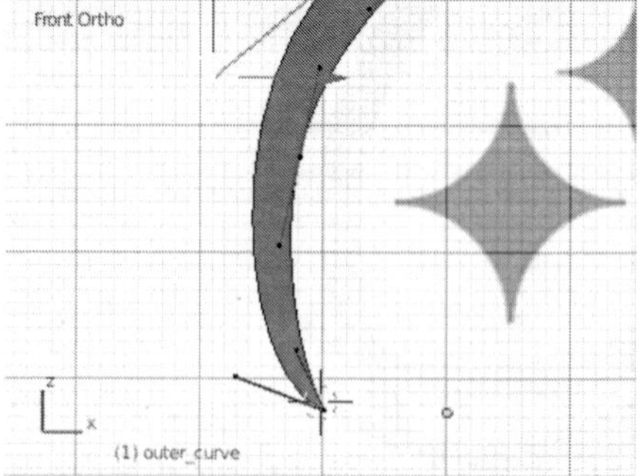

***Figure 3-54** The outer_curve filled with grey color*

Next, you will create the inner curve of the outer shape.

16. Make sure *outer_curve* is selected. Switch to **Object Mode**. Next, press SHIFT+D and then Enter. Copy of *outer_curve* is created. Rename it as *inner_Curve* using the **Outliner**.

17. Switch to **Edit Mode** and modify the shape of *inner_curve*, as shown in Figure 3-56.

    Note that you may have to change the handle types of individual control points and add some control points to get the desired curvature.

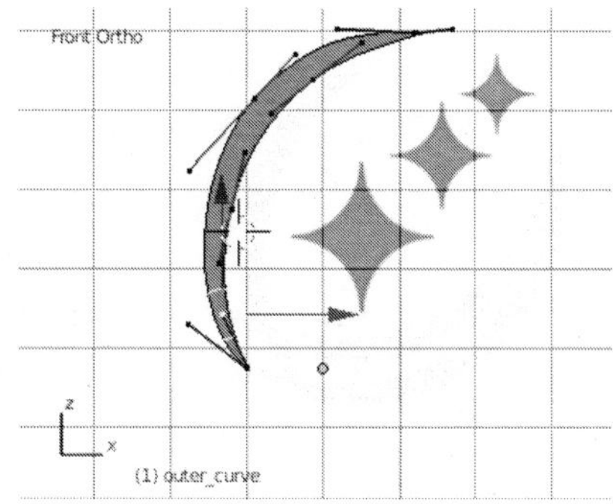

Figure 3-55 *The color of outer_curve changed*

18. Repeat the process done in steps 14 and 15 to fill *inner_curve* with the desired color, refer to Figure 3-57.

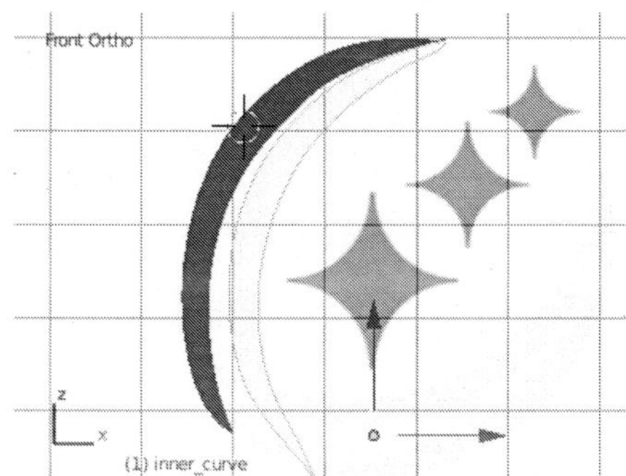

Figure 3-56 *The inner_curve created*

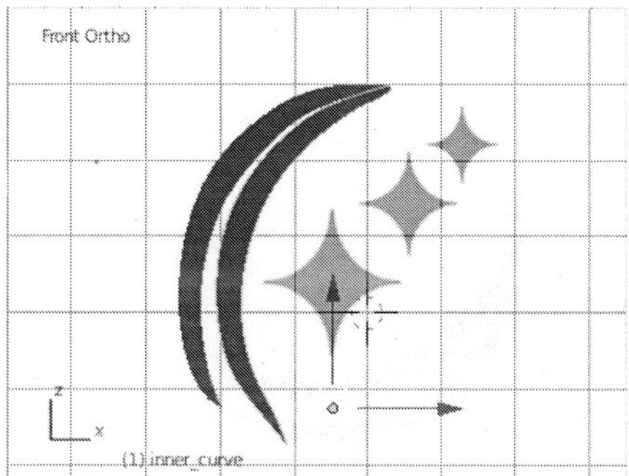

Figure 3-57 *The inner_curve filled with color*

19. Make sure *inner_curve* is selected. Next, press SHIFT+D; a copy of *inner_curve* is created with the name *inner_curve.001*. Similarly, create a copy of *outer_curve*. Next, choose the **Object** button from **Properties Editor**. Change the rotation and location values in the **Transform** panel for *inner_curve.001* and *outer_curve.001* to place them, as shown in Figure 3-58.

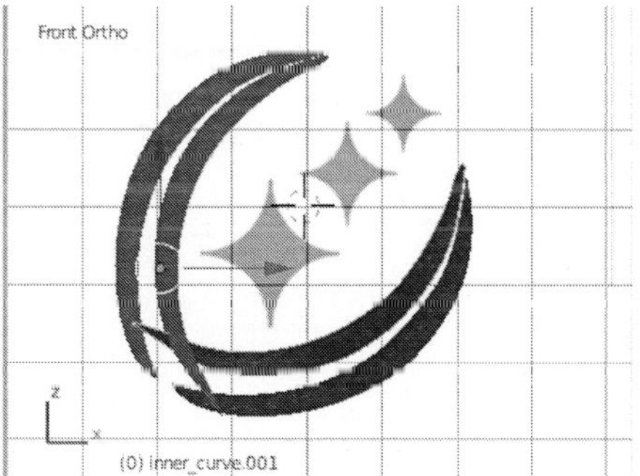

Figure 3-58 *The inner_curve.001 and outer_curve.001 placed*

Creating the Inner Shape

In this section, you will create the inner shape using the **Circle** tool. You will use new layer for the inner shape and hide all the shapes created earlier as they are created in default layer.

1. Click on the Layer 2 button; Layer 2 is selected and all the shapes created earlier get hidden as they are created in the default Layer 1.

2. Choose the **Circle** tool from the **Curve** area in the **Add primitive** panel of **Toolshelf**; the Bezier circle is created at the position of the 3D Cursor. Rename it as *ishape1*. Notice the small orange colored circle on the Layer 2 button.

3. Position *ishape1* on the reference image in the Front Ortho view, as shown in Figure 3-59.

4. Switch to **Edit Mode**. You will notice that there are four control points on *ishape1*. Select any two control points on the circle and press W; the **Specials** menu is displayed. Choose **Subdivide** from this menu; a control point is added between the two selected control points.

5. Similarly, add one control point between other default control points. Figure 3-60 shows the four control points added to *ishape1* .

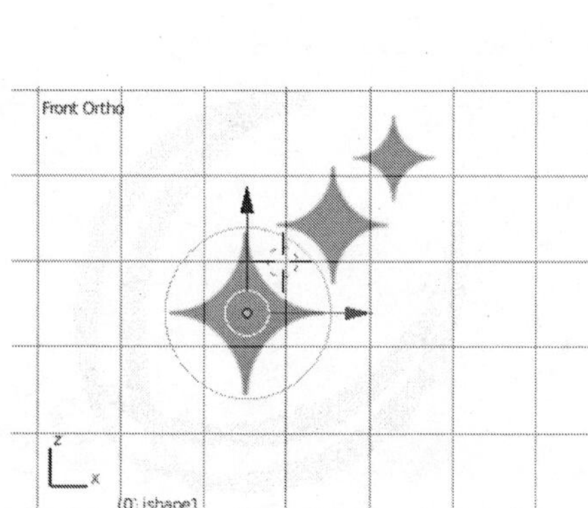

Figure 3-59 *The ishape1 positioned*

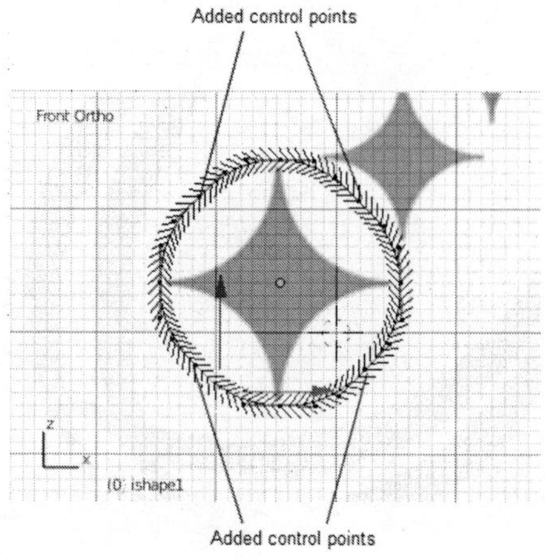

Figure 3-60 *The four control points added to ishape1*

6. Move the added control points, as shown in Figure 3-61. Next, adjust their handles and relocate the control points to get the shape, as shown in Figure 3-62.

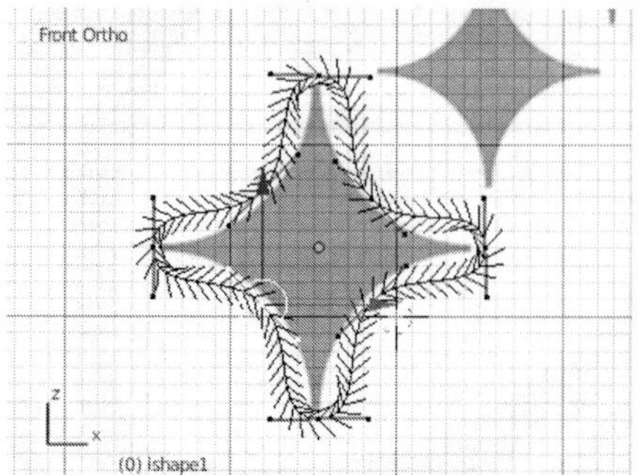

Figure 3-61 *The added control points moved*

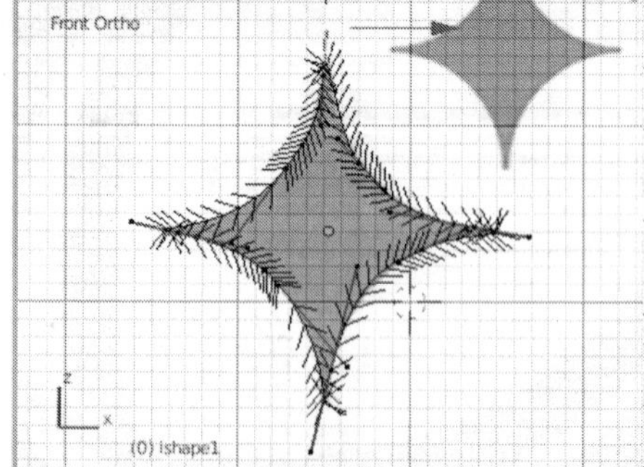

Figure 3-62 *The changed shape of ishape1*

7. Make sure the **Object Data** button is chosen in **Properties Editor**. Next, choose the **2D** button from the **Shape** panel in **Properties Editor**; *ishape1* is filled with grey color, as shown in Figure 3-63.

8. Change the color of *ishape1* to the color of your choice, as done in Tutorial 1 of Chapter 2. Figure 3-64 shows *ishape1* with color changed.

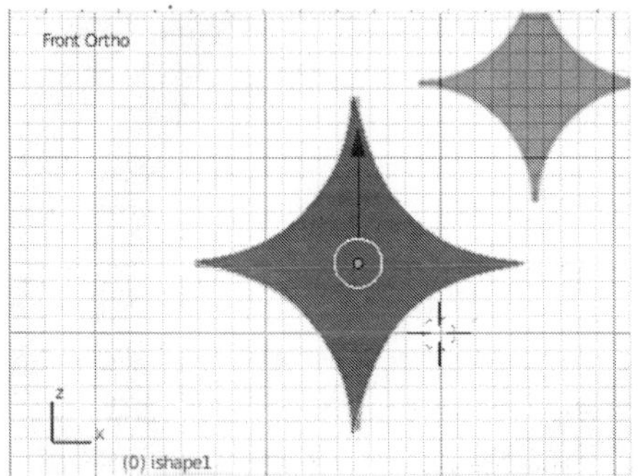

***Figure 3-63** The ishape1 filled with grey color*

***Figure 3-64** The changed color of ishape1*

9. Make sure *ishape1* is selected. Press SHIFT+D and ENTER; a copy of *ishape1* is created. Rename it as *ishape2.*

10. Make sure *ishape2* is selected. Next, move it away from *ishape1*. Choose the **Object** button from **Properties Editor**. Enter **0.7** in the **Scale** area of the **Transform** panel; *ishape2* is uniformly scaled. Place *ishape2* on the reference image, as shown in Figure 3-65.

11. Create one more copy of *ishape1*. Rename it as *ishape3*. Next, move it away from *ishape1*. Choose the **Object** button from **Properties Editor**. Enter **0.5** in the **Scale** area of the **Transform** panel; *ishape3* is uniformly scaled. Place *ishape3* on the reference image, as shown in Figure 3-66.

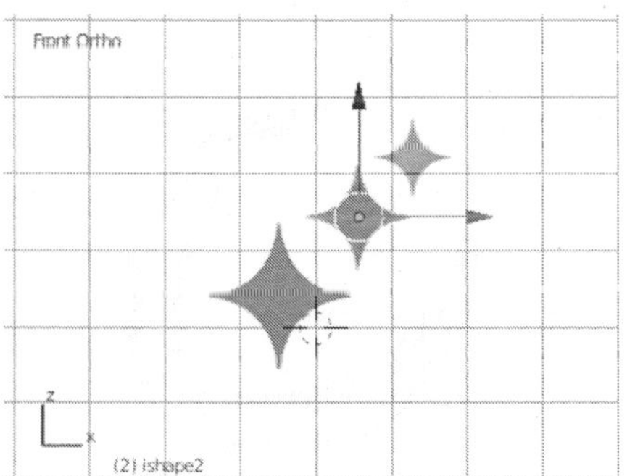

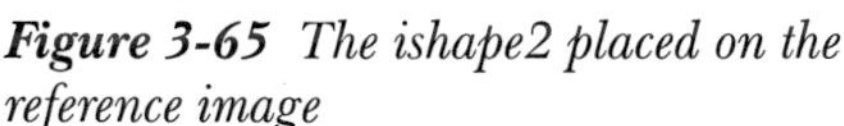

***Figure 3-65** The ishape2 placed on the reference image*

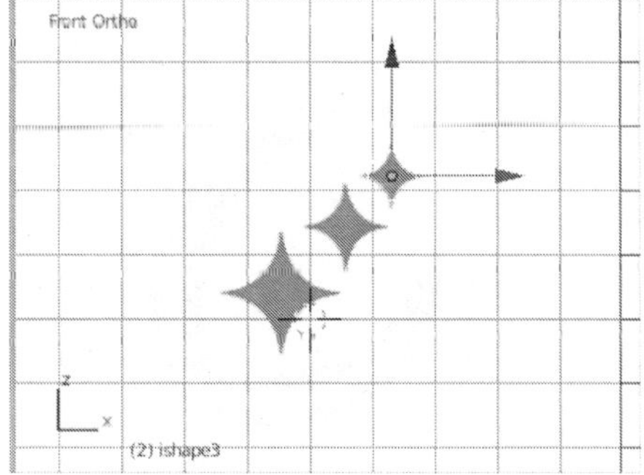

***Figure 3-66** The ishape3 placed on the reference image*

12. Select all the shapes in the view and press CTRL+J; all the shapes combine to form a single shape. Rename it as *inner_shape*.

Creating the Text

In this section, you will create the text using the **Text** tool.

1. Click on the Layer 3 button; Layer 3 is selected and *inner_shape* is hidden as it is created in layer 2.

2. Choose the **Text** tool from the **Other** area in the **Add primitive** panel of **Toolshelf**; the **Text** text is created at the position of the 3D Cursor, refer to Figure 3-67. Rename it as *logotext*. Notice the small orange colored circle on the Layer 3 button.

3. Switch to **Edit Mode**. Notice the cursor at the end of *logotext*. Press the BACKSPACE key four times and enter **Company Name**; **Text** gets replaced by **Company Name**.

4. Switch to **Object Mode**. Move *logotext* to the right of the reference image, as shown in Figure 3-68.

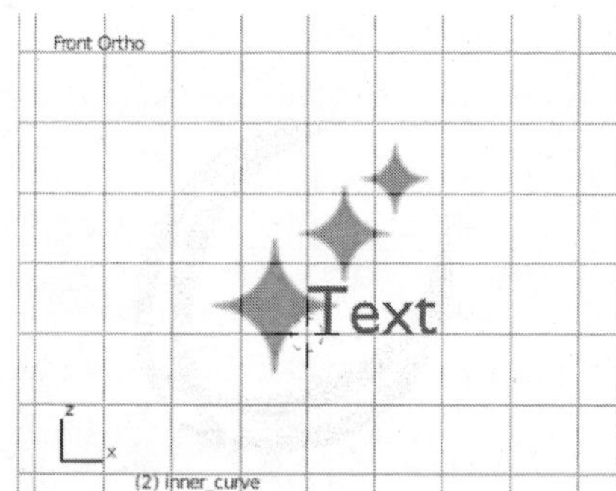

Figure 3-67 *The text created*

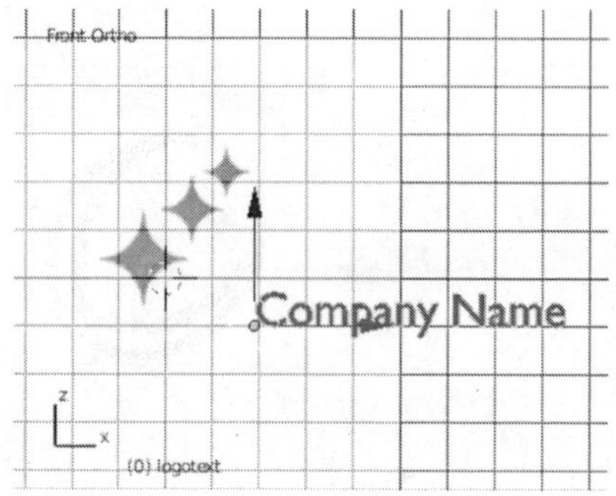

Figure 3-68 *The logotext moved to right of the reference image*

Next, you will change the font and style of *logotext*.

5. Switch to **Edit Mode** again. Choose the **Object Data** button from **Properties Editor**; various panels are displayed in **Properties Editor**, as shown in Figure 3-69.

Note

*The icon of the **Object data** button of **Properties Editor** is different for different primitives.*

6. Enter following values in the **Geometry** panel of **Properties Editor**:

   Depth: **0.025** Extrude: **0.115** Resolution: **2**

7. Choose the **Load New Font** button from the **Font** panel, refer to Figure 3-69; **File Browser** is displayed. Navigate to *c:/Windows/Fonts* and select font of your choice or navigate to the folder where fonts are saved and then choose **Open Font**; the font of *logotext* changed in the view and the name of the font is added to the **Fonts** panel at the left of the **Load New Font** button. Figure 3-70 shows *logotext* with font and style changed.

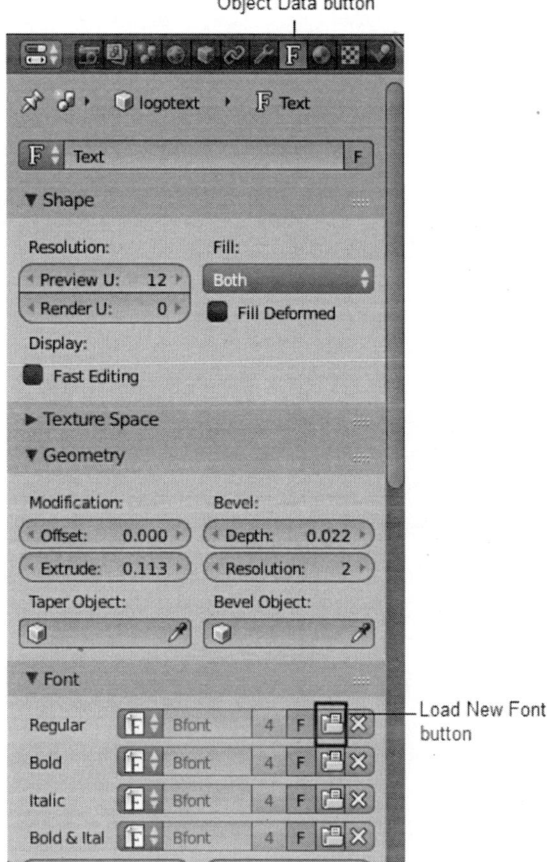

Figure 3-69 Various panels in ***Properties Editor***

Placing the Text on Curve

In this section, you will place *logotext* on the curve using the **Text on Curve** option in **Properties Editor**.

1. Switch to **Object Mode**. Next, choose the **Bezier** tool from the **Curve** area in the **Add primitive** panel of **Toolshelf**; the Bezier curve is created at the position of the 3D Cursor. Rename it as *text_curve*.

2. Switch to **Edit Mode** and modify *text_curve,* as shown in Figure 3-71.

3. Switch to **Object Mode** again and select *logotext.* Next, click on the edit box below the **Text on Curve** option in the **Font** panel of **Properties Editor**; a menu is displayed listing all the available curves in the scene, refer to Figure 3-72.

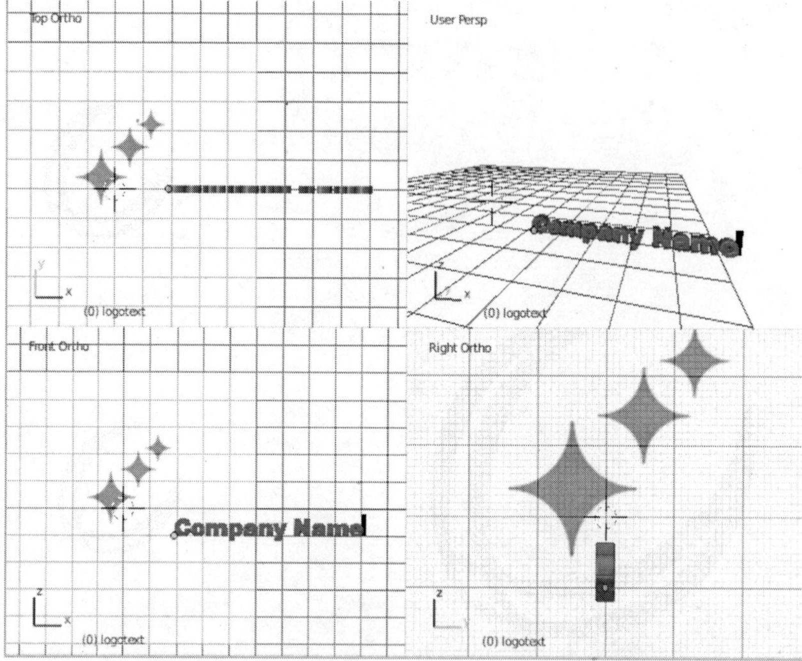

Figure 3-70 The logotext with font and style changed

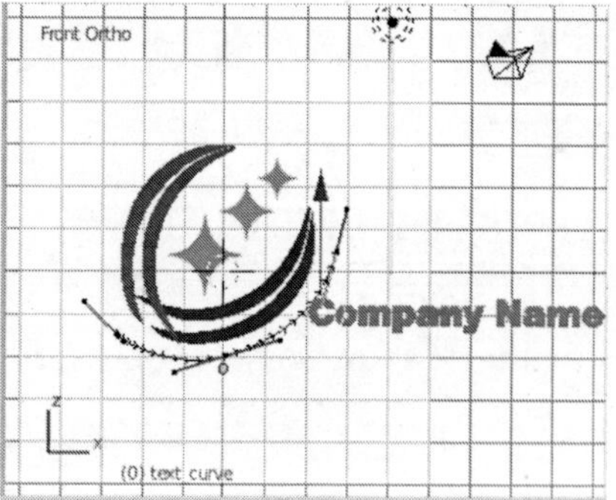

Figure 3-71 The text_curve modifed

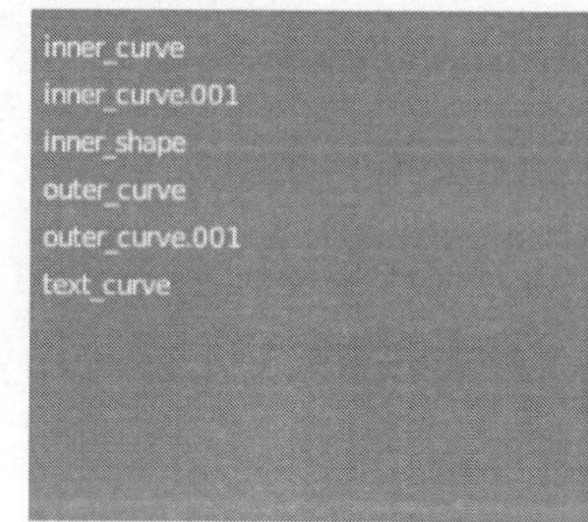

Figure 3-72 The menu displayed

4. Choose *text_curve* from the menu displayed; the shape of *logotext* is changed, as shown in Figure 3-73.

5. Align *logotext* using the **Translate** and **Rotate** tools from **3D view Editor**, as shown in Figure 3-74.

6. Change the color of *logotext* to the color of your choice, as done in Tutorial 1 of Chapter 2.

7. Click on the visibility icon next to *text_curve*, refer to Figure 3-75; *text_curve* is removed from the view.

You will now unhide all the shapes by selecting layer 1 and layer 2.

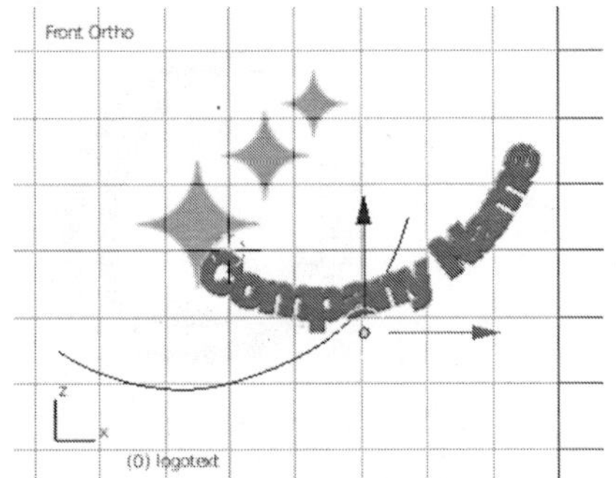

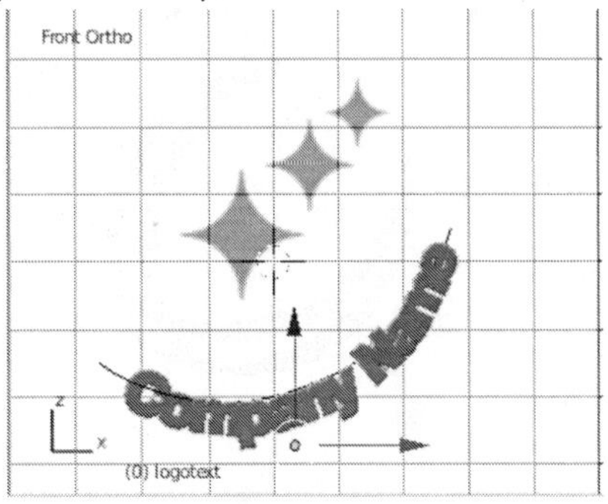

Figure 3-73 *The shape of logotext changed*

Figure 3-74 *The logotext aligned*

8. Press and hold the SHIFT key and choose the Layer1 button and the Layer 2 button; all the shapes of logo are now visible, refer to Figure 3-76.

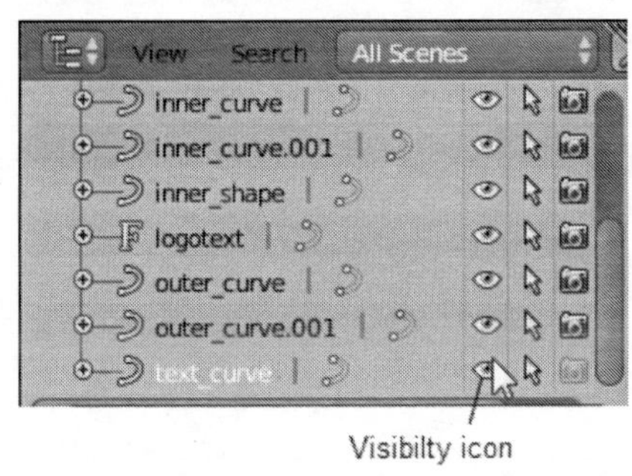

Figure 3-75 *Choosing the visibility icon from the* ***Outliner***

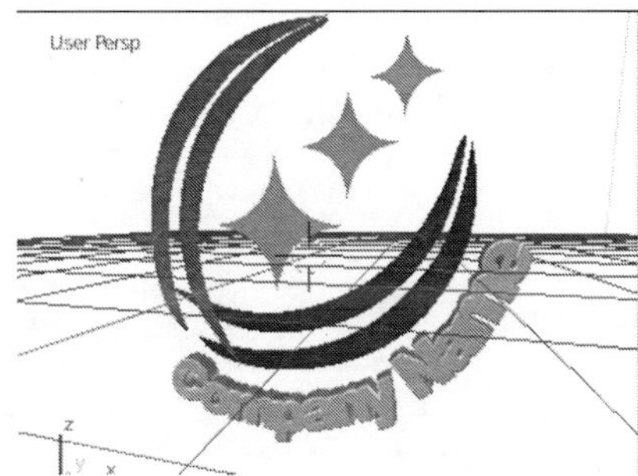

Figure 3-76 *All the shapes of logo*

Saving and Rendering the Scene

In this section, you will save the scene that you have created and then render it. You can also view the final rendered image of this model by downloading the *c03_blender2.79_rndr.zip* file from *www.cadcim.com.* The path of the file is as follows: *Textbooks > Animation and Visual Effects > Blender > Blender 2.79 for Digital Artists*

1. Change the background color of the scene as discussed in Tutorial 1 of Chapter 2.

2. Choose **File > Save** from the **Info Editor** menu bar.

3. Adjust the view in the User Persp view. Next, choose the **Open GL still image render** button from **3D View Editor**; the rendered image is displayed in the **UV/Image Editor**; refer to Figure 3-39.

Tutorial 3

In this tutorial, you will create a line art, as shown in Figure 3-77. **(Expected time: 20 min)**

Figure 3-77 *The rhino line art*

The following steps are required to complete this tutorial:

a. Create folder.
b. Add reference image.
c. Create the line art.
d. Save and render the scene.

Creating Folder

1. Navigate to *\Documents\blender2.79\c03* folder and create a new folder with the name *c03_tut3*.

2. Press CTRL+N or choose **File > New** from the **Info Editor** menu bar; a menu is displayed. Choose **Reload Start-Up File**; the menu is disappeared and the startup file is loaded.

3. Choose **File > Save** from the **Info Editor** menu bar; **File Browser** is displayed.

4. Navigate to *\Documents\blender2.79\c03\c03_tut3* folder and enter **Lineart** in the **File Name** edit box. Next, choose the **Save Blender File** button to save the file at the specified location.

Adding Reference Image

1. Choose **View > Toggle Quad View** from the **3D View Editor** menu bar or press CTRL+ALT+Q; the quad view is displayed. Hover the cursor over any of the views and press N; **Properties Region** is displayed.

2. Expand the **Background Images** panel from **Properties Region**. Next, choose the **Add Image** button from the **Background Images** panel; the **Not Set** area is added to the **Background Images** panel. Choose the **Open** button from the **Not Set** area; **File Browser** is displayed. Navigate to *\Documents\blender2.79\c03* and select the **tut3lineart** image and choose the **Open Image** button; the selected image is displayed in all the three ortho views. Also, the **Not Set** area is replaced by the **tut3lineart** area in the **Background Images** panel

of **Properties Region**. Next, choose **Front** from the **Axis** drop-down to show the image in the Front view only, refer to Figure 3-78.

3. Enter **0.4** in the **Opacity** edit box of the **tut3lineart.jpg** area; the opacity of the reference image is reduced.

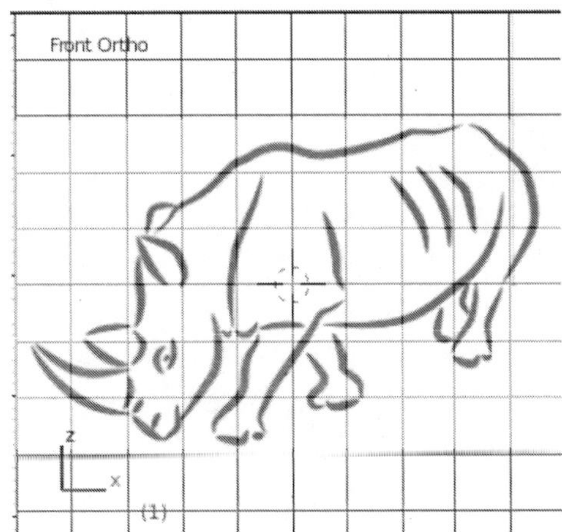

Figure 3-78 The reference image displayed

Creating the Lineart

In this section, you will create the lineart using the **Draw Curve** tool.

1. Delete **Cube** from the view. Make sure the **Create** tab is chosen in **Toolshelf**. Next, choose the **Bezier** tool from the **Curve** area in the **Add Primitive** panel of **Toolshelf**; Bezier curve is created at the center in the view.

2. Press TAB to switch to **Edit Mode**; the **Add Curves** panel is displayed in the **Create** tab of **Toolshelf**.

   Now, you need to set the parameters in the **Options** tab of **Toolshelf** and **Properties Editor** before creating the curve to achieve a desired shape.

3. Choose the **Options** tab from **Toolshelf**. Set the parameters in the **Curve Stroke** panel as follows:

   Tolerance: **15**   Taper Radius: **0.6** (in both the edit boxes)

   Choose the **Surface** button

   Offset: **0.5**

4. Choose the **Object Data** button from **Properties Editor** and choose the **3D** button from the **Shape** panel. Also, choose **Full** from the **Fill** drop-down. Next, enter **0.185** in the **Depth** slider of the **Geometry** panel.

5. Choose the **Draw Curve** tool from the **Add Curves** panel in **Toolshelf**. Next, draw the curve, refer to Figure 3-79. You may need to move the control points and handles of the curve drawn to fit it on the reference image.

6. Select the control points of the Bezier curve created earlier, refer to Figure 3-80 and press DELETE. Next, choose **Vertices** from the **Delete** pop-up; the selected control points are deleted.

7. Choose the **Draw Curve** tool again and create one more curve. Repeat this process to create all the curves on the reference image, as shown in Figure 3-81.

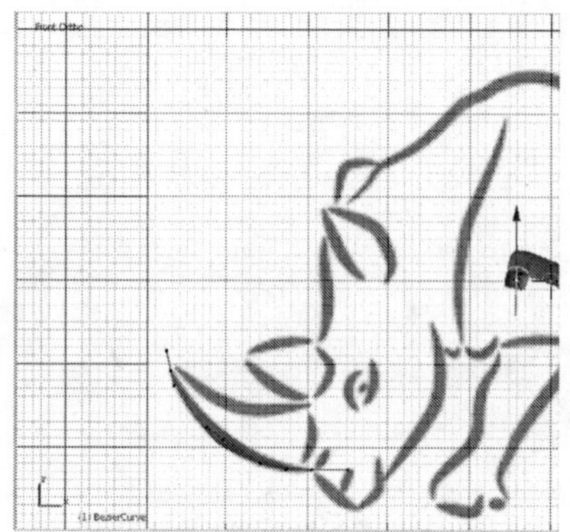

Figure 3-79 The curve drawn

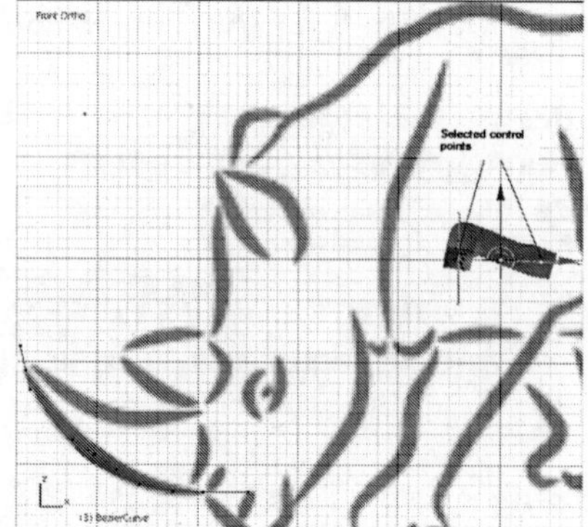

Figure 3-80 The selected control points

8. Switch to **Object Mode**. Lineart is created, as shown in Figure 3-81.

Figure 3-81 The lineart created

Saving and Rendering the Scene

In this section, you will save the scene that you have created and then render it. You can also view the final rendered image of this model by downloading the *c03_blender2.79_rndr.zip* file from *www.cadcim.com.* The path of the file is as follows: *Textbooks > Animation and Visual Effects > Blender > Blender 2.79 for Digital Artists*

1. Choose **File > Save** from the **Info Editor** menu bar.

2. Adjust the view in the User Persp view. Next, choose the **Open GL still image render** button from **3D View Editor**; the rendered image is displayed in the **UV/Image Editor**; refer to Figure 3-77.

Self-Evaluation Test

Answer the following questions and then compare them to those given at the end of this chapter:

1. Which of the following keys is used to display the **Handle** menu?

   (a) W (b) E
   (c) N (d) V

2. You need to press __________ to extend the Bezier curve.

3. The normals on the Bezier curve represent the direction and speed of the movement along the curve. (T/F)

4. A NURBS curve primitive has control points, handles, and segments. (T/F)

5. You can add control points to a NURBS surface. (T/F)

Review Questions

Answer the following questions:

1. Which of the following handle types has independent handles?

   (a) **Aligned** (b) **Free**
   (c) **Automatic** (d) **Vector**

2. The __________ option in the **Specials** menu is used to subdivide the segment in a curve.

3. You can also create and save a text file using the __________.

4. You need to press __________ to combine the selected curve primitives.

5. **Properties Editor** is used to add background images in orthographic views. (T/F)

EXERCISES

Exercise 1

Create the wall design model shown in Figure 3-82. **(Expected time: 15 min)**

Figure 3-82 The wall design model

Exercise 2

Create the wall design model shown in Figure 3-83. **(Expected time: 15 min)**

Figure 3-83 The wall design model

Answers to Self-Evaluation Test

1. d, **2.** E, **3.**T, **4.** F, **5.** F

Chapter 4

Working with Modifiers

Learning Objectives

After completing this chapter, you will be able to:

- *Use modifiers*
- *Understand the types of modifiers*
- *Create complex objects using modifiers*
- *Understand the pivot point alignment*

INTRODUCTION

Modifiers are used to modify an object by applying various effects on the object or perform operations which will help you to create complex models that would otherwise be quite difficult to create. In this chapter, you will learn about various modifiers in detail. You will also learn pivot point alignment of an object.

UNDERSTANDING THE PIVOT POINT ALIGNMENT

The pivot point of an object represents the local center of the object. When you transform an object, the pivot point acts like a center. By default, pivot point is located at the center of the object. If you select more than one object in the scene and perform some operations on these objects, by default the pivot point for this selection is set at the center of selection. To change the location of pivot point of an individual object or of the selected objects, choose the desired option from the **Pivot** drop-down in **3D View Editor**, refer to Figure 4-1. Note that active element is the last selected element in the selection and median point is the center point of the selection.

To further transform the pivot point with respect to the object and 3D cursor, press CTRL+SHIFT+ALT+C; the **Set Origin** menu will be displayed, as shown in Figure 4-2. You can choose the desired option from this menu to change the location of pivot point or the object. Alternatively, choose **Object > Transform** from the **3D View Editor** menu bar and then choose the desired option to transform the pivot point.

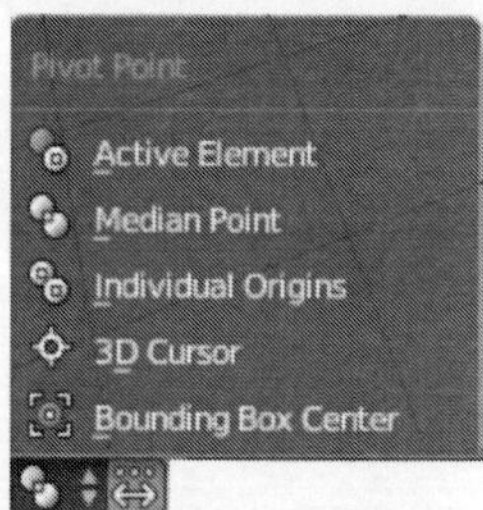

*Figure 4-1 The **Pivot** drop-down*

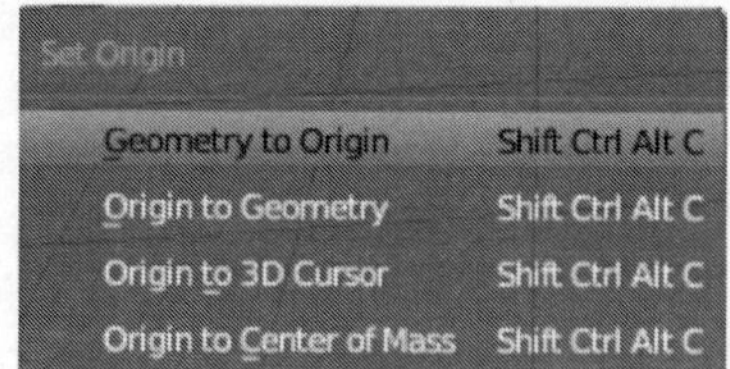

*Figure 4-2 The **Set Origin** menu*

MODIFIERS

In Blender, modifiers are classified into different categories based on the operations performed on the object. There are four major categories of modifiers: **Modify**, **Generate**, **Deform**, and **Simulate**. All these modifiers are available in **Properties Editor**. To access these modifiers, choose the **Object modifiers** button from **Properties Editor**, refer to Figure 4-3; the **Add Modifier** drop-down will be displayed. This drop-down contains various modifiers under different categories. Figure 4-3 shows modifiers in the **Add** drop-down when a mesh primitive is selected and Figure 4-4 shows modifiers in the **Add** drop-down when a curve primitive is selected.

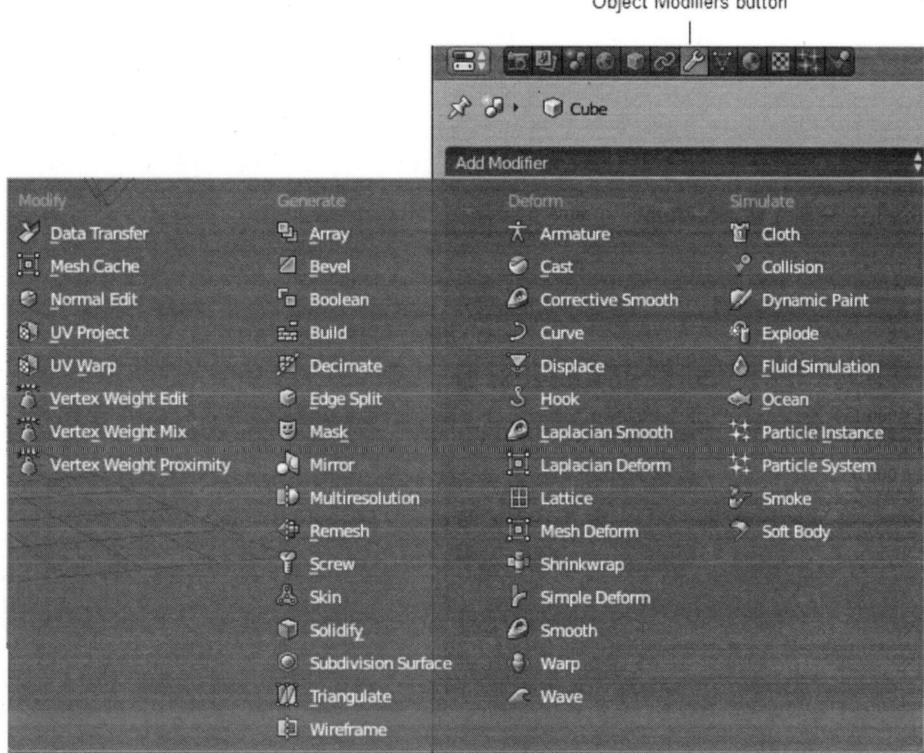

***Figure 4-3** Modifiers displayed for a mesh primitive*

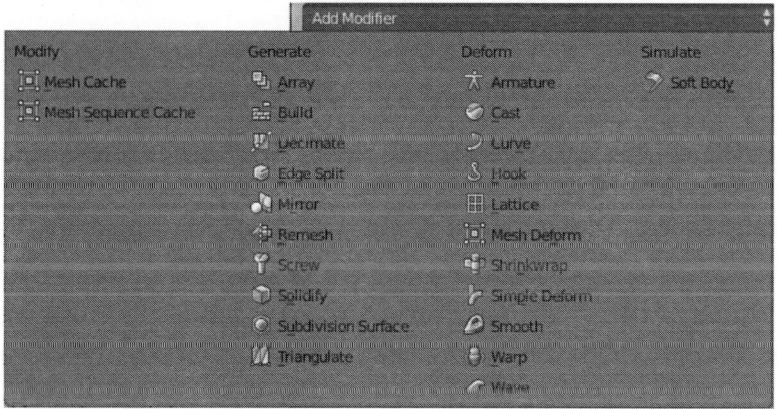

***Figure 4-4** Modifiers displayed for a curve primitive*

You can add any number of modifiers to an object. As you add a modifier to an object, it gets added to the modifier stack. Modifier stack is a place where all the modifiers are listed in a sequence in which they are added to the object. The sequence of the modifiers in the modifier stack affects the resulting shape of the object. You can change the order of the modifiers in the modifier stack by using the buttons in **Properties Editor**. The process is discussed in the next section.

In this chapter, you will learn modifiers in the **Generate** and **Deform** categories which are used for modeling complex objects. Modifiers in the **Simulate** category and the **Modify** category will be discussed in later chapters.

Generate Category

The modifiers in this category are constructive modifiers that are used to change the appearance of an object or add a new geometry to it. Note that some of the modifiers in this category are not applicable to curve primitives. To add a modifier from this category to the modifier stack of the object, select the object and choose the **Object modifiers** button from **Properties Editor**. Next, click on the **Add Modifiers** drop-down and choose the desired modifier from the **Generate** category of the list displayed. The most commonly used modifiers in this category are discussed next.

Array Modifier

As the name suggests, the **Array** modifier is used to create array of the selected object based on the parameters set for this modifier in the **Properties Editor**. Figure 4-5 shows parameters for the **Array** modifier in **Properties Editor**. Some of these parameters are common to all the modifiers in the **Generate** category and rest of the modifiers are specific to the **Array** modifier, as shown in Figure 4-5. The parameters common to all the modifiers in the **Generate** category are discussed next.

Expand/Collapse Button

This button is used to expand or collapse the modifier in the modifier stack.

Modifier Name Edit Box

This edit box is used to specify a unique name to the added modifier. This is useful when you add a modifier more than one time on the object. By default the modifier name is displayed in this edit box.

Camera Icon Button

This button is used to toggle the visibility of modifier effect on the object in the render.

Eye Icon Button

This button is used to toggle the visibility of modifier effect on the object in 3D view.

Edit Icon Button

This button is used to show modified geometry as well as original geometry of the object in **Edit Mode**.

Edit Cage Button

This button is used to show modified geometry of the object in **Edit Mode**.

Up Arrow Button

This button is used to move the modifier up in the modifier stack.

Down Arrow Button

This button is used to move the modifier down in the modifier stack.

Delete Button

This button is used to delete the modifier from the modifier stack.

Apply Button

This button is used to apply the modifier permanently to the object and remove it from the modifier stack.

Copy Button

This button is used to copy the modifier at the same position in the modifier stack.

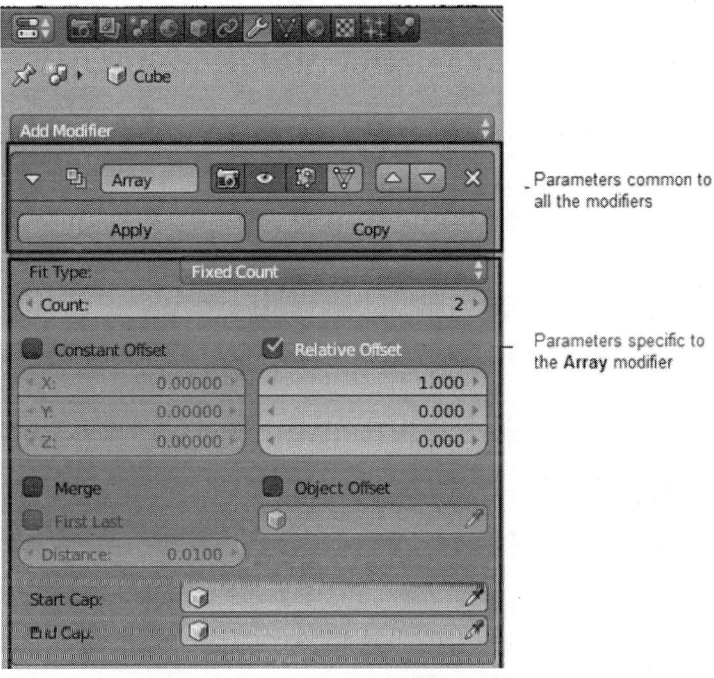

***Figure 4-5** The parameters for the **Array** modifier*

Figure 4-6 shows the **Array** modifier added to a cube with the **Count** value set to **5** with **Relative Offset** check box selected and **1.5** in the edit box located below it. You can also use constant offset or another object as an offset when you create an array of the object.

Bevel Modifier

This modifier is used to bevel all the edges of the object. It is similar to the **Bevel** option discussed in Chapter 2. Figure 4-7 shows parameters for the **Bevel** modifier in **Properties Editor** and Figure 4-8 shows the **Bevel** modifier added to a cube with change in various parameters in **Properties Editor**.

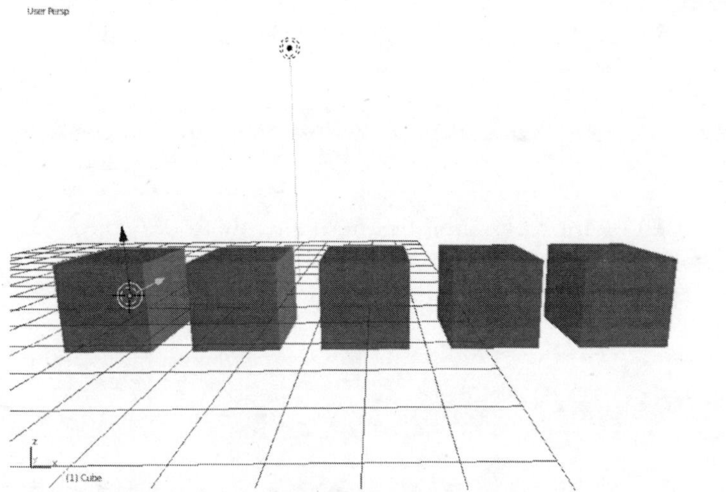

*Figure 4-6 The **Array** modifier added to a cube*

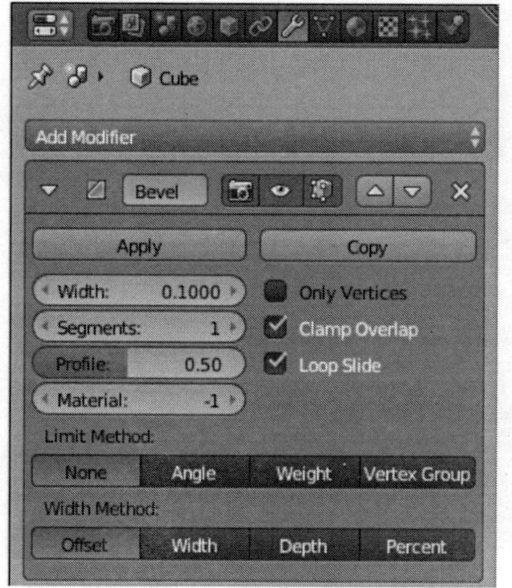

*Figure 4-7 The parameters for the **Bevel** modifier*

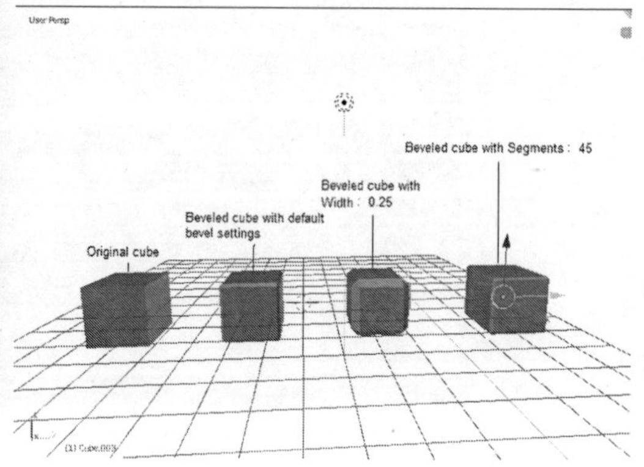

*Figure 4-8 The **Bevel** modifier added to a cube*

Boolean Modifier

This modifier is used to trim or combine two mesh primitive objects. The selected object is called as master object whereas the other object to be selected during the operation is called as target object.

To add this modifier to the modifier stack, select the master object and choose the **Object modifiers** button from **Properties Editor**. Next, choose **Boolean** from the **Generate** category in the **Add Modifiers** drop-down; the parameters for the **Boolean** modifier will be displayed in **Properties Editor**, as shown in Figure 4-9. Next, click on the **Object** text box in **Properties Editor**, refer to Figure 4-9; a menu will be displayed showing all the mesh primitive objects in the scene. Choose the desired mesh primitive to act as a target object from the menu or enter the name of target object in the **Object** text box. Next, choose the desired option from the **Operation** drop-down and choose **Apply**, refer to Figure 4-9; boolean operation will be performed on these two objects depending on the option chosen from the **Operation** drop-down. Figure 4-10 shows the boolean operation performed on a cube and a sphere using the options in the **Operation** drop-down.

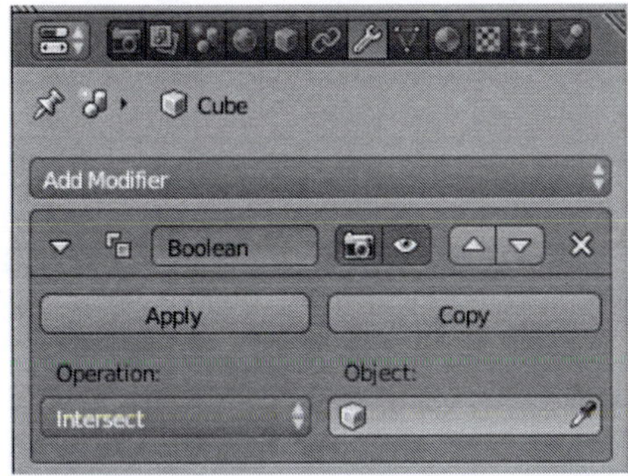

Figure 4-9 *The parameters for the* ***Boolean*** *modifier*

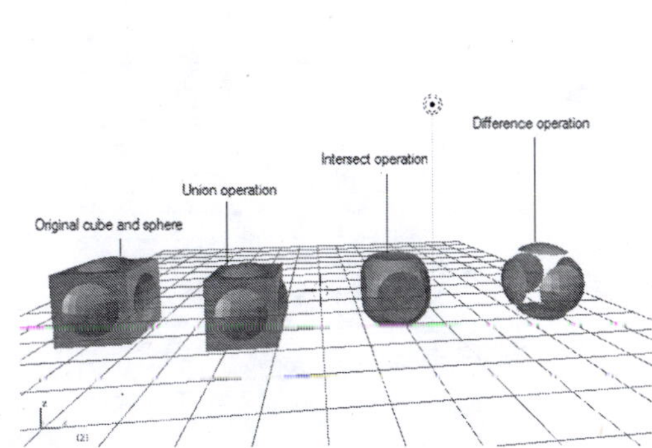

Figure 4-10 *The Boolean operation performed using various options*

Build Modifier

This modifier shows the building of faces of the object on one another over the defined time. Figure 4-11 shows parameters for the **Build** modifier in **Properties Editor**.

The **Length** slider is used to specify the time over which the object will build and the **Randomize** check box is used to randomize the building of the faces of the object, refer to Figure 4-11. Figure 4-12 shows the building of UV Sphere at frame 51 with the **Length** value set to **100**.

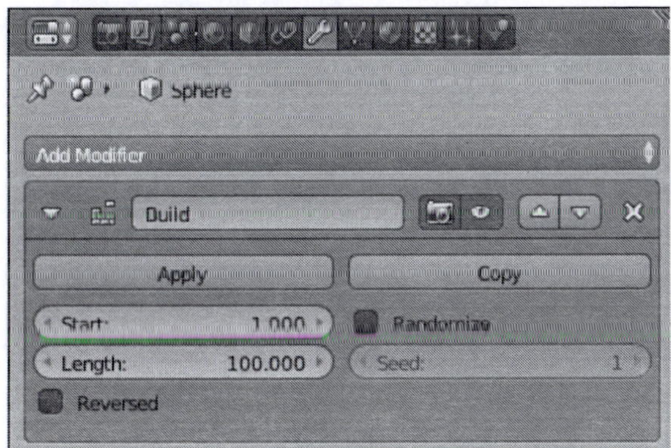

Figure 4-11 *The parameters for the* ***Build*** *modifier*

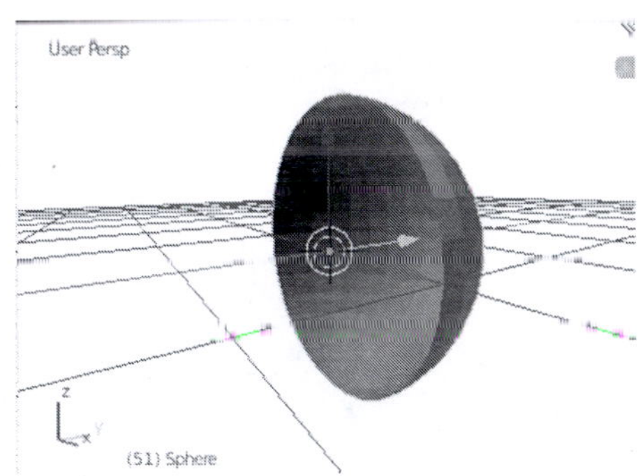

Figure 4-12 *The* ***Build*** *modifier added to a cube*

Mirror Modifier

The **Mirror** modifier is used to make the exact replica of the selected object in a specific direction. This modifier is mostly useful for creating the symmetrical models. You can create half of the model and then mirror it to complete the model. Figure 4-13 shows the parameters for the **Mirror** modifier in **Properties Editor**. In Blender, you can use the **Mirror** modifier in two ways.

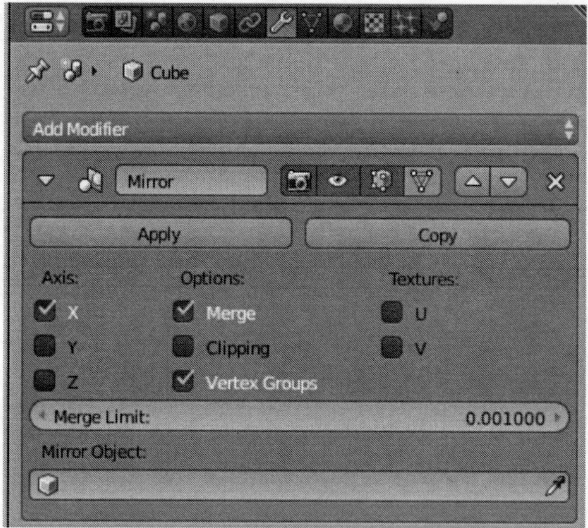

***Figure 4-13** The parameters for the **Mirror** modifier*

1. Use the pivot point of the object as the mirror center and its one of the axes as the mirror plane.

2. Use the pivot point of other object as the mirror center and its one of the axes as the mirror plane.

To mirror the object using its own pivot point and axis(s), you need to first relocate the pivot point of the object along the specific axis. To do so, left-click at a point or set the location values of 3D Cursor in the **3D Cursor** panel of **Properties Region**; 3D cursor will be placed at the specified location. Now, select the object to be mirrored and press SHIFT+CTRL+ALT+C; the **Set Origin** menu will be displayed. Next, choose the **Set Origin to 3D Cursor** option from this menu; the pivot point of the object will be relocated to the current position of 3D Cursor. Now, add the **Mirror** modifier to the selected object and specify the axis in **Properties Editor**, refer to Figure 4-13. Mirror copy of the selected object will be created along specified axis, refer to Figure 4-14.

To mirror the object using the pivot point and axis(s) of other object, select the object to be mirrored and then add the **Mirror** modifier to it. Next, click on the **Mirror Object** edit box in **Properties Editor**, refer to Figure 4-13 and select the other object from the menu displayed. Also, specify the axis in **Properties Editor**; mirror copy of the selected object will be created in the specified axis, refer to Figure 4-15.

Subdivision Surface Modifier

This modifier is used to subdivide the edges of a selected mesh primitive. Figure 4-16 shows parameters for the **Subdivision Surface** modifier in **Properties Editor**.

The **View** and **Render** sliders are used to increase the subdivision levels in view and on rendering, respectively. Figure 4-17 shows the **Subdivision Surface** modifier added to a cube with the **View** value set to **2**.

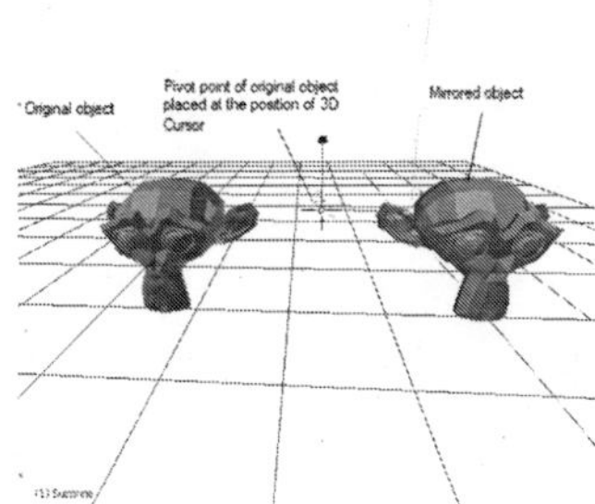

*Figure 4-14 The **Mirror** modifier added to an object using its own pivot point and axis*

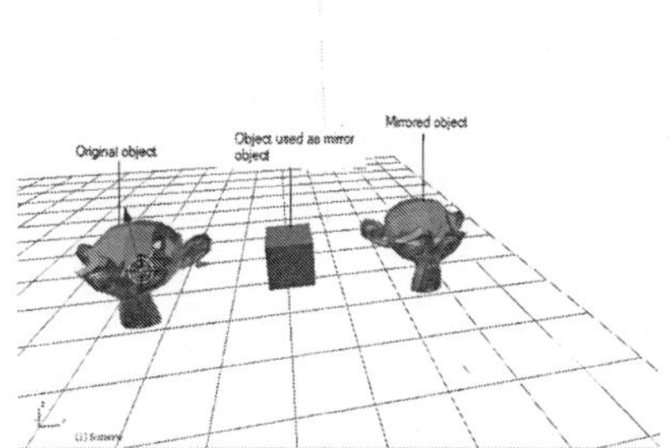

*Figure 4-15 The **Mirror** modifier added to an object using the mirror object*

*Figure 4-16 The parameters for the **Subdivision Surface** modifier*

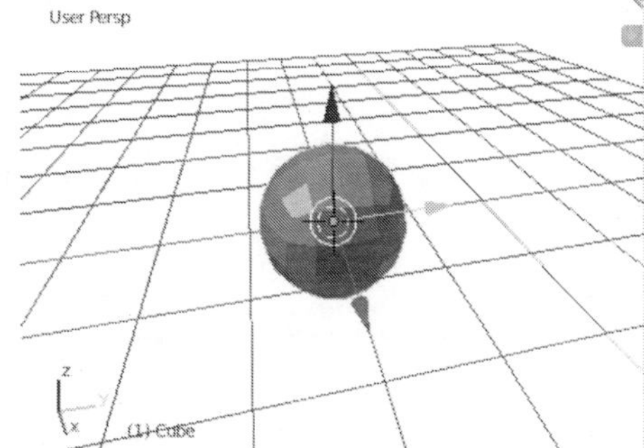

*Figure 4-17 The **Subdivision Surface** modifier added to a cube*

Remesh Modifier

This modifier is used to create the new topology for the selected object. Figure 4-18 shows parameters for the **Remesh** modifier in **Properties Editor**. You can create three types of topology using the options in the **Mode** drop-down, as shown in Figure 4-19.

Decimate Modifier

This modifier is useful for the objects that have very complex geometry. It reduces the face count of the object with minor change in the shape of the object. Figure 4-20 shows parameters for the **Decimate** modifier in **Properties Editor**. To see the effect of this modifier, choose one of the three buttons, **Collapse**, **Un-Subdivide**, or **Planar** in **Properties Editor** and then set the respective parameters below these buttons.

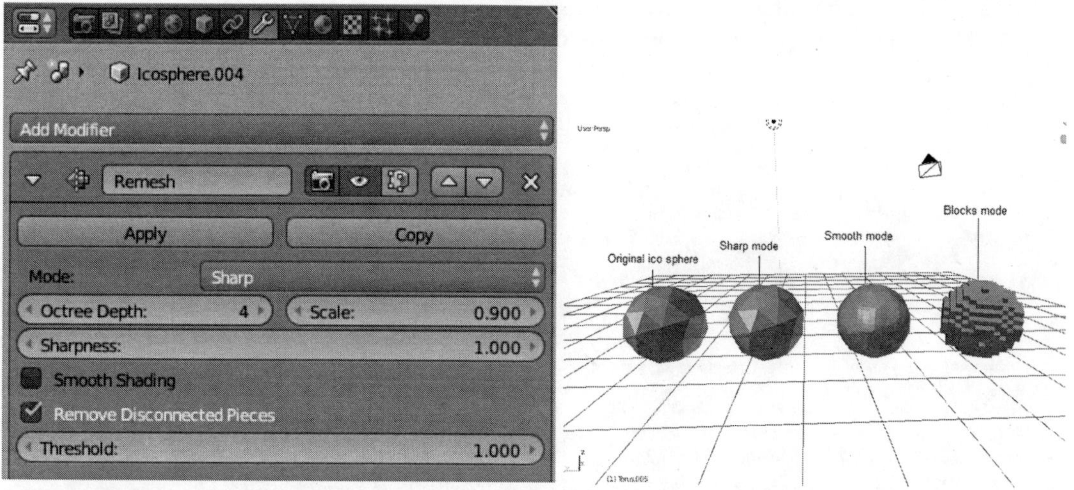

***Figure 4-18** The parameters for the **Remesh** modifier*

***Figure 4-19** The **Remesh** modifier added using options in the **Mode** drop-down*

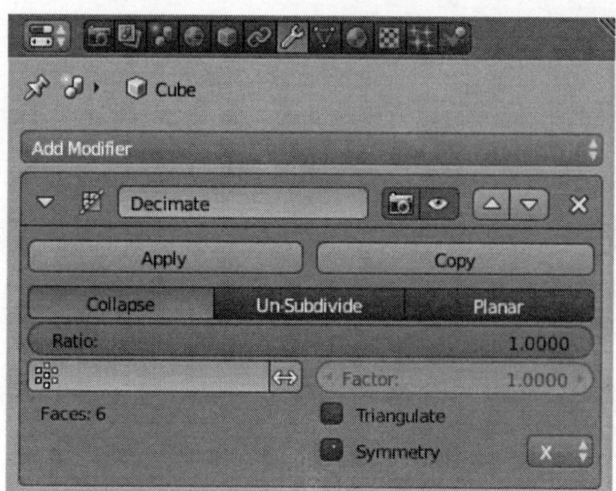

***Figure 4-20** The parameters for the **Decimate** modifier*

Multiresolution Modifier

This modifier is similar to the **Subdivision Surface** modifier with the only difference that these subdivisions can be edited in **Sculpt Mode**. You can also subdivide UVs using this modifier. Figure 4-21 shows parameters for the **Multiresolution** modifier in **Properties Editor** and Figure 4-22 shows the **Multiresolution** modifier added to a cube.

Triangulate Modifier

This modifier is used to convert all quad/N-gons to triangular faces. Figure 4-23 shows parameters for the **Triangulate** modifier in **Properties Editor**. Note that you need to switch to **Edit Mode** and choose the **Apply** button in **Properties Editor** to see the effect of the modifier. Figure 4-24 shows the **Triangulate** modifier added to a cube.

Figure 4-21 The parameters for the ***Multiresolution*** *modifier*

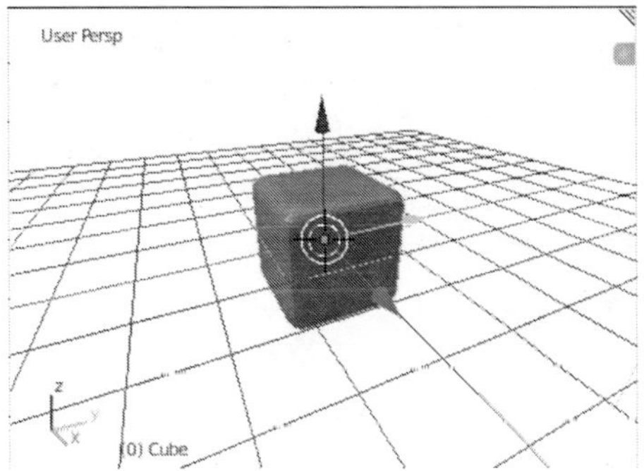

Figure 4-22 The ***Multiresolution*** *modifier added to a cube*

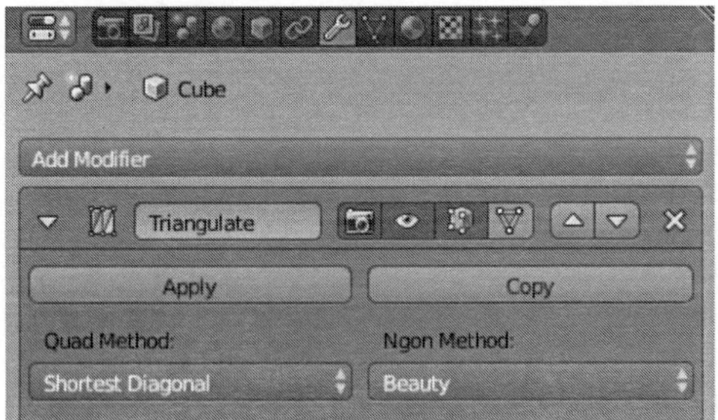

Figure 4-23 The parameters for the ***Triangulate*** *modifier*

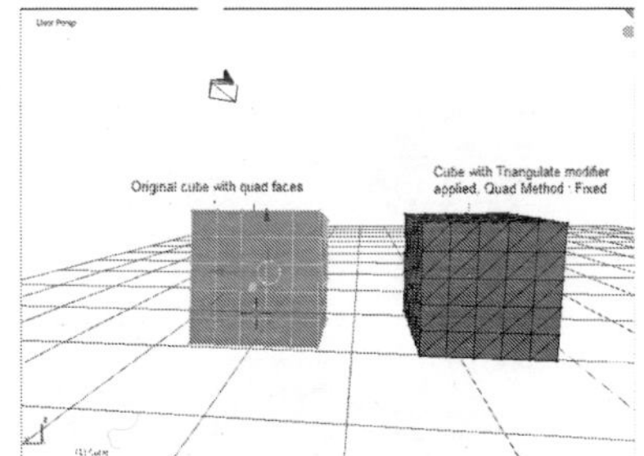

Figure 4-24 The ***Triangulate*** *modifier added to a cube*

Wireframe Modifier

This modifier converts mesh of an object into wireframe. Figure 4-25 shows parameters for the **Wireframe** modifier in **Properties Editor**. Figure 4-26 shows the **Wireframe** modifier added to a torus.

Deform Category

The modifiers in this category are used to deform the geometry of an object in such a manner that they help in creating the specific type of objects. Note that some of the modifiers in this category are not applicable to curve primitives. To add the modifier from this category to the modifier stack of the object, select the object and choose the **Object modifiers** button from **Properties Editor**. Next, choose desired modifier from the **Deform** category in the **Add Modifiers** drop-down; The most commonly used modifiers in this category are discussed next.

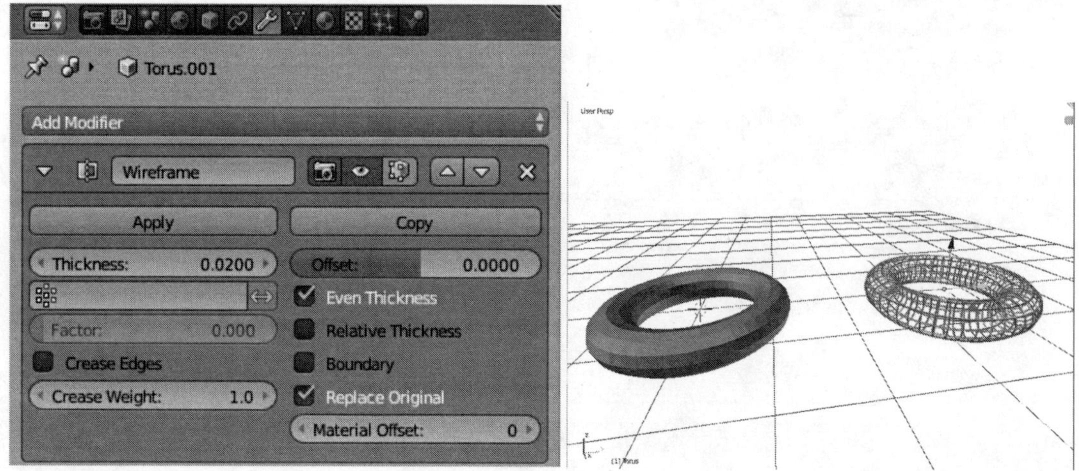

*Figure 4-25 The parameters for the **Wireframe** modifier*

*Figure 4-26 The **Wireframe** modifier added to a torus*

Curve Modifier

This modifier is used to move and deform the object along the specified curve in a specific direction. The direction is set in X, Y, Z, -X, -Y, or -Z axis. Figure 4-27 shows the parameters for the **Curve** modifier and Figure 4-28 shows the **Curve** modifier added to a cube placed near the curve and to another cube placed on the curve itself. Note that amount of deformation of an object depends on the number of subdivisions in the object.

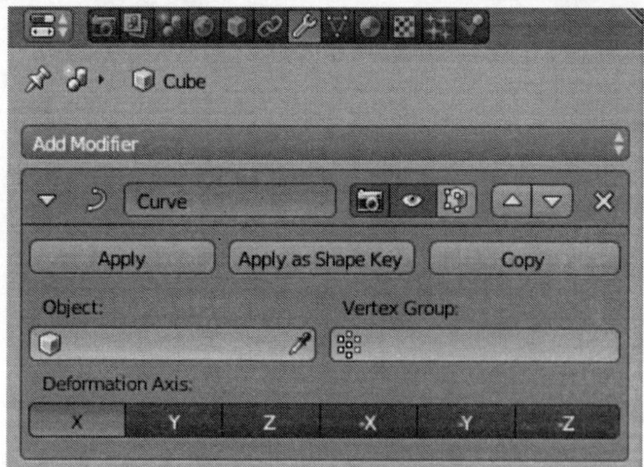

*Figure 4-27 The parameters for the **Curve** modifier*

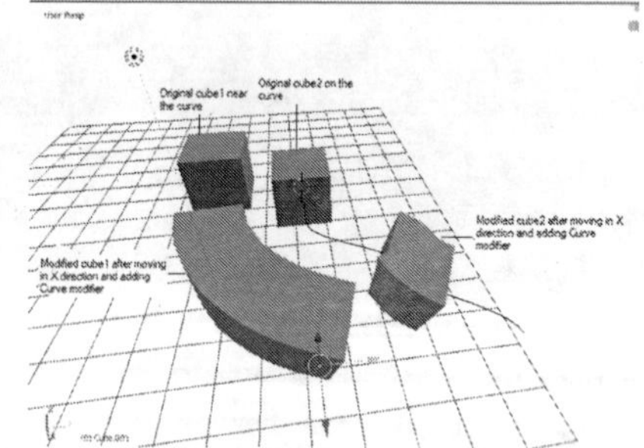

*Figure 4-28 The **Curve** modifier added to the cubes*

Laplacian Smooth Modifier

This modifier is similar to the **Smooth** modifier. It smoothens the object by removing noise on its surface with minimum changes in the shape of the object. Note that you need to subdivide the mesh of the object before applying this modifier to see the modifiers effect. Figure 4-29 shows the parameters of the **Laplacian Smooth** modifier.

Lattice Modifier

This modifier is used to deform the object by using a lattice object placed around it. To use this modifier, you need to first create a lattice object. To create the lattice object, choose **Lattice** from the **Other** area in the **Add Primitive** panel of **Toolshelf**.

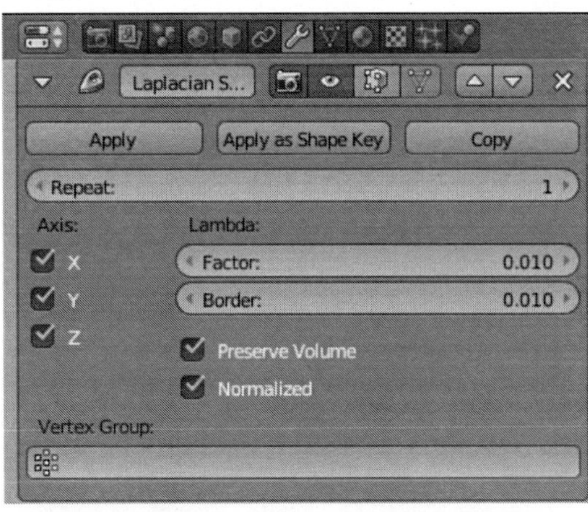

*Figure 4-29 The parameters for the **Laplacian Smooth** modifier*

To add the **Lattice** modifier to the modifier stack, select the object and choose the **Object modifiers** button from **Properties Editor**. Next, choose **Lattice** from the **Deform** category in the **Add Modifiers** drop-down; the parameters for the **Lattice** modifier will be displayed in **Properties Editor**, refer to Figure 4-30. Now, click on the **Object** edit box in **Properties Editor** and choose the lattice object from the menu displayed. Next, select the lattice object in a view and then fit it around the object to be deformed by transforming it. Make sure the lattice object is selected and then choose the **Object Data** button from **Properties Editor** and increase the control points of the lattice object by changing the values in the **U**, **V**, and **W** sliders. Now, switch to **Edit Mode** and transform control points of the lattice object to deform the object. Figure 4-31 shows the cone deformed using the **Lattice** Modifier.

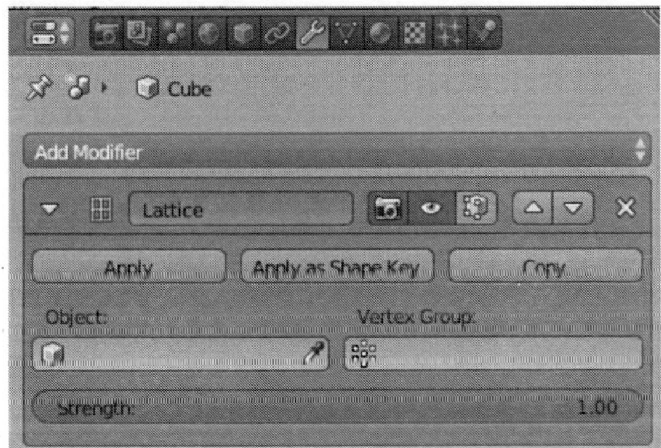

*Figure 4-30 The parameters for the **Lattice** modifier*

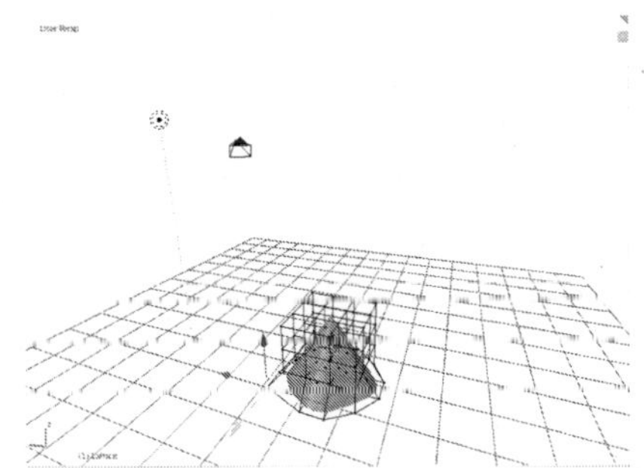

*Figure 4-31 The **Lattice** modifier added to a cone*

Smooth Modifier

This modifier is used to smoothen an object without increasing the number of vertices/edges in the object. To add this modifier to the modifier stack of the object, select the object and choose the **Object modifiers** button from **Properties Editor**. Next, click on the **Add Modifiers** drop-down and choose **Smooth** from the **Deform** category of the list displayed; the parameters for the **Smooth** modifier will be displayed in **Properties Editor**, refer to Figure 4-32. Figure 4-33 shows the **Smooth** modifier added to a icosphere. Note that if you increase or decrease the value in the **Factor** slider of **Properties Editor** by a considerable amount, the object deforms to create different shape instead of smoothing the object.

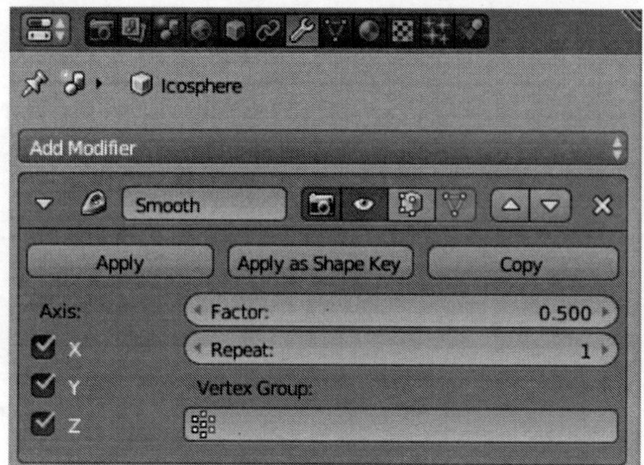

*Figure 4-32 The parameters for the **Smooth** modifier*

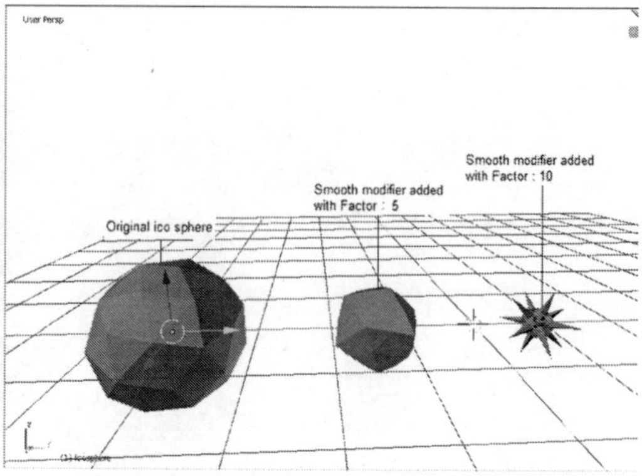

*Figure 4-33 The **Smooth** modifier added to an icosphere*

Shrinkwrap Modifier

The **Shrinkwrap** modifier is used to shrink or wrap an object around the surface of other object. Figure 4-34 shows the parameters for the **Shrinkwrap** modifier. You need to select the other object as target object. Figure 4-35 shows the **Shrinkwrap** modifier added to a plane with cylinder as the target object.

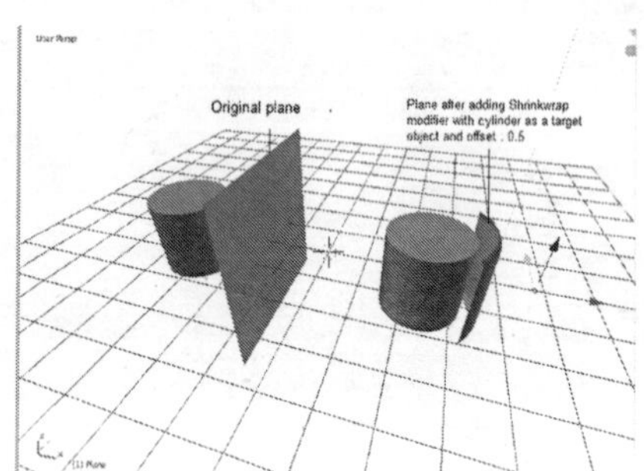

*Figure 4-34 The parameters for the **Shrinkwrap** modifier*

*Figure 4-35 The **Shrinkwrap** modifier added to a torus*

Simple Deform Modifier

This modifier is used to deform the object by twisting, bending, tapering, or stretching it. Figure 4-36 shows the parameters for the **Simple Deform** modifier. Figure 4-37 shows the **Simple Deform** modifier added to a cube.

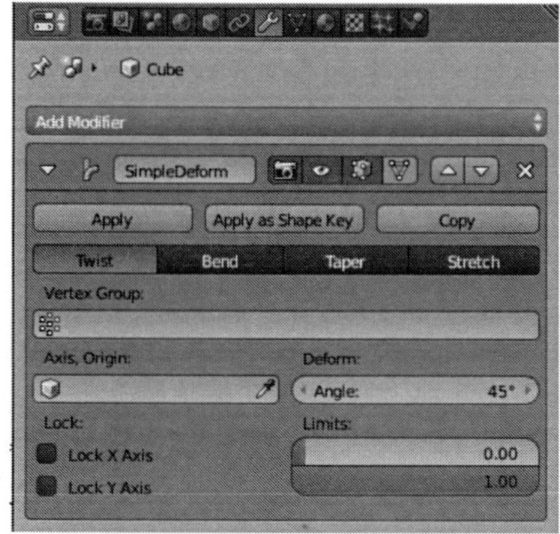

*Figure 4-36 The parameters for the **Simple Deform** modifier*

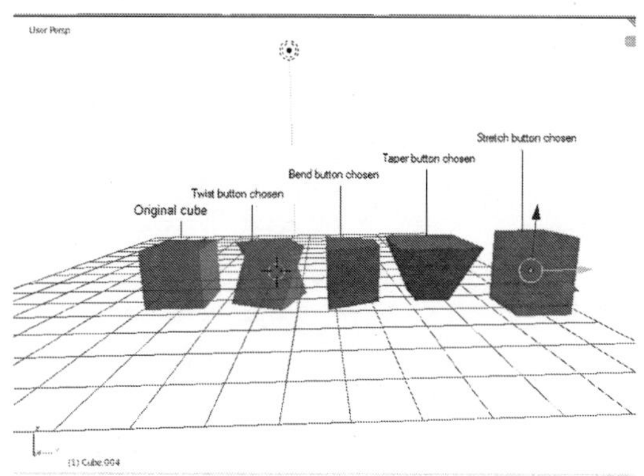

*Figure 4-37 The **Simple Deform** modifier added to a cube*

Warp Modifier

As the name suggests, this modifier is used to warp the object by using other two objects. The center of these two objects is used for setting the direction of warping. Figure 4-38 shows the parameters for the **Warp** modifier. Figure 4-39 shows the **Warp** modifier added to a plane.

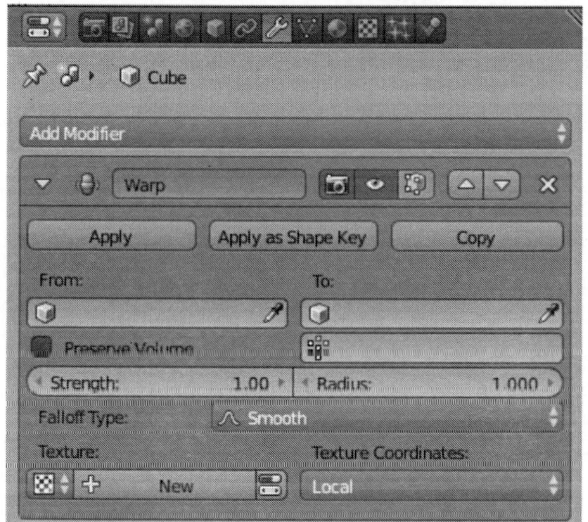

*Figure 4-38 The parameters for the **Warp** modifier*

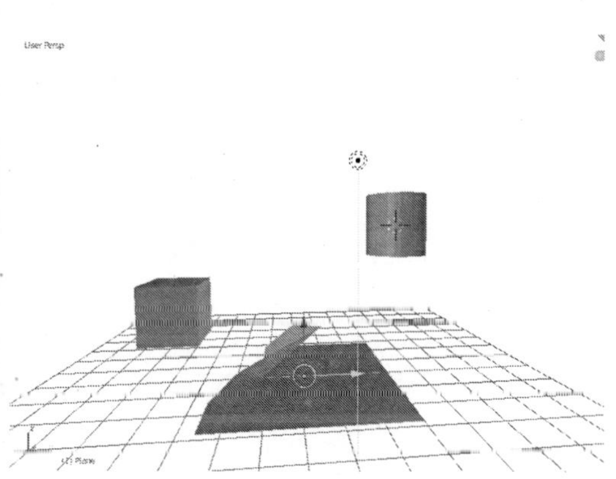

*Figure 4-39 The **Warp** modifier added to a plane*

Wave Modifier

This modifier creates wave-like effect on the geometry of object. Note that you need to subdivide the mesh of the object considerably to see this effect of this modifier. Figure 4-40 shows the parameters for the **Wave** modifier and Figure 4-41 shows the **Wave** modifier added to a plane.

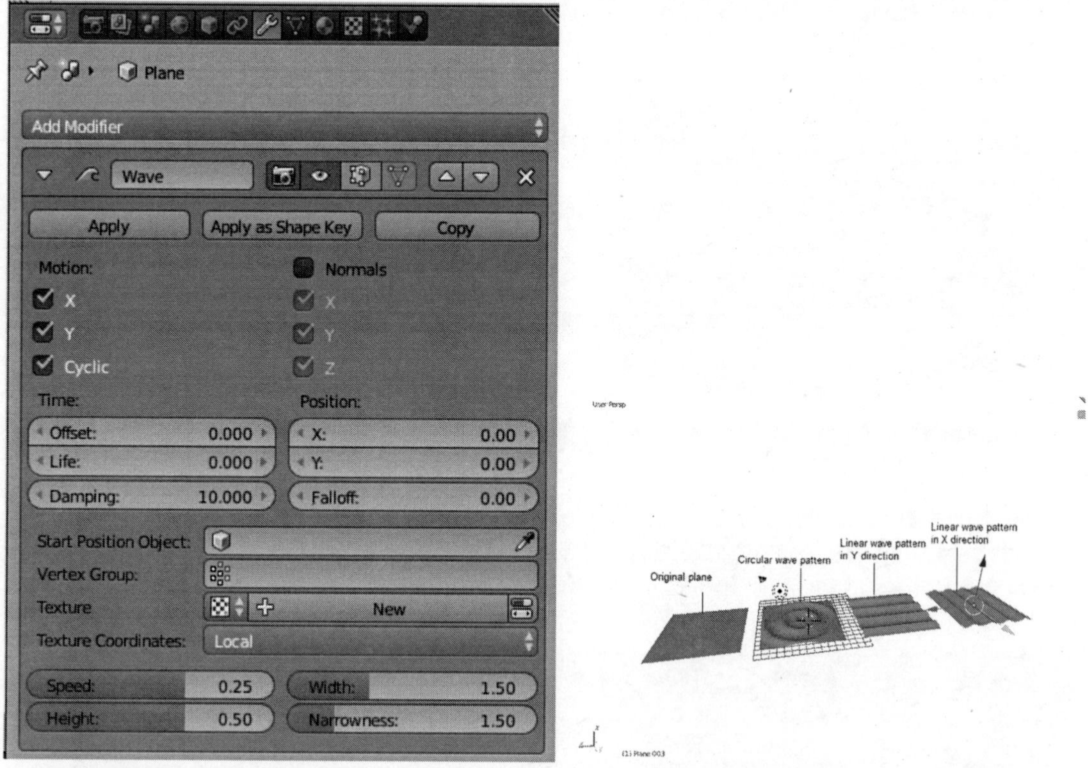

*Figure 4-40 The parameters for the **Wave** modifier*

*Figure 4-41 The **Wave** modifier added to a plane*

TUTORIALS

Before you start tutorials of this chapter, you need to download *c04_blender_2.79_tut.zip* file from *www.cadcim.com*. The path of the file is as follows: *Textbooks > Animation and Visual Effects > Blender > Blender 2.79 for Digital Artists*

Browse to *\Documents\blender2.79* and create a folder with the name *c04*. Next, extract the content of the zip file in this folder.

Tutorial 1

In this tutorial, you will create a hanging lamp using the **Wireframe** modifier, as shown in Figure 4-42. **(Expected time: 20 min)**

The following steps are required to complete this tutorial:

a. Create the folder.
b. Create the shape of the lamp cover.
c. Add the **Wireframe** modifier.
d. Create the hook.
e. Save and render the scene.

Creating the Folder

Figure 4-42 The model of a hanging lamp

1. Navigate to *\Documents\blender2.79\c04* and create a new folder with the name *c04_tut1*.

2. Press CTRL+N or choose **File > New** from the **Info Editor** menu bar; a menu is displayed. Choose **Reload Start-Up File**; the menu is disappeared and the startup file is loaded.

3. Choose **File > Save** from the **Info Editor** menu bar; the **File Browser** is displayed

4. Navigate to *\Documents\blender2.79\c04\c04_tut1* and enter **Hanging lamp** in the **File Name** edit box. Next, choose the **Save Blender File** button to save the file at the specified location.

Creating the Shape of Lamp Cover

In this section, you will create the lamp cover using the **UV Sphere** tool.

1. Make sure *Cube* is selected in the view. Next, press X; the **Delete** menu is displayed. Choose **Delete** from this menu; *Cube* is deleted.

2. Make sure the **Create** tab is chosen in **Toolshelf**. Next, choose the **UV Sphere** tool from the **Add Primitive** panel of **Toolshelf**; *Sphere* is created at the center in the view. Rename it as *lamp cover*.

3. Press CTRL+ALT+Q to change the view to quad view. Make sure the **Object** button is chosen in **Properties Editor**. Enter **1.5** in the **Z** slider of the **Scale** area in the **Transform** panel; *lamp cover* is scaled along the Z axis, as shown in Figure 4-43. You can also manually scale *lamp cover* along the Z axis in the view.

4. Switch to **Edit Mode** and choose the **Vertex Select** tool. Next, choose the **Visible Selection** tool from **3D View Editor**; all the vertices of *lamp cover* are now visible.

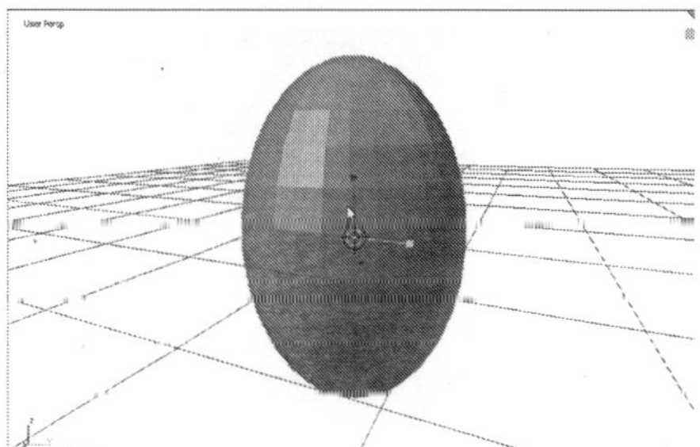

Figure 4-43 The lamp cover scaled

5. Press A to deselect all the vertices. Next, press B and select the vertices of *lamp cover* in the Front Ortho view, as shown in Figure 4-44.

6. Choose the **Scale** tool from **3D View Editor** and scale the vertices to some extent; the **Resize** panel is added to **Toolshelf**. Enter **0.75** in the **X**, **Y**, and **Z** sliders and select the **X**, **Y**, and **Z** check boxes of the **Resize** panel; selected vertices are scaled uniformly, as shown in Figure 4-45.

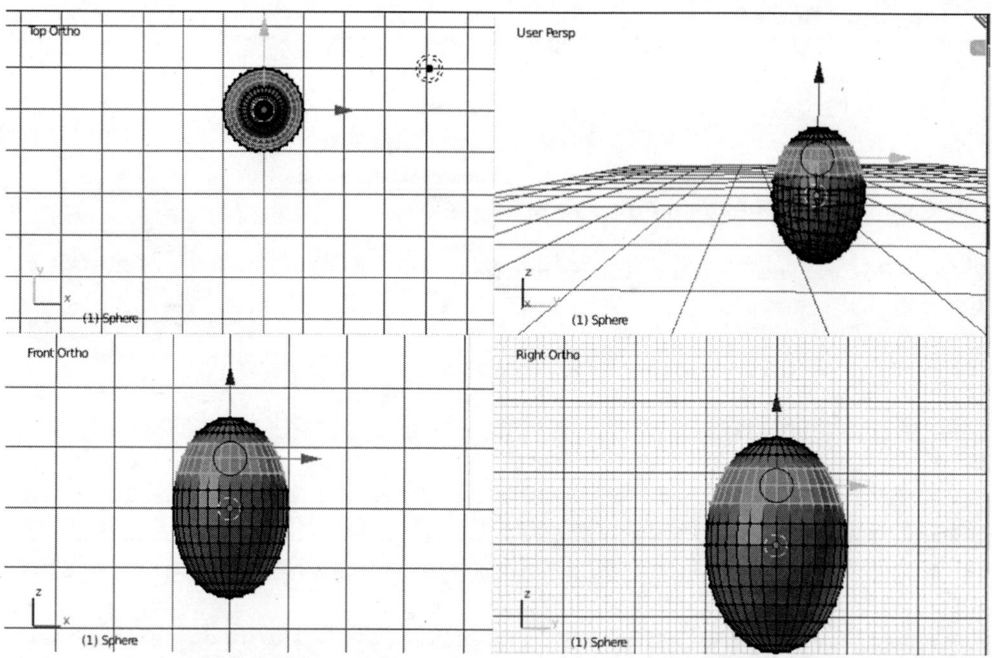

Figure 4-44 *Selected vertices of lamp cover*

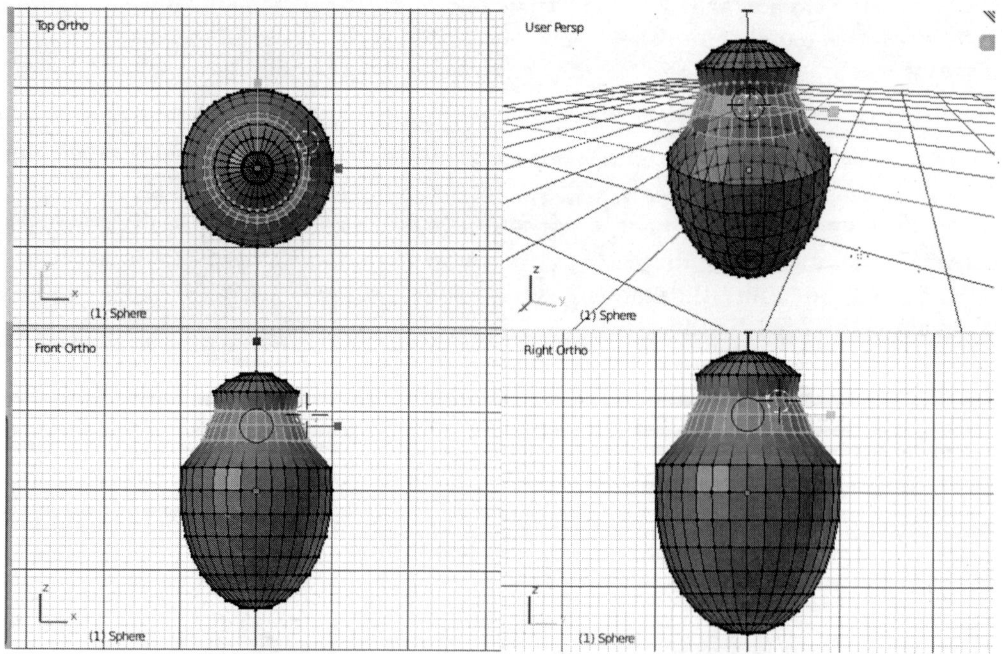

Figure 4-45 *Selected vertices of lamp cover scaled*

7. Select the topmost vertex of *lamp cover* and move it vertically upwards, as shown in Figure 4-46.

8. Make sure the **Visible Selection** tool is chosen and then select topmost edges of *lamp cover* in the Front Ortho view, as shown in Figure 4-47. Next, choose the **Tools** tab from **Toolshelf** and then choose **Subdivide** from the **Add** area in the **Mesh Tools** panel of **Toolshelf**; selected edges are subdivided, as shown in Figure 4-48.

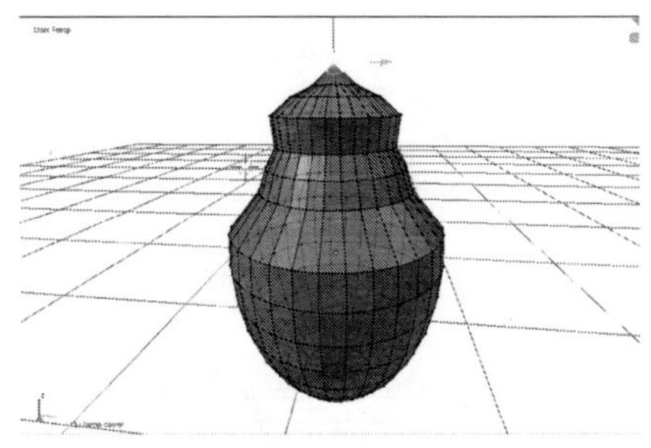

Figure 4-46 *Topmost vertex moved*

9. Select the topmost edges again and subdivide them as discussed in step 8, refer to Figure 4-49.

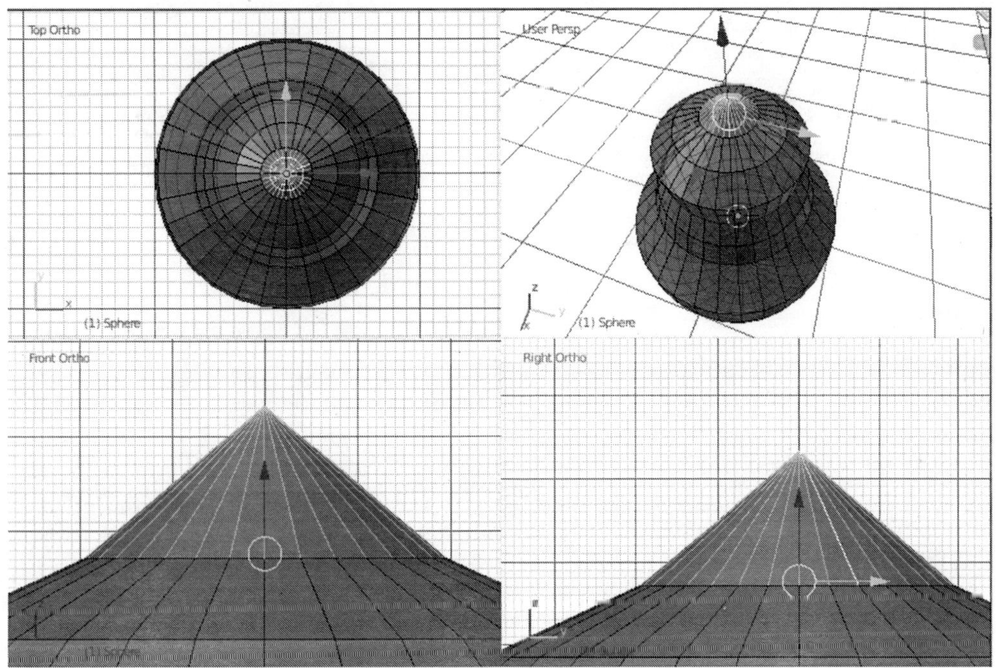

Figure 4-47 *Topmost edges selected*

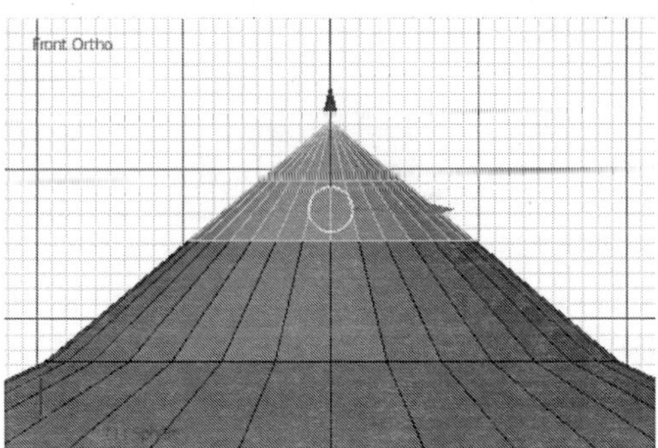

Figure 4-48 *Selected edges subdivided*

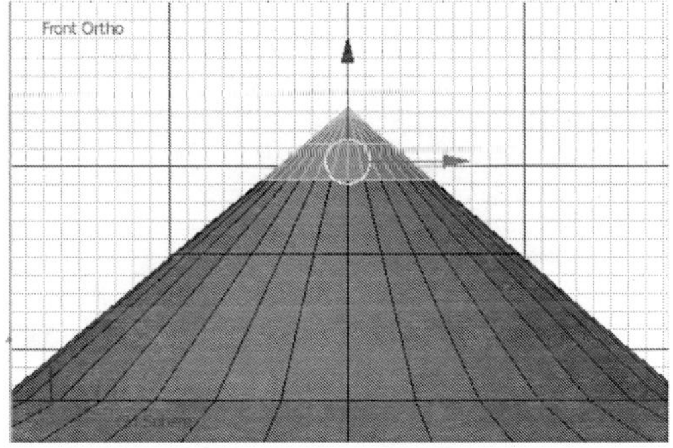

Figure 4-49 *Selected edges subdivided*

10. Select the topmost vertex again and press DELETE; the **Delete** menu is displayed. Choose **Vertices** from the **Delete** menu; the selected vertex is deleted and a hole is created at the top of *lamp cover*, refer to Figure 4-50.

11. Choose the **Visible Selection** tool again to deactivate it. Now, hover the cursor over any of the views and press CTRL+7 and then press 5 on numpad; Bottom Ortho view is displayed.

12. Choose the **Edge Select** tool from **3D View Editor**. Next, select the bottommost edges, as shown in Figure 4-51.

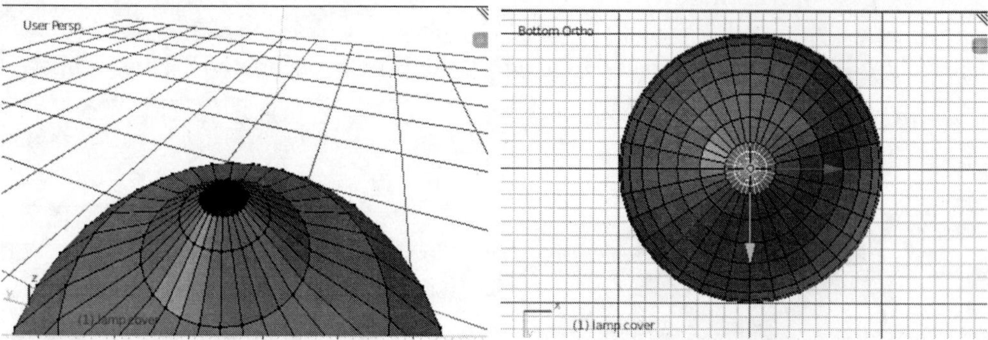

Figure 4-50 *Hole created at the top of lamp cover*

Figure 4-51 *Bottommost edges selected*

13. Press DELETE; the **Delete** menu is displayed. Choose **Edges** from the **Delete** menu; selected edges are deleted and a hole is created at the bottom of *lamp cover*, refer to Figure 4-52.

14. Press 4 and then 5 on numpad to switch back to the User Persp view.

15. Switch to **Object Mode**. Press SHIFT + D and ENTER; copy of *lamp cover* is created with the name *lamp cover001*.

Adding the Wireframe Modifier

In this section, you will add the **Wireframe** modifier to *lamp cover*.

1. Switch to **Object Mode**. Next, choose the **Object modifiers** button from **Properties Editor**. Next, choose the **Wireframe** modifier from the **Generate** category in the **Add Modifiers** drop-down; the **Wireframe** modifier is added to *lamp cover* and the parameters for this modifier are displayed in **Properties Editor**, as shown in Figure 4-53. Figure 4-54 shows *lamp cover* and *lamp cover 001* after the **Wireframe** modifier added to *lamp cover* with its default settings.

2. Enter **0.04** in the **Thickness** slider and select the **Boundary** check box in **Properties Editor**; thickness of grid of *lamp cover* is increased and the boundary at the top and bottom of *lamp cover* is closed, refer to Figure 4-55.

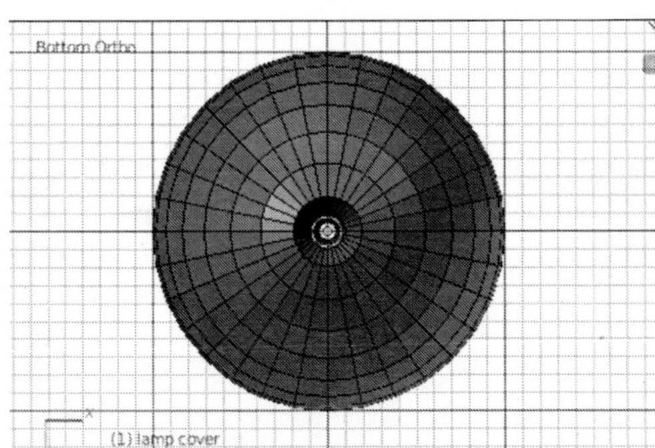

Figure 4-52 Hole created at the bottom of lamp cover

*Figure 4-53 The parameters for the **Wireframe** modifier*

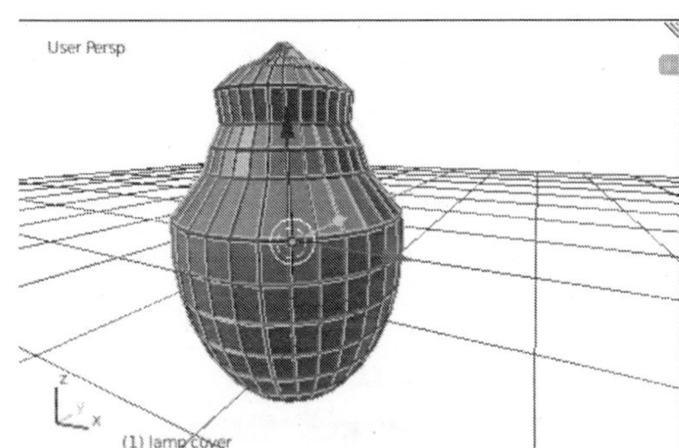

*Figure 4-54 The lamp cover with default settings of the **Wireframe** modifier*

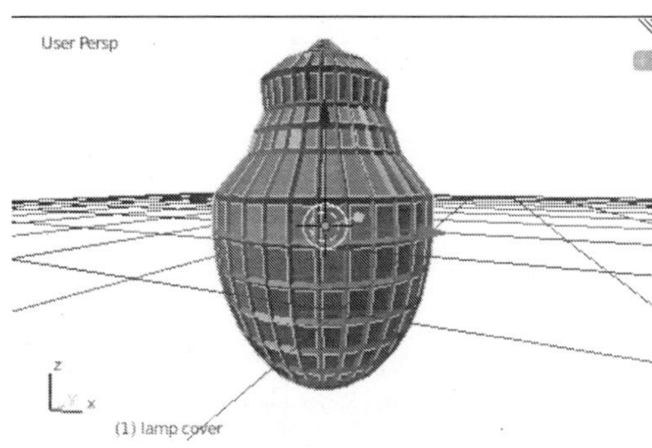

*Figure 4-55 The lamp cover with changed settings of the **Wireframe** modifier*

3. Change the color of *lamp cover* and *lamp cover001* as discussed in Tutorial 1 of Chapter 2, refer to Figure 4-56.

Note

You will learn to change the material of lamp cover 001 to a transparent glass material in a later chapter.

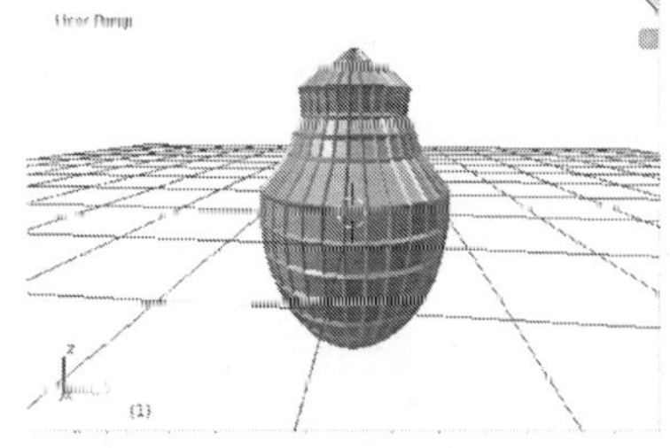

Figure 4-56 Color of lamp cover and lamp cover 001 changed

Creating the Hook

In this section, you will create a hook using the **Bezier** and **Nurbs Circle** tools.

1. Make sure the **Create** tab is chosen in **Toolshelf**. Next, choose the **Bezier** tool from the **Curve** area in the **Add Primitive** panel of **Toolshelf**; bezier curve is created in the view. Rename it as *hook*.

2. Switch to **Edit Mode** and change the shape of *hook*, as shown in Figure 4-57.

3. Choose the **Nurbs Circle** tool from the **Curve** area in the **Add Primitive** panel of **Toolshelf**; NURBs circle is created in the view and the **Add Nurbs Circle** panel is added to **Toolshelf**.

4. Enter **0.05** in the **Radius** slider of the **Add Nurbs Circle** panel in **Toolshelf**.

5. Select *hook* and then choose the **Object Data** button from **Properties Editor**. Next, click on the **Bevel Object** edit box in the **Geometry** panel of **properties Editor** and then choose **NurbsCircle** from the menu displayed; *hook* is modified, as shown in Figure 4-58.

6. Change the color of *hook* to black as discussed in Tutorial 1 of Chapter 2.

Saving and Rendering the Scene

In this section, you will save the scene that you have created and then render it. You can also view the final rendered image of this model by downloading the *c04_blender_2.79_rndr.zip* file from *www.cadcim.com.* The path of the file is as follows: *Textbooks > Animation and Visual Effects > Blender > Blender 2.79 for Digital Artists*

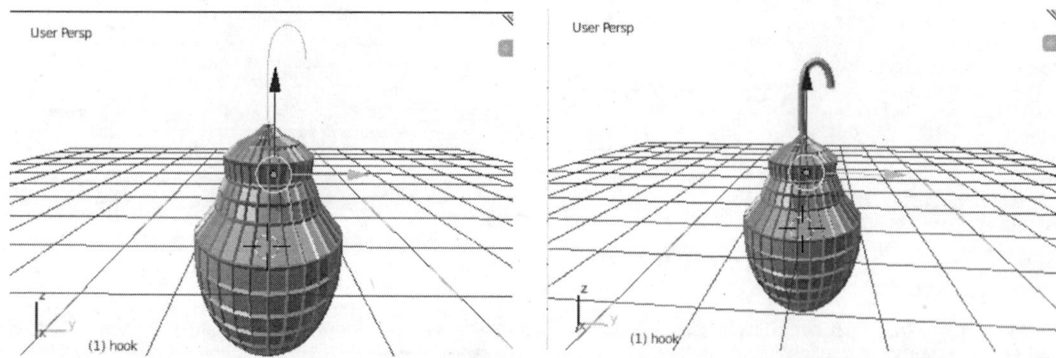

***Figure 4-57** The changed shape of hook*

***Figure 4-58** The hook modified*

1. Choose **File > Save** from the **Info Editor** menu bar.

2. Adjust the view in the User Persp view. Next, choose the **Open GL still image render** button from **3D View Editor**; the rendered image is displayed in the **UV/Image Editor**, refer to Figure 4-42.

Tutorial 2

In this tutorial, you will create flower using the **Array** modifier, as shown in Figure 4-59.

(Expected time: 20 min)

The following steps are required to complete this tutorial:

a. Create the folder.
b. Create a petal.
c. Create flower.

d. Create ovary.
e. Save and render the scene.

Figure 4-59 The model of a flower

Creating the Folder

1. Navigate to *\Documents\blender2.79\c04* and create a new folder with the name *c04_tut2.*

2. Press CTRL+N or choose **File > New** from the **Info Editor** menu bar; a menu is displayed. Choose **Reload Start-Up File**; the menu is disappeared and the startup file is loaded.

3. Choose **File > Save** from the **Info Editor** menu bar; the **File Browser** is displayed.

4. Navigate to *\Documents\blender2.79\c04\c04_tut2* and enter **Flower** in the **File Name** edit box. Next, choose the **Save Blender File** button to save the file at the specified location.

Creating a Petal

In this section, you will create a petal using the **Plane** tool and the **Multiresolution** modifier.

1. Press CTRL+ALT+Q; the quad view is displayed. Make sure *Cube* is selected in the view. Delete the cube.

2. Make sure the **Create** tab is chosen in **Toolshelf**. Choose the **Plane** tool from the **Add Primitives** panel of **Toolshelf**; *Plane* is created at the center in the view, as shown in Figure 4-60. Rename it as *petal*.

3. Switch to **Edit Mode** and choose the **Tools** tab from **Toolshelf**. Next, choose **Subdivide** twice from the **Add** area in the **Mesh Tools** panel of **Toolshelf**; *petal* is subdivided, refer to Figure 4-61.

4. Choose the **Vertex Select** tool from **3D View Editor**. Next, move the vertices of *petal* to create the petal shape, as shown in Figure 4-62.

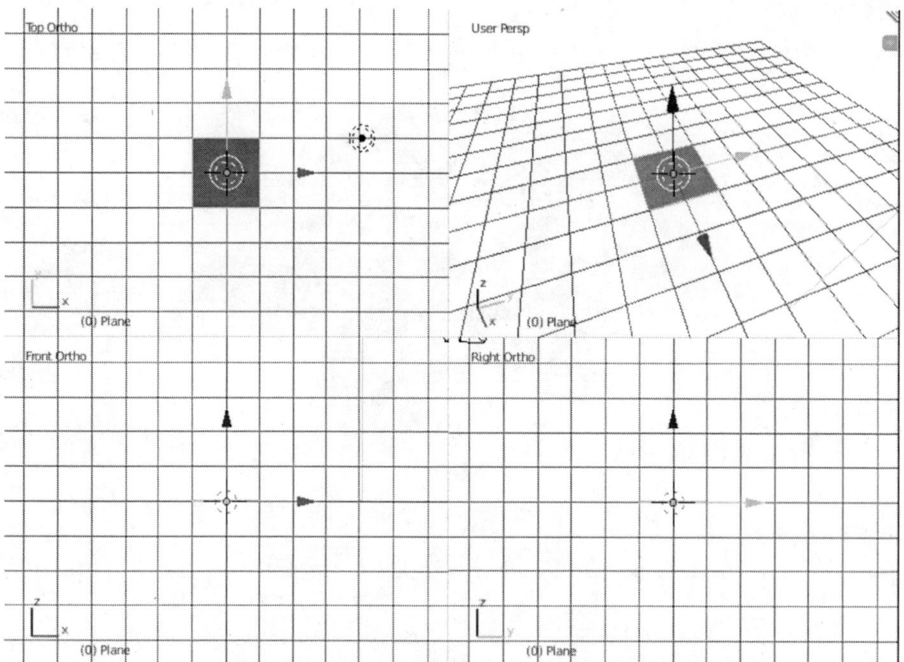

Figure 4-60 *The plane created in the view*

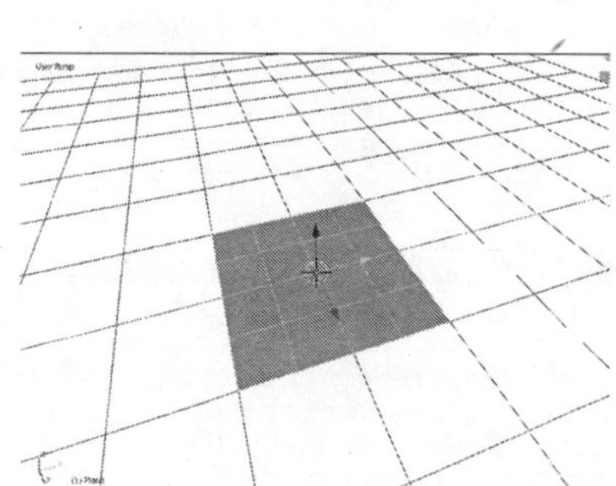

Figure 4-61 *The petal subdivided*

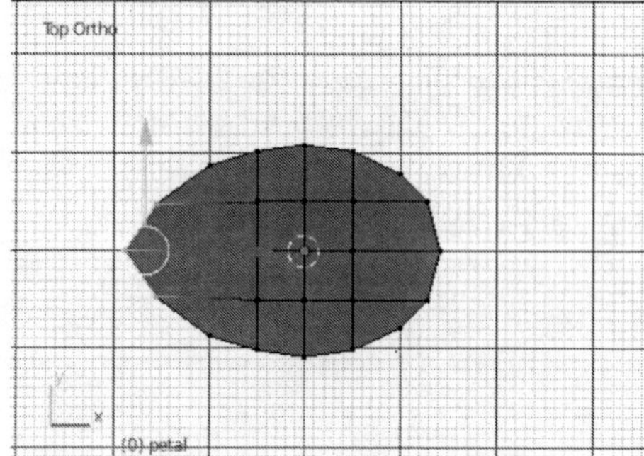

Figure 4-62 *The petal shape created*

5. Move the vertices of *petal* in Z direction, refer to Figure 4-63; 3D shape of *petal* is created.

6. Switch to **Object Mode** and choose the **Object modifiers** button from **Properties Editor**. Next, click on the **Add Modifiers** drop-down and then choose the **Multiresolution** modifier from the **Generate** category of the list displayed; the **Multiresolution** modifier is added to *petal* and the parameters for this modifier are displayed in **Properties Editor**, as shown in Figure 4-64.

7. Choose **Subdivide** twice from **Properties Editor**, refer to Figure 4-64; *petal* is subdivided to make it smoother, as shown in Figure 4-65.

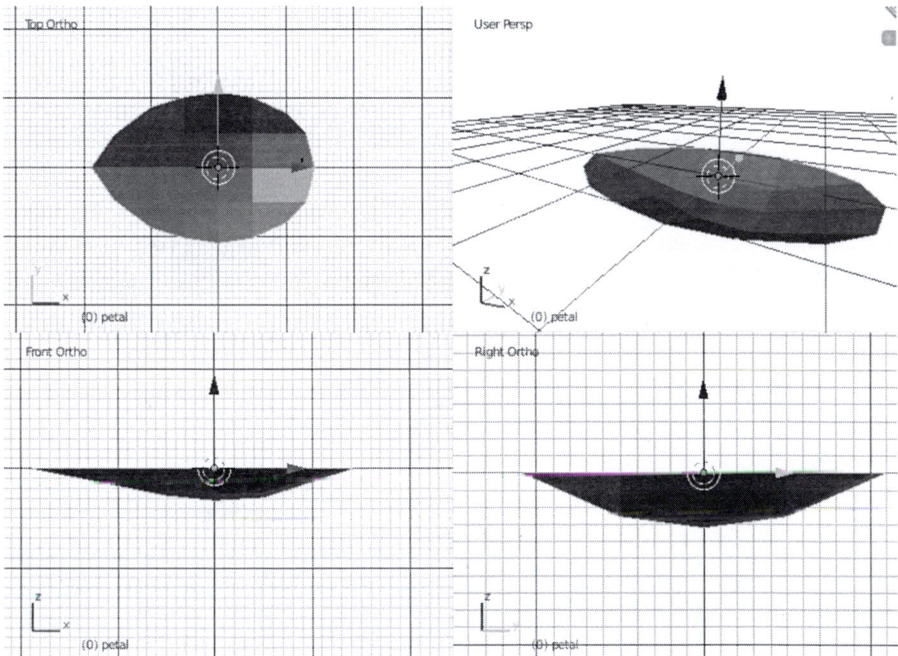

Figure 4-63 *Vertices of petal moved in Z direction*

Figure 4-64 *The parameters for the* ***Multiresolution*** *modifier*

Creating Flower

In this section, you will add the **Array** modifier to *petal* and use the Empty object to create flower.

1. Align the 3D Cursor at a point in all the views, as shown in Figure 4-66.

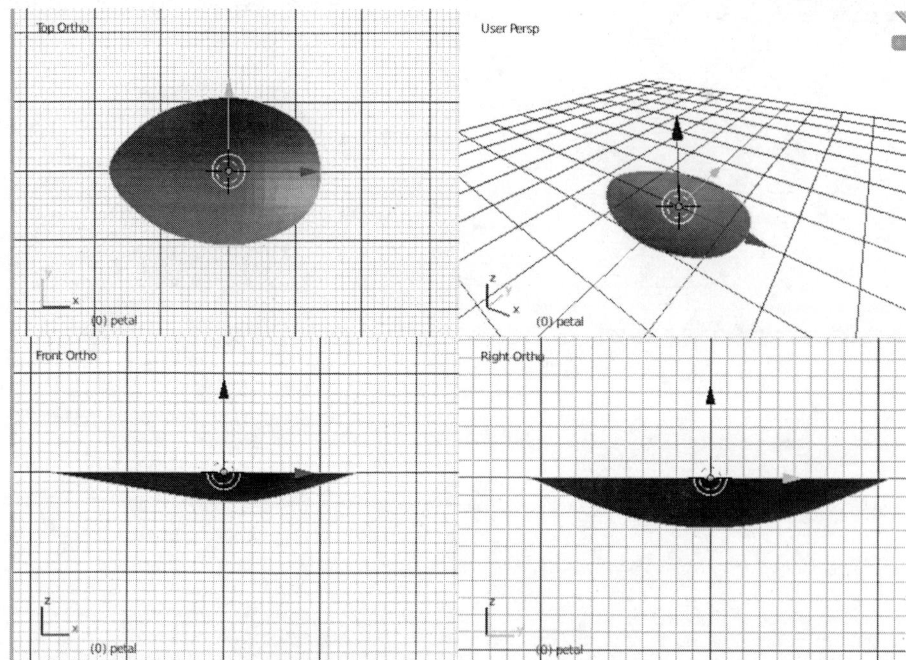

Figure 4-65 *The petal subdivided*

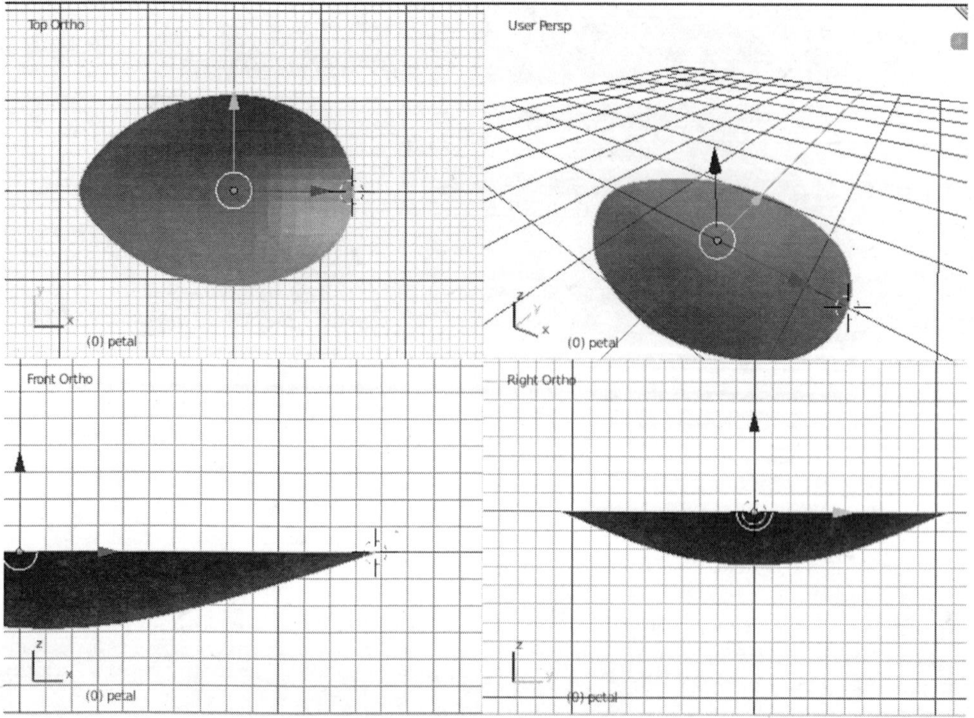

Figure 4-66 *The 3D Cursor aligned*

2. Press CTRL+ALT+SHIFT+C; the **Set Origin** menu is displayed. Choose **Origin to 3D Cursor**; pivot point of *petal* is shifted to the location of 3D Cursor, refer to Figure 4-67.

3. Make sure the **Object** button is chosen in **Properties Editor**. Enter **25** in the **Y** slider and -45 in the **Z** slider of the **Rotation** area in the **Transform** panel; *petal* is tilted as shown in Figure 4-68.

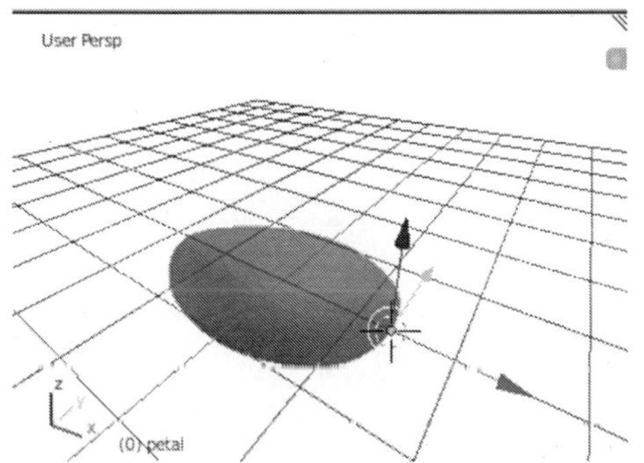

Figure 4-67 *Pivot point of petal shifted*

Figure 4-68 *The petal tilted*

4. Make sure the **Create** tab is chosen in **Toolshelf**. Next, choose **Empty** from the **Other** area in **Toolshelf**; *Empty* is created at the location of the 3D Cursor.

   The Empty object is a single coordinate point without a volume or surface. It is mainly used as a transformation handle, as a target object for constraints, and as an offset for the **Array** modifier.

5. Make sure *Empty* is selected. Next, press CTRL+A; the **Apply** menu is displayed, as shown in Figure 4-69. Choose **Rotation & Scale** from this menu; the rotation and scale values of *Empty* are reset to default value.

   Figure 4-70 shows **Empty** in all the views.

   The options in the **Apply** menu are used to set the transformation to default transformation.

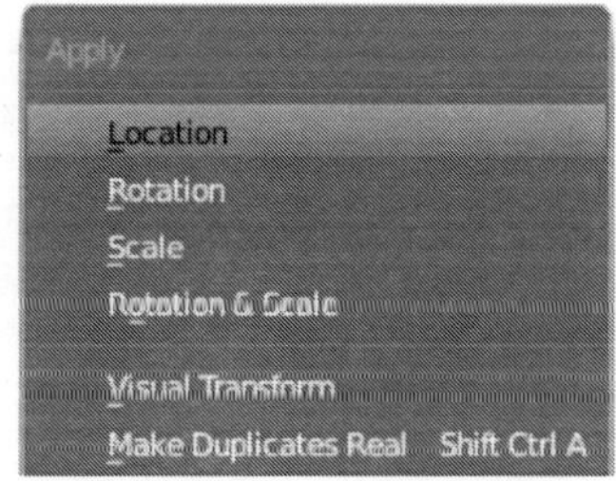

Figure 4-69 *The **Apply** menu*

6. Select *petal* and repeat the procedure in step 5 for *petal;* the rotation and scale values of *petal* are reset to default value.

7. Make sure *petal* is selected. Next, choose the **Object modifiers** button from **Properties Editor**. Next, click on the **Add Modifiers** drop-down and then choose the **Array** modifier from the **Generate** category of the list displayed; the **Array** modifier is added to *petal* and the parameters for this modifier are displayed in **Properties Editor** below the parameters of the **Array** modifier in the modifier stack, refer to Figure 4-71.

8. Clear the **Relative Offset** check box and select the **Object Offset** check box from **Properties Editor**. Next, click on the edit box located below the **Object Offset** check box and then select **Empty** from the list displayed.

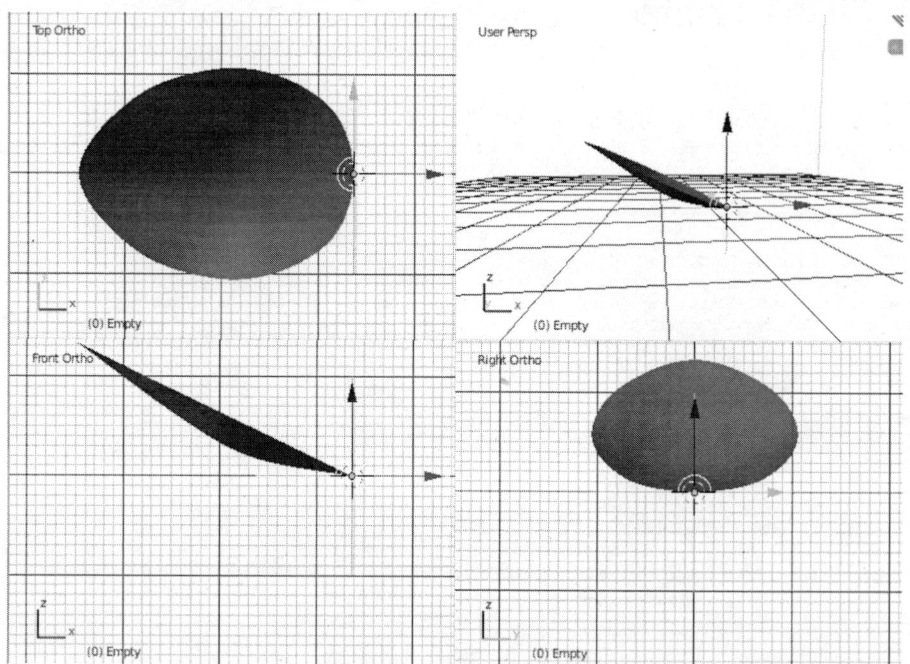

Figure 4-70 *The Empty object in all the views*

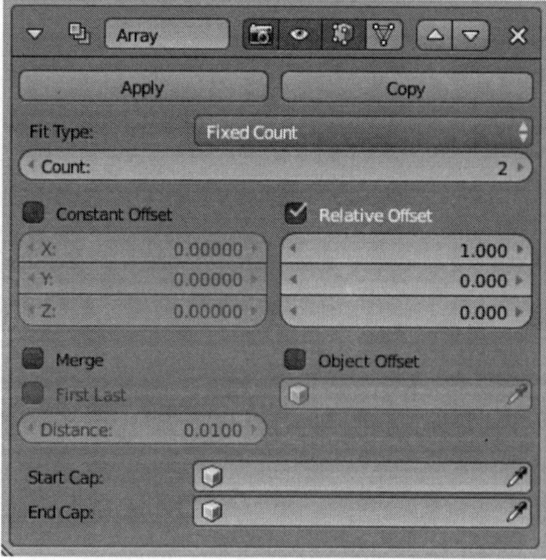

Figure 4-71 *The parameters for the* ***Array*** *modifier*

9. Select *Empty*. Make sure the **Object** button is chosen in **Properties Editor**. Next, enter **45** in the **Z** slider of the **Rotation** area in the **Transform** panel of **Properties Editor**; second petal is created and aligned, as shown in Figure 4-72.

To increase the number of petals in the flower, you need to increase the value in the **Count** slider in **Properties Editor**.

10. Select *petal* and enter **8** in the **Count** slider of **Properties Editor**; the flower is created, as shown in Figure 4-73.

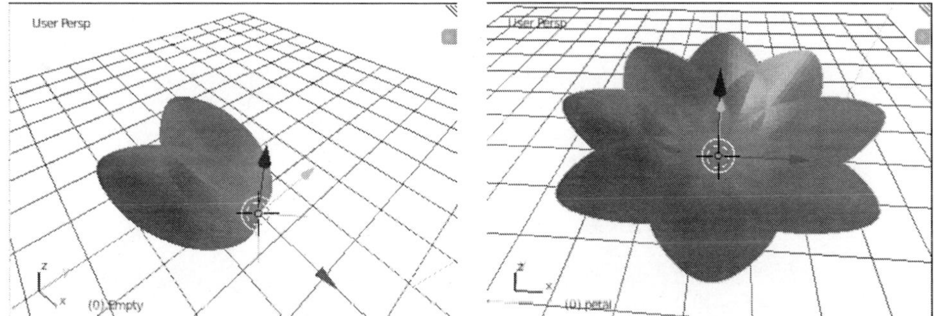

Figure 4-72 *Second petal created* ***Figure 4-73*** *The flower created*

11. Select *Empty*. To move it along the Y axis in the view, enter **-0.75** in the **Y** slider of the **Location** area in the **Transform** panel of **Properties Editor**, refer to Figure 4-74; a space is created at the center of flower to place ovary of a flower.

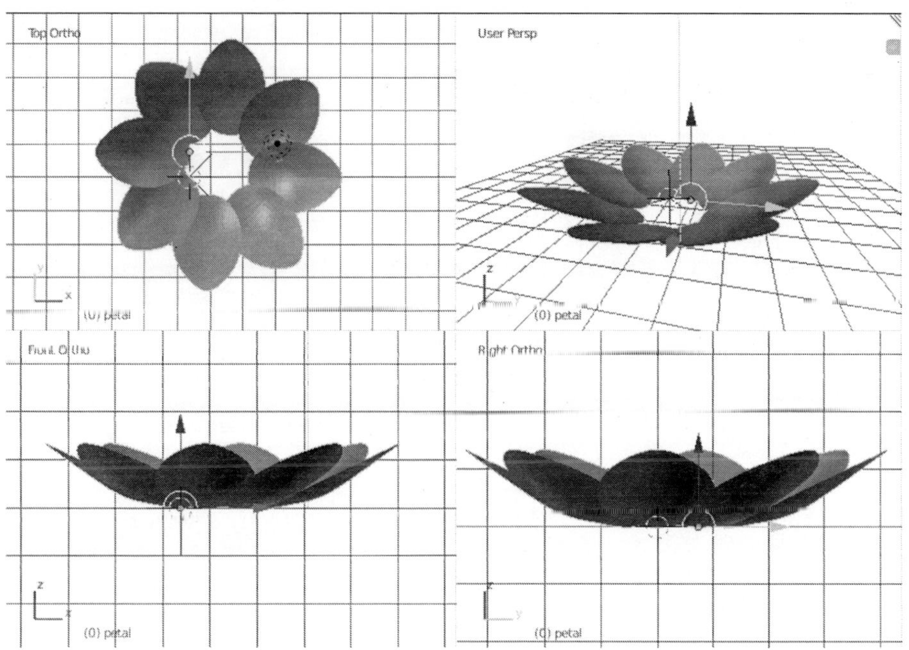

Figure 4-74 *The Empty moved along Y axis*

Creating Ovary

In this section, you will create ovary of a flower by using the **UV Sphere** tool.

1. Make sure the **Create** tab is chosen in **Toolshelf**. Next, choose the **UV Sphere** tool from the **mesh** area of the **Add Primitives** panel; a sphere is created with the name *Sphere* and the **Add UV Sphere** panel is added to **Toolshelf.**

2. Enter **1.25** in the **Size** slider of the **Add UV Sphere** panel in **Toolshelf**. Next, rename it as *ovary* and align it in all the views, as shown in Figure 4-75.

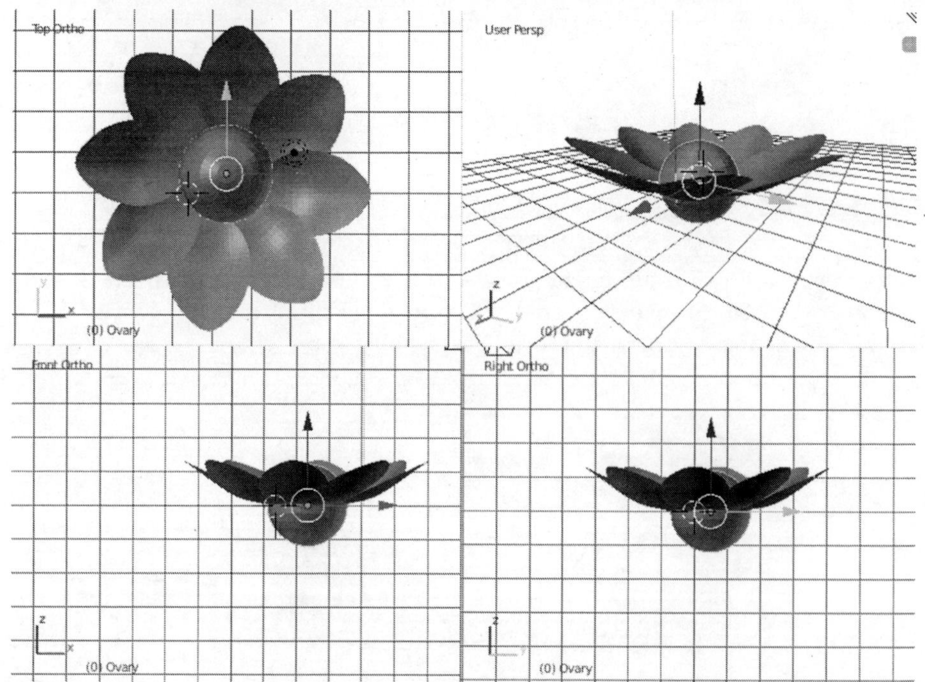

Figure 4-75 *The ovary aligned in all the views*

3. Scale and move *ovary* along the Z axis to fit it at the center of the flower, refer to Figure 4-76.

4. Change the color of *petal* and *ovary* as discussed in Tutorial 1 of Chapter 2, refer to Figure 4-77.

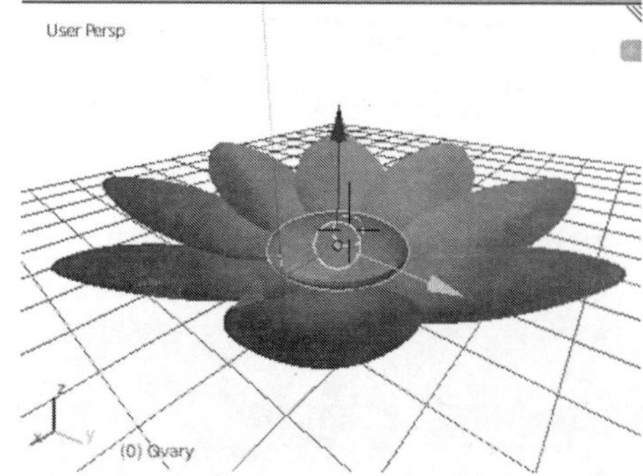

Figure 4-76 *The Ovary scaled and moved*

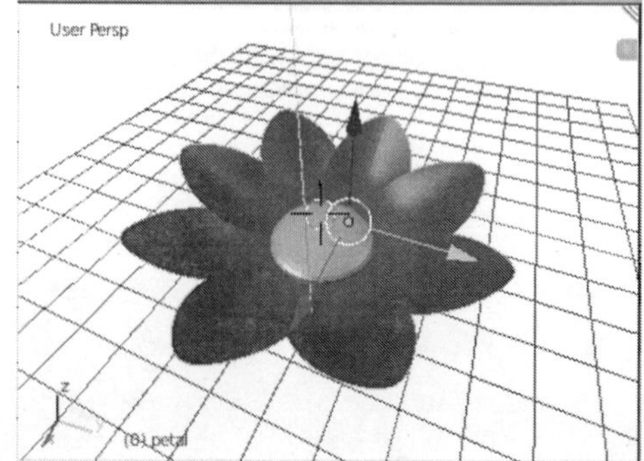

Figure 4-77 *Color of petal and ovary changed*

Saving and Rendering the Scene

In this section, you will save the scene that you have created and then render it. You can also view the final rendered image of this model by downloading the *c04_blender_2.79_rndr.zip* file from *www.cadcim.com*. The path of the file is as follows: *Textbooks > Animation and Visual Effects > Blender > Blender 2.79 for Digital Artists*

1. Choose **File > Save** from the **Info Editor** menu bar.

2. Adjust the view in the User Persp view. Next, choose the **Open GL still image render** button from **3D View Editor**; the rendered image is displayed in the **UV/Image Editor**, refer to Figure 4-59.

Self-Evaluation Test

Answer the following questions and then compare them to those given at the end of this chapter:

1. Which of the following modifiers is used to reduce the face count of the object with minimum changes in the shape of object?

   (a) **Decimate** (b) **Smooth**
   (c) **Remesh** (d) **Shrinkwrap**

2. The __________ modifier smoothens the object by removing noise from its surface.

3. The __________ modifier is used to show the building of faces of the object on one another over the defined time.

4. The subdivisions created in an object using the __________ modifier can be edited in **Sculpt Mode**.

5. The **Smooth** modifier smoothens the object without increasing the number of vertices/edges in the object. (T/F)

Review Questions

Answer the following questions:

1. Which of the following combination of shortcut keys is used to invoke the **Set Origin** menu?

   (a) CTRL+ALT+SHIFT+A (b) CTRL+ALT+SHIFT+S

   (c) CTRL+ALT+SHIFT+C (d) CTRL+ALT+SHIFT+W

2. The __________ modifier is used to shrink or wrap an object around the surface of other object.

3. You cannot change the order of the modifiers in the modifier stack. (T/F)

4. The **Remesh** modifier is used to trim or combine two mesh primitive objects. (T/F)

5. You can add any number of modifiers to an object. (T/F)

EXERCISES

Exercise 1

Create a sofa set using the **Boolean**, **Subdivision Surface**, and the **Multiresolution** modifiers, refer to Figure 4-78. **(Expected time: 25 min)**

Figure 4-78 *Model of a sofa set*

Exercise 2

Create a fruit basket using the **Wireframe** modifier, refer to Figures 4-79 and 4-80. **(Expected time: 15 min)**

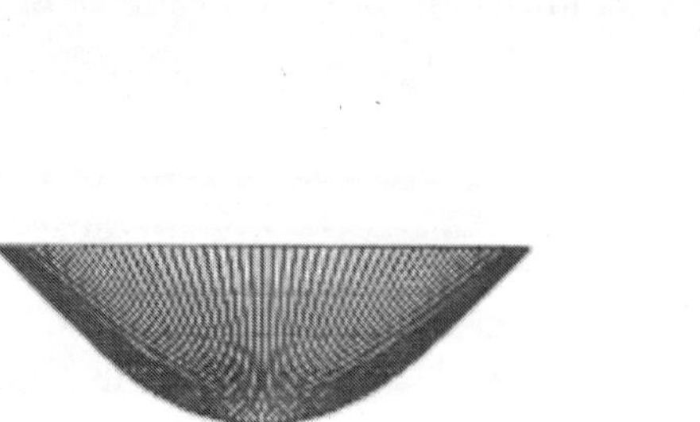

Figure 4-79 *Side view of a fruit basket*

Figure 4-80 *Top view of a fruit basket*

Answers to Self-Evaluation Test

1. a, **2. Laplacian Smooth**, **3. Build**, **4. Multiresolution**, **5.** T

Chapter 5

Digital Sculpting Techniques

Learning Objectives

After completing this chapter, you will be able to:

- *Understand Sculpt Mode*
- *Understand types of brushes and strokes*
- *Understand the Spin tool*

INTRODUCTION

Digital Sculpting is a modeling technique similar to clay modeling. In this technique, instead of using vertices, edges, or faces, objects are created or modified by using various brushes and strokes on specific area of an object. In this chapter, you will learn to create and modify objects using various sculpting techniques.

SCULPT MODE

In Blender, **Sculpt Mode** is used to create or modify an object by using various types of brushes and strokes. To activate **Sculpt Mode**, create an object and select it. Next, choose the **Sculpt Mode** option from the **Mode** drop-down in **3D View Editor**. Alternatively, activate the pie menu and press the TAB key; the **Mode** pie menu will be displayed. Press 8 or choose **Sculpt Mode** from the pie menu. The procedure to activate pie menus is discussed in Chapter 1.

As you switch to **Sculpt Mode**, a red circle gets attached to the cursor and all the menus except the **View** menu in the **3D View Editor** menu bar get changed. Also, various panels such as the **Brush**, **Texture**, and **Stroke** related to sculpting are displayed in **Toolshelf** in the **Tools** tab, refer to Figure 5-1. You need to set the values of parameters in these panels at the time of sculpting objects. Also, if you choose the **Options** tab in **Toolshelf**, the **Overlay**, **Appearance**, and **Options** panels are displayed. The options in the **texture** panel are discussed in Chapter 7. Rest of the panels are discussed next.

Note

*1. **Sculpt Mode** is available only for mesh primitive objects.*

*2. You need to subdivide the object considerably before sculpting to get better results in **Sculpt Mode**.*

Brush Panel

The **Brush** panel is the topmost panel in **Toolshelf**. Figure 5-2 shows the options in the **Brush** panel. As the name suggests, the options in the **Brush** panel are used to set the parameters of a brush to be used for sculpting. These options are discussed next.

Brush Type

The currently selected brush type is specified at the top in the **Brush** panel with its image and name. By default, the name and image of the **SculptDraw** brush is displayed. To change the brush type, click on the current brush type image; a flyout will be displayed, as shown in Figure 5-3. Choose the desired brush type from the flyout; the name and the image of the brush type chosen will be displayed in the **Brush** panel.

Note

*To make the names of the options clearly visible in the panel, you may need to increase size of the panel in **Toolshelf** by dragging its boundary to right.*

Radius

The **Radius** slider is used to specify the radius of the red circle attached to the cursor. You can move the slider or click on the slider and enter a value to change the radius of the circle. You can also interactively change the radius of a circle by using the F key. To do so, press the F key;

a blurred black circle will be displayed inside the red circle, refer to Figure 5-4. Now, drag the cursor towards the center of circle or away from it to decrease or increase the radius, respectively, refer to Figure 5-5. Alternatively, use] or [key to increase or decrease the radius of a circle.

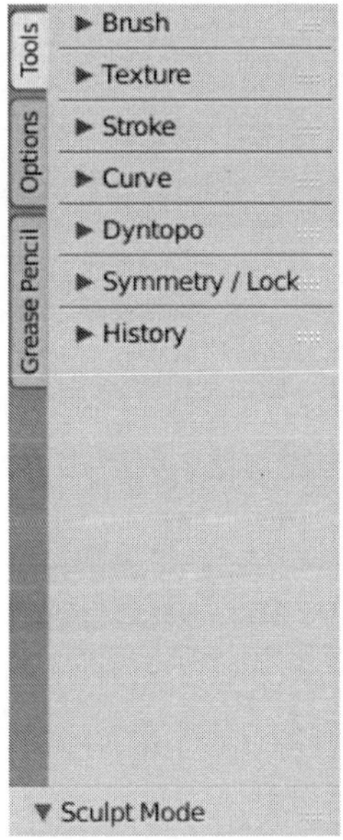

Figure 5-1 *Various panels in the* ***Tools*** *tab*

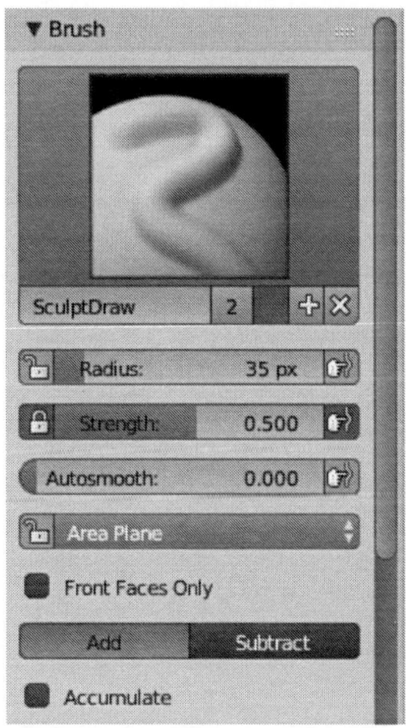

Figure 5-2 *The options in the* ***Brush*** *panel*

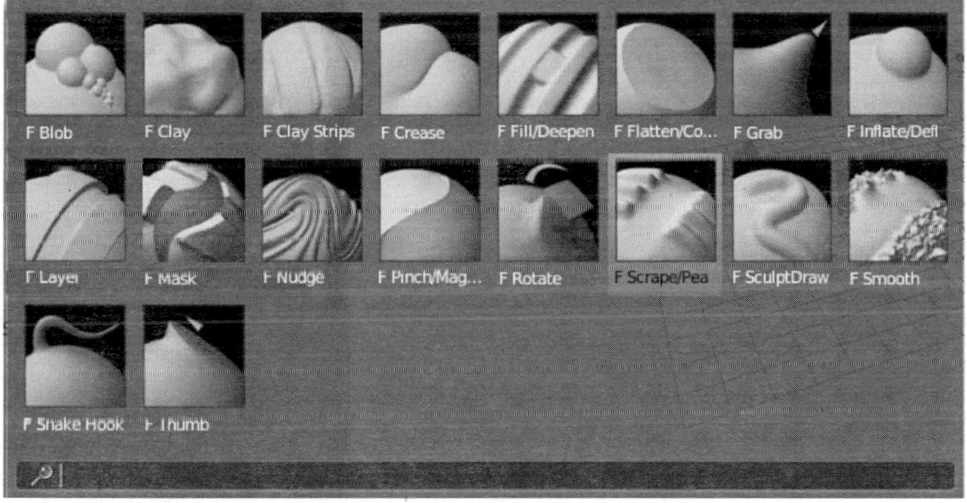

Figure 5-3 *The Flyout displaying various brush types*

The lock icon on the left of the **Radius** slider locks the brush size. As a result, the change in object size on changing the zoom level in the view does not affect the brush size. When unlocked, brush size is given in pixels.

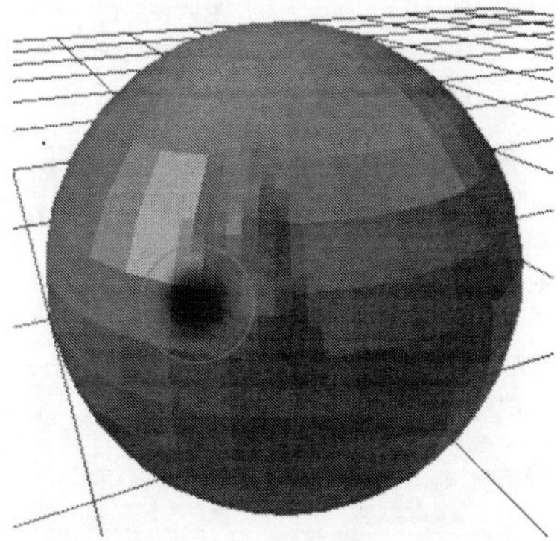

Figure 5-4 A blurred black circle displayed

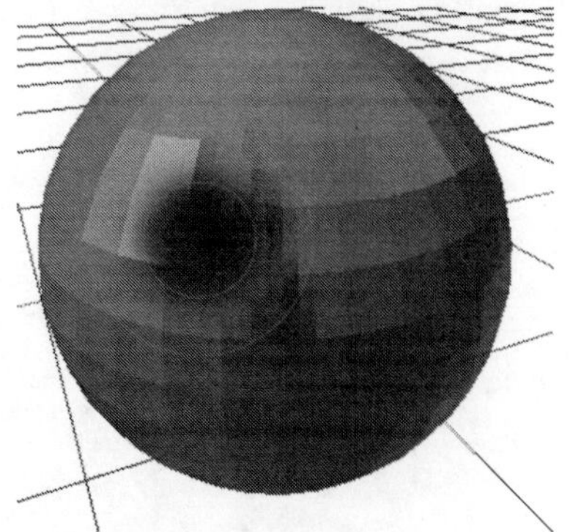

Figure 5-5 Dragging the cursor

Strength

The **Strength** slider is used to change the strength of a brush to be applied on the object. Note that the effect of brush strength on an object depends on its size. If the size of the object is small then even moderate strength will also affect the object. But if the object is too large then you need to scale it first to see the effect of brush strength on it.

The lock icon on the left of the **Strength** slider is used to automatically adjust the strength that gives consistent results for different spacings.

Autosmooth

The **Autosmooth** edit box is used to smoothen the strokes applied using the brush. The range of the value in this edit box varies from 0 to 1.

Area Plane

The options in the **Sculpt Plane** drop-down are used to specify the plane for sculpting. By default, **Area Plane** is chosen in this drop-down. Figure 5-6 shows the **Sculpt Plane** drop-down.

Front Faces Only

The **Front Faces Only** check box when selected, sculpting is restricted to the front faces of the object.

Add/Subtract

If the **Add** button chosen and the CTRL key is pressed, then on moving the cursor on the object, the strokes on the object are applied inward. If the **Subtract** button chosen and the CTRL key is pressed, then on moving the cursor on the object, the strokes on the object are applied outward.

Accumulate

When you select the **Accumulate** check box, the strokes applied on the same area of the object get accumulated over one another.

Stroke Panel

The options in the **Stroke** panel are used to further manipulate the stroke applied on the object, refer to Figure 5-7. These options are discussed next.

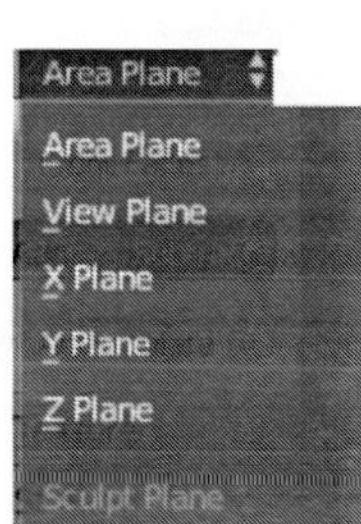

***Figure 5-6** The **Sculpt Plane** drop-down*

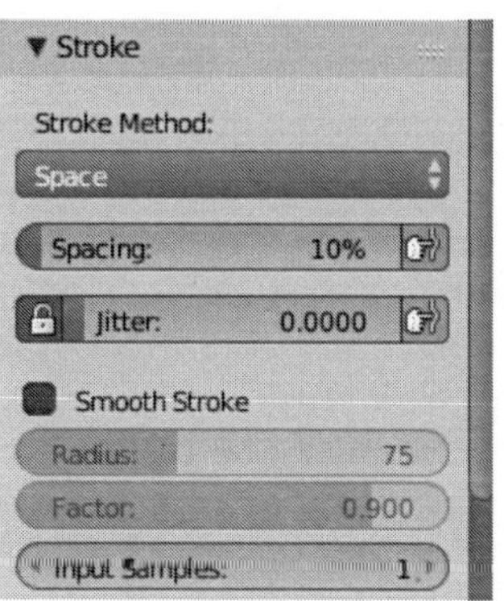

***Figure 5-7** The **Stroke** panel*

Stroke Method

The options in the **Stroke Method** drop-down, refer to Figure 5-8, are used to specify the way of applying the brush strokes on the object. For some of these options, specific parameters are displayed below this drop-down. The options in this drop-down and parameters specific to these options are discussed next.

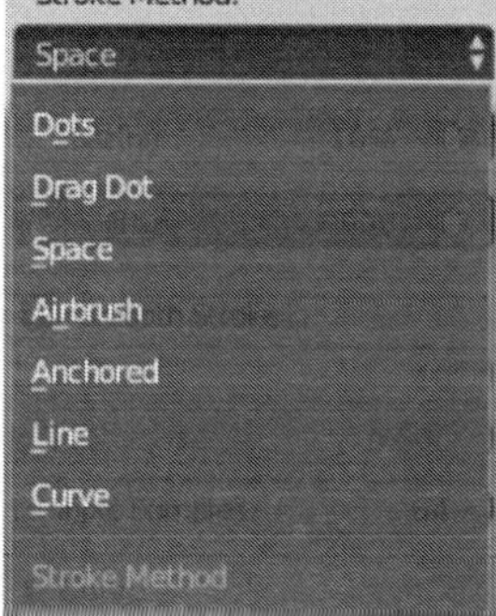

***Figure 5-8** The **Stroke Method** drop-down*

Space

By default, this option is chosen in the **Stroke Method** drop-down. and the **Spacing** slider is displayed below this drop-down. Brush strokes are applied as a series of dots and the spacing between them is specified in the **Spacing** slider.

Dots

When you choose this option, standard brush strokes are applied on the object.

Drag Dot

When you choose this option, a single stroke is applied at a time on dragging.

Anchored

When you choose this option and click and drag the cursor on the surface of the object, stroke will be applied to that point and brush diameter will change depending on the dragging direction. Note that the **Edge to Edge** check box is displayed below the **Stroke** drop-down on choosing this option. If you select this check box, brush diameter of a circle is specified by two points where the first point is the point you click for the first time and the second point is the point you drag and click again.

Airbrush

When you choose this option, brush strokes similar to the strokes in the **Dots** option are applied but the amount of stroke depends on the value in the **Rate** slider displayed on choosing the **Airbrush** option.

Jitter

This slider specifies the offset of the brush position on the object.

Smooth Stroke

This check box is used to add smoothness to the stroke applied on the object. When you select this check box, the **Radius** and **Factor** sliders are activated. The value in the **Radius** slider specifies minimum distance of a single stroke and value in the **Factor** slider specifies the smoothing amount.

Curve Panel

The **Curve** panel is shown in Figure 5-9. The curve and buttons in this panel are used to modify the intensity of the stroke from center to the circumference of a circle. Buttons located at the top of this panel are used to zoom in, zoom out, set the handles of curve points, delete curve points and so on whereas buttons located at the bottom of this panel are used to change the shape of a curve in the panel. You can manually change the shape of a curve by adding points and moving existing points. To add a point to the curve, you need to click at a desired point on the curve.

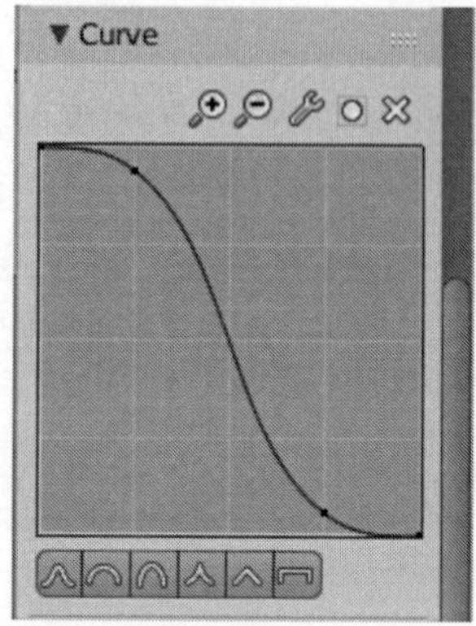

*Figure 5-9 The **Curve** panel*

Dyntopo Panel

The **Dyntopo** panel uses the dynamic tessellation method for sculpting. You need to select the **Dyntopo** check box to activate parameters in the **Dyntopo** panel, refer to Figures 5-10 and 5-11. Using this panel, detailing is carried out on the object at the time of sculpting. You can use one of the options from the **Detail Method** drop-down. Next, refine the details by choosing an option from the **Detail Refine** drop-down. You need to also set the value in the **Detail Size** slider based on the requirement. To set the direction of symmetry, choose desired option from the **Direction** drop-down and choose the **Symmetrize** button located below it.

Symmetry/Lock Panel

The options in the **Symmetry/Lock** panel are used at the time of sculpting to set symmetry or lock the sculpting of object along specific axis(es), refer to Figure 5-12. These options are discussed next.

Mirror

The **X**, **Y**, and **Z** buttons in this area are used to mirror brush strokes applied around respective axes.

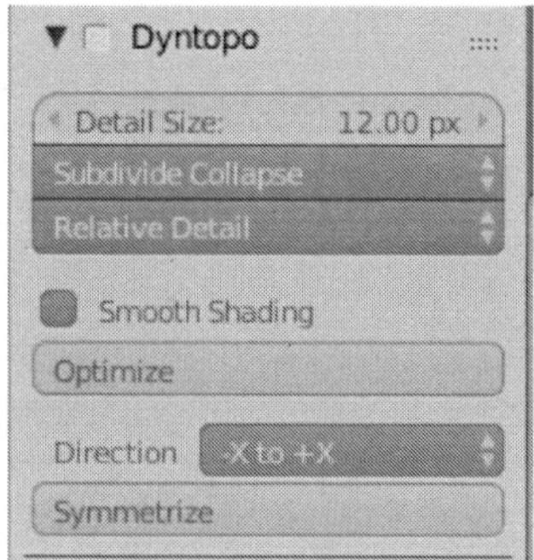

*Figure 5-10 The **Dyntopo** panel*

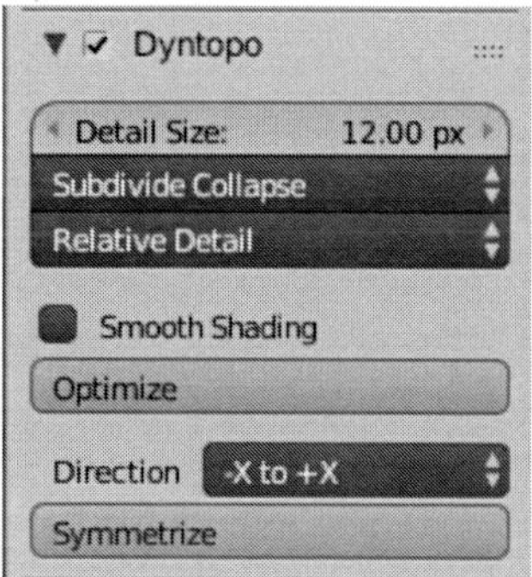

*Figure 5-11 The **Dyntopo** panel on selecting the **Dyntopo** check box*

Radial
The **X**, **Y**, and **Z** sliders in this area are used to set the symmetry and number of strokes repeated in radial direction along respective axes.

Feather
This check box is used to reduce the brush stroke strength in the areas where the symmetry planes overlaps each other.

Lock
The **X**, **Y**, and **Z** buttons in this area are used to prevent the sculpting of the object along respective axis.

Tiling
The **X**, **Y**, and **Z** buttons in this area are used to tile the brush strokes along respective axes.

*Figure 5-12 The **Symmetry/Lock** panel*

Tile Offset
The **X**, **Y**, and **Z** sliders in this area are used to change the tile offset along respective axes.

History Panel
The **History** panel is used to undo or redo the last action, repeat the last action, or show the history of commands executed so far. Figure 5-13 shows the **History** panel.

Overlay Panel
The **Overlay** panel is only visible in **Toolshelf** when you choose the **Options** tab, refer to Figure 5-14. The parameters in this tab are used to show or hide the brush texture in the view and adjust its transparency. The brush icons on the right of these parameters are used to turn off the texture in the view at the time of applying the strokes.

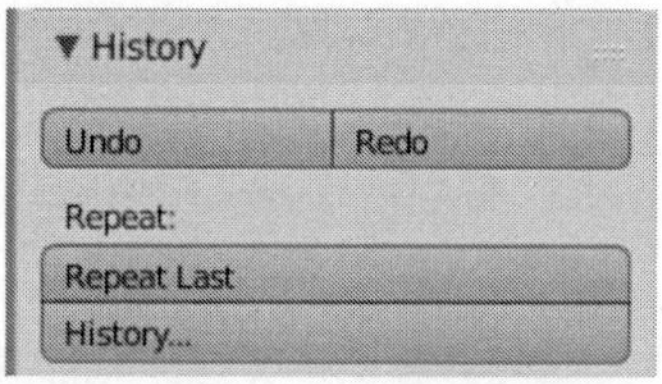

*Figure 5-13 The **History** panel*

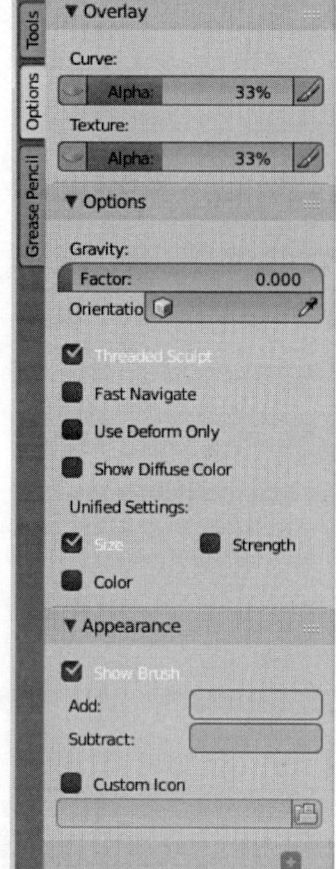

*Figure 5-14 Various panels in the **Options** tab*

Options Panel

The parameters in the **Options** panel are used to set gravity for brush, navigate fast in the view, and set uniform size/strength of the brush. Also, these options allow you to define the color of brushes, show the diffuse color in shading, and limit the use of activated modifiers.

Appearance Panel

You can toggle the visibility of a circle along with cursor and change its color using this panel.

TUTORIALS

Before you start tutorials of this chapter, you need to download *c05_blender_2.79_tut.zip* file from *www.cadcim.com*. The path of the file is as follows: *Textbooks > Animation and Visual Effects > Blender > Blender 2.79 for Digital Artists*

Browse to *\Documents\blender2.79* and create a folder with the name *c05*. Next, extract the content of the zip file in this folder.

Tutorial 1

In this tutorial, you will sculpt a candle using sculpting tools, as shown in Figure 5-15.

(Expected time: 20 min)

Figure 5-15 The sculpted candle

The following steps are required to complete this tutorial:

a. Create the folder.
b. Create the base of the candle.
c. Sculpt the candle.
d. Create the wick of the candle.
e. Save and render the scene.

Creating the Folder

1. Navigate to *\Documents\blender2.79\c05* and create a new folder with the name *c05_tut1*.

2. Press CTRL+N or choose **File > New** from the **Info Editor** menu bar; a menu is displayed. Choose **Reload Start-Up File** from the menu; the menu disappears and the startup file is loaded.

3. Choose **File > Save** from the **Info Editor** menu bar; **File Browser** is displayed

4. Navigate to *\Documents\blender2.79\c05\c05_tut1* and enter **Candle** in the **File Name** edit box. Next, choose the **Save Blender File** button to save the file at the specified location.

Creating the Base of the Candle

In this section, you will create the base of the candle using the **Cylinder** tool.

1. Make sure *Cube* is selected. Next, delete *Cube*. Choose the **Cylinder** tool from the **Mesh** area in the **Add Primitive** panel of **Toolshelf**; a cylinder is created in the view and the **Add Cylinder** panel is added to **Toolshelf**. Rename it as *candle*.

2. In the **Add Cylinder** panel of **Toolshelf**, enter the following values.

   Vertices: **128** Depth: **3.5**

   Figure 5-16 shows *candle* in the view.

Sculpting the Candle

In this section, you will sculpt *candle* using various sculpting tools.

1. Click on the **Mode** drop-down and choose **Sculpt Mode** from the options in the drop-down. Alternatively, if the pie menus are activated, press TAB and choose **Sculpt Mode** from the **Mode** pie menu displayed; various panels are displayed in **Toolshelf**.

2. Enter the following values in the **Brush** panel of **Toolshelf**.

   Radius: **6** Strength: **1** Autosmooth: **1**

3. Expand the **Stroke** panel and choose **Line** from the **Stroke Method** drop-down. Next, enter **1** in the **Spacing** slider.

4. Expand the **Dyntopo** panel and select the **Dyntopo** check box; the parameters below it are activated. Choose **Constant Detail** from the **Detail** drop-down and then make sure 100 is displayed in the **Resolution** slider.

5. In the **Mirror** area of the **Symmetry/Lock** panel, activate the **X**, **Y**, and **Z** buttons. In the Front Ortho view, apply the stroke, as shown in Figure 5-17.

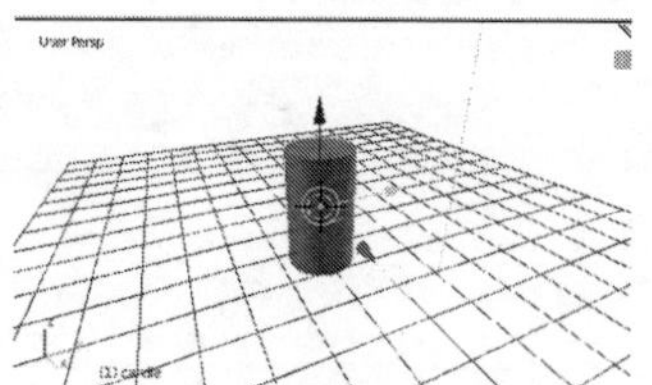

Figure 5-16 *The candle displayed*

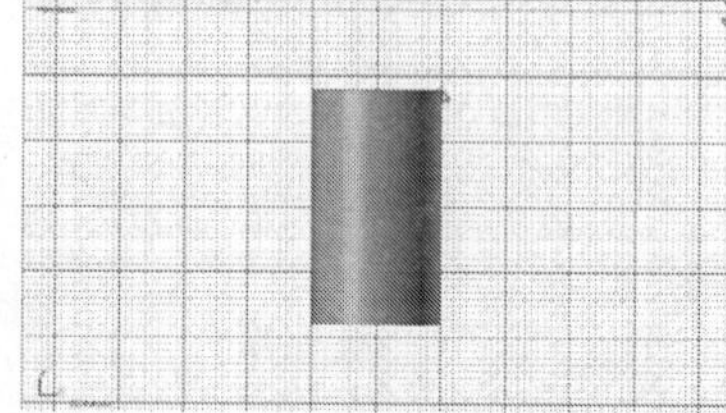

Figure 5-17 *Applying the stroke in the Front Ortho view*

6. In the Right Ortho view, join the stroke to create a ring; two rings are created that smoothens top and bottom circular edges of *candle*, refer to Figures 5-18 and 5-19.

   Next, you will sculpt the top face of *candle*.

7. In the **Brush** panel, increase the radius of brush to about 75 pixels. Next, enter **0.1** in the **Strength** slider. Also, choose **Dots** from the **Stroke Method** drop-down in the **Stroke** panel. Next, make sure that **Dyntopo** check box is selected in the **Dyntopo** panel.

8. In the **Mirror** area of the **Symmetry/Lock** panel, make sure all the buttons are deactivated. Apply the strokes on the top face of *candle*, refer to Figure 5-20. Note that you may need to change the brush radius depending on the zoom level in the view.

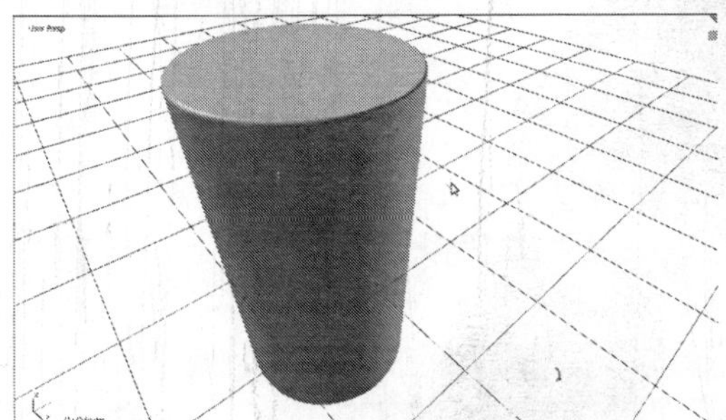

Figure 5-18 Top circular edge smoothened

Figure 5-19 Bottom circular edge smoothened

Note

To pull down surface, press CTRL and apply strokes.

Next, you will further sculpt one side of *candle*.

9. In the **Brush** panel, increase the radius of brush to about 25 pixels. Next, enter **0.5** in the **Strength** slider. Also, choose **Space** from the **Stroke Method** drop-down in the **Stroke** panel and enter **10** in the **Spacing** slider. Next, make sure that the **Disable Dyntopo** button is displayed in the **Dyntopo** panel. If not, choose **Enable Dyntopo** button in this panel.

10. In the **Mirror** area of the **Symmetry/Lock** panel, make sure all the buttons are deactivated. Press CTRL and apply the strokes on the top circular edge of *candle*, refer to Figure 5-21. Note that you may need to change the brush radius depending on the zoom level in the view.

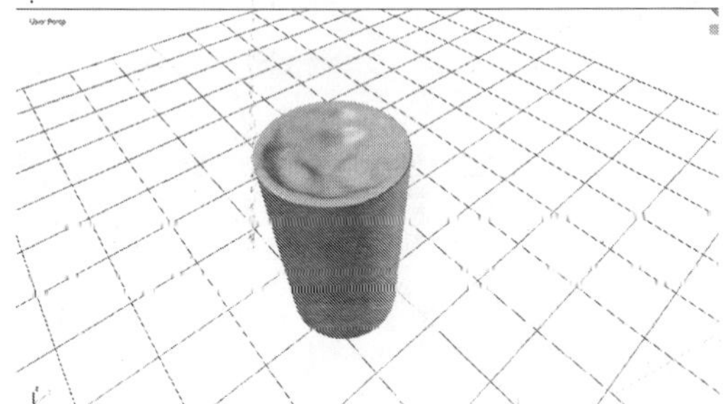

Figure 5-20 Strokes applied on the top face of candle

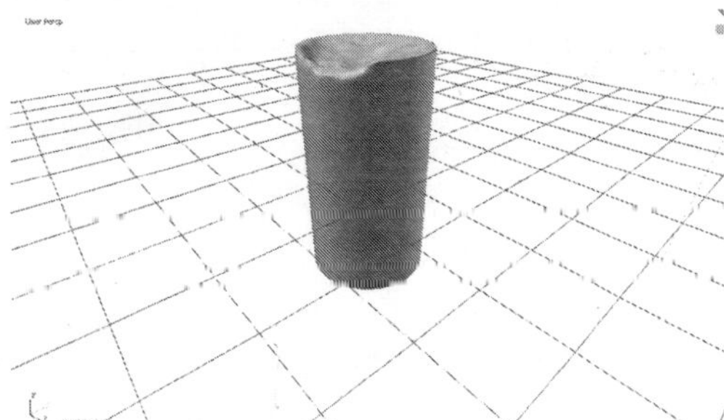

Figure 5-21 Strokes applied on the top circular edge of candle

11. Similarly, apply strokes on *candle* with and without using the CTRL key, as shown in Figure 5-22.

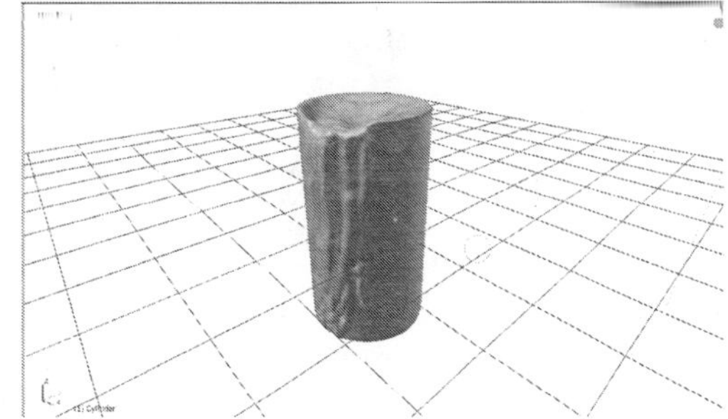

Figure 5-22 Strokes applied on candle

Creating the Wick of the Candle

In this section, you will create the wick of *candle* using the **F Grab** brush.

1. In the **Brush** panel, click on a current brush type image; a flyout is displayed, as shown in Figure 5-23. Choose **F Grab** from the flyout; the name and the image of the **F Grab** brush is displayed in the **Brush** panel.

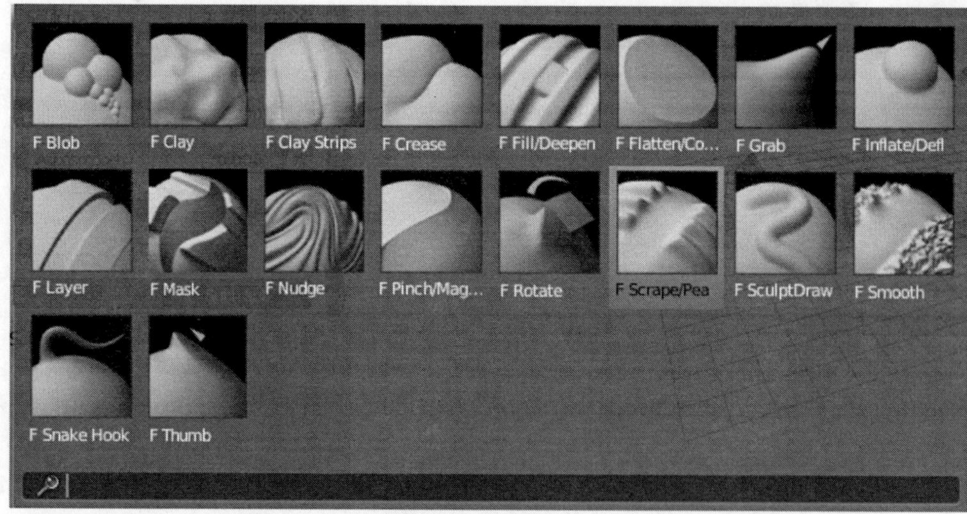

Figure 5-23 *The Flyout displayed on clicking the current brush type image*

2. Enter **10** and **1** in the **Radius** and **Normal Weight** sliders, respectively, of the **Brush** panel.

3. In the User Persp view, adjust the view of *candle,* as shown in Figure 5-24. Next, click at the center of the top face of *candle* and drag slightly upward; wick of *candle* is created, as shown in Figure 5-25.

4. Change the color of *candle* as discussed in Tutorial 1 of Chapter 2, refer to Figure 5-26.

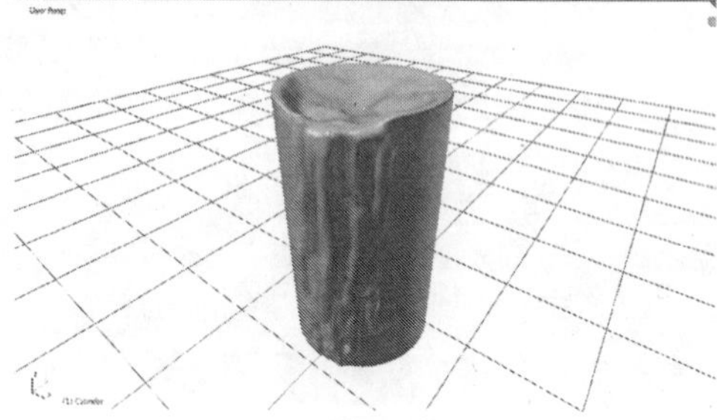

Figure 5-24 *Adjusting the view of candle*

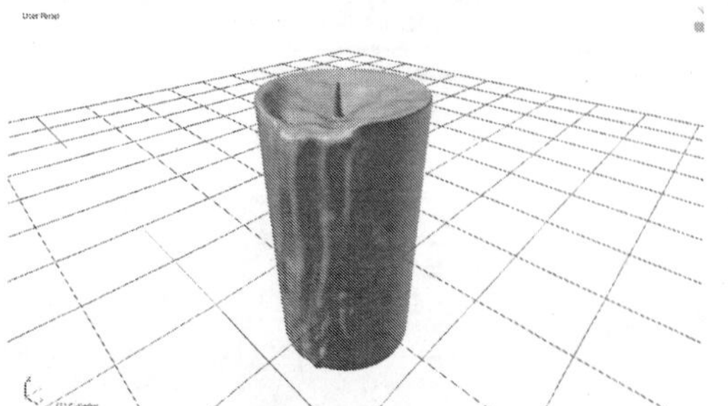

Figure 5-25 *Wick of candle created*

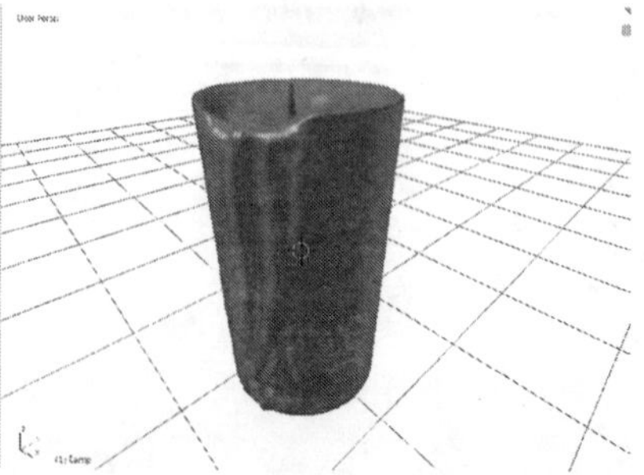

Figure 5-26 *Color of candle changed*

Saving and Rendering the Scene

In this section, you will save the scene that you have created and then render it. You can also view the final rendered image of this model by downloading the *c05_blender_2.79_rndr.zip* file from *www.cadcim.com*. The path of the file is as follows: *Textbooks > Animation and Visual Effects > Blender > Blender 2.79 for Digital Artists*

1. Choose **File > Save** from the **Info Editor** menu bar.

2. Adjust the view in the User Persp view. Next, choose the **Open GL still image render** button from **3D View Editor**; the rendered image is displayed in the **UV/Image Editor**, refer to Figure 5-15.

Tutorial 2

In this tutorial, you will create a decorative pot using the **Spin** tool and then sculpt it using the sculpting tools, refer to Figures 5-27 and 5-28. **(Expected time: 25 min)**

The following steps are required to complete this tutorial:

a. Create the folder.
b. Create the pot.
c. Apply modifiers to the pot.
d. Sculpt the pot.
e. Save and render the scene.

Figure 5-27 *The sculpted pot (view 1)*

Figure 5-28 *The sculpted pot (view 2)*

Creating the Folder

1. Navigate to *\Documents\blender2.79\c05* and create a new folder with the name *c05_tut2*.

2. Press CTRL+N or choose **File > New** from the **Info Editor** menu bar; a menu is displayed. Choose **Reload Start-Up File**; the menu disappears and the startup file is loaded.

3. Choose **File > Save** from the **Info Editor** menu bar; the **File Browser** is displayed.

4. Navigate to *\Documents\blender2.79\c05\c05_tut2* and enter **pot** in the **File Name** edit box. Next, choose the **Save Blender File** button to save the file at the specified location.

Adding the Reference Image

1. Choose **View > Toggle Quad View** from the **3D View Editor** menu bar or press CTRL+ALT+Q; the quad view is displayed. Hover the cursor over any of the views and Press N; **Properties Region** is displayed.

2. Expand the **Background Images** panel from **Properties Region**. Next, choose the **Add Image** button from the **Background Images** panel; the **Not Set** area is added to the **Background Images** panel, refer to Figure 5-29. Choose the **Open** button from the **Not Set** area; the **File Browser** is displayed. Navigate to *\Documents\blender2.79\c05* and select the **tut2pot** image and choose the **Open Image** button; the selected image is displayed in all the three ortho views, as shown in Figure 5-30. Also the **Not Set** area is replaced by the **tut2pot** area in the **Background Images** panel of **Properties Region.**

*Figure 5-29 The **Not Set** area in the **Background Images** panel*

3. Enter **0.3** in the **Opacity** edit box of the **tut2pot** area; the opacity of the reference image is reduced.

Creating the Pot

In this section, you will create the pot using the **Spin** tool.

1. Press CTRL+ALT+Q; the quad view is displayed. Make sure *Cube* is selected in the view. Delete *Cube*.

2. Make sure the **Create** tab is chosen in **Toolshelf**. Choose the **Plane** tool from the **Add Primitives** panel of **Toolshelf**; *Plane* is created at the center in the view. Rename it as *pot*.

3. Make sure the **Object** button is chosen in **Properties Editor**. Next, enter **90** in the **X** slider of the **Rotation** area of the **Transform** panel; plane gets rotated, as shown in Figure 5-31.

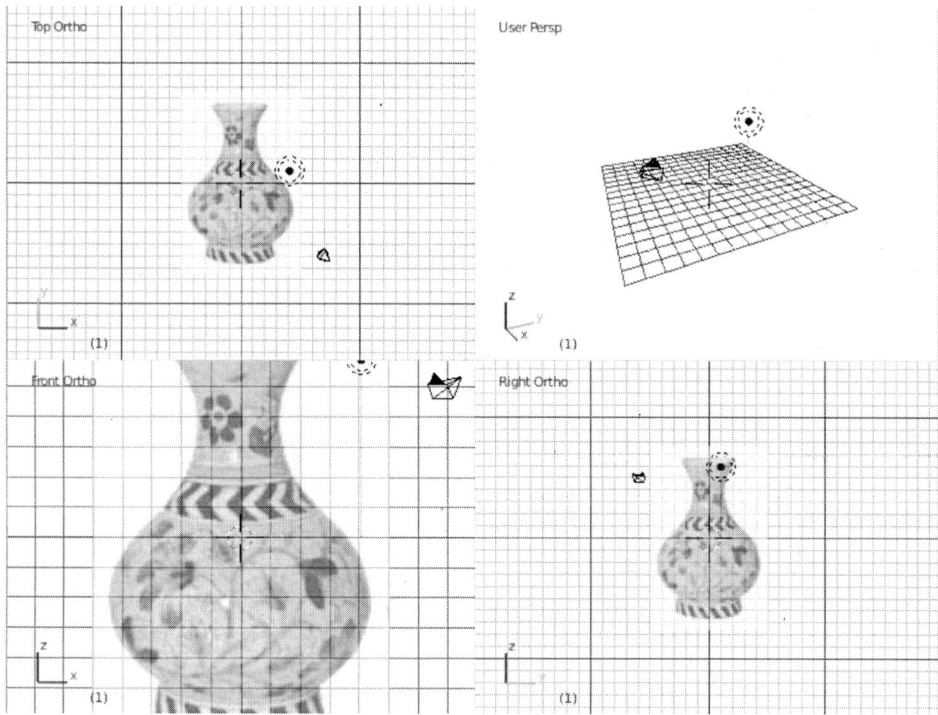

Figure 5-30 *The selected image in ortho views*

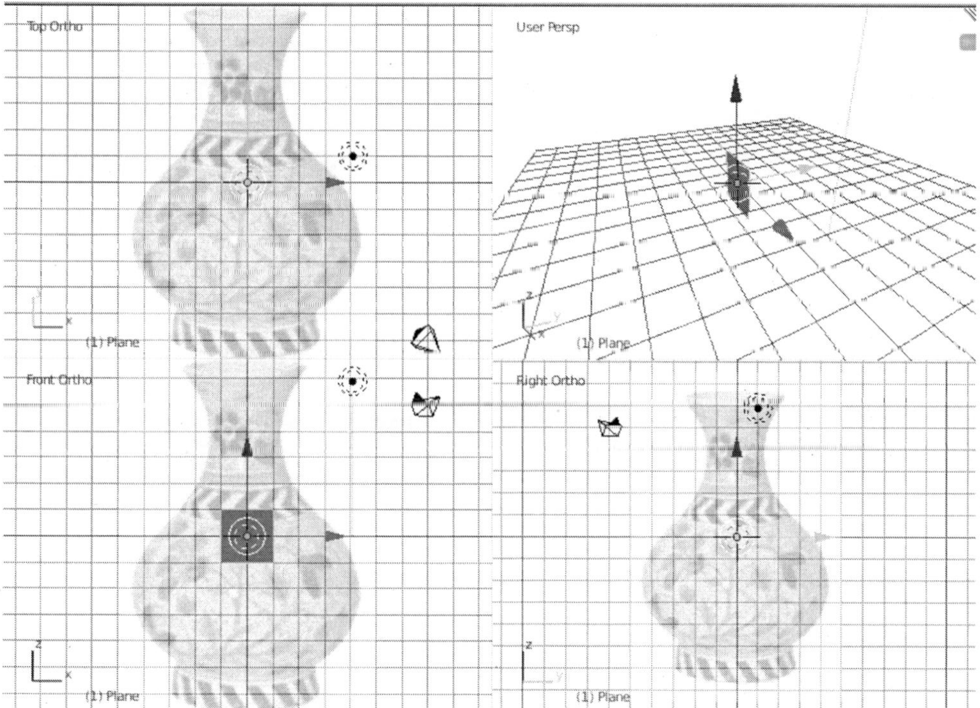

Figure 5-31 *The rotated plane*

4. Switch to **Edit Mode**. Next, press A to deselect the vertices. Now, select two vertices of *pot* in the Front Ortho view, as shown in Figure 5-32. Next, press delete; the **Delete** menu is displayed. Choose **Vertices** from this menu. You will notice that now there are only two vertices of *pot*.

5. Place the two vertices on the reference image, as shown in Figure 5-33.

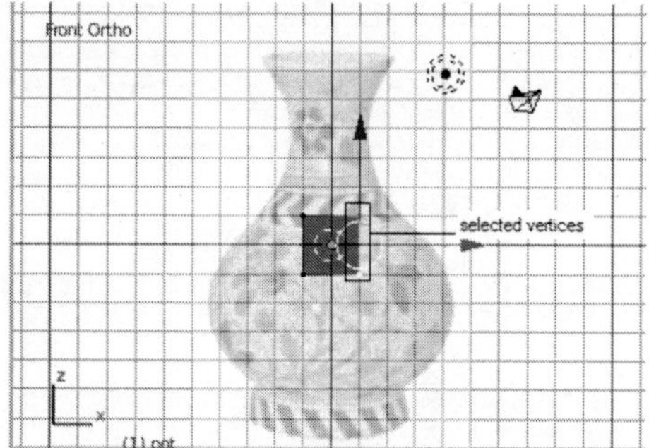

Figure 5-32 *Selected vertices of pot*

Figure 5-33 *Two vertices of pot placed*

6. Select the leftmost vertex and press E; line is extruded along with the vertex at the end. Next, place the vertex, as shown in Figure 5-34.

7. Similarly, create the profile for the pot by extruding the last vertex, as shown in Figure 5-35.

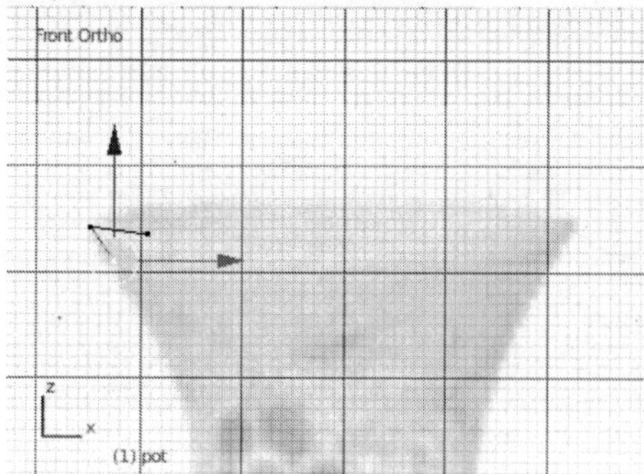

Figure 5-34 *The vertex placed*

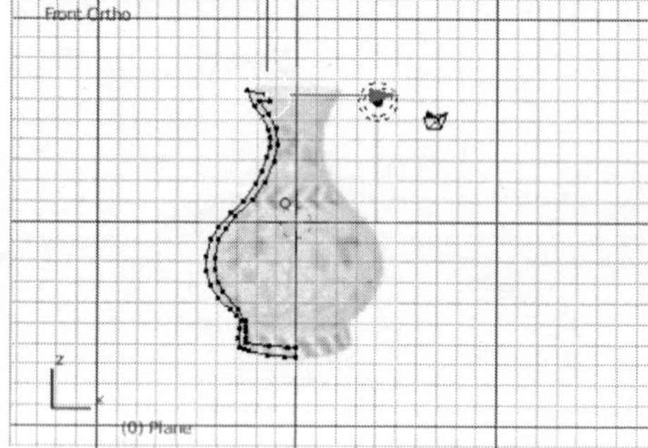

Figure 5-35 *The profile created*

8. Select the first and last vertices of the profile and then click on the **Merge** drop-down in the **Remove** area of the **Mesh Tools** panel in **Toolshelf** and choose **At Center** from the **Merge** drop-down; two vertices are joined at center, refer to Figure 5-36.

9. Select all the vertices of *pot,* as shown in Figure 5-37 and make sure that the 3D Cursor is at the center of the grid floor. If not, press SHIFT+C to place it at the center.

10. Choose **Spin** from the **Add** area in the **Mesh Tools** panel of **Toolshelf**; the profile is revolved around 3D Cursor and the **Spin** panel is added to **Toolshelf**. You will notice that the profile is not correctly revolved. To correct it, enter **360** and **0** in the **Angle** and **Y** sliders, respectively, of the **Axis** area in the **Spin** panel; the pot is created, as shown in Figure 5-38.

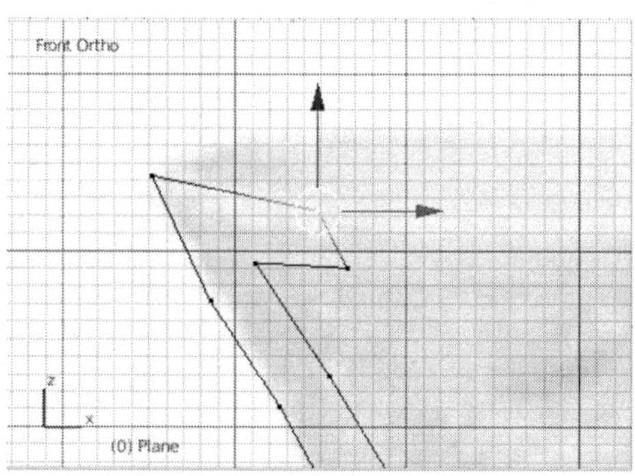

Figure 5-36 Two vertices of pot joined

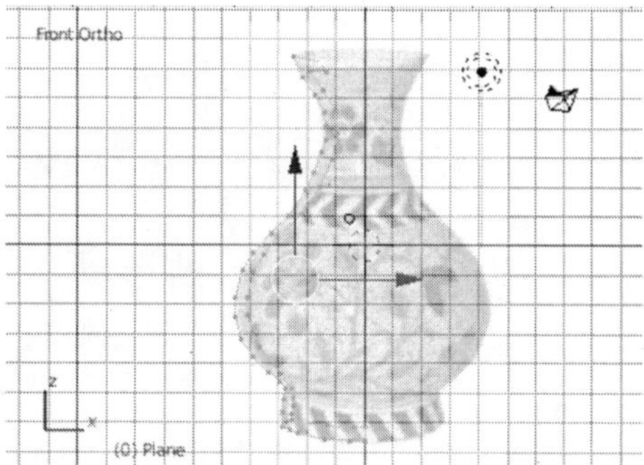

Figure 5-37 Selecting all the vertices of pot

Note

*The **Spin** tool is available for mesh primitive objects only.*

11. Enter **24** in the **Steps** slider of the **Spin** panel; the smoothness of *pot* increases, refer to Figure 5-39.

12. Choose the **Visible Selection** tool from **3D View Editor** and select all the vertices of *pot*. Next, choose **Remove Doubles** from the **Remove** area in the **Mesh Tools** panel of **Toolshelf**; the vertices that are very close to each other are merged.

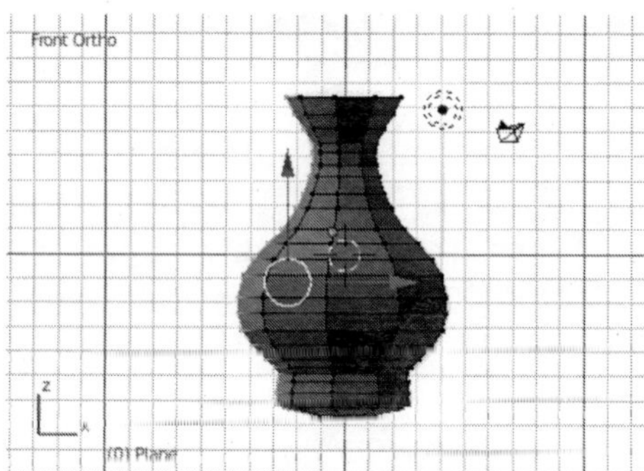

Figure 5-38 The pot created

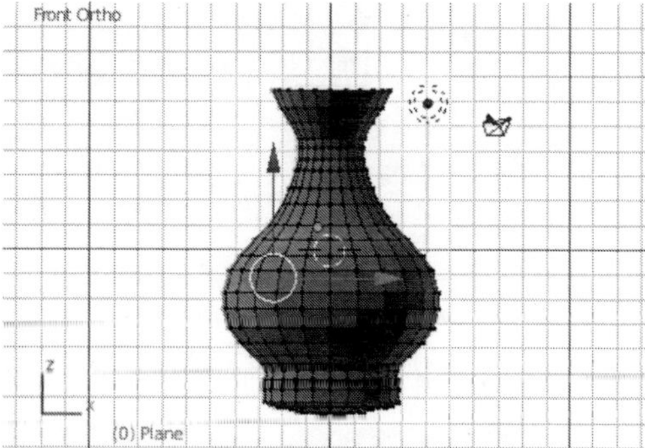

Figure 5-39 Smoothness of pot increased

Applying Modifier to Pot

In this section, you will apply the **Multiresolution** modifier to *pot*.

1. Switch to **Object Mode**. Next, choose the **Object Modifiers** button from **Properties Editor**. Next, click on the **Add Modifiers** drop-down and then choose **Multiresolution** from the **Generate** category of the list displayed; the **Multiresolution** modifier is applied to *pot* and the parameters for this modifier are displayed in **Properties Editor**, as shown in Figure 5-40.

2. Choose **Subdivide** thrice from **Properties Editor**; *pot* is smoothened, as shown in Figure 5-41. Next, choose **Apply** from **Properties Editor**; the modifier is applied to *pot* permanently and removed from the Modifier Stack.

Figure 5-40 *The parameters of the* ***Multiresolution*** *modifier*

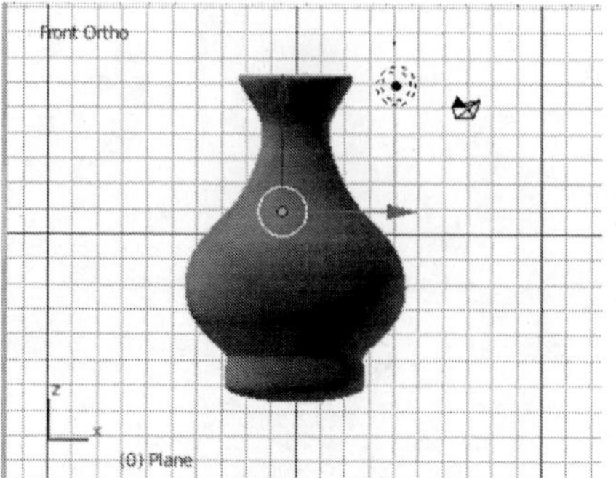

Figure 5-41 *The pot smoothened*

Sculpting the Pot

In this section, you will sculpt *pot* using various sculpting tools.

1. Click on the **Mode** drop-down and choose **Sculpt Mode** from the options in the drop-down. Alternatively, if the pie menus are activated, press TAB and choose **Sculpt Mode** from the **Mode** pie menu displayed; various panels are displayed in **Toolshelf**.

2. Enter the following values in the **Brush** panel of **Toolshelf**.

   Radius: **7** Strength: **1** Autosmooth: **1**

3. Expand the **Stroke** panel and choose **Line** from the **Stroke Method** drop-down. Next, enter **1** in the **Spacing** slider. Now, expand the **Dyntopo** panel and select the **Dyntopo** check box; the parameters below it are activated. Choose **Relative Detail** from the **Detail** drop-down and then enter **1** in the **Detail Size** slider.

4. Expand the **Symmetry/Lock** panel. In the **Mirror** area, click on the **X** button to deactivate it and click on the **Z** button to activate it. In the Front Ortho view, press the CTRL key and apply the stroke, refer to Figure 5-42. Figure 5-43 shows the stroke on *pot*. Note that same stroke is also applied on the back side of *pot*.

5. Apply the second stroke at the bottom of first stroke, as shown in Figure 5-44.

6. In the Right Ortho view, apply the strokes, as shown in Figure 5-45. Next, choose **Dots** from the **Stroke Method** drop-down in the **Stroke** panel. Also, set the following parameters in the **Brush** panel.

   Radius: **16** Strength: **0.5**

   In the **Mirror** area of the **Symmetry/Lock** panel, choose the **Z** button to deactivate it.

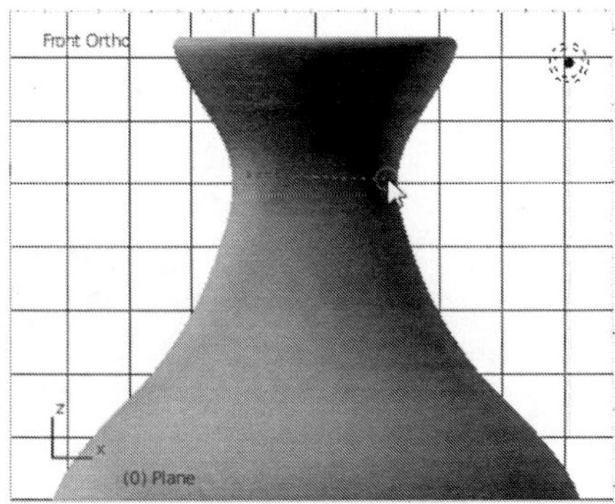

Figure 5-42 *Applying the stroke*

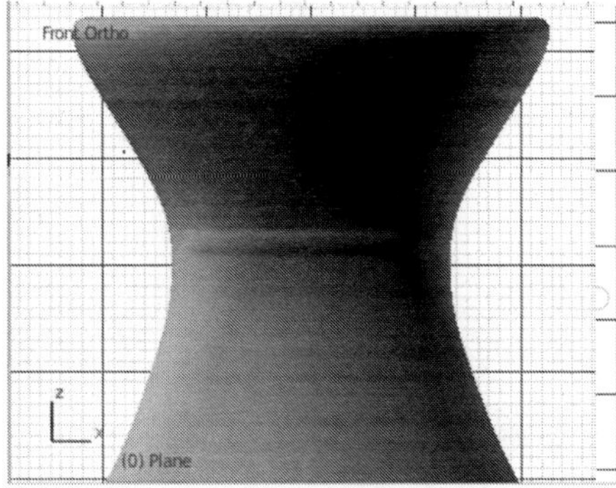

Figure 5-43 *The stroke on pot*

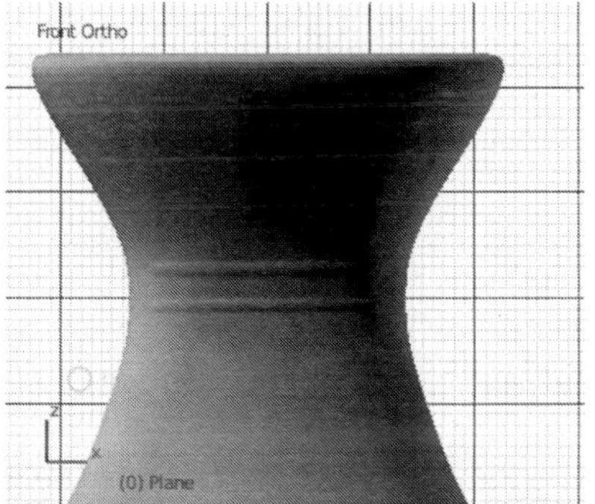

Figure 5-44 *Second stroke at the bottom of first stroke*

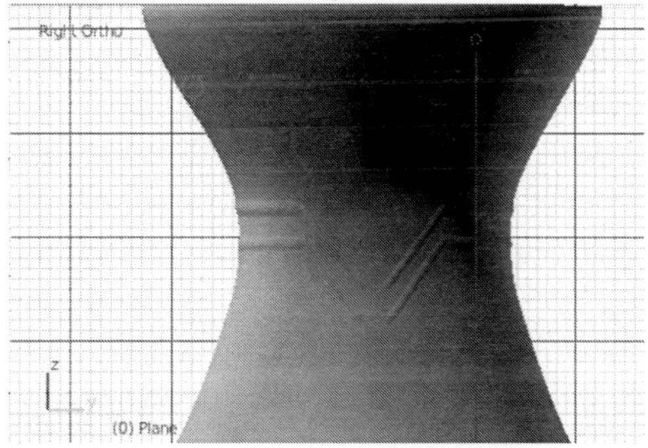

Figure 5-45 *Strokes applied in the Right Ortho view*

7. Press the CTRL key and click on *pot* at two places to create dots, as shown in Figure 5-46.

8. Press 3 and then 5 to switch to Left ortho view from the User Persp view. Now, apply the same strokes as applied in the Right Ortho view. Next, press 4 and then 5 to switch back to User Persp view.

   Next, you will apply strokes on the top face of *pot*.

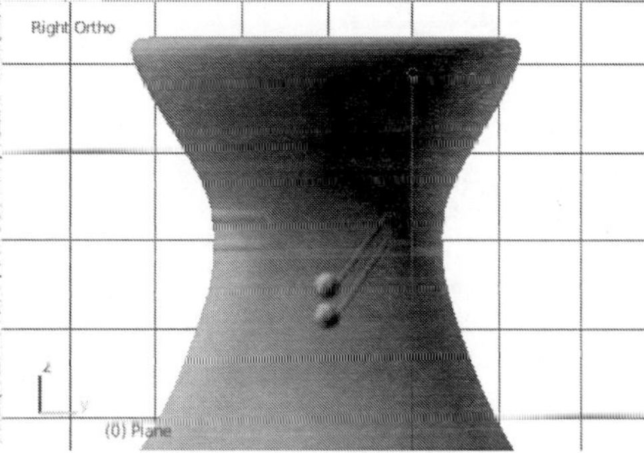

Figure 5-46 *Dots created on pot*

9. Enter **26** in the **Radius** slider of the **Brush** panel. Make sure **Dots** is chosen in the **Stroke Method** drop-down.

10. In the **Mirror** area of the **Symmetry/Lock** panel, make sure the **Z** button is activated. Next, press CTRL and apply the stroke, as shown in Figure 5-47. Apply the strokes on the top face of *pot*, as shown in Figure 5-48.

Note

If zoom level of the view is changed, you may need to change the radius of brush to achieve the strokes shown in Figure 5-48.

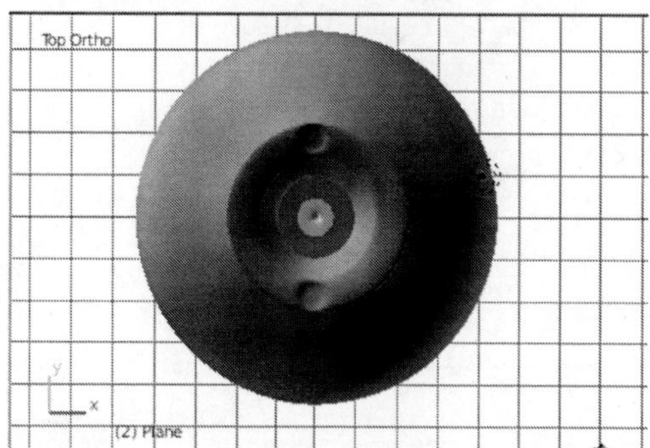

Figure 5-47 *Stroke applied on the top face of pot*

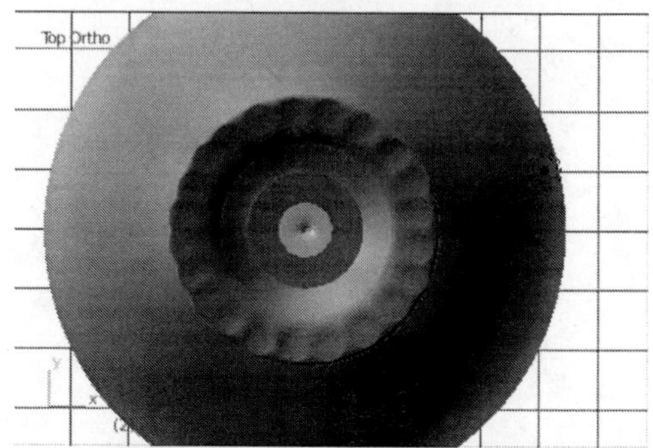

Figure 5-48 *Strokes applied on the top face of pot*

Next, you will apply strokes at the bottom side of *pot.*

11. Enter the following values in the **Brush** panel of **Toolshelf**.

    Radius: **5** Strength: **0.5** Autosmooth: **1**

12. Expand the **Stroke** panel and choose **Line** from the **Stroke Method** drop-down. Next, enter **5** in the **Spacing** slider

13. Make sure the **Disable Dyntopo** button is activated in the **Dyntopo** panel. If not, choose **Enable Dyntopo** panel. In the **Mirror** area of the **Symmetry/Lock** panel, make sure the **Z** button is activated.

14. In the Front Ortho view, apply the strokes, as shown in Figure 5-49. Next, join these strokes in the Right and Left ortho view to create two rings.

15. Similarly, apply the strokes on *pot* to create the design, refer to Figures 5-50 and 5-51. Note that do not press the CTRL key when you apply stroke to create inward stroke.

16. Change the color of *pot* as discussed in Tutorial 1 of Chapter 2, refer to Figure 5-52.

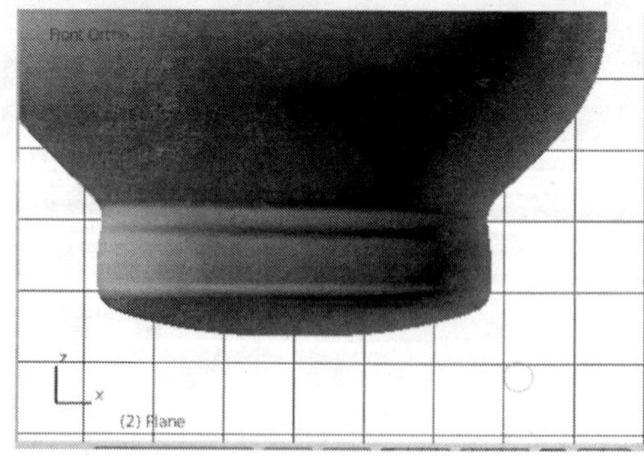

Figure 5-49 *Strokes applied on pot*

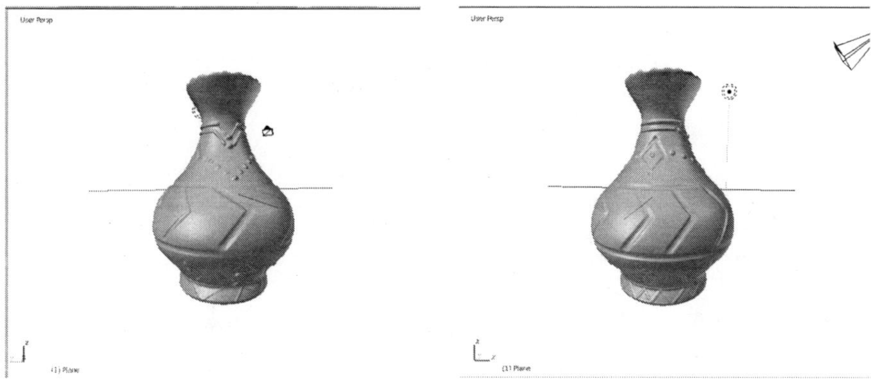

Figure 5-50 Design created on pot (view 1)

Figure 5-51 Design created on pot (view 2)

Saving and Rendering the Scene

In this section, you will save the scene that you have created and then render it. You can also view the final rendered image of this model by downloading the *c05_blender_2.79_rndr.zip* file from *www.cadcim.com.* The path of the file is as follows: *Textbooks > Animation and Visual Effects > Blender > Blender 2.79 for Digital Artists*

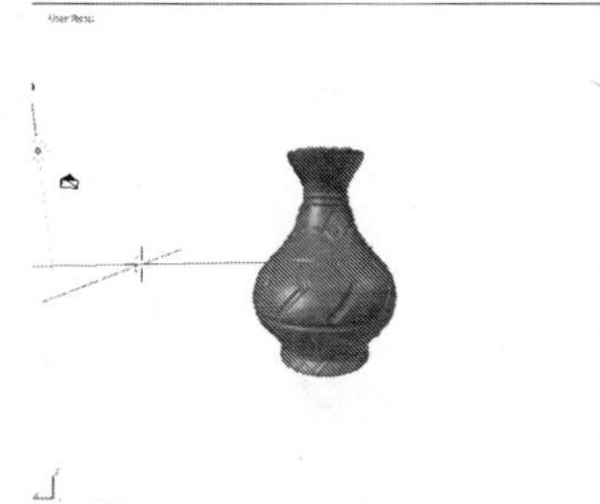

Figure 5-52 Color of pot changed

1. Choose **File > Save** from the **Info Editor** menu bar.

2. Adjust the view in the User Persp view. Next, choose the **Open GL still image render** button from **3D View Editor**; the rendered image is displayed in **UV/Image Editor**, refer to Figures 5-27 and 5-28.

Self-Evaluation Test

Answer the following questions and then compare them to those given at the end of this chapter:

1. Which of the following panels use dynamic tessellation method for sculpting?

   (a) **Brush** (b) **Dyntopo**
   (c) **Symmetry/Lock** (d) **Stroke**

2. The __________ panel are used to modify the intensity of the stroke from center to the circumference of a circle.

3. The __________ check box in the **Brush** panel is used to accumulate the strokes over one another on the same area of the object.

4. **Sculpt Mode** is available for mesh primitive objects only. (T/F)

5. There should be substantial subdivisions in an object to get better results in **Sculpt Mode**. (T/F)

Review Questions

Answer the following questions:

1. Which of the following keys is used to change the radius of the circle attached to cursor in **Sculpt Mode**?

(a) E (b) R
(c) D (d) F

2. If the pie menus are activated, then you can activate **Sculpt Mode** by first pressing the _________ key and then the _________ key.

3. The _________ tool is used to revolve the profile around 3D Cursor.

4. The **Spin** tool is available for mesh primitive objects only. (T/F)

EXERCISES

Exercise 1

Create a mug and sculpt it using sculpting tools, refer to Figure 5-53.

(Expected time: 15 min)

Figure 5-53 *Model of a sculpted mug*

Exercise 2

Create a photoframe and sculpt it using sculpting tools, refer to Figure 5-54.

(Expected time: 15 min)

Figure 5-54 *Model of a sculpted photoframe*

Answers to Self-Evaluation Test

1. b, **2. Curve**, **3. Accumulate**, **4.** T, **5.** T

Chapter 6

Working with Materials - I

Learning Objectives

After completing this chapter, you will be able to:

- ***Understand the*** *Blender Render* ***and*** *Cycles Render* ***engines***
- ***Create, assign, modify, and delete materials***
- ***Apply textures to the object***
- ***Apply multiple materials to the object***
- ***Apply multiple textures to the object***
- ***Create background for the scene***

INTRODUCTION

Materials and textures are used to simulate various types of surfaces that make the scene more realistic. Materials define reflection in an object. In Blender, there are numerous ways of creating materials and applying textures such as using the parameters in **Properties Editor**, using **Node Editor**, using the **Vertex Paint** mode, and using the **Texture Paint** mode. In this chapter, you will learn to create materials and apply textures using the parameters in **Properties Editor**. You will also learn about render engines in brief.

In addition, you will learn to create environment by setting an image as background of a scene.

BLENDER RENDER ENGINE

The Blender Render engine is the default render engine in Blender. It is fast and produces non-photorealistic but noiseless images. To change the default render engine, click on and choose the desired engine from the **Engine** drop-down in **Info Editor**, refer to Figure 6-1.

Creating a Material using the Blender Render Engine

To create material for an object using the Blender Render engine, select the object and choose the **Material** button from **Properties Editor**; modified **Properties Editor** will be displayed, as shown in Figure 6-2. Choose **New** from **Properties Editor**; a new material will be created and added to the **Material** drop-down and to **Material Stack**, refer to Figure 6-3. Also, the **New** button is replaced by a text box displaying the name of the newly created material and three small buttons, refer to Figure 6-3. The **F** button is used to add a fake user to a material created. The **+** button is used to add more materials to the scene. The **X** button is used to delete the material displayed in the text box.

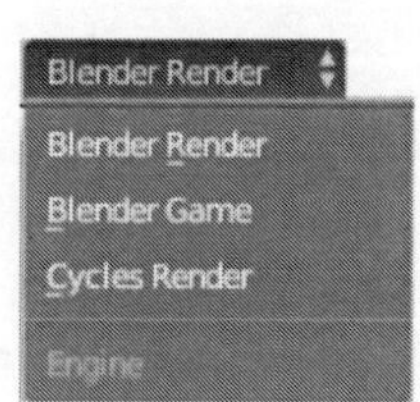

***Figure 6-1** The **Engine** drop-down*

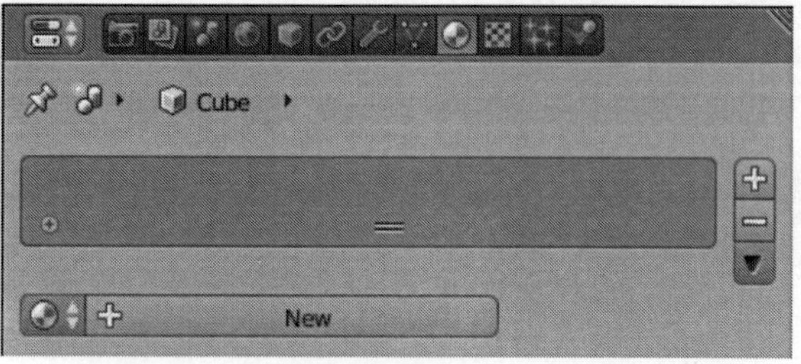

***Figure 6-2** Modified **Properties Editor** on choosing the **Material** button*

Note

*1. In Blender, the **F** button is used to create a fake user for a material in order to retain it in the scene even after reloading, even if it is not assigned to any of the objects in the scene.*

*2. To rename the created material, double-click on its name in the **Material Slot** box or click on its name in the text box located next to the **Material** drop-down and type the desired name.*

Material Stack is a box in which you can add slots for materials created. To add a material slot to **Material Stack**, click on the **+** button on its right side; a new slot will be created. You can add as many slots as you need. To remove a slot, select the slot from **Material Stack** and choose the **-** button on its right side. To add a material or to replace an existing material from the existing slot, select the slot and choose the desired material from the **Material** drop-down. Note that if a material slot is selected and you are creating a new material, the existing material applied to the object will be replaced by the newly created material in the selected slot of **Material Stack**. You can also change the order of materials in **Material Stack** by using the **Up Arrow** and the **Down Arrow** buttons on its right side.

In addition, **Properties Editor** will display various panels and buttons below the **Material** drop-down, as shown in Figure 6-3. You need to scroll down to see all the panels. Most commonly used panels are discussed next.

Figure 6-3** New material created in **Properties Editor

Surface

By default, the **Surface** button is chosen in **Properties Editor**. As a result, objects in the scene are rendered as surface, refer to Figure 6-3.

Wire

If you choose this button, edges of the object are only rendered. refer to Figure 6-4. Note that raytracing is not supported in this type of rendering.

Volume

If you choose this button, the objects will be rendered as a volume, refer to Figure 6-5 and panels such as **Density**, **Shading**, and **Lighting** that are specific to volume rendering will be displayed in **Properties Editor**. You can assign different values to the parameters in these panels to change the density of a volume, amount of light scattered or emitted by a volume, and so on.

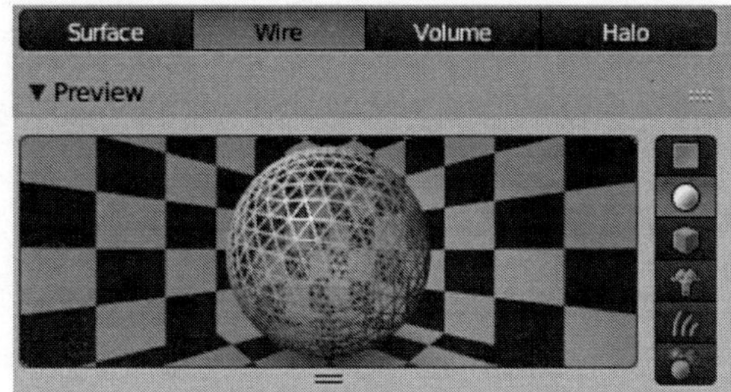

Figure 6-4 *Preview of rendered edges of the object*

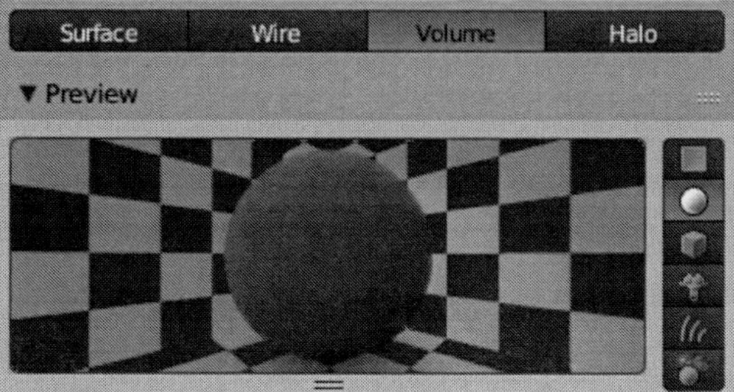

Figure 6-5 *Preview of render on choosing the **Volume** button*

Halo

If you choose this button, the objects will be rendered as halo particles, refer to Figure 6-6. Halo particles are glowing dots on the vertices of the object which can be used to simulate various particles and lens flares.

Preview

The **Preview** panel has a Preview window to get a quick visualization of the material being created. It has five buttons on its right to specify the shape used for displaying the preview.

Diffuse

The options in the **Diffuse** panel are used to set intensity and color of a diffuse material, to specify type of shader, and to set the specified shader parameters. The **Ramp** check box in this panel is used to set color gradient for the material. As you select the **Ramp** check box, some parameters are added to the **Diffuse** panel to define the color gradient for the material in a precise way, refer to Figure 6-7. The options available in the **Diffuse Shader** drop-down are used to provide different effects to the material after rendering. These options are discussed next.

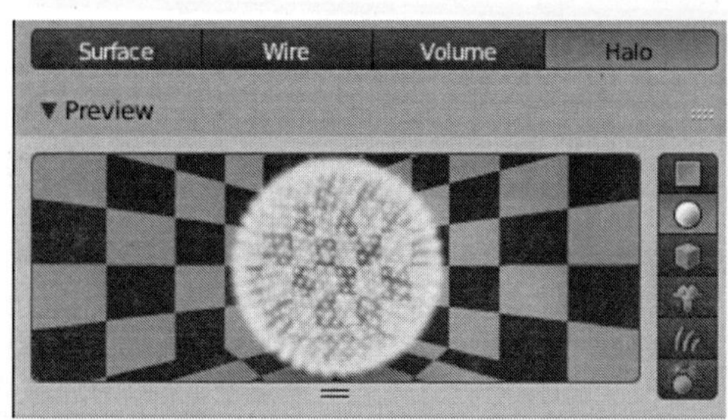

Figure 6-6 *Preview of render on choosing the **Halo** button*

Figure 6-7 *Parameters added to the **Diffuse** panel*

Lambert
The **Lambert** option is the default option chosen in the **Diffuse Shader** drop-down. The Lambert shader is a general purpose shader used for the material with less specular reflection.

Fresnel
If you choose the **Fresnel** option, the incidence angle determines the amount of reflected light. It means that the part of the object facing towards the incoming light will be darker compared to the part that is perpendicular to the incoming light.

Minnaert
When the Minnaert option is chosen and the value in the Darkness slider is set to 1, the material applied will be same as that applied in the Lambert option. If the value in the **Darkness** slider is less than 1, edges of the object will be lighter in shade and vice versa.

Toon
The **Toon** option is used to achieve non-photorealistic material used mostly in cartoon style rendering.

Oren-Nayar
The **Oren-Nayar** option is similar to the **Lambert** option with the difference in the amount of roughness in the material that is controlled by setting the value in the **Roughness** slider.

Specular
The options available in the **Specular** panel are used to create bright highlights to make a surface glossy. The options in the **Specular Shader** drop-down are used to create specific type of surfaces like **Cook Torr** is used to create shiny plastic surfaces, **Phong** is used to create organic surfaces, and so on.

Shading
The **Shading** panel has some more options to set the shading of material.

Transparency
The options available in the **Transparency** panel are used to set the transparency of an object. You need to select the **Transparency** check box to activate the options in the **Transparency** panel and then choose one of the three buttons **Mask**, **Z Transparency**, or **Raytrace** to set the transparency. If you choose the **Mask** button, the options displayed are used to mask the background. The amount of masking depends on the value in the **Alpha** slider. If you choose the **Z Transparency** button, alpha buffer will be used to make the faces transparent but refractions will not be calculated. Similarly, if you choose the **Raytrace** button, complex refractions and falloff will be calculated using raytracing.

Mirror
The options available in the **Mirror** panel are used to simulate the mirror. Select the **Mirror** check box to activate the options in the **Mirror** panel. You need to set a value in the Reflectivity slider to get desired amount of reflection from the object. If you set **1** in the **Reflectivity** slider and retain default values for all the other parameters in the **Mirror** panel, you will get a perfect mirror. The **Fresnel** slider sets the fresnel effect on the object. The fresnel effect depends on the

angle between the surface normal to the object and the viewing direction. You can also simulate metals like chrome, copper, and so on by setting the other options in the **Mirror** panel.

Subsurface Scattering

Penetration of some amount of light through the surface of an object that has some transparency on its surface and subsequent scattering of light inside the object is called as subsurface scattering. To enable subsurface scattering, select the **Subsurface Scattering** check box; the parameters in the **Subsurface Scattering** panel are activated. Various options are available in the **SSS Presets** drop-down to simulate apple, skin, marble, ketchup, and so on. As you choose a preset option, **IOR** and **RGB** values are set accordingly and you need to set other parameters in the panel as they may vary as per the size of the object.

Shadow

The parameters in the **Shadow** panel are used to control the effect of applied material on the shadow of the object. For example, if you select the **Receive Transparency** check box, the object with transparent material will cast a transparent shadow.

CYCLES RENDER ENGINE

The Cycles Render engine produces photorealistic rendered images. When you use the Cycles Render engine, light rays are traced from camera and not from light source. A scene rendered using the Cycles Render engine needs to be sampled a number of times to reduce noise. As you switch to the Cycles Render engine, parameters in **Properties Editor** change and you need to enable nodes. Also, nodes will be automatically created in **Node Editor** as you set parameters in **Properties Editor**. Material creation using **Node Editor** is discussed in detail in Chapter 7. In the next section, you will learn to create material using the Cycles Render Engine using parameters in **Properties Editor**.

Creating a Material using the Cycles Render Engine

To create a material using the Cycles Render engine, select the object and choose **Cycles Render** from the **Engine** drop-down in **Info Editor**, refer to Figure 6-1. Next, choose the **Material** button from **Properties Editor**; **Properties Editor** will be modified. Choose **New** from **Properties Editor**; a new material will be created and added to the **Material** drop-down and to **Material Stack**, refer to Figure 6-8. Also, the **New** button is replaced by a text box displaying the name of the newly created material and three small buttons, as shown in Figure 6-8. The use of the **F**, **+**, and **X** buttons and **Material Stack** are already discussed in the previous section. Next, choose the **Use Nodes** button from the **Surface** panel; **Properties Editor** will be modified, as shown in Figure 6-9. Most commonly used panels are discussed next.

Note

*If you start a new session in Blender and choose **Cycles Render** from the **Engine** drop-down, on choosing the **Material** button, modified **Properties Editor** shown in Figure 6-9 will be displayed directly.*

Surface

Parameters in this panel are used to specify the surface shader by setting interaction of light through surface of the object. The options in the **Surface** drop-down are used to define the type of bidirectional scattering distribution function, refer to Figure 6-10. Other parameters in this panel depend on the option chosen from the **Surface** drop-down. Figures 6-11 and 6-12 shows the effect of **Diffuse BSDF** and **Transparent BSDF**, respectively, on the surface of the object (with same color set in **Color** swatch and default values for other parameters) on rendering.

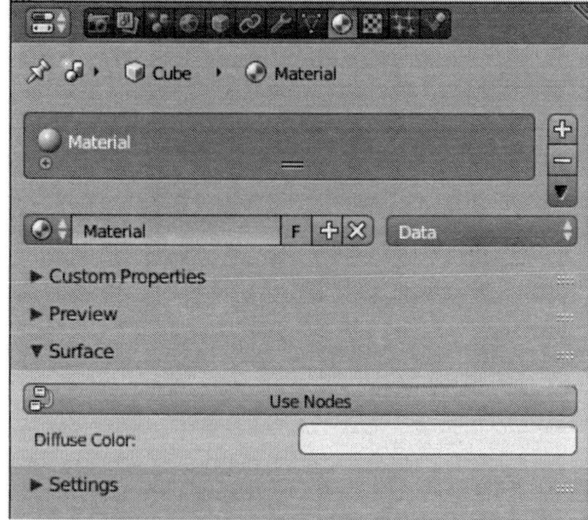

***Figure 6-8** Default parameters in **Properties Editor** for the Cycles Render engine*

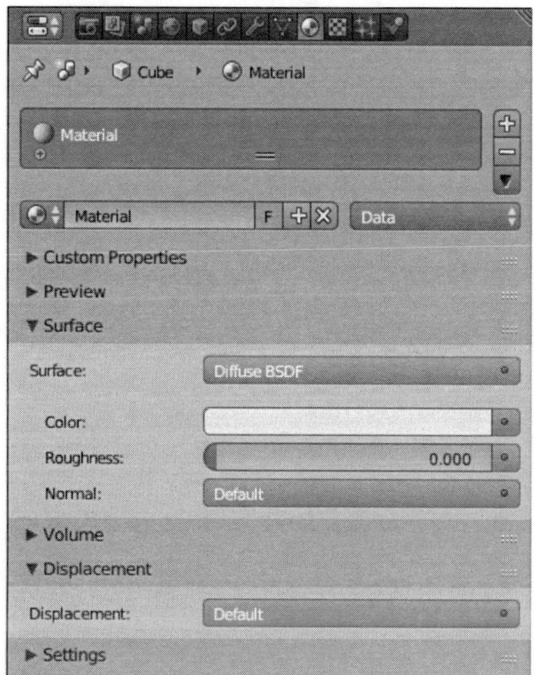

***Figure 6-9** Modified **Properties Editor** for the Cycles Render engine*

***Figure 6-10** The options in the **Surface** drop-down*

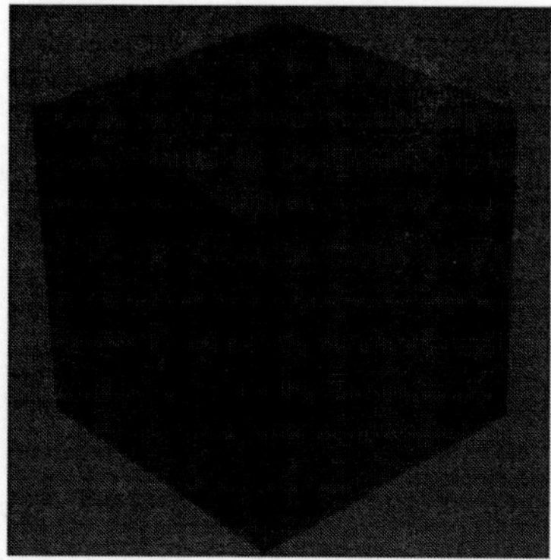

Figure 6-11 ***Diffuse BSDF*** *appiled to an object*

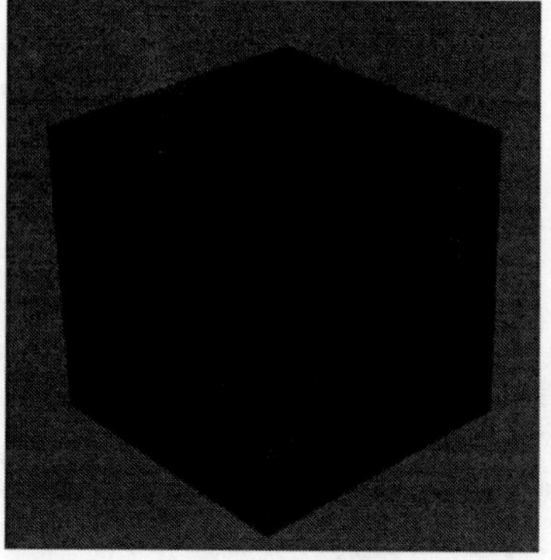

Figure 6-12 ***Transparent BSDF*** *appiled to an object*

Note

1. To display material in 3D view, choose ***Material*** *from the* ***Viewport Shading*** *drop-down in* ***3D View Editor****, refer to Figure 6-13.*

2. To display material on rendering, press F12. Alternatively, choose the ***Render*** *button from* ***Properties Editor*** *and then choose the* ***Render*** *button from the* ***Render*** *panel, refer to Figure 6-14. If you render a scene using the* ***Open GL still image render*** *button in* ***3D View Editor,*** *you will not be able to see the materials in the rendered image.*

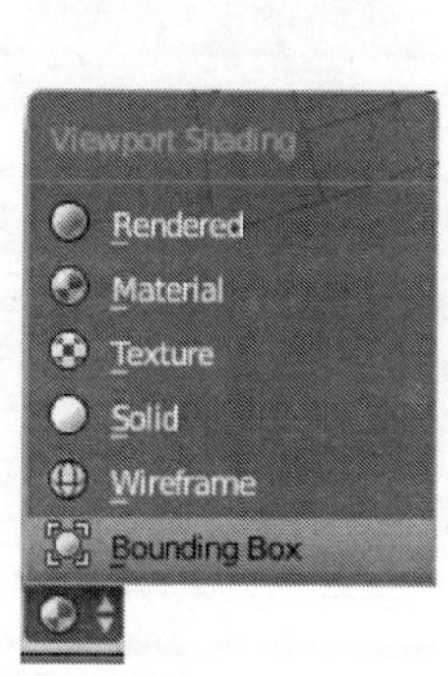

Figure 6-13 *The* ***Viewport Shading*** *drop-down*

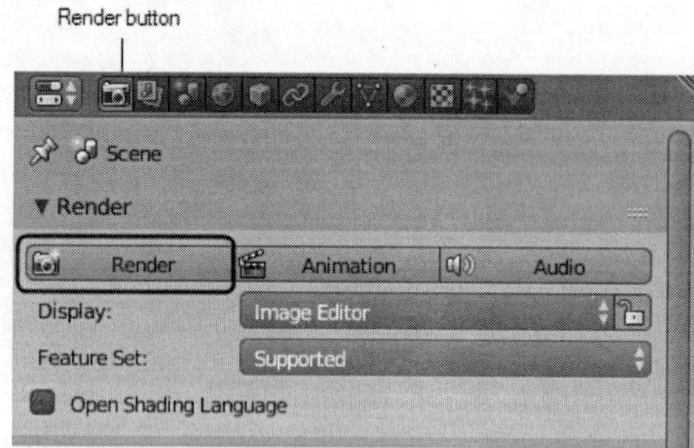

Figure 6-14 *The* ***Render*** *button in the* ***Render*** *panel*

Volume

This panel is used to specify volume shader for an object by setting interaction of the light passing through the volume of object. By default, **None** is chosen in the **Volume** drop-down. As a result, volume shader is not set for the object. As you set type of volume shader, related parameters will be displayed in the **Volume** panel. Figure 6-15 shows the parameters set in the **Surface** and **Volume** panels of **Properties Editor** to create a material. Figure 6-16 shows rendered image of a UV Sphere to which the same material applied.

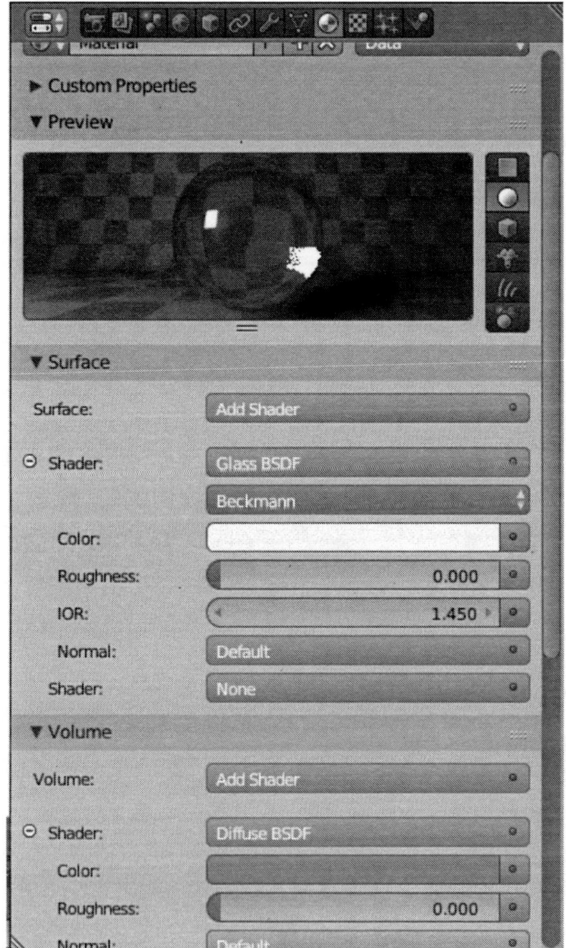

*Figure 6-15 The **Glass BSDF** and **Diffuse BSDF** shaders and their parameters in **Properties Editor***

Figure 6-16 Rendered image of a sphere

Displacement

The parameters in this panel are used to add various types of displacement shaders to an object. As you choose the type of displacement from the **Displacement** drop-down, related parameters will be displayed in the **Displacement** panel. Figure 6-17 shows the **Brick Texture**, **Diffuse BSDF**, and **Tangent** options chosen in the **Displacement**, **Surface**, and **Normal** drop-downs respectively in **Properties Editor** to create a material for a UV sphere. Figure 6-18 shows rendered image of the material created.

Assigning a Material

To assign a material to an object, select the object and create the material as discussed in the previous section. To assign existing material to an object, select the object and choose desired option from the **Material** drop-down.

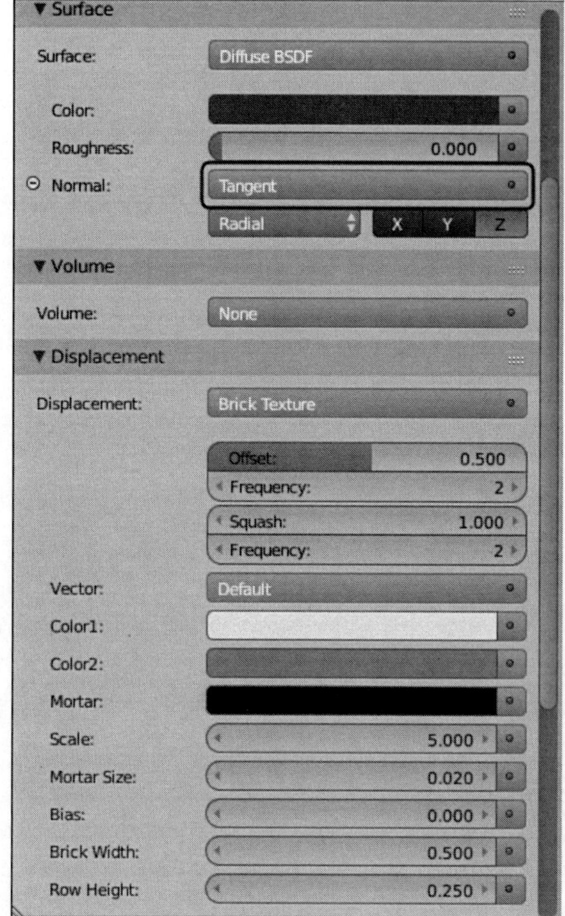

Figure 6-17** The **Diffuse BSDF** and **Brick Texture** shaders and their parameters in **Properties Editor

***Figure 6-18** The rendered image*

Deleting a Material

To delete a material from an object, select the object and click on **X** located next to the **Material** drop-down, refer to Figure 6-8; material will be removed from the object but will not be removed from the **Material** drop-down. Also, if the same material is assigned to other objects, it will be retained for those objects.

If the material to be deleted is not assigned to any other object(s), it will be there in the material list for the current session. To retain the material for the next session also, press the **F** button before deleting it so that it links to a fake user.

Creating Background

In Chapter 2, you learned about changing the background color of a scene in a rendered image. Also, you learned to setup an image as a reference image in orthographic views for modeling purpose. Now, you will learn to set up an image that will act as background of a scene on rendering.

To create background when the Blender Render engine is active, you need to follow the steps given next:

1. Create a scene and adjust its camera view.

2. Choose the **World** button from **Properties Editor**. Next, select the **Paper Sky** check box from the **World** panel, refer to Figure 6-19. 

3. Choose the **Texture** button from **Properties Editor**; **Properties Editor** is modified. Choose **New** from **Properties Editor**; new texture will be created and added to the **texture** drop-down and to Texture Stack. Also, the **New** button is replaced by a text box displaying the name of the newly created texture.

4. Double-click on the texture name in Texture Stack and enter **background** to rename the texture.

5. Choose **Open** from the **Image** panel; **File Browser** is displayed. Navigate to the location where the background image is located. Select it and choose **Open Image** from **File Browser**.

6. In the **Influence** panel of **Properties Editor**, select the **Horizon** check box, refer to Figure 6-20. Press F12; the selected image is displayed as a background of the scene, Figure 6-21 shows background image of a scene that has a plane.

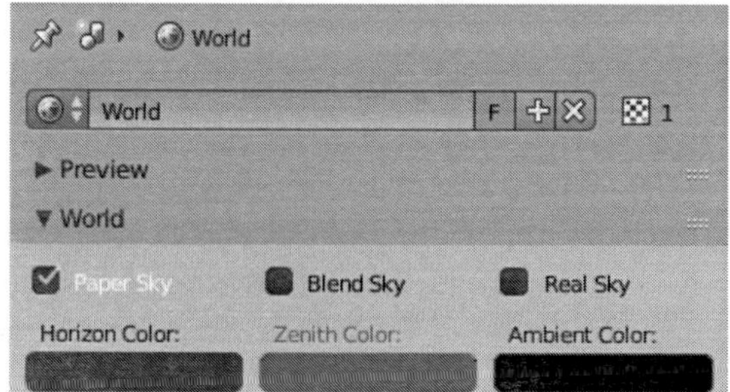

*Figure 6-19 The **Paper Sky** check box in the **World** panel*

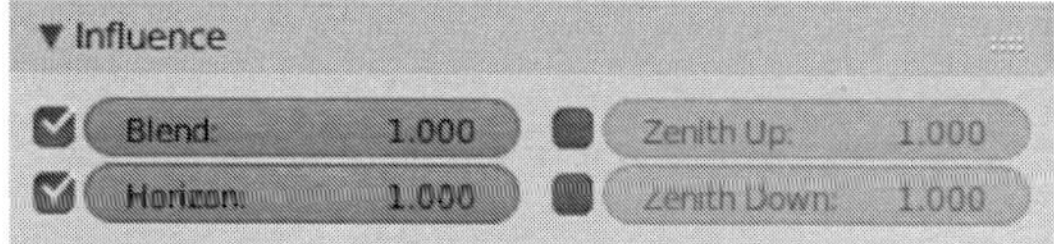

*Figure 6-20 The **Horizon** check box in the **Influence** panel*

Note

*If you want to add background as a gradient, you need to select the **Paper Sky**, **Blend Sky**, and **Real Sky** check boxes from the **World** panel in different combinations and set colors in the **Horizon Color**, **Zenith Color**, and **Ambient Color** swatches to get desired color ramp.*

To create background when the Cycles Render engine is active, you need to follow the steps given next:

1. Choose the **World** button from **Properties Editor**. Choose **Use Nodes** from the **Surface** panel; parameters in the **Surface** panel will be modified and the **Background** shader is displayed in the **Surface** drop-down, refer to Figure 6-22.

Figure 6-21 Rendered image of a scene

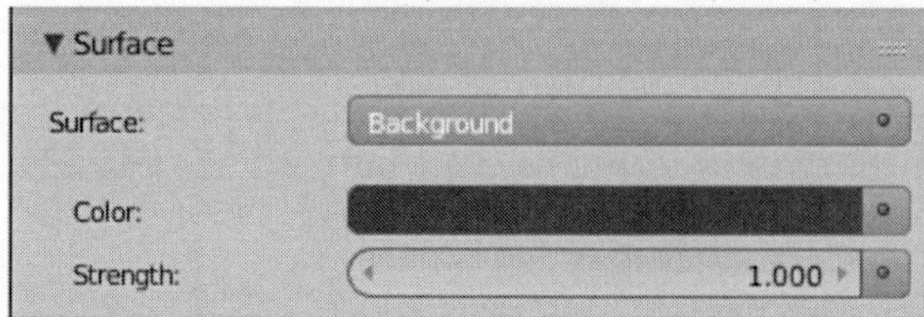

*Figure 6-22 The **Surface** panel modified*

2. Choose the Dot button next to the **Color** swatch and choose **Environment Texture** from the flyout displayed, as shown in Figure 6-23.

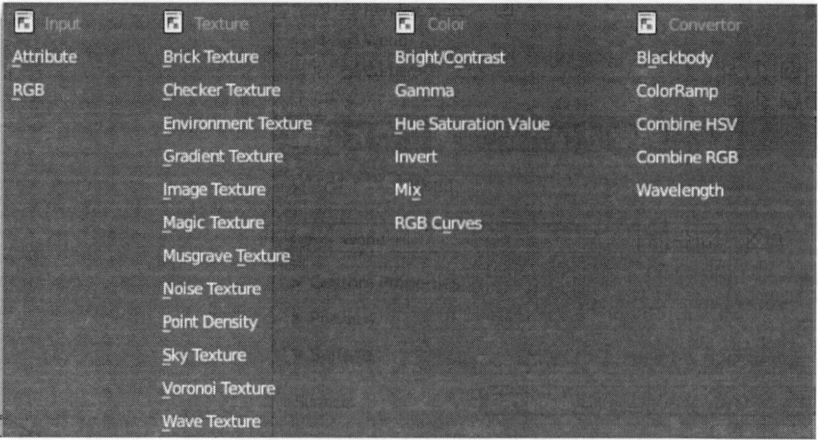

Figure 6-23 The flyout displayed

3. Choose the **Open** button; **File Browser** is displayed. Navigate to the image to be used as background and then choose **Open Image** from **File Browser**.

4. Press F12; the rendered image will be displayed with the selected image as its background. Figure 6-24 shows rendered image of a scene with sphere.

***Figure 6-24** Rendered image of the scene*

Assigning Multiple Materials to an object

In Blender, you can assign multiple materials to an object at the face level. To do so, choose the Blender Render engine and follow the steps given next:

1. Select the object and create a material as discussed earlier; the material will be displayed in a view. This material will act as the base material.

2. Make sure the object is selected and then create second material; the second material will be assigned to the object.

3. Choose the base material from the **Material** drop-down. You will notice that base material will be displayed on the object. Switch to **Edit Mode**; three buttons, **Assign**, **Select**, and **Deselect** will be added to **Properties Editor** above the **Material** drop-down.

4. Choose the **Face Select** button from **3D View Editor**. Next, select the faces on which second material is to be assigned.

5. Choose the + button on the right of the **Material Slot** box; a new material slot will be created below the existing material slot.

6. Make sure the new material slot is selected in the **Material Slot** box. Next, choose the second material from the **Material** drop-down and then choose the **Assign** button; second material will be assigned to the selected faces. You will notice that base material is displayed on non-selected faces of the object. In this way, you can assign more than two materials to an object. Figure 6-25 shows a UV sphere with two materials applied to it.

Figure 6-25 The UV Sphere with two materials applied

Note

*To assign multiple materials to an object when the Cycles Render engine is active, select the object and choose the **Use Nodes** button in the **Surface** panel and then follow the steps given above.*

TEXTURES

Textures are used to define specific pattern on the surface of an object. In Blender, you need to assign material to an object before applying texture on it. You can also blend more than one textures to create customized patterns.

Applying Texture in Blender Render Engine

To apply texture on an object using the Blender Render engine, select the object and choose the **Material** button from **Properties Editor**. Next, choose **New** from **Properties Editor**; new material will be assigned to the object. Now, choose the **Texture** button from **Properties Editor**; **Properties Editor** will be modified, as shown in Figure 6-26. Next, choose the **New** button from it; a new texture will be displayed in the selected slot of **Texture Stack** and will be added to the **Texture** drop-down. Also, the **New** button will be replaced by a text box and three small buttons, **F**, **+**, and **X**. The use of these buttons is explained in the **Creating a Material** section. In addition, various panels and the **Type** drop-down will be displayed in **Properties Editor**, refer to Figure 6-27.

The use of **Texture Stack**, the **Type** drop-down, and various panels are discussed next.

Texture Stack

Texture Stack is a box in which slots are available for adding textures in it. To add a texture to a slot, select the slot and choose desired texture from the **Texture** drop-down or choose **New** to add a new texture. Note that if a texture slot is selected and you are adding a new texture, the existing texture will be automatically replaced by the newly added texture in the selected slot. You can also change the order of materials in **Material Stack** by using the **Up Arrow** and the **Down Arrow** buttons on its right side.

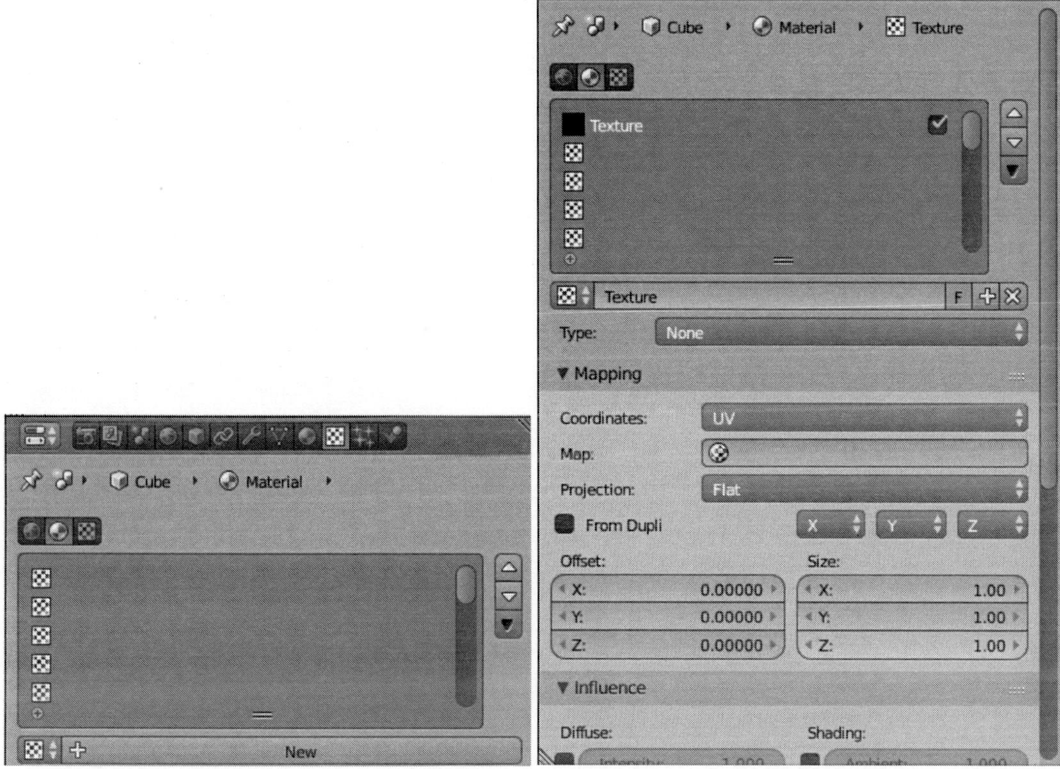

*Figure 6-26 Modified **Properties Editor***

*Figure 6-27 Various panels and the **Type** drop-down in **Properties Editor***

Type Drop-down

The **Type** drop-down consists of procedural textures, volumetric textures, and environment maps, refer to Figure 6-28. As you choose any of these textures, **Preview**, **Colors**, **Mapping**, **Influence**, **Custom Properties** panels will be displayed in **Properties Editor** in addition to the specific panel for each of the option chosen.

To use external images or videos as textures, choose the **Image or Movie** option from the **Type** drop-down. Note that when you choose this option, two additional panels, **Image Sampling** and **Image Mapping** are added to **Properties Editor** along with the **Image** panel. Most commonly used panels are discussed next.

Preview

The **Preview** panel has a Preview window to get quick visualization of the texture. The **Texture** button displays only the texture, the **Material** button displays only the material, and the **Both** button displays both the texture and the material side by side in the Preview window.

Colors

The options in this panel are used to adjust brightness, contrast, and saturation, and to tint the color of the texture.

Mapping

The **Mapping** panel specifies the mapping coordinates which in turn determines the wrapping technique of a texture around the object. Using the options in this panel, you can adjust the type, size, location, and projection of these coordinates on the object. The **Coordinates** drop-down is used to specify the type of coordinates, refer to Figure 6-29. Also, there are four types of projections available in the **Projection** drop-down, as shown in Figure 6-30. To offset the location of the mapping coordinates, set required value in the **X**, **Y**, and **Z** sliders of the **Offset** area whereas to change the size of the coordinates, set the value in the **X**, **Y**, and **Z** sliders of the **Size** area.

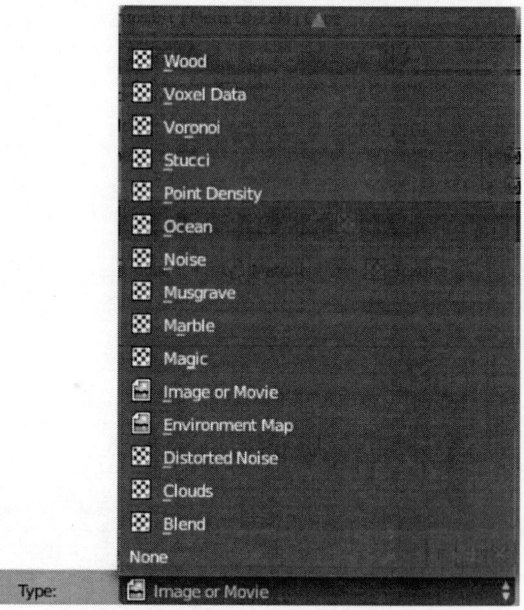

*Figure 6-28 The **Type** drop-down*

Some objects in the scene are duplicated as an instance of the original objects. To inherit the texture coordinates from the original objects, select the **From Dupli** check box.

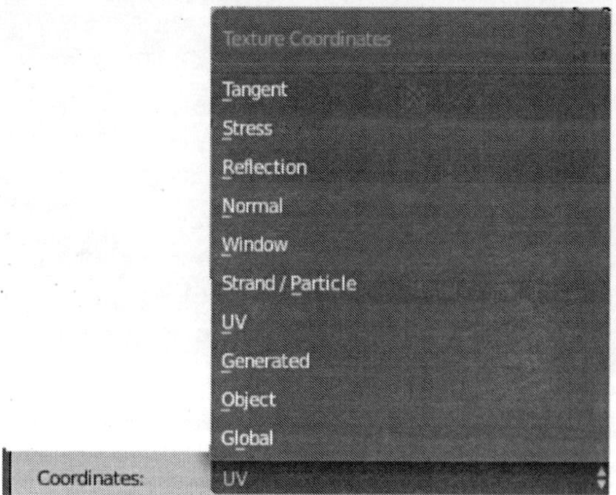

*Figure 6-29 The **Coordinates** drop-down*

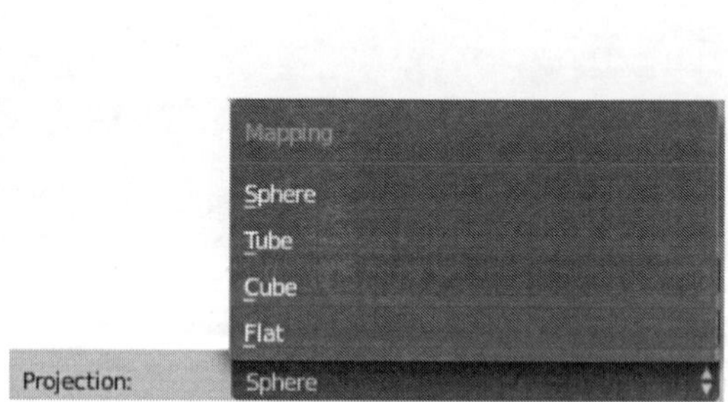

*Figure 6-30 The **Projection** drop-down*

Influence

The parameters in the **Influence** panel are used to set different aspects of a material in detail. To have a particular influence on the texture, you need to select respective check box at the left of these parameters.

The **Normal** slider in the **Geometry** area is used for bump mapping. As you activate this slider, parameters in the **Bump Mapping** area (**Method** and **Space** drop-downs) will be activated. You can choose required options from these drop-downs to achieve desired illusion of bump on the surface of an object.

The **Normal** and **Displace** sliders are used for displacement mapping. In displacement mapping, vertices appear to be displaced from their original position on rendering. Note that there will not be any displacement in actual geometry of the object. Also, mesh should be considerably subdivided before using the displacement map to get better results.

Note that the parameters in this panel may change depending on the button chosen (**Surface**, **Wire**, **Volume**, or **Halo**) in **Properties Editor** at the time of setting the material for the texture. You have already learned about the use of these buttons in the **Creating a Material** section.

Image

The **Image** panel is displayed in **Properties Editor** if the **Image or Movie** option is chosen from the **Type** drop-down, refer to Figure 6-31. If you choose the **Open** button from this panel; **File Browser** will be displayed. You need to select the image or video from the computer to use it as a texture. On doing so, the **Image Panel** will be modified, as shown in Figure 6-32. The parameters in this panel are discussed next.

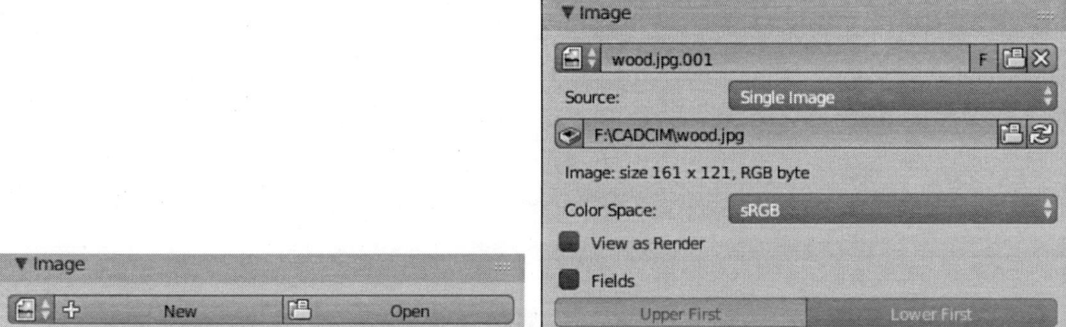

Figure 6-31 *The* ***Image*** *panel*   ***Figure 6-32*** *Modified* ***Image*** *panel*

The name of the loaded image will be displayed on the top in the panel. You can rename the image by clicking on its name. At the right of the image name three buttons, **F**, **Open Image**, and **X** are available. The **F** button is used to create the fake user for the image to retain it even if it is not used for the objects in the scene. The **Open Image** button is used to navigate to the computer and change the loaded image, if required. The **X** button is used to remove the image.

The **Source** drop-down shows the type of source used, refer to Figure 6-33. If you select an image from the computer, the **Single image** option will be displayed and if you select a video from the computer, the **Video** option will be displayed in the **Source** drop-down.

The **Open** button located below the **Source** drop-down is used to open **File Browser**. Also, if you press and hold SHIFT and click on this button, the image will be displayed in the default picture viewer and if you press and hold ALT and click on this button; the Windows Explorer will be displayed showing the folder in which the loaded image is available. Choose the desired color space from the options in the **Color Space** drop-down, refer to Figure 6-34.

The **Image Sampling** and **Image Mapping** panels are also displayed in **Properties Editor** when you choose the **Image or Movie** option from the **Type** drop-down. The parameters in these panels are used to further manipulate the image and control the mapping of an image on the surface of the object.

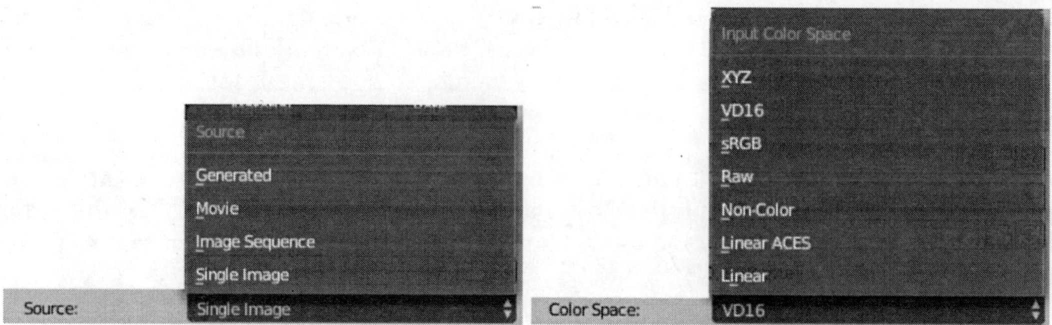

*Figure 6-33 The **Source** drop-down* *Figure 6-34 The **Color Space** drop-down*

Applying Texture in Cycles Render Engine

To apply texture on an object in the Cycles Render engine, select the object and choose the **Material** button from **Properties Editor**. Next, choose **New** from **Properties Editor**; new material will be assigned to the object and various panels are displayed in **Properties Editor**. To apply texture, choose the Dot button on the right of the respective parameters in **Properties Editor**, refer to Figure 6-35; a flyout will be displayed, as shown in Figure 6-36.

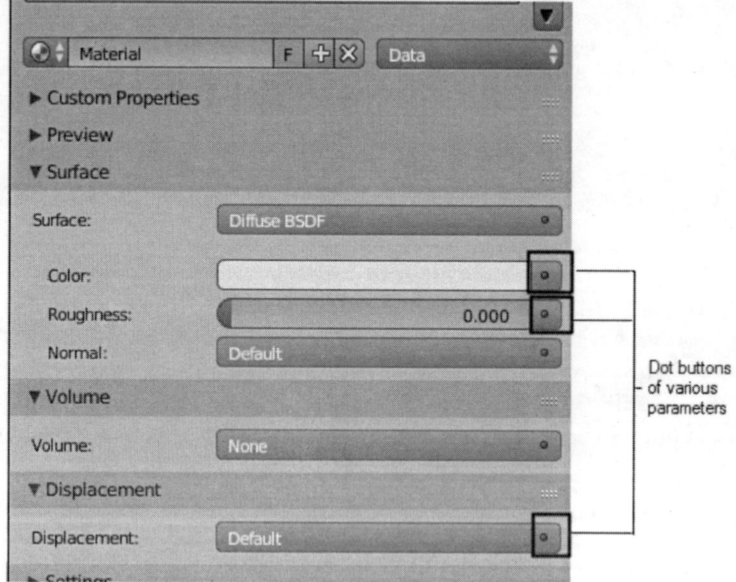

Figure 6-35 Dot buttons in various panels

Choose the desired texture from the flyout; the parameters related to the selected texture will be displayed in **Properties Editor**. You need to set these parameters to achieve the desired texture effect on the object.

You can also use **Node Editor** to apply textures in the Cycles Render engine. This process is discussed in detail in Chapter 7.

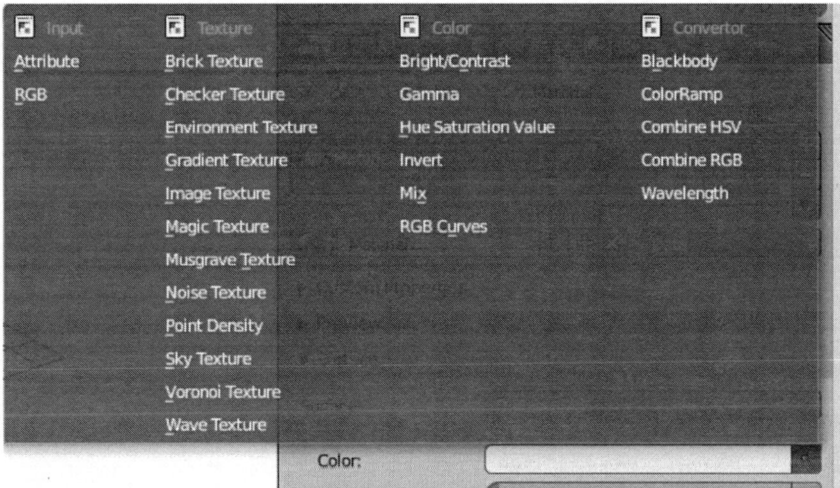

***Figure 6-36** The flyout displayed*

TUTORIALS

Before you start tutorials of this chapter, you need to download *c06_blender_2.79_tut.zip* file from *www.cadcim.com*. The path of the file is as follows: *Textbooks > Animation and Visual Effects > Blender > Blender 2.79 for Digital Artists*

Browse to *\Documents\blender2.79* and create a folder with the name *c06*. Next, extract the content of the zip file in this folder.

Tutorial 1

In this tutorial, you will create an environment by setting a background image and create a water surface, as shown in Figure 6-37. **(Expected time: 20 min)**

***Figure 6-37** The Water surface*

The following steps are required to complete this tutorial:

a. Open and save the File.
b. Create an environment.
c. Create water surface.
d. Save and render the scene.

Opening and Saving the File

1. Choose **File > Open** from **Info Editor**; **File Browser** is displayed.

2. In **File Browser**, browse to *\Documents\blender2.79\c06\c06_tut1_start* and then choose the **Open Blender File** button; the *c06_tut1_start.blend* file is displayed in 3D view, as shown in Figure 6-38.

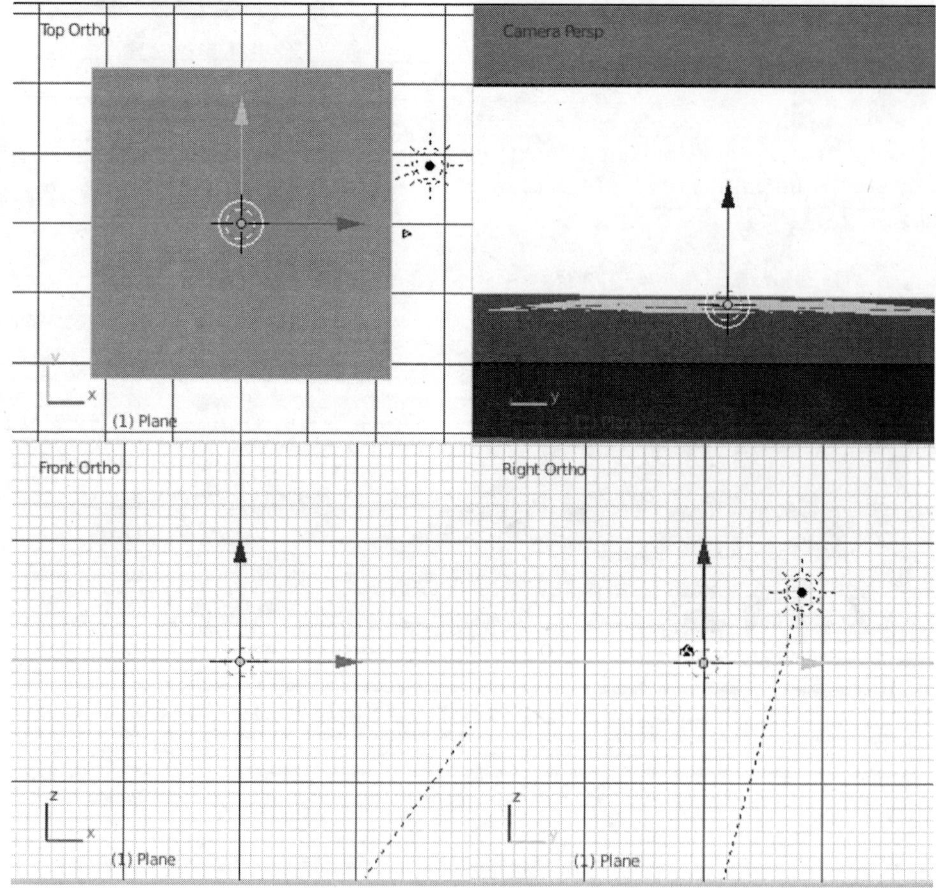

Figure 6-38 *The c06_tut1_start file*

3. Navigate to *\Documents\blender2.79\c06* and create a new folder with the name *c06_tut1*.

4. Choose **File > Save As** from the **Info Editor** menu bar; **File Browser** is displayed.

5. Navigate to *\Documents\blender2.79\c06\c06_tut1* and enter **Water scene** in the **File Name** edit box. Next, choose the **Save Blender File** button to save the file at the specified location.

Creating Environment

In this section, you will create an environment by setting a background image. You will use the Blender Render engine.

1. Choose the **World** button from **Properties Editor**. Next, select the **Paper Sky** and **Blend Sky** check boxes from the **World** panel, refer to Figure 6-39.

***Figure 6-39** Selected check boxes in the **World** panel*

2. Choose the **Texture** button from **Properties Editor**; **Properties Editor** is modified. Choose **New** from **Properties Editor**; new texture is created and added to the **texture** drop-down and to **Texture Stack**. Also, the **New** button is replaced by a text box displaying the name of the newly created texture.

3. Double-click on the **Texture** drop-down and enter **background** to rename the texture.

4. Choose **Open** from the **Image** panel; **File Browser** is displayed. Navigate to *\Documents\blender2.79\c06\c06_tut1* and select **sky.jpg** and choose **Open Image** from **File Browser**.

5. In the **Influence** panel of **Properties Editor**, select the **Horizon** check box. Press F12; the selected image is displayed as background of the scene.

Creating Water Surface

In this section, you will create the water surface by applying modifiers to the plane in the scene and then assign material and texture to it to simulate water effect.

1. Select **Plane** from **Outliner** or 3D View. Note that it is subdivided to achieve desired modifiers effect on it.

2. Choose the **Object modifiers** button from **Properties Editor**. Choose **Displace** from the **Deform** category in the **Add Modifiers** drop-down; the **Displace** modifier is applied

to *Plane* and the parameters for this modifier are displayed in **Properties Editor**, as shown in Figure 6-40.

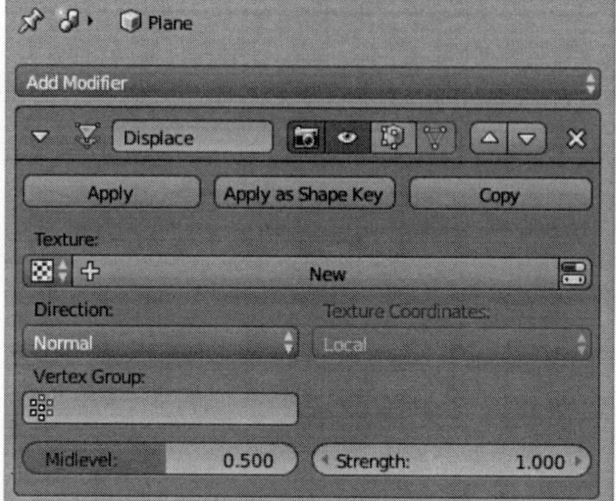

***Figure 6-40** The parameters of the **Displace** modifier*

3. Choose **New** from **Properties Editor**, refer to Figure 6-40; a new texture with the name **Texture** is added to replace the **New** button. Now, choose the **Texture** button from **Properties Editor**; the newly added texture **Texture** is displayed.

4. Choose **Clouds** from the **Type** drop-down. Now, choose the **Object modifiers** button from **Properties Editor** again. Next, enter **0.045** in the **Strength** edit box.

   You will now create material such that *Plane* simulates the water surface.

5. Choose the **Material** button from **Properties Editor**. Next, choose **New** from it; a new material with the name *Material* is created. Rename it as *Water material*.

6. In the **Specular** panel, enter **0.2** in the **Intensity** edit box. Next, choose **Blinn** from the **Specular Shader** drop-down. Also, enter **1.33** in the **IOR** edit box.

7. Select the **Mirror** check box in the **Mirror** panel; the parameters in this panel are activated. Enter **1** in the **Reflectivity** edit box, **0.7** in the **Amount** edit box, and **0.557** in the **Threshold** edit box.

8. Choose the **Texture** button from **Properties Editor**. Next, choose the **New** button; a new texture is added to the **Texture** drop-down. Make sure **Image or Movie** is chosen in the **Type** drop-down.

9. Choose the **Open** button from the **Image** panel; **File Browser** is displayed. Navigate to *\Documents\blender2.79\c06* and select the **sky.jpg** image and choose the **Open Image** button; the selected image is displayed as texture in the **Preview** window of the **preview** panel.

Saving and Rendering the Scene

In this section, you will save the scene that you have created and then render it. You can also view the final rendered image of this model by downloading the *c06_blender_2.79_rndr.zip* file from *www.cadcim.com*. The path of the file is as follows: *Textbooks > Animation and Visual Effects > Blender > Blender 2.79 for Digital Artists*

1. Choose **File > Save** from the **Info Editor** menu bar.

2. Choose the **Render** button from **Properties Editor**. Next, choose the **Render** button from the **Render** panel or press F12; the rendered image is displayed in **UV/Image Editor**; refer to Figure 6-37.

Tutorial 2

In this tutorial, you will create material for hanging lamp, as shown in Figure 6-41,

(Expected time: 20 min)

Figure 6-41 *Hanging lamp with material*

The following steps are required to complete this tutorial:

a. Open and save the file.
b. Create material for inner cover.
c. Create material for outer cover.
d. Create material for hook.
e. Save and render the scene.

Opening and Saving the File

1. Choose **File > Open** from **Info Editor**; **File Browser** is displayed.

2. In **File Browser**, browse to *\Documents\blender2.79\c06\c06_tut1_start.blend* and choose the **Open Blender File** button; the *c06_tut1_start.blend* file is displayed in Camera Persp view, as shown in Figure 6-42.

3. Navigate to *\Documents\blender2.79\c06* and create a new folder with the name *c06_tut1*.

Figure 6-42 The c06_tut1_start file

4. Choose **File > Save As** from the **Info Editor** menu bar; **File Browser** is displayed

5. Navigate to *\Documents\blender2.79\c06\c06_tut1* and enter **Hanging lamp_material** in the **File Name** edit box. Next, choose the **Save Blender File** button to save the file at the specified location.

Creating Material for Wall

In this section, you will first switch over to the Cycles render engine and create material for walls.

1. Choose **Cycles Render** from the **Blender Engine** drop-down.

2. Make sure *wall01* is selected. Next, choose the **Material** button from **Properties Editor**; **Properties Editor** is modified.

3. Choose **New** from **Properties Editor**; a new material with the name **Material** is created. Double-click on **Material** in the Material Stack and enter **wall material** to rename it. Now, choose **Mix Shader** from the **Surface** drop-down in the **Surface** panel, as shown in Figure 6-43; the **Surface** panel is modified, as shown in Figure 6-44.

4. Choose **Diffuse BSDF** from the first **Shader** drop-down;related parameters are displayed below the drop-down. Click on the **Color** swatch and enter **0.3**, **0.35**, and **0.05** in the in the **R**, **G**, and **B** edit boxes, respectively, of the Color window displayed; base color of *wall01* is set to green.

5. Choose **Glossy BSDF** from the second **Shader** drop-down; parameters related to **Glossy BSDF** are displayed below the **Shader** drop-down. Also, choose **Beckmann** from the drop-down located below the second **Shader** drop-down. Click on the **Color** swatch and enter **0.3**, **0.35**, and **0.05** in the in the **R**, **G**, and **B** edit boxes, respectively, of the Color window displayed; glossiness is added to *wall01*.

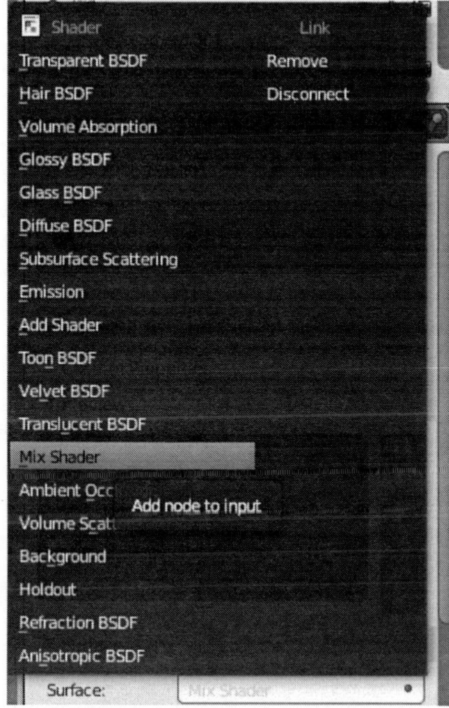

Figure 6-43 *Choosing* ***Mix Shader*** *from the* ***Surface*** *drop-down*

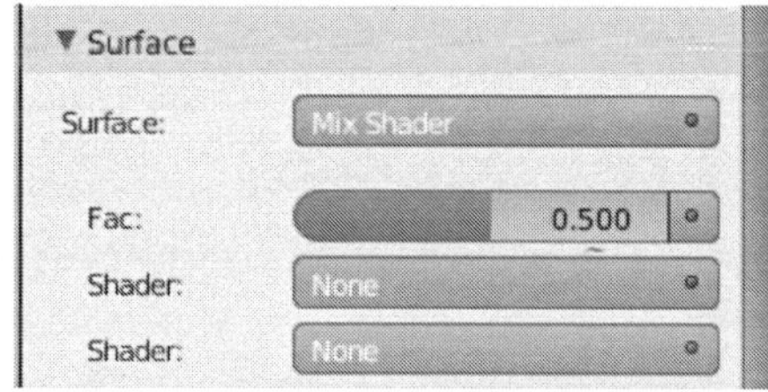

Figure 6-44 *The modified* ***Surface*** *panel*

6. Expand the **Displacement** panel. Choose **Noise Texture** from the **Displacement** drop-down. Next, enter **400** and **15** in the **Scale** and **Detail** sliders, respectively. The Noise texture is added to *wall material.*

   Notice preview of *wall material* in the **Preview** panel.

7. Select *wall02* from **Outliner**. Next, choose the **Material** button from **Properties Editor**. Choose **wall material** from the **Material** drop-down; *wall material* is assigned to *wall02*. Press F12; rendered image of the scene is displayed, as shown in Figure 6-45.

Figure 6-45 *The rendered image*

Creating Material For Outer Lamp Cover

In this section, you will create transparent material for the outer lamp cover using the Cycles Render engine.

1. Select *outer lamp cover* from **Outliner**. Next, choose the **Material** button from **Properties Editor**.

2. Choose **New** from **Properties Editor**; a new material with the name **Material** is created. Double-click on **Material** in the Material Stack and enter **outer lamp cover material** to rename it.

3. Choose **Mix Shader** from the **Surface** drop-down; the **Surface** panel is modified.

4. Choose **Diffuse BSDF** from the first **Shader** drop-down; related parameters are displayed below the drop-down. Click on the **Color** swatch and enter **0.8**, **0.8**, and **0.1** in the in the **R**, **G**, and **B** edit boxes, respectively, of the Color window displayed; base color of *outer lamp cover* is set to yellow.

5. Choose **Glossy BSDF** from the second **Shader** drop-down; related parameters are displayed below the drop-down. Also, choose **Beckmann** from the drop-down located below the second **Shader** drop-down. Click on the **Color** swatch and enter **0.8**, **0.8**, and **0.1** in the in the **R**, **G**, and **B** edit boxes, respectively, of the Color window displayed; glossiness is added to *outer lamp cover*.

6. Press F12; a rendered image of the scene is displayed, as shown in Figure 6-46.

Creating Material for Inner Lamp Cover

In this section, you will create transparent material for the inner lamp cover using the Cycles Render engine.

1. Select *inner lamp cover* from **Outliner**. Next, choose the **Material** button from **Properties Editor**.

Figure 6-46 *The rendered image*

2. Choose **New** from **Properties Editor**; a new material with the name **Material** is created. Double-click on **Material** in the Material Stack and enter **inner lamp cover material** to rename it.

3. Choose **Transparent BSDF** from the **Surface** drop-down in the **Surface** panel; the **Surface** panel is modified, as shown in Figure 6-47.

Figure 6-47 *The **Surface** panel for the **Transparent BSDF** shader*

4. Click on the **Color** swatch and enter **0.85, 0.75,** and **0.45** in the **R, G,** and **B** edit boxes, respectively, of the Color window displayed; color of *inner lamp cover* is set to transparent yellow shade. Figure 6-48 shows the rendered image.

Creating Material for Hook

In this section, you will create the metal material for hook.

1. Select *hook_part1* from **Outliner**. Next, choose the **Material** button from **Properties Editor**.

Figure 6-48 *The rendered image*

2. Choose **New** from **Properties Editor**; a new material with the name **Material** is created. Double-click on **Material** in the Material Stack and enter **metal material** to rename it.

3. Choose **Mix Shader** from the **Surface** drop-down; the **Surface** panel is modified.

4. Choose **Glossy BSDF** from the first **Shader** drop-down ; parameters related to **Glossy BSDF** are displayed below the **Shader** drop-down.

5. Choose **Beckmann** from the drop-down located below the first **Shader drop-down**.

6. Choose the Dot button located next to the **Color** swatch and choose **Color Ramp** from the flyout displayed;related parameters are displayed below the drop-down, as shown in Figure 6-49.

7. Click on the first color stop, refer to Figure 6-49. Next, choose the color swatch located below it; the Color Window is displayed. Enter **1** in the **R, G,** and **B** edit boxes; color of the first color stop is changed to white.

8. Click on the second color stop. Next, choose the color swatch located below it; the Color Window is displayed. Enter **0** in the **R, G,** and **B** edit boxes; color of the first color stop is

changed to black. Also, enter **0.273** in the **Position** edit box; the second color stop position is changed, as shown in Figure 6-50.

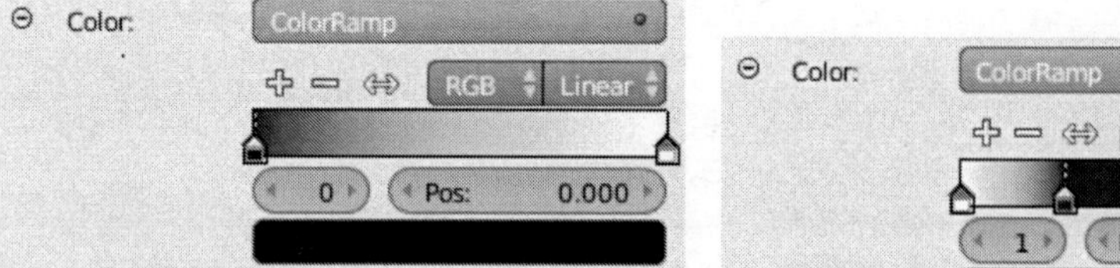

Figure 6-49 *Parameters related to* ***Color Ramp***

Figure 6-50 *Position of second color stop changed*

9. Choose the Dot button next to **Fac**; a flyout is displayed. Choose **Facing** from it. Next, enter **0.850** in the **Blend** edit box located below **Fac**.

10. Choose **Glossy BSDF** from the second **Shader** drop-down; related parameters are displayed below the drop-down.

11. Choose the Dot button located next to the **Color** swatch and choose **Image Texture** from the flyout displayed. Next, choose **Open**; **File Browser** is displayed. Navigate to *\Documents\blender2.79\c06\c06_tut2* and select **metal.jpg** from it and then choose **Open Image** button from **File Browser**.

12. Select *hook_part2* from **Outliner**. Next, choose the **Material** button from **Properties Editor.** and then choose **metal material** from the **Material** drop-down; *metal material* is assigned to *hook_part2*.

13. Select *hook_part3* and *hook_part4* one by one and assign *metal material* to them as done in step 12.

Saving and Rendering the Scene

In this section, you will save the scene that you have created and then render it. You can also view the final rendered image of this model by downloading the *c06_blender_2.79_rndr.zip* file from *www.cadcim.com.* The path of the file is as follows: *Textbooks > Animation and Visual Effects > Blender > Blender 2.79 for Digital Artists*

1. Choose **File > Save** from the **Info Editor** menu bar.

2. Choose the **Render** button from **Properties Editor**. Next, choose the **Render** button from the **Render** panel or press F12; the rendered image is displayed in the **UV/Image Editor**; refer to Figure 6-41.

Self-Evaluation Test

Answer the following questions and then compare them to those given at the end of this chapter:

1. Which of the following buttons is used to render only the edges of an object?

   (a) **Surface** (b) **Wire**
   (c) **Halo** (d) **Volume**

2. The __________ engine is the default render engine in Blender.

3. The __________ engine is used to render photorealistic render images.

4. In Blender, you can assign multiple materials to a single object. (T/F)

5. In Blender, you need to assign a material to an object before applying texture to it. (T/F)

Review Questions

Answer the following questions:

1. Which of the following shaders is used to achieve non-photorealistic material used in cartoon style rendering.

   (a) **Lambert** (b) **Oren Nayer**
   (c) **Toon** (d) **Fresnel**

2. The __________ button in **Properties Editor** is used to create a fake user for a material.

3. Choose __________ from the **Viewport Shading** drop-down in **3D View Editor** to display material in 3D view.

4. If a material is removed from an object, it will also be removed from the **Material** drop-down. (T/F)

5. The options displayed on choosing the __________ button in **Properties Editor** are used to set background for a scene.

EXERCISES

Exercise 1

Create a model of a tea cup and a floor. Next, create copper material for the tea cup and apply floor texture of your choice to the floor, refer to Figure 6-51. **(Expected time: 15 min)**

***Figure 6-51** The model of a tea cup with copper material and a floor with a texture*

Exercise 2

Create a scene as shown in Figure 6-52. Next, create steel material for cups, glass material for glasses, and a brick texture for walls, refer to Figure 6-52. **(Expected time: 15 min)**

***Figure 6-52** Scene with materials and textures applied*

Answers to Self-Evaluation Test

1. b, **2.** Blender Render, **3.** Cycles Render, **4.** T, **5.** T

Chapter 7

Working with Materials - II

Learning Objectives

After completing this chapter, you will be able to:

- *Use Node Editor to create various materials*
- *Use Node Editor to apply various textures*
- *Use the Vertex Paint mode*
- *Understand UV unwrapping techniques*
- *Use the Texture Paint mode*

INTRODUCTION

In chapter 6, you learned in detail about applying materials and textures to objects using the parameters in **Properties Editor**. In this chapter, you will learn to create and modify materials and apply textures using **Node Editor**. You will also learn to unwrap objects and use the **Vertex Paint** and **Texture Paint** modes to apply textures.

NODE EDITOR

Node Editor is not displayed by default in the Blender interface. To display it, choose **Compositing** from the **Screen Layout** drop-down in **Info Editor**, as shown in Figure 7-1; default blender interface will change to a Compositing layout, as shown in Figure 7-2. The Compositing layout consists of **Node Editor, UV/Image Editor, 3D View Editor** with the Camera Persp view, and **Properties Editor**.

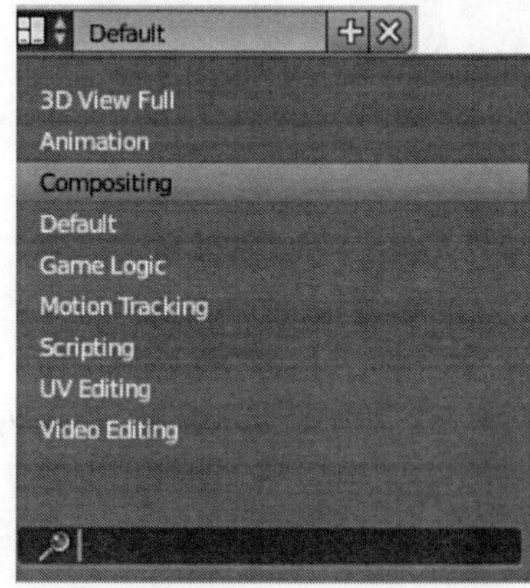

***Figure 7-1** Choosing **Compositing** from the **Screen Layout** drop-down*

The advantage of using the Compositing layout over the default layout is that you can have a scene in Camera Perspective view, node flow, properties of the selected nodes and objects, and rendered image displayed side by side in one screen. Three types of nodes can be created in **Node Editor**: material nodes, texture nodes, and composite nodes. You need to create a node tree of material nodes to create and modify material. Similarly, you need to create a node tree of texture nodes to apply texture to an object. In the next section, you will learn to create material and then apply texture to the object using **Node Editor** and the Cycles Render engine.

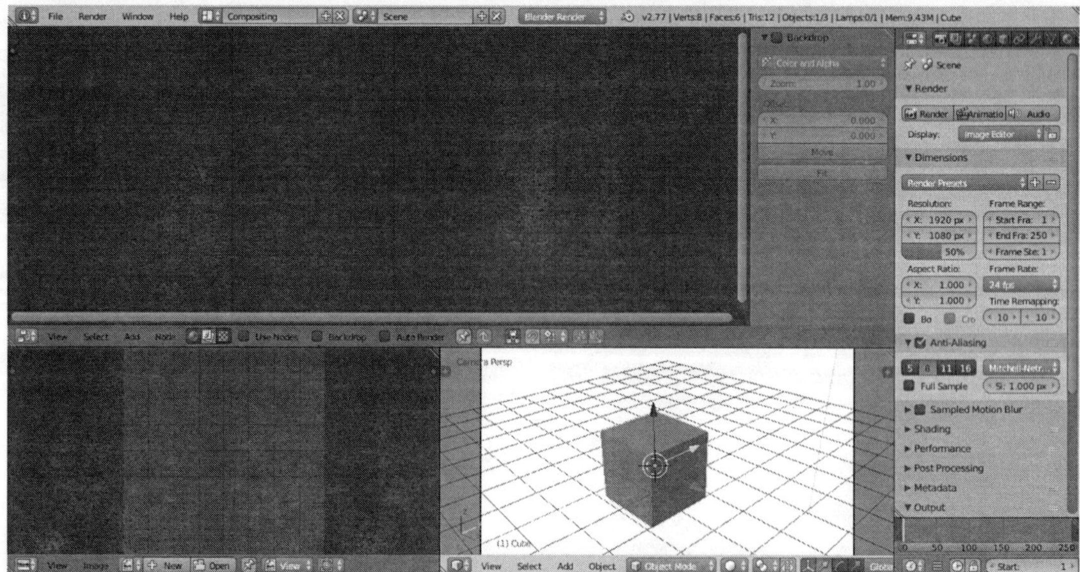

***Figure 7-2** The Compositing layout*

Note

*If you want to retain default Blender interface and use **Node Editor** in it, choose **Node Editor** from the **Editor Type** drop-down of **Timeline**, refer to Figure 7-3.*

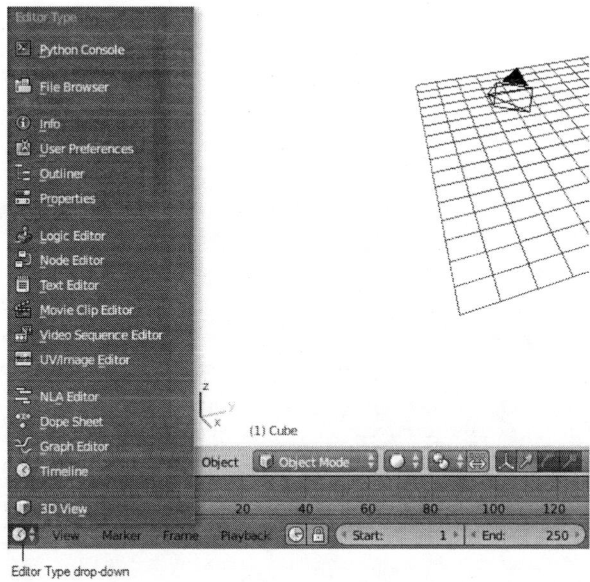

Figure 7-3 The ***Editor Type*** *drop-down*

Creating Materials and Applying Textures Using Node Editor

To create a material using **Node Editor**, follow the steps given next:

1. Choose **Cycles Render** from the **Engine** drop-down.

2. Choose **Compositing** from the **Screen Layout** drop-down in **Info Editor**, default, Blender interface will change into the Compositing layout, refer to Figure 7-2. Figure 7-4 shows components of **Node Editor**.

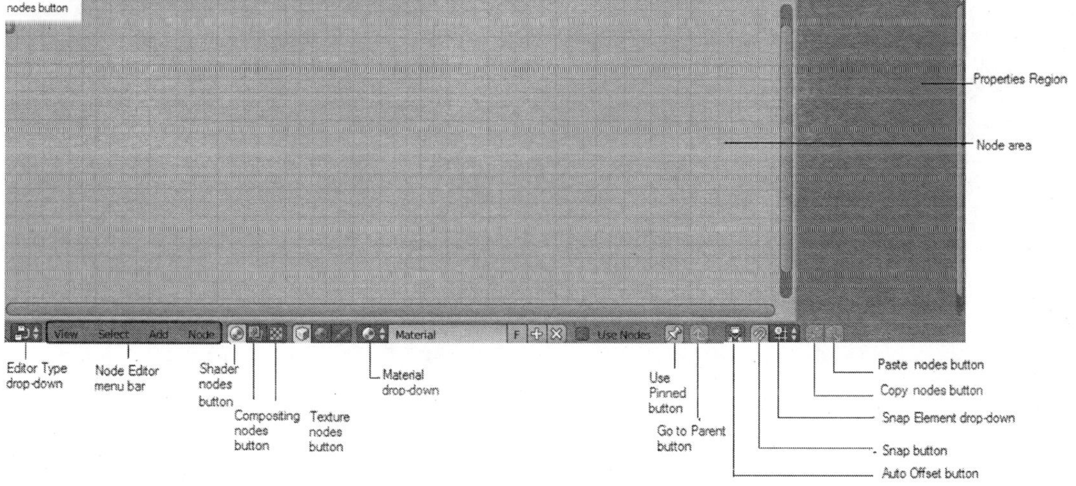

Figure 7-4 Components of ***Node Editor***

3. Make sure the **Shader nodes** button is chosen in **Node Editor**. Select the **Use Nodes** check box; the **Diffuse BSDF** and **Material Output** nodes will be added to **Node Editor**, as shown in Figure 7-5.

Note

*1. **Node Editor** has **Properties Region** on its right. By default, **Properties Region** is empty. As you create nodes and select a node from the node tree, properties of that node and some settings related to **Node Editor** are displayed in **Properties Region**. You can toggle the display of **Properties Region** by pressing N.*

*2. **Node Editor** has **Toolshelf** on its left. By default, **Toolshelf** is not displayed. To display it, hover the cursor over the **+** sign on the left and drag the cursor toward right or press T; **Toolshelf** will be displayed with a number of tabs for creating various nodes. The **Grease Pencil** tab is chosen by default in **Toolshelf**, refer to Figure 7-5.*

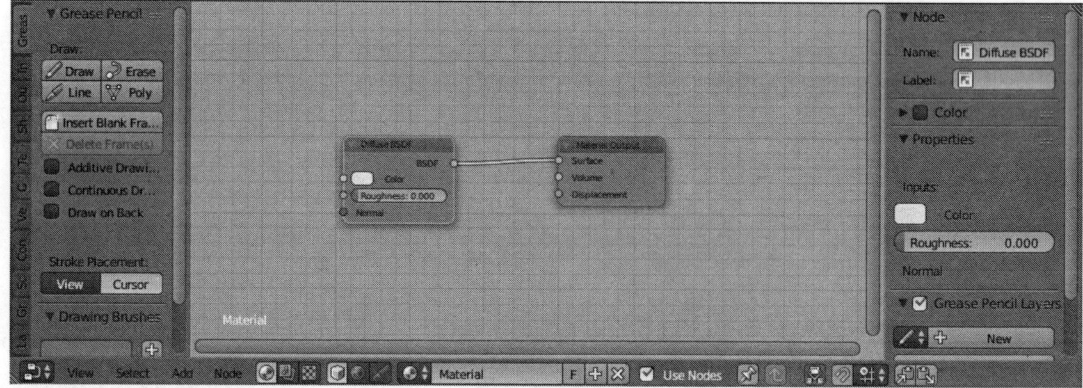

***Figure 7-5** The **Material** and **Output** nodes added to **Node Editor** with the **Material** node selected*

4. To add more nodes, hover the cursor in the Node area and press SHIFT + A; the **Add** menu will be displayed, as shown in Figure 7-6. The **Add** menu has all the node types. Hover the cursor on the desired node type; a cascading menu will be displayed, refer to Figure 7-7. Next, choose desired node from the cascading menu; the chosen node will be attached to the cursor. Next, place it at a point in the Node area.

Note

*The node types in the **Add** menu can also be accessed from the **Add** menu of the **Node Editor** menu bar.*

5. Add all the desired nodes and connect their input and output points to each other as per requirement.

6. To add texture, hover the cursor in the Node area and press SHIFT + A. Next, choose **Texture** from the **Add** menu displayed. Choose the desired texture type from the cascading menu displayed, refer to Figure 7-8.

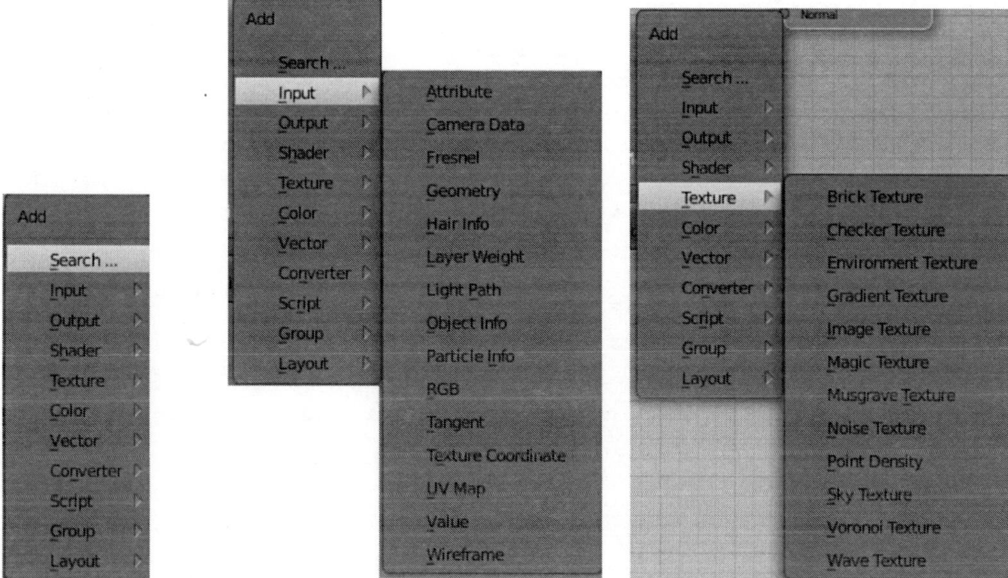

***Figure 7-6** The **Add** menu* ***Figure 7-7** The cascading menu* ***Figure 7-8** The cascading menu*

VERTEX PAINT MODE

The **Vertex Paint** mode is used to paint vertices of an object using brush. It is mainly used when you need to have multicolored material on the object, refer to Figure 7-9. To activate the **Vertex Paint** mode, choose the **Vertex Paint** option from the **Mode** drop-down. Alternatively, activate the pie menu and press the TAB key; the **Mode** pie menu will be displayed. Press 7 or choose the **Vertex Paint** mode from the pie menu. The procedure to activate pie menus is discussed in Chapter 1.

***Figure 7-9** The multicolored cube*

Note

*You can also press V to switch to the **Vertex Paint** mode from **Object Mode**.*

As you switch to the **Vertex Paint** mode, a red circle will be attached to the cursor and all the menus in the **3D View Editor** menu bar will change except the **View** menu. Also, various panels related to vertex painting such as the **Brush**, **Texture**, and **Stroke** will be displayed in **Toolshelf** of the **Tools** tab, refer to Figure 7-10. Also, if you choose the **Options** tab in **Toolshelf**, the **Overlay**, **Appearance**, and **Options** panels will be displayed, as shown in Figure 7-11. You need to set the parameters in these panels and then apply brush strokes on the surface of the object in the **Vertex Paint** mode. These panels are similar to the panels in **Sculpt Mode** and are discussed in Chapter 5. The parameters in the **Brush** panel are discussed next.

Brush Panel

As the name suggests, the options in the **Brush** panel are used to set the parameters of a brush to be used for vertex painting. Figure 7-12 shows the options in the **Brush** panel. The type of brush is specified at the top in the **Brush** panel with its image and name. By default, the name and image of the **Draw** brush is displayed. To change the brush type, click on a current brush type image; a flyout will be displayed, as shown in Figure 7-13. Choose the desired brush type from the flyout; the name and the image of the brush type chosen will be displayed in the **Brush** panel.

*Figure 7-10 The panels in the **Tools** tab*

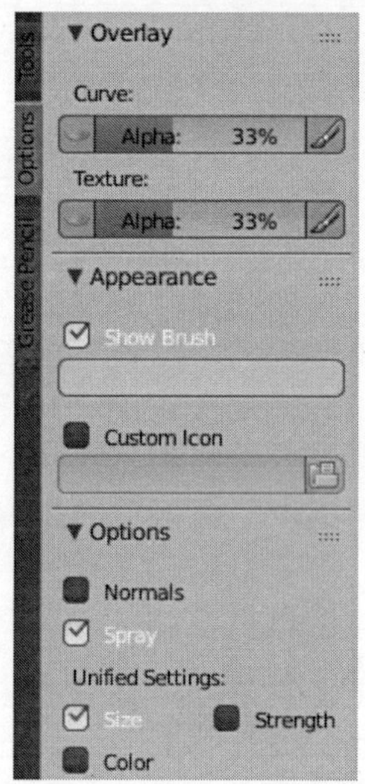

*Figure 7-11 The panels in the **Options** tab*

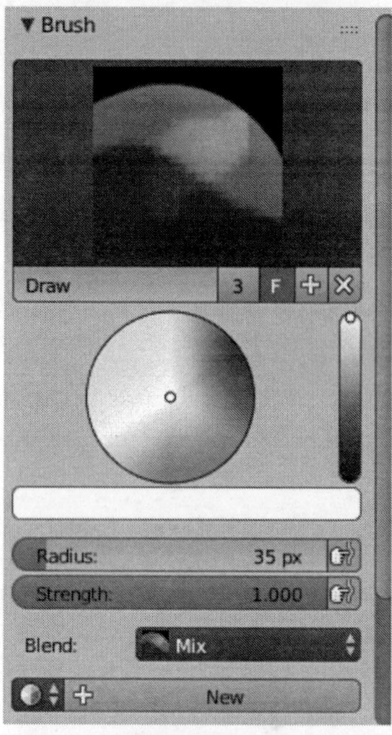

*Figure 7-12 The options in the **Brush** panel*

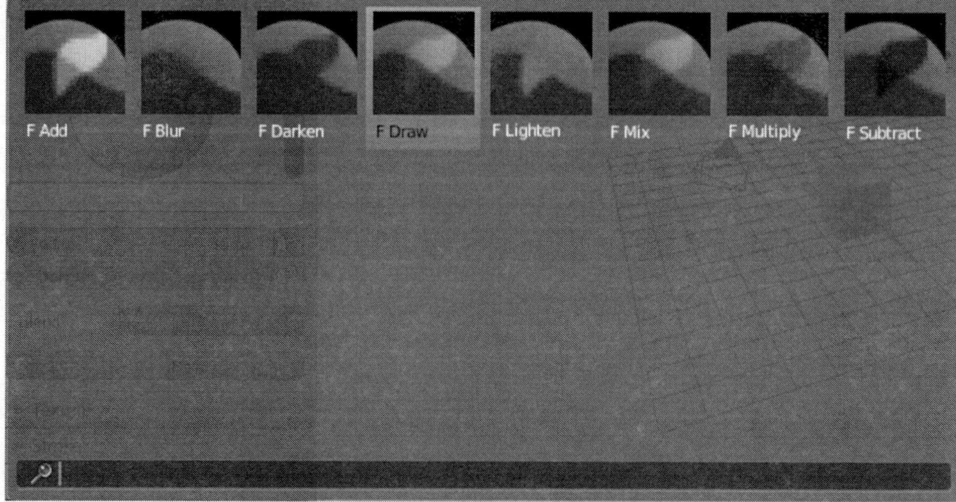

Figure 7-13 The flyout displayed

You can change the radius and strength of the brush using the **Radius** and **Strength** sliders, respectively. The options in the **Blend** drop-down are used to blend, add, or subtract the selected color with the underlying color and to lighten, darken, or blur the vertex colors of the object.

Rendering of a Vertex Painted Object

If you are using the Blender Render engine, make sure the vertex painted object is selected. Choose the **Material** button from **Properties Editor** and then choose **New** to create a new material for the object. Next, select the **Vertex Color Paint** check box in the **Options** panel. Now, press F12 to render the vertex painted objects. Note that same material is to be assigned to all the vertex painted objects in a scene.

If you are using the Cycles Render engine then after painting the object in the **Vertex Paint** mode, you need to switch to the Compositing layout. Next, make sure the object in the scene is selected. Now, select the **Use Nodes** check box in **Node Editor** and press SHIFT+A. Choose **Input > Attribute** from the menu displayed; the **Attribute** node will be added to **Node Editor**. Connect the **Color** output of the **Attribute** node to the **Color** input of the **Diffuse BSDF** node and enter **Col** in the text box of the **Attribute** node. Note that you need to follow this process for each painted object using the **Vertex Paint** mode. Now, press F12; the rendered image will be displayed in **UV/Image Editor**.

Note

***Col** is the default name of the vertex color layer. If you want to rename it, choose the **Object Data** button from **Properties Editor**. Next, double-click on **Col** in the **Vertex Colors** panel.*

UV UNWRAPPING AND TEXTURE PAINT MODE

If the geometry of object is complex or if you want to put multiple textures on object, you need to unwrap the object. The UVs of unwrapped object are displayed in **UV/Image Editor**. You can then paint the UVs in **UV/Image Editor** to create the desired texture.

The **Texture Paint** mode is used to paint the surface of an object in **3D view Editor** or in **UV/Image Editor**. You can also load an external image to **UV/Image Editor** and then edit it by painting it in **3D view Editor** or in **UV/Image Editor**. This modified image can be used as a texture for the object. To activate the **Texture Paint** mode, choose the **Texture Paint** option from the **Mode** drop-down. Alternatively, activate the pie menu and then press the TAB key; the **Mode** pie menu will be displayed. Press 1 or choose the **Texture Paint** mode from the pie menu.

The steps for creating texture using the unwrapping technique and the **Texture Paint** mode in the Cycles Render engine are similar and are discussed next.

1. Select the object. Switch to **Edit Mode** and make sure the whole object is highlighted. Next, choose the **Shading/UVs** tab from **Toolshelf**; the **Shading** and **UVs** panels will be displayed in **Toolshelf**, refer to Figure 7-14.

2. Choose an option from the **UV Mapping** drop-down depending on the geometry of the object, refer to Figure 7-15.

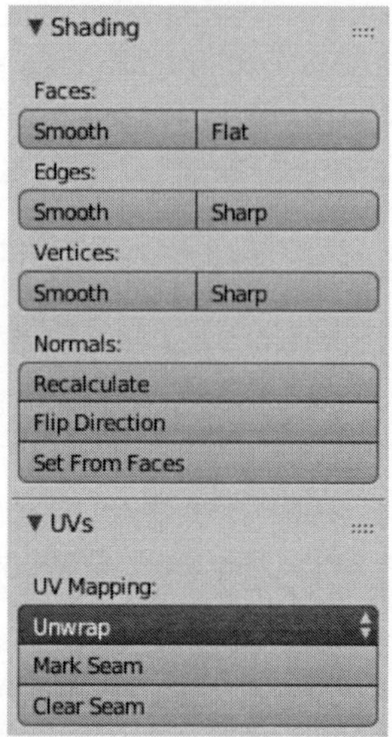

*Figure 7-14 The **Shading** and **UVs** panel in **Toolshelf***

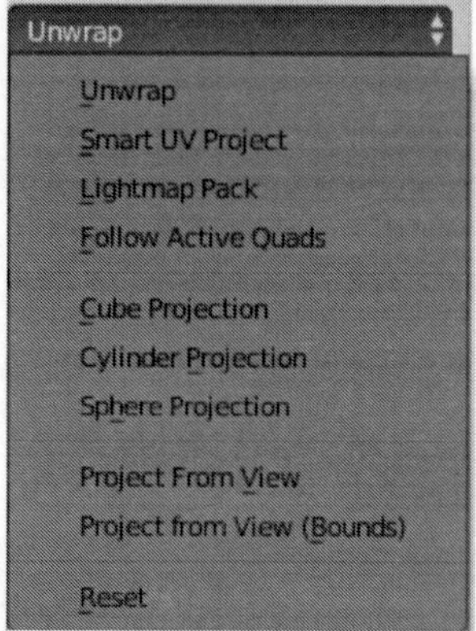

*Figure 7-15 Options in the **UV Mapping** drop-down*

3. Choose **Compositing** from the **Screen Layout** drop-down in **Info Editor**; the unwrapped geometry of the object will be displayed in **UV/Image Editor**.

4. Choose **New** from **UV/Image Editor**; the **New Image** window will be displayed, as shown in Figure 7-16. Enter desired name in the **Name** text box and choose **OK** in the **New Image** window.

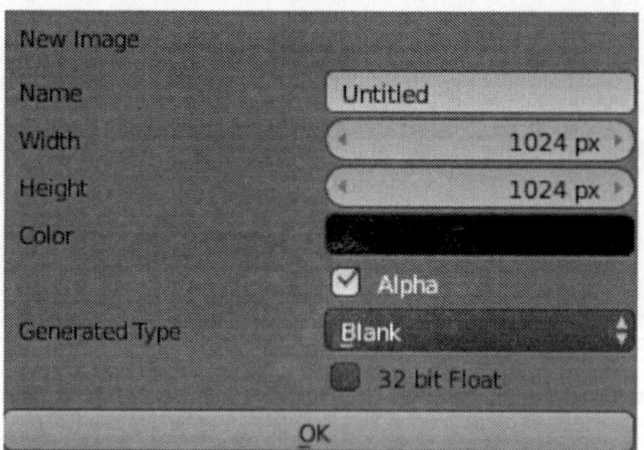

*Figure 7-16 The **New Image** window*

5. Hover the cursor in **UV/Image Editor** and press T; **Toolshelf** of **UV/Image Editor** will be displayed. You will notice that various panels are displayed in **Toolshelf** to paint UVs of the object.

6. Choose the **Shader Nodes** button from **Node Editor**. Next, select the **Use Nodes** button; two default nodes will be displayed in the Node area. Hover the cursor in the Node area and press Shift + A; the **Add** menu will be displayed. Choose **Texture > Image Texture** from the menu; the **Image Texture** node will be attached to the cursor. Place it in **Node Editor**. Connect the **Color** output of the **Image Texture** node to the **Color** input of the **Diffuse BSDF** node.

7. Paint the UVs as desired in **UV/Image Editor**.

   You need to follow step 8 only if you are creating texture using the **Texture Paint** mode.

8. Choose **Texture Paint** from the **Mode** drop-down in **3D View Editor**. Now, paint on the object surface in 3D View.

9. Choose **Image > Save as Image** from the **UV/Image Editor** menu bar to save the changes in the image; **File Browser** will be displayed. Navigate to the desired location and save the image.

10. Choose **Open** from the **Image Texture** node; **File Browser** will be displayed. Browse to the location where the painted image is saved and select the image. You will notice that the painted image is used as a texture for the object. Press F12; the rendered image of the object will be visible in **UV/Image Editor**.

    You can also paint the object in 3D view using the options in **Toolshelf**. After painting, follow the next step.

11. Save the image again in **UV/Image Editor**. Next, choose the **Open Image** from the **Image Texture** node and select the updated image from **File Browser**. Next, press F12 to view the rendered image.

TUTORIALS

Before you start tutorials of this chapter, you need to download *c07_blender_2.79_tut.zip* file from *www.cadcim.com*. The path of the file is as follows: *Textbooks > Animation and Visual Effects > Blender > Blender 2.79 for Digital Artists*

Browse to *\Documents\blender2.79* and create a folder with the name *c07*. Next, extract the content of the zip file in this folder.

Tutorial 1

In this tutorial, you will create material for the center table and glass, as shown in Figure 7-17. **(Expected time: 20 min)**

Figure 7-17 *Textured center table and glass*

The following steps are required to complete this tutorial:

a. Open and Save the file.
b. Create material for top.
c. Create material for legs and rings.
d. Create material for glass.
e. Save and render the scene.

Opening and Saving the File

1. Choose **File > Open** from **Info Editor**; **File Browser** is displayed.

2. In **File Browser**, browse to*\Documents\blender2.79\c07\c07_tut1_start* and then choose the **Open Blender File** button; the *c07_tut1_start.blend* file is displayed in Camera Persp view, as shown in Figure 7-18.

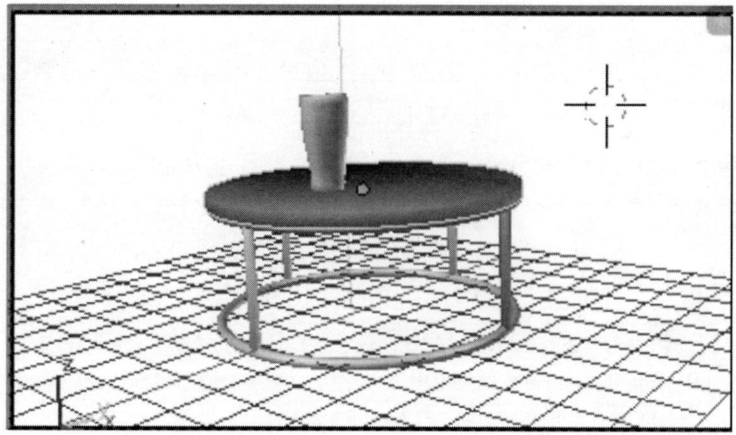

Figure 7-18 *The c07_tut1_start file*

3. Navigate to *\Documents\blender2.79\c07* and create a new folder with the name *c07_tut1*.

4. Choose **File > Save As** from the **Info Editor** menu bar; **File Browser** is displayed.

5. Navigate to *\Documents\blender2.79\c07\c07_tut1* and enter **center table_material** in the **File Name** edit box. Next, choose the **Save Blender File** button to save the file at the specified location.

Creating Material for Top

In this section, you will create material for top of the center table using **Node Editor**.

1. Choose **Compositing** from the **Screen Layout** drop-down; the layout is changed. Select *top* from 3D View.

2. Choose the **Shader nodes** button in **Node Editor**. Next, select *top* from 3D View. 

3. Choose **New** from **Node Editor**; a new material is created and the **Diffuse BSDF** and **Material**

Output nodes are displayed in **Node Editor**. Enter **wood Material** in the text box located on the left of the **Material** drop-down in **Node Editor**.

4. Hover the cursor in **Node Editor** and press SHIFT+A; the **Add** menu is displayed. Choose **Texture > Image Texture** from the menu; the **Image Texture** node is attached to the cursor. Place this node on the left of the **Diffuse BSDF** node.

5. Choose **Open** from the **Image Texture** node; **File Browser** is displayed. Navigate to *\Documents\blender2.79\c07\c07_tut1* and select **wood.jpg** from it and then choose **Open Image** button from **File Browser**; the **Open** button in the **Image Texture** node is replaced by *wood.jpg*.

6. Connect the **Color** output of the **Image Texture** node with the **Color** input of the **Diffuse BSDF** node, as shown in Figure 7-19.

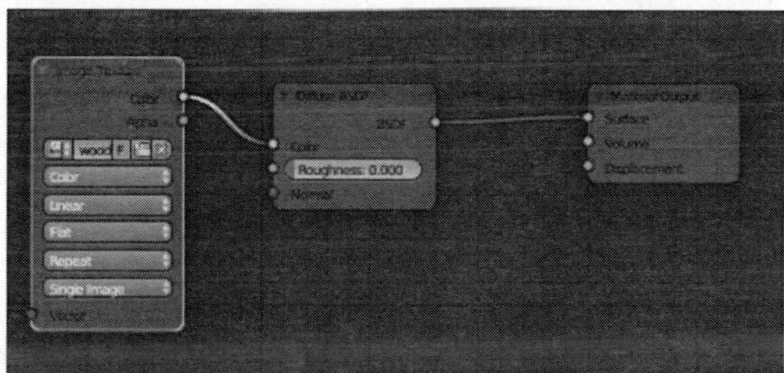

Figure 7-19 *Connected* ***Image Texture*** *node and* ***Diffuse BSDF*** *node displayed*

7. Hover the cursor in **Node Editor** and press SHIFT+A; the **Add** menu is displayed. Choose **Vector > Mapping** from the menu; the **Mapping** node is attached to the cursor. Place this node in between the **Image Texture** node and the **Diffuse BSDF** node such that the **Vector** input of the **Mapping** node is connected to the **Color** output of the **Image Texture** node and the **Vector** output of the **Mapping** node is connected to the **Color** input of the **Diffuse BSDF** node.

Note

To preview the material being created, choose the ***Material*** *button from* ***Properties Editor****. Next, expand the* ***Preview*** *panel.*

8. Hover the cursor in **Node Editor** and press SHIFT+A; the **Add** menu is displayed. Choose **Input > Texture Coordinate** from the menu; the **Texture Coordinate** node is attached to the cursor. Place this node on the left of the **Image Texture** node.

9. Connect the **Generated** output of the **Texture Coordinate** node to the **Vector** input of the **Image Texture** node.

10. Select the **Image Texture** node and press Ctrl+C. Next, press CTRL +V; Copy of the **Image Texture** node is created at the same place as that of the original **Image Texture** node. Place the copy of the **Image Texture** node at the bottom in **Node Editor**.

11. Hover the cursor in **Node Editor** and press SHIFT+A; the **Add** menu is displayed. Choose **Vector > Bump** from the menu; the **Bump** node is attached to the cursor. Place this node on the right of the copied **Image Texture** node.

12. Connect the **Color** output of the copied node to the **Height** input of the **Bump** node. Also connect the **Normal** output of the **Bump** node to the **Normal** input of the **Diffuse BSDF** node.

13. Hover the cursor in **Node Editor** and press SHIFT+A; the **Add** menu is displayed. Choose **Shader > Glossy BSDF** from the menu; the **Glossy BSDF** node is attached to the cursor. Place this node on the right of the **Bump** node.

14. Hover the cursor in **Node Editor** and press SHIFT+A; the **Add** menu is displayed. Choose **Shader > Mix Shader** from the menu; the **Mix Shader** node is attached to the cursor. Place this node on the right of the **Glossy BSDF** node.

15. Connect the **BSDF** output of the **Diffuse BSDF** node to the first **Shader** input of the **Mix Shader** node. Also, connect the **BSDF** output of the **Glossy BSDF** node to the second **Shader** input of the **Mix Shader** node. Enter **0.1** in the **Fac** slider of the **Mix Shader** node.

16. Connect the **Shader** output of the **Mix Shader** node to the **Surface** output of the **Material Output** node. Figure 7-20 shows the node flow for *wood material* applied to *top*.

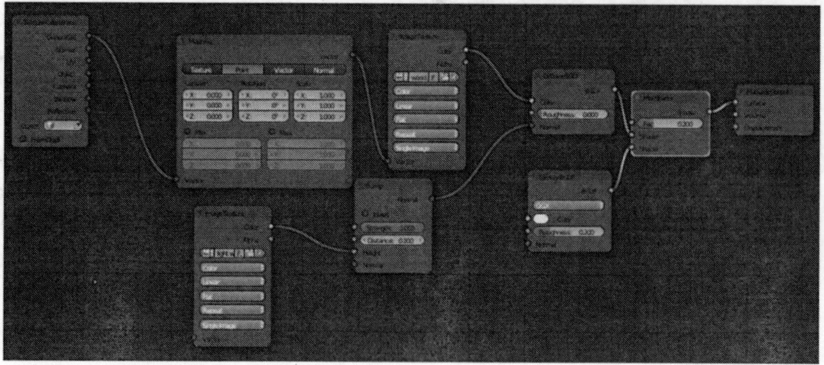

***Figure 7-20** Node flow for the wood material*

17. Press F12; center table is displayed with *wood material* applied to its top, refer to Figure 7-21.

***Figure 7-21** The rendered image*

Creating Material for Legs and Rings

In this section you will create metal material for the legs and rings of center table.

1. Make sure the **Shader nodes** button is chosen in **Node editor**. Next, select *upper ring* from Camera Persp View. 

2. Choose **New** from **Node Editor**; a new material is created and the **Diffuse BSDF** and **Material Output** nodes are displayed in **Node Editor**. Enter **metal material** in the text box located on the left of the **Material** drop-down in **Node Editor**.

3. Hover the cursor in **Node Editor** and press SHIFT+A; the **Add** menu is displayed. Choose **Texture > Image Texture** from the menu; the **Image Texture** node is attached to the cursor. Place this node on the left of the **Diffuse BSDF** node.

4. Choose **Open** from the **Image Texture** node; **File Browser** is displayed. Navigate to *\Documents\blender2.79\c07\c07_tut1* and select **metal.jpg** from it and then choose **Open Image** button from **File Browser**; the **Open** button in the **Image Texture** node is replaced by *metal.jpg*.

5. Connect the **Color** output of the **Image Texture** node with the **Color** input of the **Diffuse BSDF** node.

6. Hover the cursor in **Node Editor** and press SHIFT+A; the **Add** menu is displayed. Choose **Shader > Glossy BSDF** from the menu; the **Glossy BSDF** node is attached to the cursor. Place this node below the **Diffuse BSDF** node.

7. Hover the cursor in **Node Editor** and press SHIFT+A; the **Add** menu is displayed. Choose **Shader > Mix Shader** from the menu; the **Mix Shader** node is attached to the cursor. Place this node on the right of the **Glossy BSDF** node. Choose **Beckmann** from the drop-down in the **Glossy BSDF** node.

8. Connect the **BSDF** output of the **Diffuse BSDF** node to the first **Shader** input of the **Mix Shader** node. Also, connect the **BSDF** output of the **Glossy BSDF** node to the second **Shader** input of the **Mix Shader** node.

9. Hover the cursor in **Node Editor** and press SHIFT+A; the **Add** menu is displayed. Choose **Input > Layer weight** from the menu; the **Layer Weight** node is attached to the cursor. Place this node above the **Diffuse BSDF** node.

10. Connect the **Facing** output of the **Layer Weight** node to the **Fac** input of the **Mix Shader** node. Figure 7-22 shows the node flow for *metal material.*

11. Select *lower ring* from Camera Persp view. Choose **metal material** from the **Material** drop-down; *metal material* is applied to *lower ring.*

12. Select *leg1*, *leg2*, *leg3*, and *leg4* from Camera Persp view one by one and apply *metal material* to them as done in step 12.

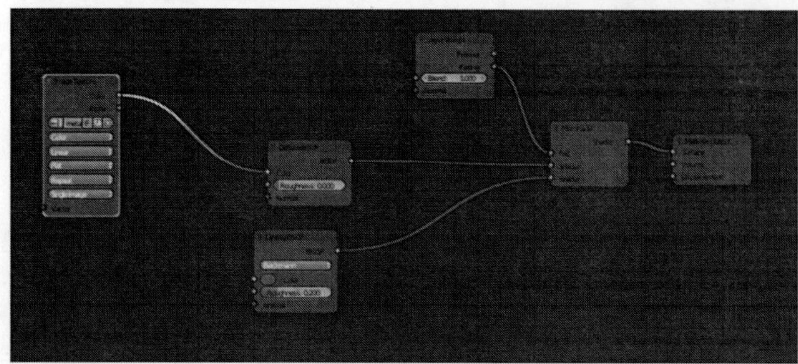

Figure 7-22 Node flow for metal material

13. Press F12; center table is displayed with *wood material* and *metal material* applied, refer to Figure 7-23.

Figure 7-23 The rendered image

Creating Material for Glass

In this section, you will create material for glass using the **UV/Image Editor**.

1. Choose the **X** button from **UV/Image Editor**. Next, choose **Default** from the **Screen Layout** drop-down; default layout is displayed.

2. Select *glass* from Camera Persp view. Switch to **Edit Mode**. Next, choose the **Face Select** button. Make sure all the faces of *glass* are selected.

3. Choose **Shading/UVs** tab from **Toolshelf**; the **Shading** and **UVs** panels are displayed in **Toolshelf**.

4. Choose **Smart UV Project** from the **UV Mapping** drop-down in the **UVs** panel, refer to Figure 7-24; the **Smart UV Project** window is displayed, as shown in Figure 7-25.

5. Enter **0.25** in the **Island Margin** edit box and choose **OK** to close the **Smart UV Project** window.

Note

*The amount in the **Island Margin** edit box is used to provide space between the UVs displayed in **UV/Image Editor**.*

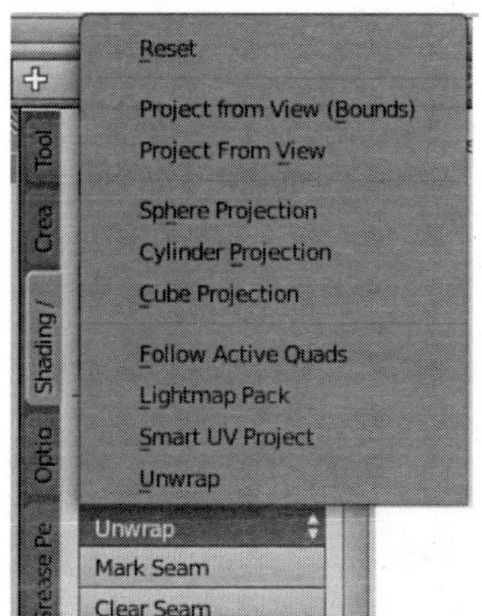

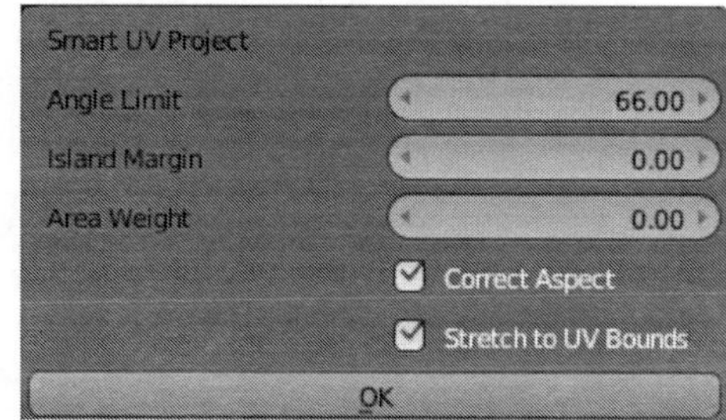

*Figure 7-24 The **UV Mapping** drop-down* *Figure 7-25 The **Smart UV Project** window*

6. Switch to the **Compositing** layout again. You will notice the UVs of *glass* displayed in **UV/ Image Editor,** refer to Figure 7-26.

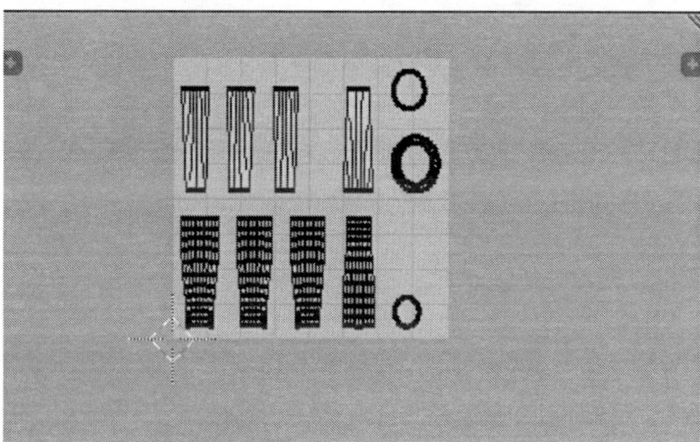

Figure 7-26 UVs of glass

7. Choose **New** from **UV/Image Editor**; the **New Image** window is displayed, as shown in Figure 7-27. Enter **glasspaint** in the **Name** text box and choose **OK** to close the window.

   You will notice black background for the UVs in **UV/Image Editor**. Also, the *glasspaint* image name is displayed in the edit box of **UV/Image Editor**.

8. Choose **Paint** from the **Mode** drop-down of **UV/Image Editor**, refer to Figure 7-28. Next, hover the cursor in **UV/Image Editor** and press T; various panels are displayed in **Toolshelf**.

9. Paint the UVs of *glass* as per choice, refer to Figure 7-29.

10. Make sure the **Shader nodes** button is chosen in **Node editor**. Choose **New** from **Node Editor**; the **Diffuse BSDF** and **Material Output** nodes are displayed in the Node area.

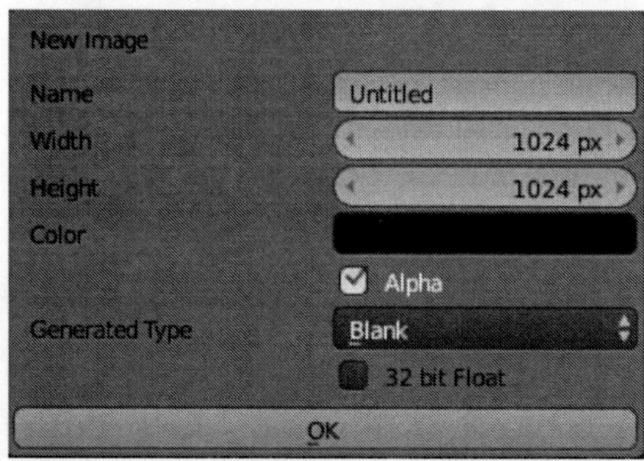

Figure 7-27 The ***New Image*** *window*

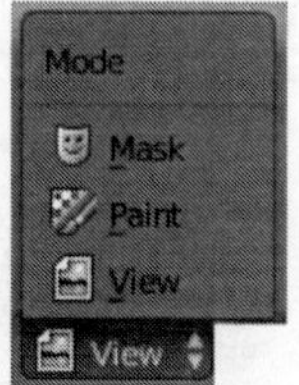

Figure 7-28 The ***Mode*** *drop-down*

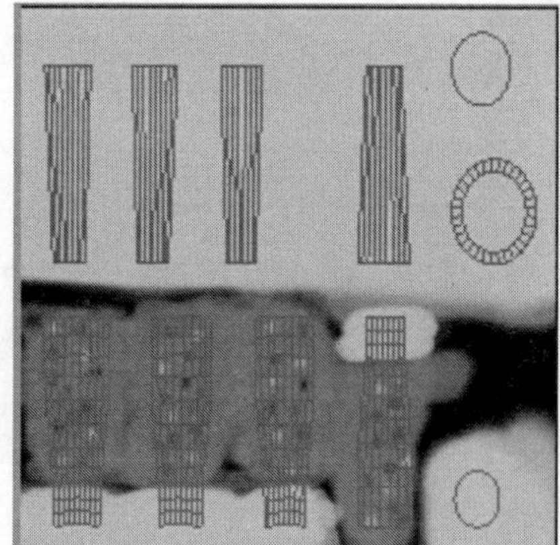

Figure 7-29 Painted UVs of glass

11. Hover the cursor in **Node Editor** and press SHIFT+A; the **Add** menu is displayed. Choose **Texture > Image Texture** from the menu; the **Image Texture** node is attached to the cursor. Place this node on the left of the **Diffuse BSDF** node.

12. Choose **Open** from the **Image Texture** node; **File Browser** is displayed. Navigate to *\Documents\blender2.79\c07\c07_tut1* and select **glasspaint.png** from it and then choose **Open Image** button from **File Browser**; the **Open** button in the **Image Texture** node is replaced by *glasspaint.png*.

13. Connect the **Color** output of the **Image Texture** node with the **Color** input of the **Diffuse BSDF** node, as shown in Figure 7-30.

14. Choose the **X** button in **UV/Image Editor**.

Saving and Rendering the Scene

In this section, you will save the scene that you have created and then render it. You can also view the final rendered image of this model by downloading the *c07_blender_2.79_rndr.zip* file from *www.cadcim.com*. The path of the file is as follows: *Textbooks > Animation and Visual Effects > Blender > Blender 2.79 for Digital Artists*

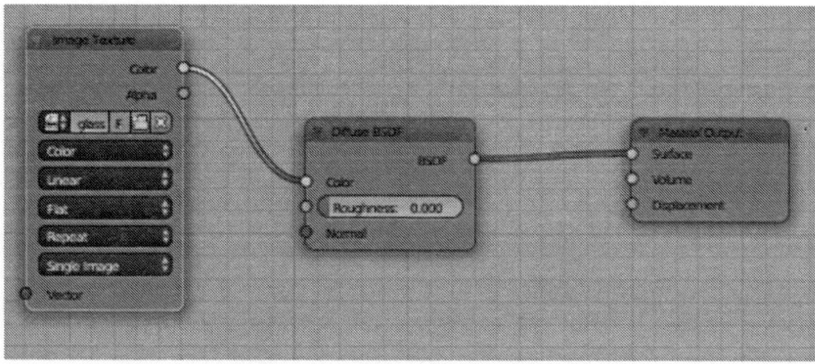

*Figure 7-30 Connected **Image Texture** node and **Diffuse BSDF** node*

1. Choose **File > Save** from the **Info Editor** menu bar.

2. Choose the **Render** button from **Properties Editor**. Next, choose the **Render** button from the **Render** panel or press F12; the rendered image is displayed in the **UV/Image Editor**; refer to Figure 7-17.

Tutorial 2

In this tutorial, you will texture flower using the **Vertex Paint** mode, as shown in Figure 7-31.

(Expected time: 20 min)

Figure 7-31 Textured flower using vertex paint

The following steps are required to complete this tutorial:

a. Open and save the scene.
b. Paint the petals and ovary.
c. Make the vertex paint visible on rendering.
d. Change the background color of the scene.
e. Save and render the scene.

Opening and Saving the File

1. Choose **File > Open** from **Info Editor**; **File Browser** is displayed.

2. In **File Browser**, browse to *\Documents\blender2.79\c07\c07_tut2_start.blend* and choose the **Open Blender File** button; the *c07_tut2_start.blend* file is displayed in Camera Persp view, as shown in Figure 7-32.

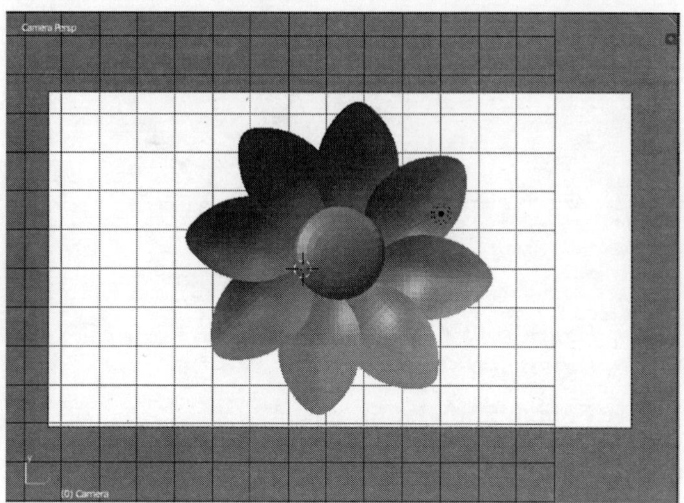

Figure 7-32 The c07_tut2_start file dispalyed

3. Navigate to *\Documents\blender2.79\c07* and create a new folder with the name *c07_tut2*.

4. Choose **File > Save As** from the **Info Editor** menu bar; **File Browser** is displayed

5. Navigate to *\Documents\blender2.79\c07\c07_tut2* and enter **Flower_vertexpaint** in the **File Name** edit box. Next, choose the **Save Blender File** button to save the file at the specified location.

Note
The Cycles Render engine is chosen in the c07_tut2_start.blend file.

Painting Petals and Ovary

In this section, you will paint petals and ovary of flower using the **Vertex Paint** mode.

1. Make sure *petal* is selected. Press V to choose the **Vertex Paint** mode; various panels are displayed in **Toolshelf**.

2. Click on the color swatch in the **Brush** panel; Color window is displayed. Enter **1, 0.693, 0.693** in the **R, G,** and **B** edit boxes; peach color is displayed in the color swatch.

3. Enter **10** in the **Radius** slider. Apply the strokes on petal near the ovary, refer to Figure 7-33.

Figure 7-33 Strokes applied on petal

4. Click on the brush image in the **Brush** panel and choose **F Mix** from the flyout displayed, refer to Figure 7-34; the brush type is changed.

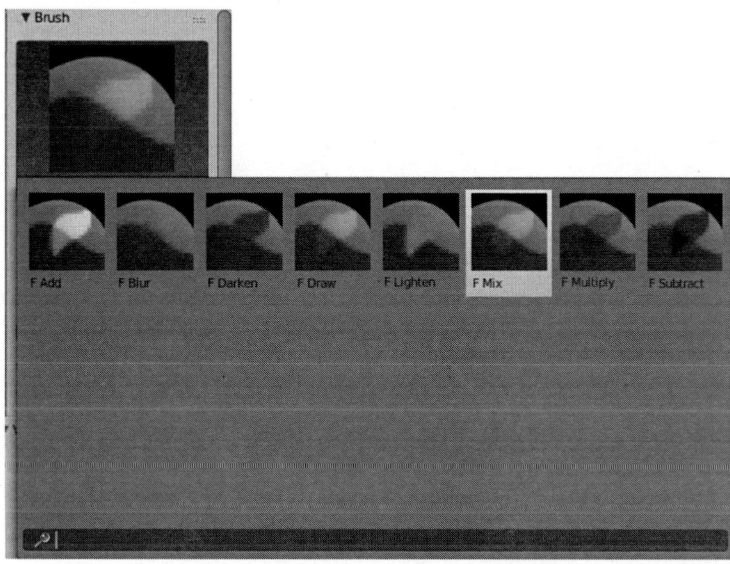

Figure 7-34 *Choosing **F Mix** from the flyout*

5. Click on the color swatch in the **Brush** panel; Color window is displayed. Enter **0.350, 0.043, 0.182** in the **R**, **G**, and **B** edit boxes, respectively; color is changed in the color swatch.

6. Enter **20** in the **Radius** slider. Apply the strokes on petal, as shown in Figure 7-35.

7. Click on the color swatch in the **Brush** panel; Color window is displayed. Enter **1**, **0.364**, **0.499** in the **R**, **G**, and **B** edit boxes, respectively; color is changed in the color swatch.

8. Enter **20** in the **Radius** slider. Apply the strokes on petal, as shown in Figure 7-36.

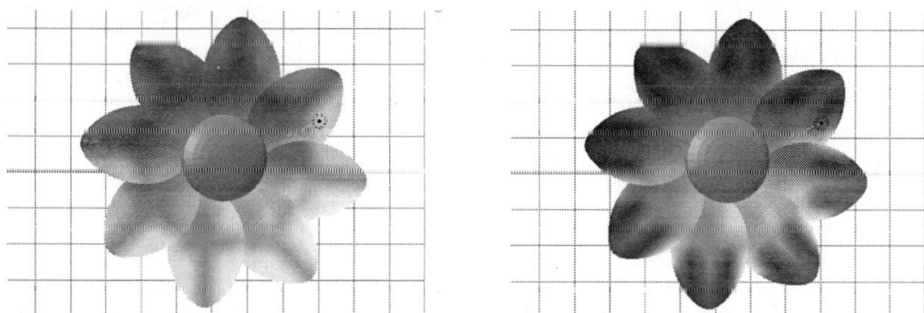

Figure 7-35 *Strokes applied on petal* ***Figure 7-36*** *Strokes applied on petal*

9. Click on the color swatch in the **Brush** panel; Color window is displayed. Enter **0.420, 0.022, 0.205** in the **R**, **G**, and **B** edit boxes, respectively; color is changed in the color swatch.

10. Apply the strokes on petal, as shown in Figure 7-37.

11. Press 4 and then 5 on Numpad; the view is changed to the User Persp view. Press and hold the middle mouse button and rotate the view to see the back side of *petal*. Use appropriate color and apply strokes on *petal* where there is no color.

12. Switch to **Object Mode** and select *ovary* from **Outliner**. Next, press V to switch to the **Vertex Paint** mode.

13. In the **Brush** panel, choose color of your choice from the color swatch and paint *ovary*, refer to Figure 7-38. Also, switch to the User Persp view and paint remaining part of *ovary* by rotating the view. Press 0 to switch back to the Camera Persp view.

Figure 7-37 *Strokes applied on petal*

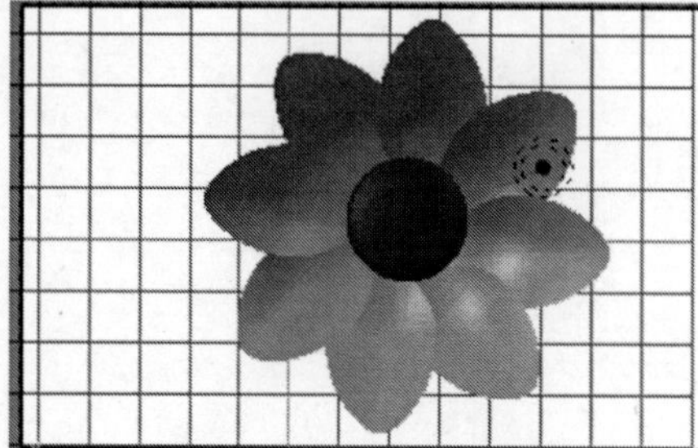

Figure 7-38 *Strokes applied on ovary*

14. Press F12; rendered image is displayed. You will notice that vertex painting on flower is not visible on rendering.

Making the Vertex Paint Visible on Rendering

In this section, you will add a node in **Node Editor** so that the vertex paint on flower is visible on rendering.

1. Choose **Compositing** from the **Screen Layout** drop-down in **Info Editor**, as shown in Figure 7-39.

2. Switch to **Object Mode**. Make sure *ovary* is selected in 3D View. Next, choose the **Shader Nodes** button from **Node Editor**.

3. Choose **New** from **Node Editor**; the **Diffuse BSDF** and **Material Output** nodes are displayed in the Node area of **Node Editor**.

4. Hover the cursor in the Node area and press SHIFT + A; the **Add** menu is displayed. Choose **Input > Attribute** from the **Add** menu; the **Attribute** node is attached to the cursor.

5. Place the **Attribute** node on the left of the **Diffuse BSDF** node and connect the **Color** output of the **Attribute** node to the **Color** input of the **Diffuse BSDF** node. Next, enter **Col** in the **Name** text box of the **Attribute** node,refer to Figure 7-40.

6. Press F12; the vertex paint on *ovary* is now visible in the rendered image in **UV/Image Editor**, refer to Figure 7-41.

7. Select *petal.* Repeat steps 3 to 5 to make the vertex paint on *petal* visible on rendering.

8. Press F12; the vertex paint is now visible on *petal* as well in the rendered image in **UV/Image Editor**, refer to Figure 7-42.

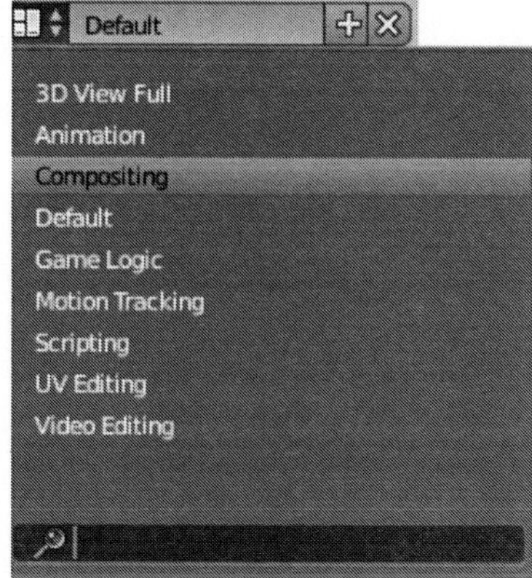

*Figure 7-39 Choosing **Compositing** from the **Screen Layout** drop-down*

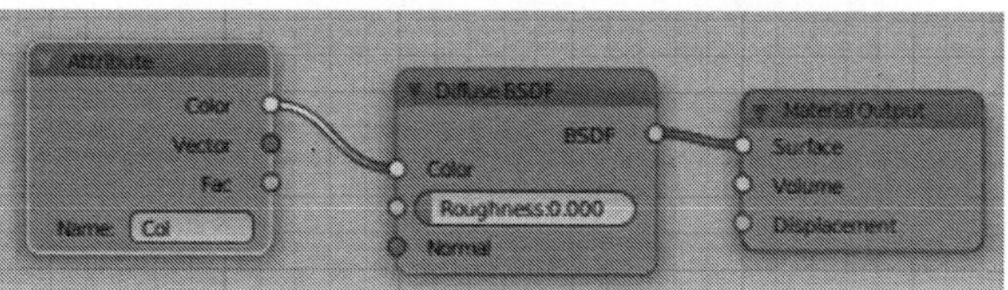

***Figure 7-40** Attribute node added to Node area*

***Figure 7-41** Vertex paint on ovary visible in the rendered image*

***Figure 7-42** Vertex paint on petal visible in the rendered image*

Changing the Background Color of the Scene

In this section, you will change the background color of the scene which uses the Cycles Render engine for rendering.

1. Choose the **World** button from **Properties Editor**; **Properties Editor** is modified.

2. Click on the **Color** swatch in the **Surface** panel; the color window is displayed. Choose the white color in the color window; the background displays the white color on rendering.

Saving and Rendering the Scene

In this section, you will save the scene that you have created and then render it. You can also view the final rendered image of this model by downloading the *c07_blender_2.79_rndr.zip* file from *www.cadcim.com.* The path of the file is as follows: *Textbooks > Animation and Visual Effects > Blender > Blender 2.79 for Digital Artists*

1. Choose **File > Save** from the **Info Editor** menu bar. Next, choose the **Render** button from **Properties Editor**. Next, choose the **Render** button from the **Render** panel or press F12; the rendered image is displayed in the **UV/Image Editor**; refer to Figure 7-31.

Self-Evaluation Test

Answer the following questions and then compare them to those given at the end of this chapter:

1. Which of the following areas display properties of a node selected in the Node area?

   (a) **Properties Editor** (b) **Properties Region**
   (c) **Toolshelf** (d) **Node Editor**

2. The __________ mode is used to paint vertices of an object.

3. The __________ key is used as shortcut key to switch from **Object Mode** to the **Vertex Paint** mode.

4. The __________ node is necessary to make the vertex paint visible on rendering when Cycles Render engine is used.

5. The **Vertex Paint** mode is used to paint on the surface of an object in **3D view Editor** or in **UV/Image Editor**. (T/F)

Review Questions

Answer the following questions:

1. Which of the following combinations of shortcut keys is used to display the **Add** menu.?

   (a) SHIFT + C (b) SHIFT + D
   (c) SHIFT + N (d) SHIFT + A

2. The __________ and __________ nodes are the default nodes in the Node area when a new material is created using the Cycles Render engine.

3. You need to select the __________check box in the **Options** panel of **Properties Editor** to make vertex painting visible on rendering in the Blender Render engine.

4. The amount in the __________ edit box of the **Smart UV Project** window is used to provide space between the UVs displayed in **UV/Image Editor**.

5. In the **Texture Paint** mode, you can load an external image in **UV/Image Editor** and then edit it by painting it in **3D view Editor** or in **UV/Image Editor**. (T/F)

EXERCISES

Exercise 1

Use the model of a sofa set created in Chapter 4 and then create a plane as the floor. Next, create velvet material for the sofa set and apply wooden flooring texture of your choice to the floor, refer to Figure 7-43. **(Expected time: 15 min)**

Figure 7-43 *The model of a sofa set with velvet material and a floor with a texture*

Exercise 2

Create a bowl as shown in Figure 7-44. Next, create texture for bowl using unwrapping technique and an external image of your choice, refer to Figure 7-44.

(Expected time: 15 min)

Figure 7-44 *Textured bowl*

Answers to Self-Evaluation Test

1. b, **2. Vertex Paint**, **3.** V, **4. Attribute**, **5.** F

Chapter 8

Lights and Cameras

Learning Objectives

After completing this chapter, you will be able to:

- *Understand various types of lamps*
- *Understand mesh lighting*
- *Understand light portals*
- *Understand camera*
- *Constrain a camera to an object*

INTRODUCTION

Lights are used to illuminate a scene and thereby making it more realistic. In Blender, lights are referred to as lamps. Cameras are used to adjust a particular view in a scene. In this chapter, you will learn the use of lamps and camera in detail.

TYPES OF LAMPS

There are five types of lamps in Blender. Each lamp has specific use in a scene. All these lamps are discussed next.

Note

The parameters of the lamp differ for the ***Blender Render*** *and* ***Cycles Render*** *engines. In this chapter, the* ***Cycles Render*** *engine is used throughout as a render engine.*

Point

The point lamp is the lamp used in the default interface of Blender. It is an omni directional point source of light that simulates a light bulb. To create a point lamp, make sure **Object Mode** is chosen. Also, make sure the **Create** tab is chosen in **Toolshelf**. Now, choose the **Point** tool from the **Lamp** area in the **Add Primitive** panel. Alternatively, hover the cursor in the view and press SHIFT+ A; the **Add** menu will be displayed. Choose **Lamp > Point** from this menu, refer to Figure 8-1; the **Add Lamp** panel will be added to **Toolshelf**. In this panel, you can change size, type, and transformation values for the lamp. Also, the **Object Data** button will be added to **Properties Editor**. On choosing this button, various panels such as **Preview**, **Lamp**, **Nodes**, and **Custom Properties** will be displayed, as shown in Figure 8-2. These panels are discussed next.

Preview

As the name suggests, this panel has a Preview window that displays the effect of the lamp settings made in the other panels.

Lamp

This panel has all the parameters that are used for the lamp settings. Five buttons available at the top are used to change the type of lamp. Other parameters in this panel may vary with the type of lamp used. The value in the **Size** edit box is used to specify the softness in shadows. Larger the value, softer the shadows will be. The value in the **Maximum Bounces** edit box determines the number of times light is allowed to bounce. As the name suggests, the **Cast Shadows** option enables shadow casting. The **Multiple Importance** check box enables indirect light sampling which helps in reducing noise.

Nodes

With the help of this panel, you can add various nodes to get desired lamp output. In this panel, when you choose the **Use Nodes** button, the **Surface** and **Strength** parameters are added to the panel. Also, if you switch to the Compositing layout, and select the **Use Nodes** check box and choose the **Shader nodes** button in **Node Editor**, you will notice that the output of the **Emission** node is connected to the **Surface** input of the **Lamp Output** node by default. You can change the type of input node connected to the **Lamp Output** node. To do so, choose **Emission** from **Properties Editor**; a flyout will be displayed. Next, choose an option from this flyout.

Alternatively, use **Node Editor** to change the input nodes as discussed in Chapter 7. The **Color** swatch is used to change the color of the selected lamp.

Figure 8-1 *Choosing* ***Point*** *from the* ***Add*** *menu*

Figure 8-2 *Various panels in* ***Properties Editor***

Figure 8-3 shows the point lamp with **Strength=300** in the **Node** panel and Figure 8-4 shows the effect of this lamp in the rendered image of the scene.

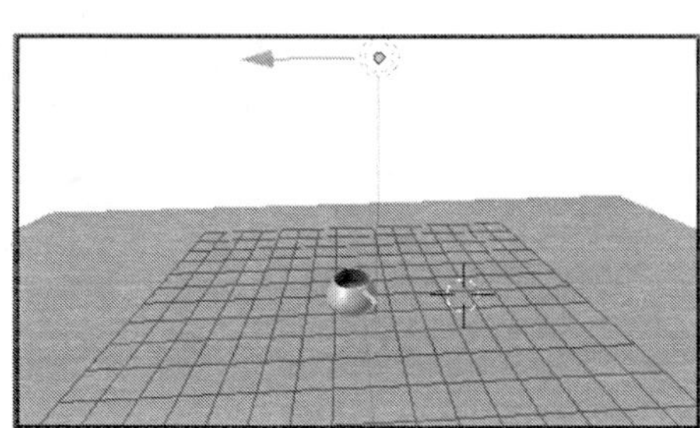

Figure 8-3 *Point lamp placed in the scene*

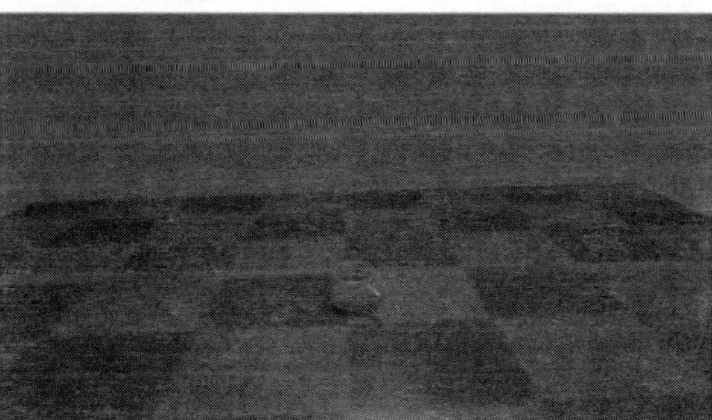

Figure 8-4 *The Rendered image*

Sun

As the name suggests, this lamp is used to simulate sunlight. As location of this lamp does not affect the light in a scene, you can place this lamp at any point in a scene. However, rotational values affect the placement of shadow of the objects in the scene.

To create a sun lamp, make sure **Object Mode** is chosen. Also, make sure the **Create** tab is chosen in **Toolshelf**. Now, choose the **Sun** tool from the **Lamp** area in the **Add Primitive** panel. Alternatively, hover the cursor in a view and press SHIFT+ A; the **Add** menu will be displayed. Choose **Lamp > Sun** from this menu; the **Add Lamp** panel will be added to **Toolshelf**. In this panel, you can change size, type, and transformation values of a lamp. Also, the **Object Data** button will be added to **Properties Editor**. On choosing this button, various panels such as **Preview**, **Lamp**, **Nodes**, and **Custom Properties** will be displayed, as shown in Figure 8-2. All these panels are same as those discussed in point light.

Figure 8-5 shows the sun lamp placed in the scene with strength=**1** in the **Node** panel and Figure 8-6 shows the effect of this lamp in the rendered image of the scene.

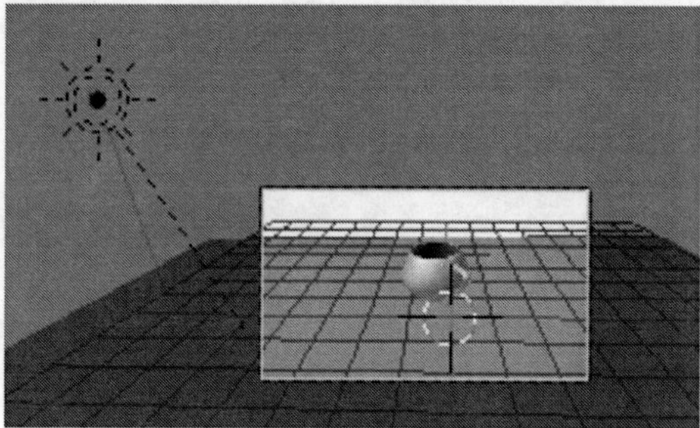

Figure 8-5 *Sun lamp placed in the scene*

Figure 8-6 *The rendered image*

Spot

The spot lamp is used to create spot lights. A spot light projects the rays in a particular direction. To create a spot lamp, make sure **Object Mode** is chosen. Also, make sure the **Create** tab is chosen in **Toolshelf**. Now, choose the **Spot** tool from the **Lamp** area in the **Add Primitive** panel. Alternatively, hover the cursor in a view and press SHIFT+ A; the **Add** menu will be displayed. Choose **Lamp > Spot** from this menu, refer to Figure 8-1; the **Add Lamp** panel will be added to **Toolshelf**. In this panel, you can change size, type, and transformation values of a lamp. Also, the **Object Data** button will be added to **Properties Editor**. On choosing this button, various panels such as **Preview**, **Lamp**, **Nodes, Spot Shape**, and **Custom Properties** will be displayed. All the panels except the **Spot Shape** panel are same as those discussed in point light. The **Spot Shape** panel is discussed next.

Spot Shape

The **Size** edit box is used to specify the size of the cone whereas the **Show Cone** check box is used to show the transparent cone in a view to know the objects covered in the spot light cone. The **Blend** edit box is used to soften the light at the edges of the cone.

Figure 8-7 shows the spot lamp placed in the scene with **Strength=250** in the **Node** panel and Figure 8-8 shows the effect of this lamp in the rendered image of the scene.

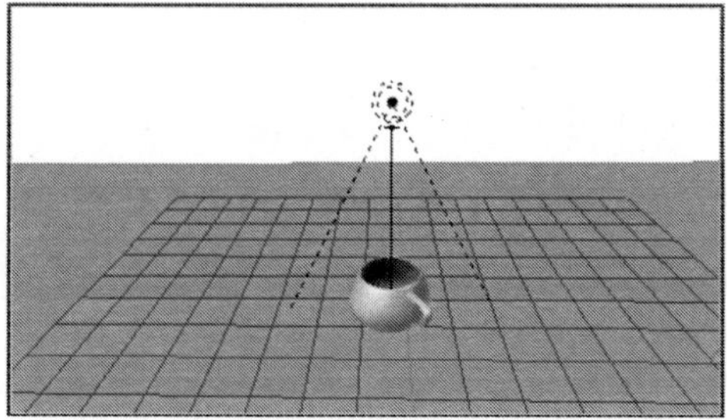

Figure 8-7 *Spot lamp placed in the scene*

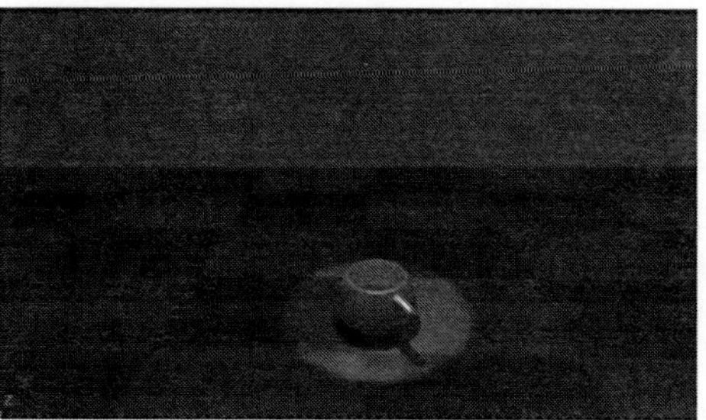

Figure 8-8 *The rendered image*

Hemi

The hemi lamp yields same result as the sun lamp as it is not supported in the **Cycles Render** engine.

Area

The area lamp is used to create light in a rectangular or square area. To create an area lamp, make sure **Object Mode** is chosen. Also, make sure that the **Create** tab is chosen in **Toolshelf.** Now, choose the **Area** tool from the **Lamp** area in the **Add Primitive** panel. Alternatively, hover the cursor in a view and press SHIFT+ A; the **Add** menu will be displayed. Choose **Lamp > Area** from this menu, refer to Figure 8-1; the **Add Lamp** panel will be added to **Toolshelf.** In this panel, you can change size, type, and transformation values of a lamp. Also, the **Object Data** button will be added to **Properties Editor**. On choosing this button, various panels such as **Preview**, **Lamp**, **Nodes**, and **Custom Properties** will be displayed. All these panels except the **Lamp** panel are same as those discussed in the point light.

Figure 8-9 shows the area lamp placed in the scene with **Strength=115** in the **Node** panel and Figure 8-10 shows the effect of this lamp in the rendered image of the scene.

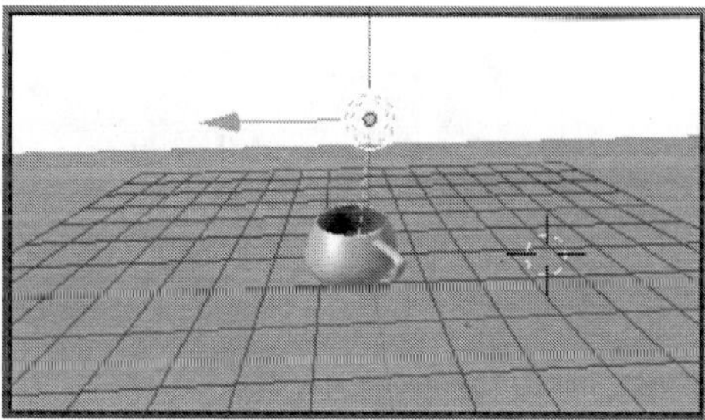

Figure 8-9 *Area lamp placed in the scene*

Figure 8-10 *The rendered image*

The **Lamp** panel of area lamp has an additional drop-down. You can choose rectangular or square area from this drop-down. You can also set dimensions of this area in this panel. The Portal check box in this panel is used to add light portals.

Light Portals

Light portals are used to reduce noise in the rendered image. These are placed in interior scenes at a window, door, or a place from where light enters the scene. Light portals are not useful in exterior scenes. Light portals increase efficiency of the render when the **Cycles Render** engine is used. You can use multiple light portals in a scene provided they are the main sources of light.

To add a light portal in a scene, create an area lamp and select the **Portal** check box from the **Lamp** panel in **Properties Editor**. Next, place it at the center of the opening of the interior scene. Now, adjust the size of the area lamp such that it matches the size of the opening by changing the parameters in the **Lamp** area. Figures 8-11 and 8-12 show the rendered image of the scene when the light portal is not used and when it is used.

Figure 8-11 *Scene without light portal*

Figure 8-12 *Scene with light portal*

Mesh lighting

In Blender, an object in a scene can act as a source of light by using the **Emission** shader. To do so, select an object in the scene and choose the **Material** button in **Properties Editor**. Next, choose **New** from **Properties Editor**. Now, choose **Emission** from the **Surface** drop-down in the **Surface** panel, refer to Figure 8-13. You can set the color and strength of the light that is emitted from the object using the **Color** and **Strength** parameters in the **Surface** panel.

Note

*To add **Emission** shader in **Node Editor**, add the **Emission** node and connect its **Emission** output to the **Surface** input of the **Material Output** node, refer to Figure 8-14.*

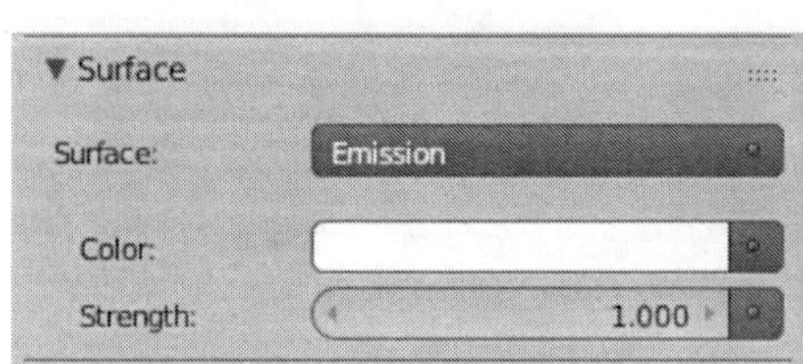

Figure 8-13 *The **Emission** shader chosen in the **Surface** drop-down*

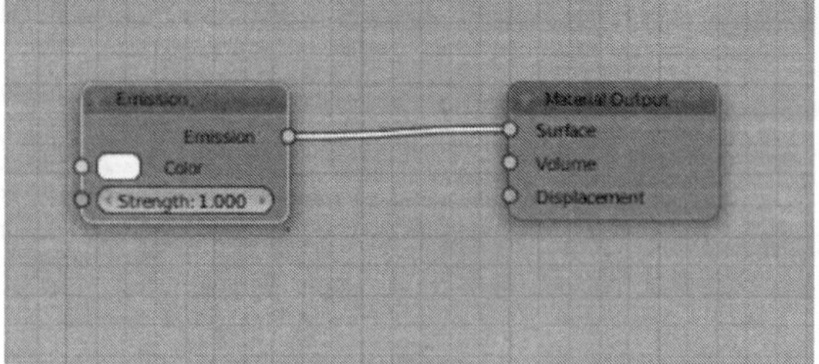

Figure 8-14 *The **Emission** node connected to the **Material Output** node*

Figure 8-15 shows the rendered image of the scene in which a plane is acting as a light source with **Strength=10** and Figure 8-16 shows the rendered image of the scene with bluish tint.

*Figure 8-15 The rendered image of the scene with **Strength=10***

Figure 8-16 The rendered image of the scene with bluish tint

CAMERA

Camera is the most important component in a scene. Placement of camera in a scene largely affects how lighting and materials in a scene are reflected in a rendered image or a sequence. In Blender, a default camera is available when you create a new scene.

To change various parameters of the camera such as lens type, focal length, and so on, select the camera. Next, choose the **Object Data** button from **Properties Editor**; various panels such as **Lens**, **Camera**, **Depth of Field**, and so on will be displayed, as shown in Figure 8-17. To position the camera, manually transform it in 3D view and change the parameters in **Properties Editor**.

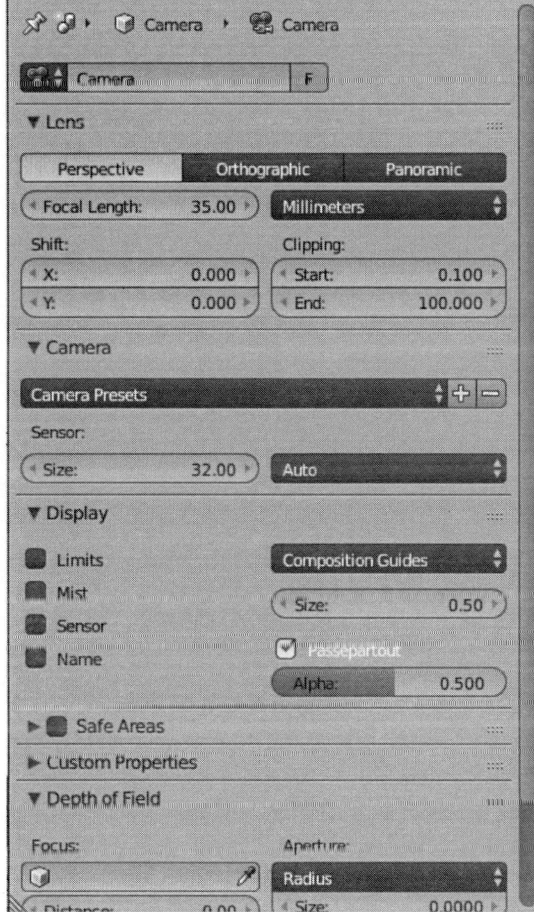

*Figure 8-17 Various panels in **Properties Editor***

Constraining a Camera to an Object

You can constrain a camera in such a way that it always points to an object or a specific area in a scene. The empty object can also be used as a target to constrain the camera. To constrain a camera to an object, select the camera. Next, choose the **Object Constraints** button from **Properties Editor**; various panels will be displayed in **Properties Editor**. Choose **Track to** from the **Tracking** category of the **Add Object Constraint** drop-down, refer to Figure 8-18; the **Track To** panel will be displayed in **Properties Editor**, as shown in Figure 8-19.

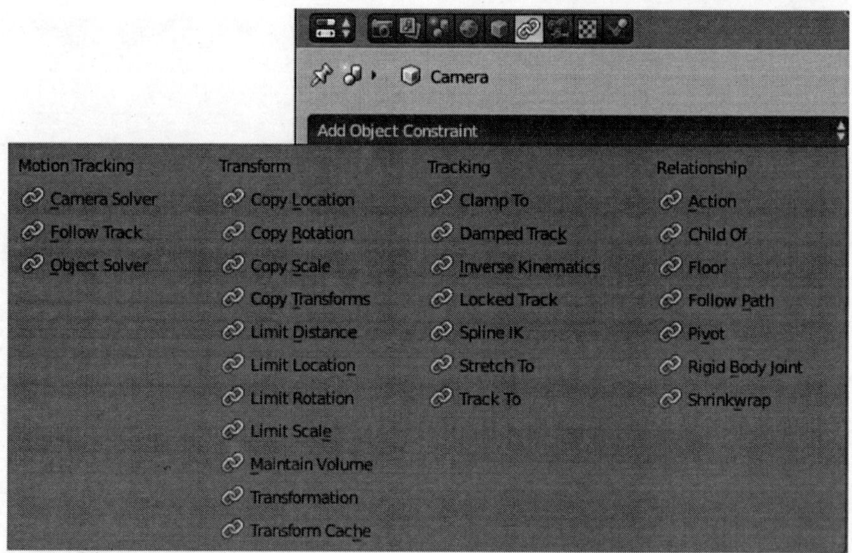

Figure 8-18 *The* ***Add Object Constraint*** *drop-down*

Choose the **-Z** button located next to the **To** parameter and then choose **Y** from the **Up** drop-down. Now, click on the **Target** edit box and select the desired object from the list displayed. You will notice that the camera and the selected object are connected with a dotted line, refer to Figure 8-20. Also notice that on moving the selected object, camera will also orient to the object as it is constrained to the object.

Figure 8-19 *The* ***Track To*** *panel in* ***Properties Editor***

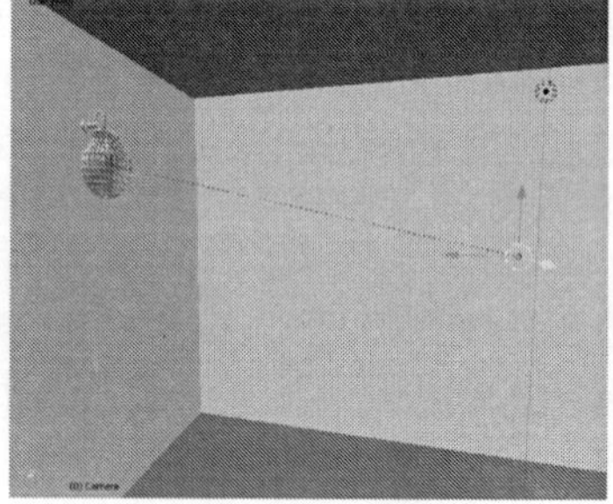

Figure 8-20 *Camera constrained to lamp*

You can also use various options in the **View** menu of the **3D View Editor** menu bar to align the camera in the scene, refer to Figure 8-21.

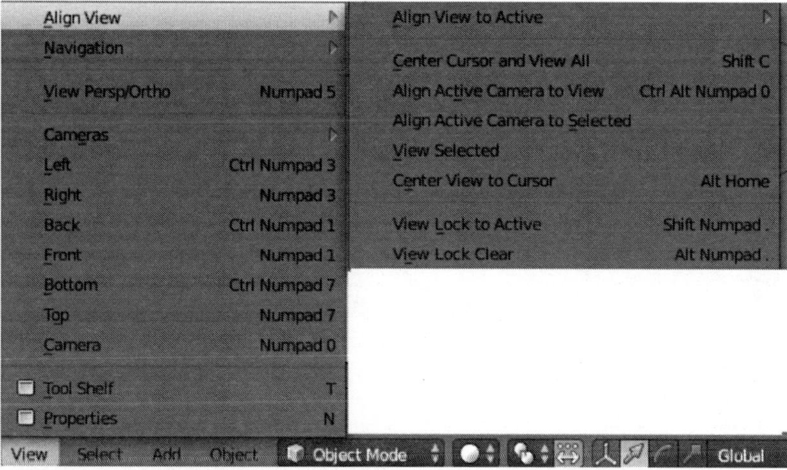

***Figure 8-21** The options in the **View** menu*

TUTORIALS

Before you start tutorials of this chapter, you need to download *c08_blender_2.79_tut.zip* file from *www.cadcim.com*. The path of the file is as follows: *Textbooks > Animation and Visual Effects > Blender > Blender 2.79 for Digital Artists*

Browse to *\Documents\blender2.79* and create a folder with the name *c08*. Next, extract the content of the zip file in this folder.

Tutorial 1

In this tutorial, you will illuminate an interior scene, as shown in Figure 8-22.

(Expected time: 25 min)

***Figure 8-22** The illuminated interior scene*

The following steps are required to complete this tutorial:

a. Open and save the file.
b. Illuminate using point lamps.
c. Illuminate using spot lamps.
d. Use light portal.
e. Save and render the scene.

Opening and Saving the File

1. Choose **File > Open** from **Info Editor**; **File Browser** is displayed.

2. In **File Browser**, browse to *\Documents\blender2.79\c08\c08_tut1_start.blend* file and then choose the **Open Blender File** button; the *c08_tut1_start.blend* file is displayed in 3D view, as shown in Figure 8-23.

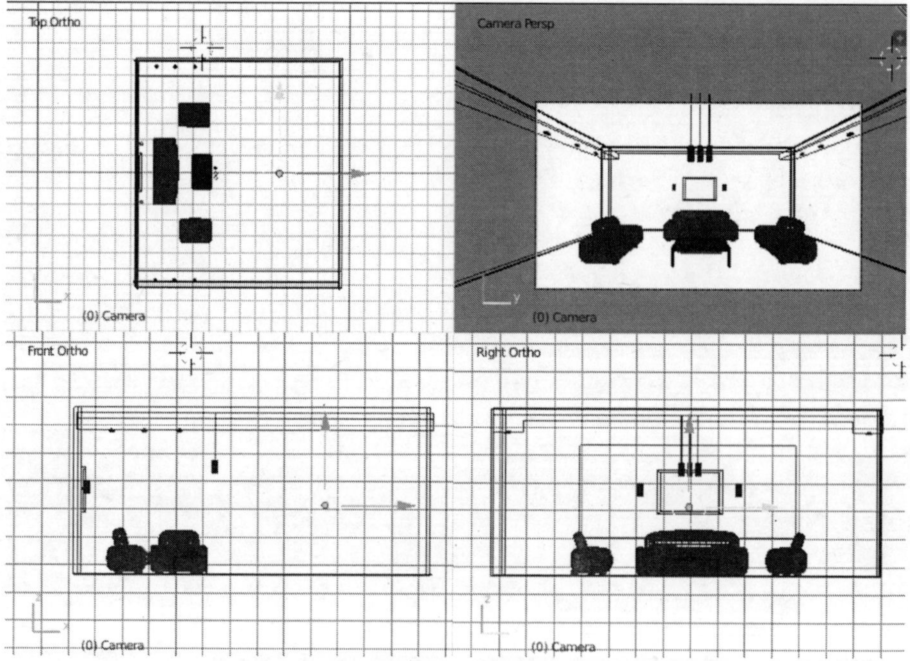

Figure 8-23 *The c08_tut1_start file*

3. Navigate to *\Documents\blender2.79\c08* and create a new folder with the name *c08_tut1*.

4. Choose **File > Save As** from the **Info Editor** menu bar; **File Browser** is displayed.

5. Navigate to *\Documents\blender2.79\c08\c08_tut1* and enter **Interior scene** in the **File Name** edit box. Next, choose the **Save Blender File** button to save the file at the specified location.

Illuminating using Point Lamp

1. Make sure the **Create** tab is chosen in **Toolshelf**. Next, choose **Point** from the **Lamp** area in the **Add Primitive** panel; a point lamp is created. Next, align it at the left of the photoframe in all the views, as shown in Figure 8-24.

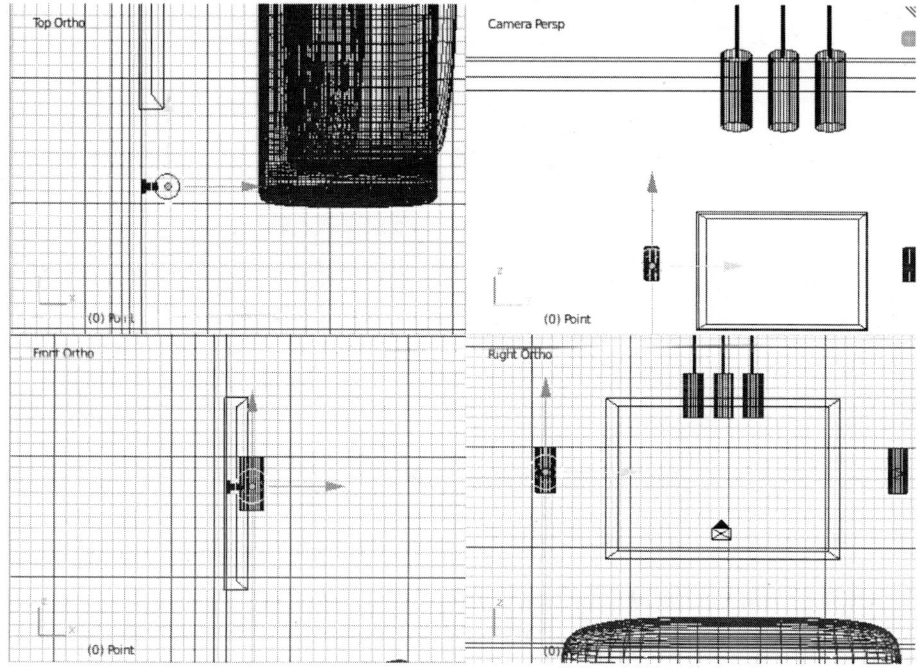

Figure 8-24 *The point lamp aligned*

2. Rename *Point* lamp as *wall light1*. Make sure *wall light1* is selected. Next, choose the **Object Data** button from **Properties Editor**. 

3. Enter **200** in the **Strength** slider of the **Nodes** panel. Also, make sure that the **Cast Shadows** and **Multiple Importance** check boxes are selected.

   Now, you will assign new material to *lampholder1*.

4. Select *lampholder1* from **Outliner**. Next, choose the **Material** button from **Properties Editor**. Choose **+** from **Properties Editor** located at the right of the **Material** drop-down. Rename it as *newlampholder material*. 

5. Choose **Emission** from the **Surface** drop-down of the **Surface** panel.

6. Select *wall light1*. Press SHIFT+D; a copy of *wall light1* is created. Rename it as *wall light2* and align it, as shown in Figure 8-25.

7. Assi

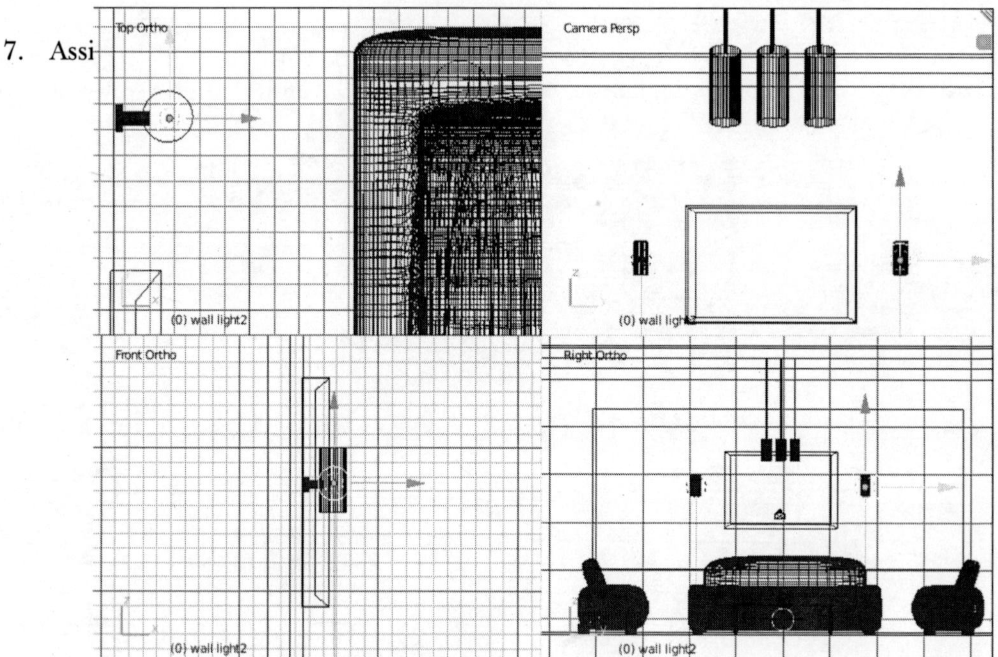

Figure 8-25 *The wall light2 aligned*

8. Create 3 copies of *wall light1*. Rename them as *hanging light1, hanging light2,* and *hanging light3*. Next, align all these lights at the bottom of *lampholder3*, *lampholder4*, and *lampholder5, respectively*, as shown in Figure 8-26.

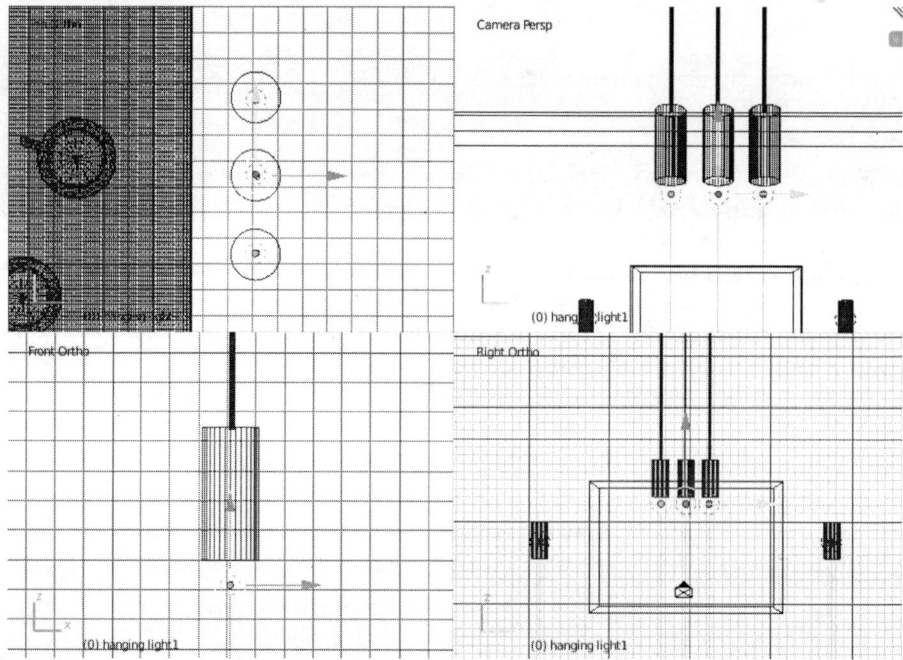

Figure 8-26 *The hanging lights aligned*

9. Select *hanging light1*. Choose the **Object Data** button from **Properties Editor**. 

10. Enter **1000** in the **Strength** slider of the **Nodes** panel. Also, make sure that the **Cast Shadows** and **Multiple Importance** check boxes are selected.

11. Assign *newlampholder material* to *lampholder3*, *lampholder4*, and *lampholder5*. Press F12; the rendered image is displayed in **UV Image Editor**, as shown in Figure 8-27.

Figure 8-27 *The rendered image*

Illuminating using Spot Lamp

1. Make sure the **Create** tab is chosen in **Toolshelf**. Next, choose **Spot** from the **Lamp** area in the **Add Primitive** panel; a spot lamp is created. Next, align it at the bottom of *rooflightholder1* in all the views, as shown in Figure 8-28.

2. Rename *Spot* lamp as *spot light1*. Make sure *spot light1* is selected. Next, choose the **Object Data** button from **Properties Editor**. 

3. Enter **2000** in the **Strength** slider of the **Nodes** panel. Also, make sure that the **Cast Shadows** and **Multiple Importance** check boxes are selected.

4. Enter **0.7** in the **Blend** slider of the **Spot Shape** panel. Notice the change in the inner ring of *spot light1* cone in Top Ortho view

   As you increase the value in the **Blend** slider, light becomes more softer at the edges of the cone.

5. Select *lampholder1* and assign *newlampholder material* to it.

6. Press F12; the rendered image is displayed, as shown in Figure 8-29.

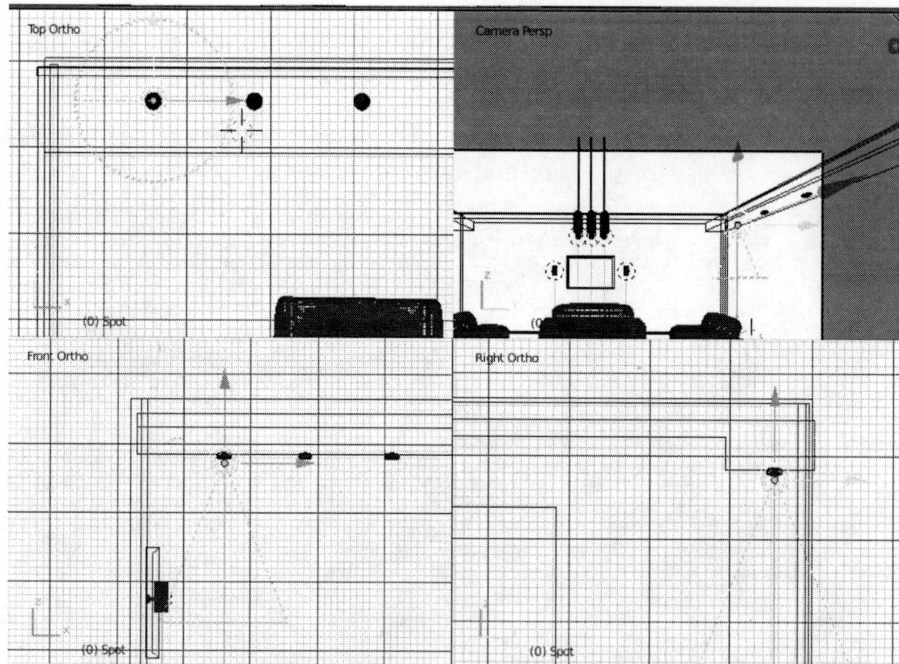

***Figure 8-28** The spot light1 aligned*

***Figure 8-29** The rendered image*

7. Create 5 copies of *spot light1* and rename them as *spot light2* through *spot light6*. Next, align them below *rooflightholder2* through *rooflightholder6*, respectively, refer to Figure 8-30.

8. Assign *newlampholder material* to *rooflightholder2* through *rooflightholder6*.

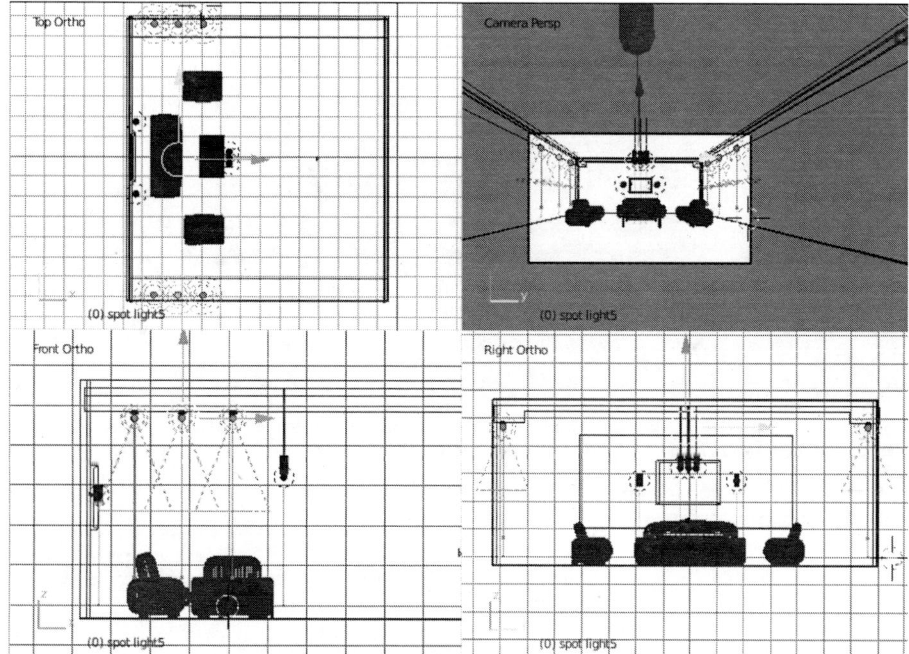

Figure 8-30 *Other spot lights aligned*

Saving and Rendering the Scene

In this section, you will save and then render the scene created. You can also view the final rendered image of this model by downloading the *c08_blender_2.79_rndr.zip* file from *www.cadcim.com.* The path of the file is as follows: *Textbooks > Animation and Visual Effects > Blender > Blender 2.79 for Digital Artists*

1. Choose **File > Save** from the **Info Editor** menu bar.

2. Choose the **Render** button from **Properties Editor**. Next, choose the **Render** button from the **Render** panel or press F12; the rendered image is displayed in **UV/Image Editor**; refer to Figure 8-22.

Tutorial 2

In this tutorial, you will illuminate an exterior scene, as shown in Figure 8-31.

(Expected time: 15 min)

The following steps are required to complete this tutorial:

a. Open and save the file.
b. Illuminate with sun lamp.
c. Illuminate with spot lamp.
d. Save and render the scene.

Figure 8-31 *The illuminated exterior scene*

Opening and Saving the File

1. Choose **File > Open** from **Info Editor**; **File Browser** is displayed.

2. In **File Browser**, browse to *\Documents\blender2.79\c08\c08_tut2_start.blend* file and then choose the **Open Blender File** button; the *c08_tut2_start.blend* file is displayed in 3D view, as shown in Figure 8-32.

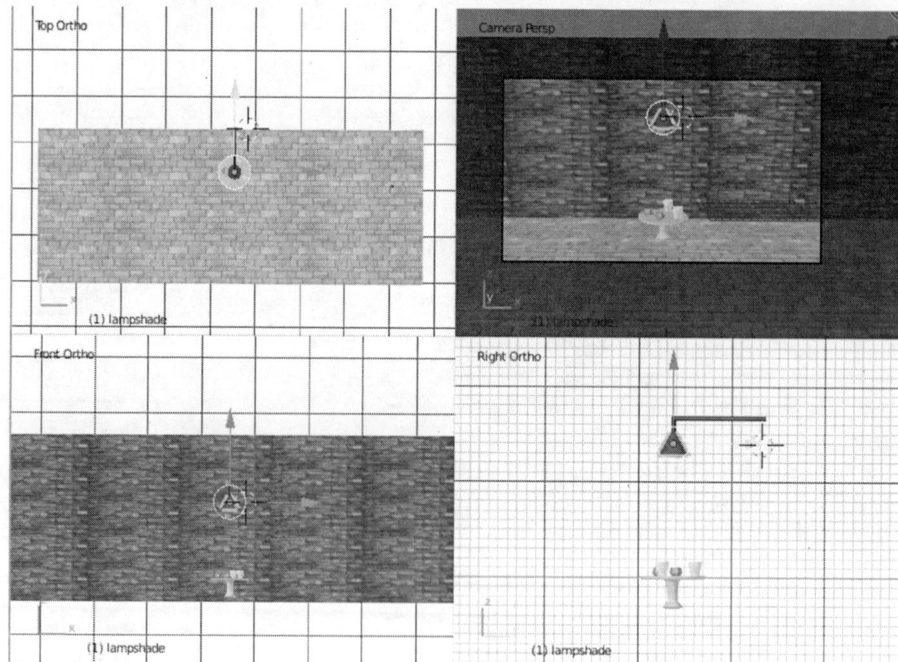

Figure 8-32 *The c08_tut2_start file*

3. Navigate to *\Documents\blender2.79\c08* and create a new folder with the name *c08_tut2*.

4. Choose **File > Save As** from the **Info Editor** menu bar; **File Browser** is displayed.

5. Navigate to *\Documents\blender2.79\c08\c08_tut2* and enter **Exterior scene** in the **File Name** edit box. Next, choose the **Save Blender File** button to save the file at the specified location.

Illuminating with Sun Lamp

1. Make sure the **Create** tab is chosen in **Toolshelf**. Next, choose **Sun** from the **Lamp** area in the **Add Primitive** panel; a sun lamp is created.

   Note that you can place sunlight at any place in the scene as its location does not affect the light in the scene.

2. Rename *Sun* lamp as *sunlight*. Make sure *sunlight* is selected. Next, choose the **Object Data** button from **Properties Editor**. Make sure that the **Cast Shadows** and **Multiple Importance** check boxes are selected. 

3. Choose the **Object** button from **Properties Editor**. Enter **45** in the **Y** slider of the **Rotation** area in the **Transform** panel; *sunlight* is rotated, refer to Figure 8-33.

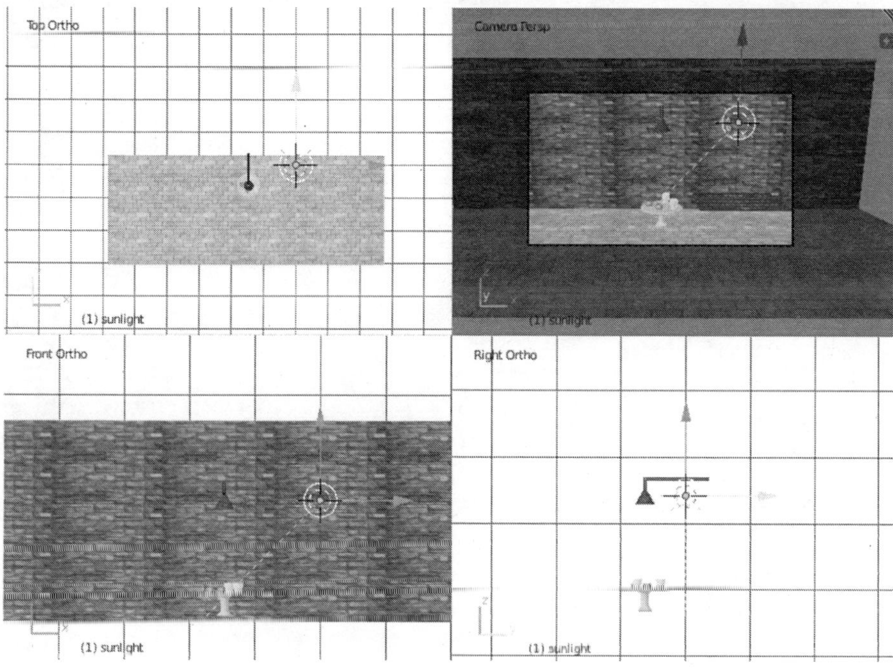

Figure 8-33 The sunlight rotated

4. Press F12. Notice that scene is illuminated with bright sun light in the rendered image, refer to Figure 8-34.

Illuminating with Spot Lamp

1. Make sure the **Create** tab is chosen in **Toolshelf**. Next, choose **Spot** from the **Lamp** area in the **Add Primitive** panel; a spot lamp is created. Next, align it at the bottom of *lampshade* in all the views, as shown in Figure 8-35.

Figure 8-34 The rendered image

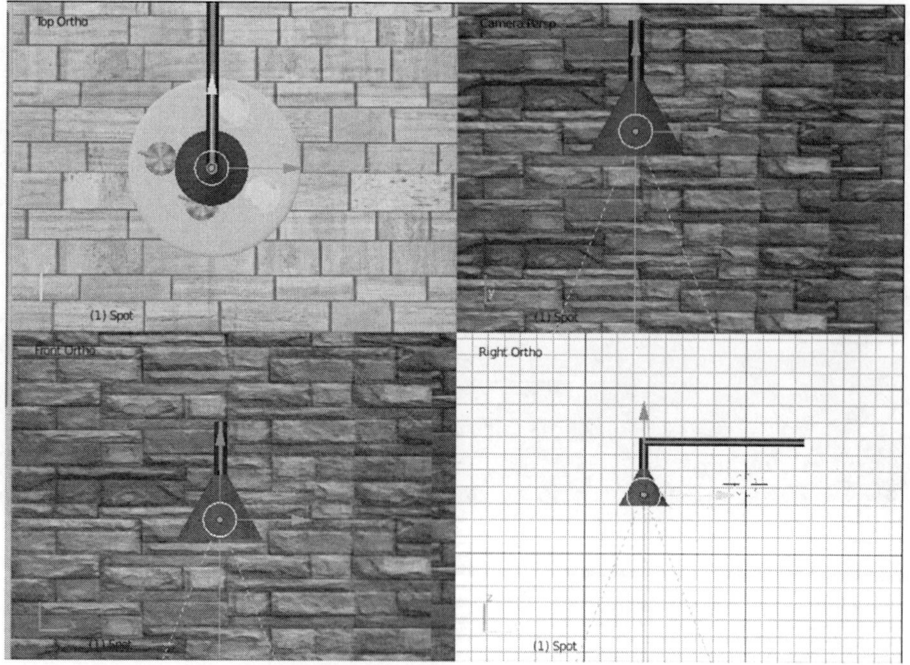

Figure 8-35 The spot light aligned

2. Rename *Spot* lamp as *spot light*. Make sure *spot light* is selected. Next, choose the **Object Data** button from **Properties Editor**. 

3. Enter **2000** in the **Strength** slider of the **Nodes** panel. Also, make sure that the **Cast Shadows** and **Multiple Importance** check boxes are selected.

4. Enter **125** in the **Size** slider and **0.45** in the **Blend** slider of the **Spot Shape** panel.

5. Choose the **World** button from **Properties Editor**. Choose **Volume Scatter** from the **Volume** drop-down in the **Volume** panel. 

6. Click on the color swatch in the **Volume** panel. In the color window displayed, enter **0.8**, **0.375**, and **0.155** in the **R**, **G**, and **B** sliders, respectively; light orange color is displayed in the color swatch. Enter **0.02** in the **Density** slider.

7. Select the check box in the **Ambient Occlusion** panel and enter **0.1** in the **Factor** slider.

8. Select the **Homogeneous** check box in the **Settings** panel.

9. Select *lampshade*. Assign *newlampholder material* to it.

Saving and Rendering the Scene

In this section, you will save the scene that you have created and then render it. You can also view the final rendered image of this model by downloading the *c08_blender_2.79_rndr.zip* file from *www.cadcim.com.* The path of the file is as follows: *Textbooks > Animation and Visual Effects > Blender > Blender 2.79 for Digital Artists*

1. Choose **File > Save** from the **Info Editor** menu bar.

2. Choose the **Render** button from **Properties Editor**. Next, choose the **Render** button from the **Render** panel or press F12; the rendered image is displayed in **UV/Image Editor**; refer to Figure 8-31.

Self-Evaluation Test

Answer the following questions and then compare them to those given at the end of this chapter:

1. Which of the following shaders is used for an object to act as a source of light?

   (a) **Subsurface Scattering** (b) **Volume absorption**
   (c) **Emission** (d) **Refraction BSDF**

2. Point lamp is an __________ directional point source of light that simulates a light bulb.

3. __________ lamp is used to simulate the sunlight.

4. The __________ edit box in the **Spot Shape** panel is used to soften the spot light at the edges of the cone.

5. Location of the sun lamp affects the light in a scene. (T/F)

6. Light portals are placed in interior scenes where light enters the scene. (T/F)

Review Questions

Answer the following questions:

1. Which of the following lights projects the rays in a particular direction?

   (a) **Spot** (b) **Area**
   (c) **Halo** (d) **Point**

2. __________ values of the sun lamp affect the placement of shadow of the objects in the scene.

3. You can change the softness in shadows by changing the value in the **Size** edit box of the **Lamp** panel. (T/F)

4. Light portals are used to reduce __________ in the rendered image.

5. The camera in the scene can be aligned with the options in the __________ menu of the **3D View Editor** menu bar.

6. Light portals are useful in exterior scenes. (T/F)

EXERCISES

Exercise 1

Create a scene and illuminate it using the point and spot lamps, refer to Figure 8-36.

(Expected time: 15 min)

Exercise 2

Create a wall with lamps, refer to Figure 8-37, and illuminate it using the point and spot lamps.

(Expected time: 15 min)

Figure 8-36 *The scene illuminated with spot lights*

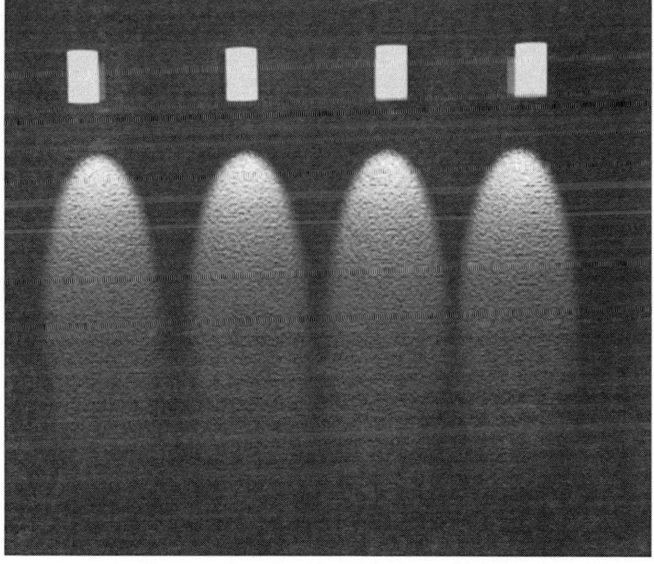

Figure 8-37 *Wall illuminated by spot lamps*

Answers to Self-Evaluation Test

1. c, **2.** omni, **3.** Sun, **4.** **Blend**, **5.** F, **6.** T

Chapter 9

Basics of Rigging and Animation

Learning Objectives

After completing this chapter, you will be able to:

- *Understand the concept of rigging*
- *Apply constraints*
- *Work with Timeline, Dope Sheet, and Graph Editor*
- *Create path animation*

INTRODUCTION

Rigging is the process of preparing an object or a character for animation. Animation is an act of giving life to a 3D object or character in the scene. To animate an object, you need to define scaling, rotation, and different positions of an object at different frames. On playing an animation, all frames are displayed one after another in quick succession to create an illusion of movement.

RIGGING

To rig an object, you can use constraints, armature, and the lattice object. The lattice object and the **Lattice** modifier are used to deform the object using the control points in the lattice object. The process of deforming an object using the lattice object is discussed in Chapter 4 in detail. Constraints and armature are discussed next.

Constraints

Constraints are used to restrict the movement of an object. To add a constraint to an object, select the object and choose the **Object constraints** button from **Properties Editor**. Next, click on the **Add Object Constraint** drop-down and then choose desired constraint from the list displayed, refer to Figure 9-1. There are four categories of constraints: **Motion Tracking**, **Transform**, **Tracking**, and **Relationship**.

Motion Tracking	Transform	Tracking	Relationship
Camera Solver	Copy Location	Clamp To	Action
Follow Track	Copy Rotation	Damped Track	Child Of
Object Solver	Copy Scale	Inverse Kinematics	Floor
	Copy Transforms	Locked Track	Follow Path
	Limit Distance	Spline IK	Pivot
	Limit Location	Stretch To	Rigid Body Joint
	Limit Rotation	Track To	Shrinkwrap
	Limit Scale		
	Maintain Volume		
	Transformation		
	Transform Cache		

***Figure 9-1** The **Add Object Constraint** drop-down*

Figure 9-2 shows a scene with cube as master object and a sphere as target object and Figure 9-3 shows a cube with the **Track To** constraint applied to it.

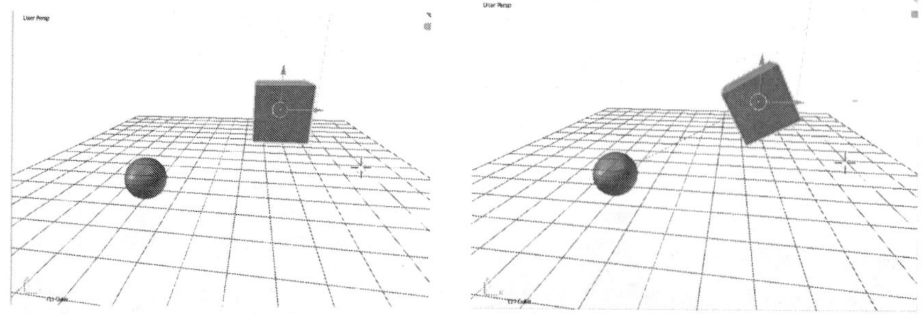

***Figure 9-2** The cube and sphere*

***Figure 9-3** The cube with the **Track to** constraint applied*

Armature

The armature object is a bone like structure used in rigging. To create an armature object, choose the **Create** tab from **Toolshelf**. Next, choose **Armature** from the **Other** area in the **Add Primitive** panel; armature will be created. It consists of three parts: root, body, and tip, refer to Figure 9-4.

When you select an armature, three modes are displayed in the **Mode** drop-down of **3D View Editor**, as shown in Figure 9-5. **Edit Mode** is used to setup a bone structure for an object and **Pose Mode** is used to setup poses for the object. To add a bone to armature, make sure **Edit Mode** is chosen. Next, select tip of the armature object and press E; bone will be added to the armature, refer to Figure 9-6.

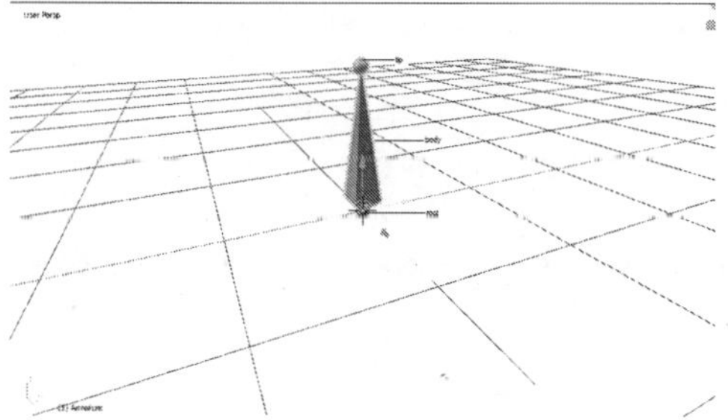

Figure 9-4 The parts of armature

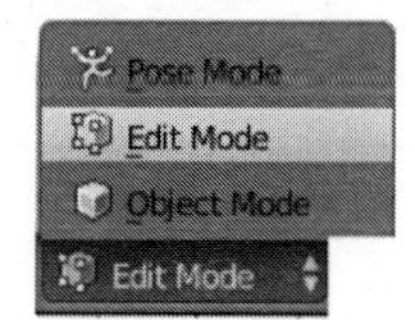

Figure 9-5 The **Mode** drop-down

To create parent child relationship between armatures, select the armature that will act as child. Next, press SHIFT and then select the armature that will act as parent. Next, press CTRL+P; the armature selected last will act as parent of the former selected armature and the **Make Parent** menu will be displayed, as shown in Figure 9-6. If you choose **Connected** from the **Make Parent** menu; the selected armatures will get connected to each other. If you choose **Keep Offset** from the **Make Parent** menu, there will be an offset between the parent and the child armature.

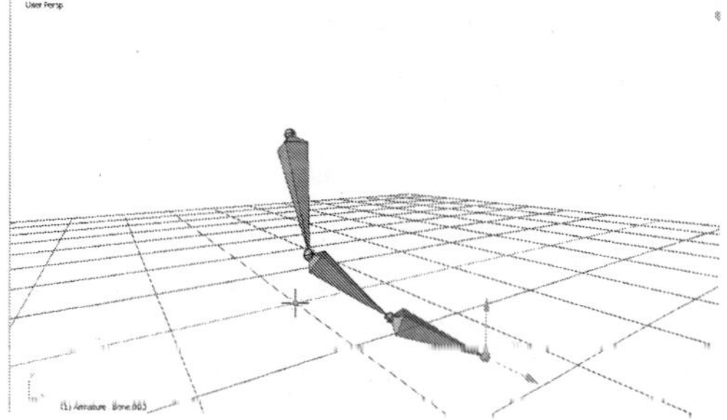

Figure 9-6 Bones added to armature

ANIMATION

There are four animation editors in Blender: **Timeline**, **Graph Editor**, **Dope Sheet**, and **NLA Editor**. Also, the Animation layout is available to set up animation of objects in the scene. The Animation layout consists of **Timeline, Dope Sheet, Graph Editor**, 3D view, Camera Persp view, **Outliner**, and **Properties Editor**, refer to Figure 9-7. The advantage of using the Animation layout over the default layout is that you have almost all the animation editors and other important editors side by side on the screen that saves the time of switching to various editors at the time of setting an animation. In this section, you will learn about all the animation editors in brief.

Timeline

Timeline is the basic editor to create animation in Blender, refer to Figure 9-8. Most commonly used options, buttons, and terminologies in **Timeline** are discussed next.

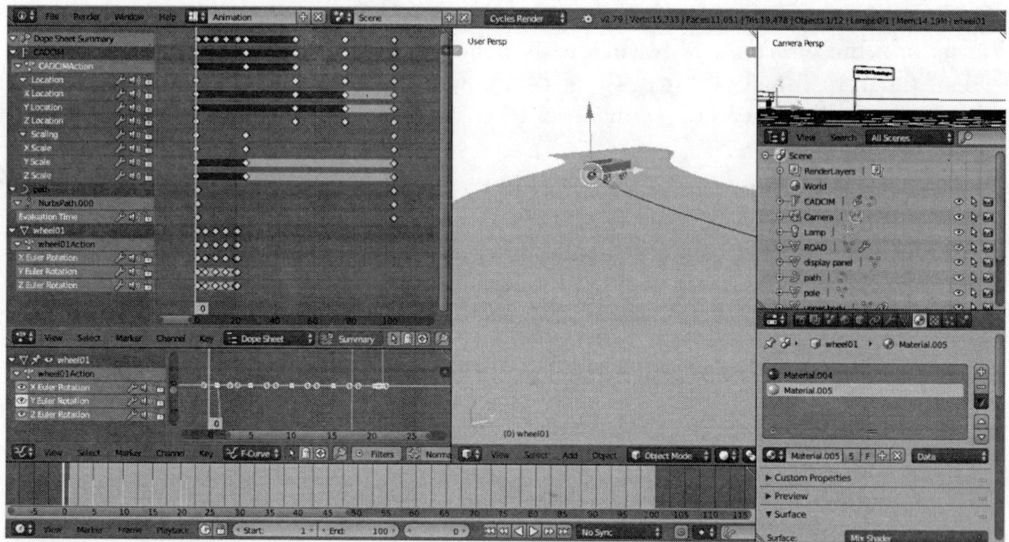

Figure 9-7 The Animation layout

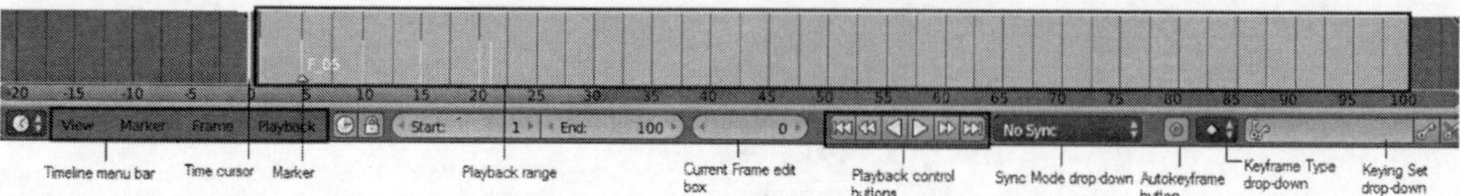

Figure 9-8 The Timeline

Time Cursor

The time cursor is located at frame 0 by default. When you click at a position on **Timeline**, the time cursor moves to that position. The keyframe is set at the current position of the time cursor. You can also attach frame number to the time cursor. To do so, choose **Number Indicator** from the **View** menu of the **Timeline** menu bar.

Markers

Markers are small triangles at the bottom of keyframes. These are generally named as per the specific use of keyframes in animation like jump, walk, and so on.

Playback Range

The playback range is specified in light grey color in **Timeline**. The **Start** and **End** edit boxes are used to display the start and end frames of the playback range. By default, the playback range is from frame 1 to frame 200. The **Current Frame** edit box is used to set/specify the current frame.

Timeline Menu Bar

The **Timeline** menu bar has four menus: **View**, **Marker**, **Frame**, **Playback**. The options in the **View** menu are used to toggle the visualization of seconds, subframes, number indicator, all frames, and so on in **Timeline**. The options in the **Marker** menu are used to add, delete, duplicate, and rename markers. The options in the **Frame** menu are used to set the start and end frames, set and clear preview range, and to set autokeyframing mode. The options in the **Playback** menu are used to toggle the updation of various editors at the time of playing the animation.

Playback Control Buttons

The playback control buttons are used to play the animation in forward and backward directions, jump to the next and previous frames, and jump to the first and last frames in the playback range.

Auto Keyframe Button

If the **Auto Keyframe** button is chosen and you transform an object in 3D View, keyframe gets automatically added at the time cursor. Also, a button with a two keys icon is added on the right of this button. If you choose this newly added button, keyframes for the properties in the active keying set are automatically added.

Keyframe Type Drop-down

The options in this drop-down are used to specify the type of keyframe to be inserted, refer to Figure 9-9. Each type of keyframe has specific color for identification.

Keying Set Drop-down

There are various keying sets available in the **Keying Set** drop-down, refer to Figure 9-10. These keying sets are the groups of properties of the object. To insert keyframes for a keying set, choose the desired keying set from the **Keying Set** drop-down. Next, press I in 3D view and choose the button with the key icon that is located next to the **Keying Set** drop-down. To delete keyframes for a keying set, choose the desired keying set from the **Keying Set** drop-down. Next, choose the button with the crossed key icon.

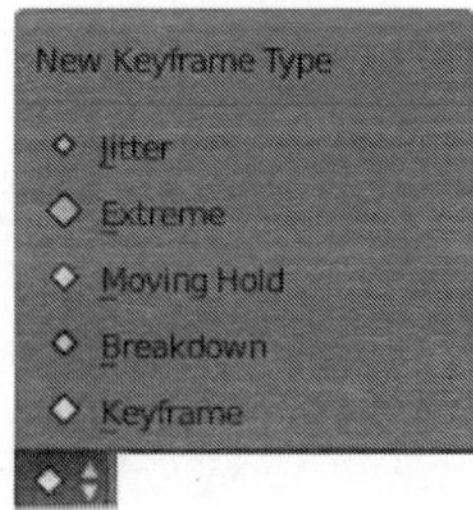

*Figure 9-9 The **Keyframe Type** drop-down*

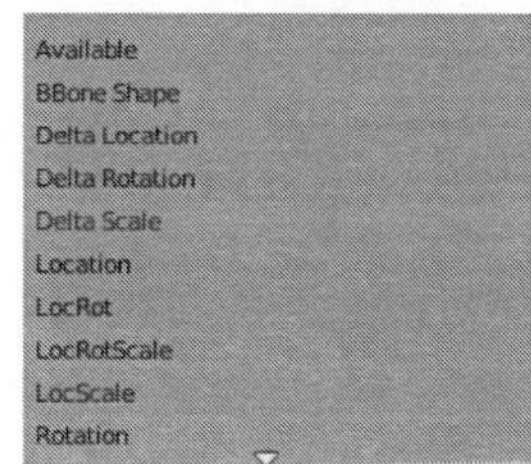

*Figure 9-10 The **Keying Set** drop-down*

Graph Editor

Graph Editor is used to modify the animation using F-curves. F-curves are the curves representing various properties of the animated object. Figure 9-11 shows **Graph Editor** with the location animation curves of an object. Properties are listed on the left and corresponding curves are on the right in **Graph Editor**. Select the desired property from the list on the left; curve for the selected property will be highlighted in green color, refer to Figure 9-11. The options in the **View** and **Marker** menus of the **Graph Editor** menu bar are similar to those of the **Timeline** menus. The options in the **Select** menu are used to select the keyframes in various possible ways. The options in the **Key** menu are used for copying and pasting keyframes, changing interpolation type for individual keyframes, inserting and deleting keyframes, and so on.

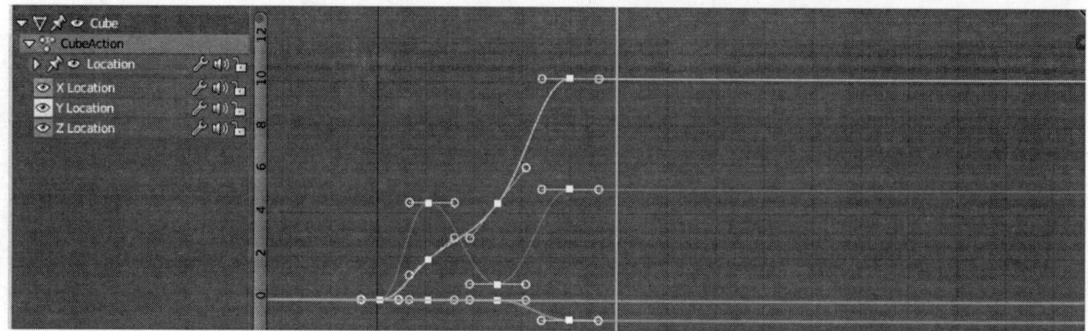

*Figure 9-11 The **Graph Editor***

Dope Sheet

Dope Sheet is also used to modify animation. In **Dope Sheet**, keyframes are marked as diamonds, refer to Figure 9-12. Most of the options in the **Dope Sheet** menus are similar to those of the **Graph Editor** menus. The **Mode** drop-down in **Dope Sheet** allows you to switch to various modes. Figure 9-12 shows **Dope Sheet** for an animated cube.

*Figure 9-12 The **Dopesheet***

NLA Editor

NLA Editor is used to blend more than one action of an object like rotation and movement of the object. It is mainly used in character animation to save time. You can make layers for motions of different parts of the body, combine them, and reuse the motions created earlier.

TUTORIALS

Before you start tutorials of this chapter, you need to download *c09_blender_2.79_tut.zip* file from *www.cadcim.com*. The path of the file is as follows: *Textbooks > Animation and Visual Effects > Blender > Blender 2.79 for Digital Artists*

Browse to *\Documents\blender2.79* and create a folder with the name *c09*. Next, extract the content of the zip file in this folder.

Tutorial 1

In this tutorial, you will create a rig for a cartoon animal, as shown in Figure 9-13.

(Expected time: 25 min)

The following steps are required to complete this tutorial:

a. Open and save the file.
b. Create rig for a front leg.

c. Copy front leg rig to other legs.
d. Bind the rig.
e. Save the scene.

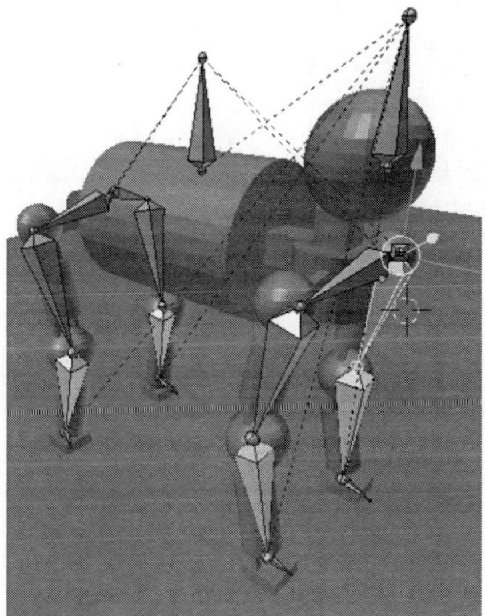

Figure 9-13 *The rig of a cartoon animal*

Opening and Saving the File

1. Choose **File > Open** from **Info Editor**; **File Browser** is displayed.

2. In **File Browser**, browse to *\Documents\blender2.79\c09\c09_tut1_start.blend* file and choose the **Open Blender File** button; the *c09_tut1_start.blend* file is displayed in 3D view, as shown in Figure 9-14.

3. Navigate to *\Documents\blender2.79\c09* and create a new folder with the name *c09_tut1*.

4. Choose **File > Save As** from the **Info Editor** menu bar; **File Browser** is displayed

5. Navigate to *\Documents\blender2.79\c09\c09_tut1* and enter **Cartoon animal_rig** in the **File Name** edit box. Next, choose the **Save Blender File** button to save the file at the specified location.

Creating Rig for a Front Leg

1. Make sure the **Create** tab is chosen in **Toolshelf**. Next, choose **Armature** from the **Other** area in the **Add Primitive** panel; *Armature* is created at the position of cursor.

2. Choose the **Object Data** button from **Properties Editor**. Next, select the **X-Ray** check box from the **Display** panel to make it visible even if it is inside the mesh.

3. Switch to **Edit Mode**. Select body of *Armature* and align it in all the views, as shown in Figure 9-15.

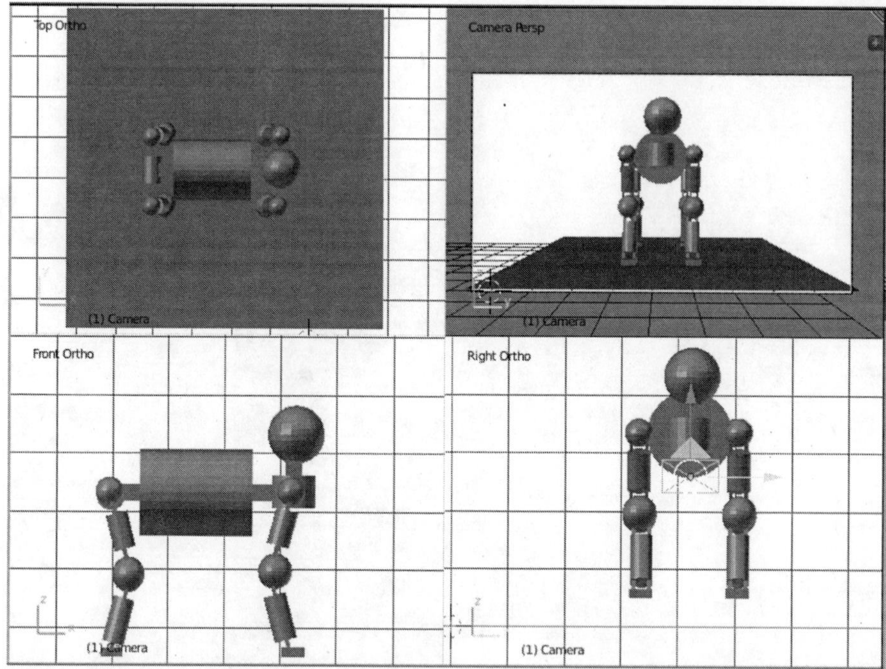

Figure 9-14 *The c09_tut1_start file*

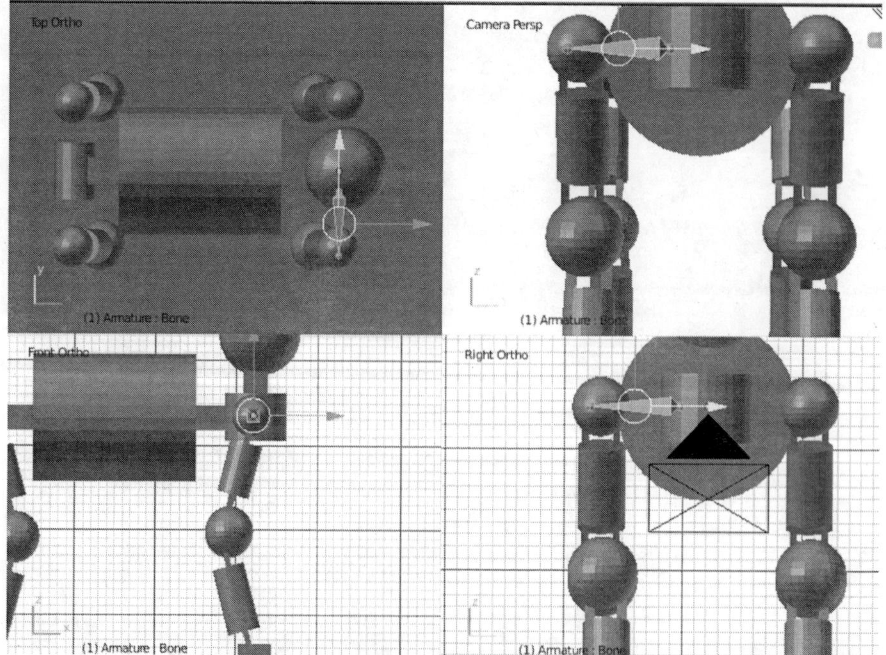

Figure 9-15 *The Armature aligned*

4. Select the tip of *Armature* and align it, as shown in Figure 9-15. Make sure the tip of *Armature* is selected. Next, Press E; *Armature* is extruded with additional bone. Align it, as shown in Figure 9-16.

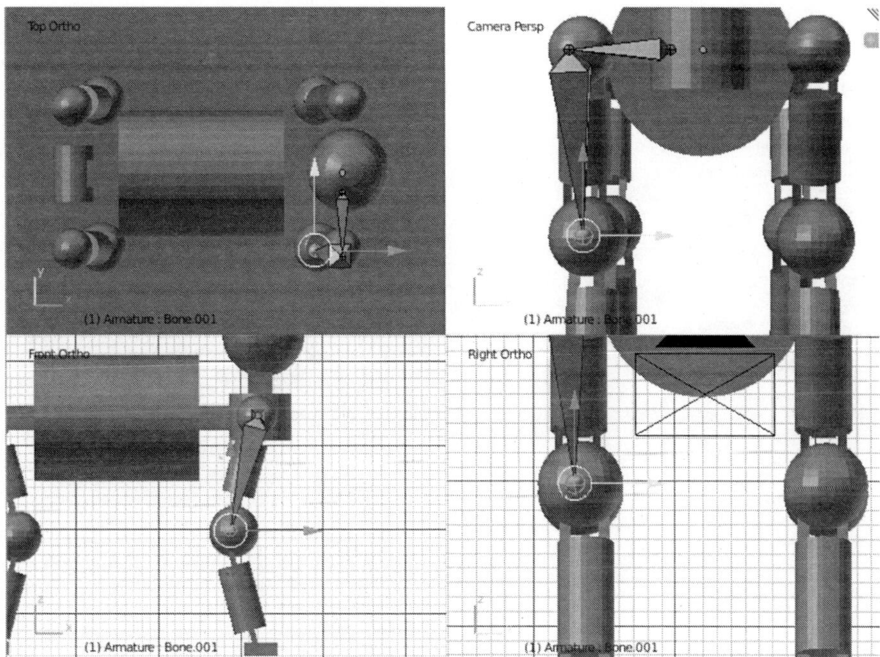

Figure 9-16 *Extruded Armature aligned*

5. Make sure the tip of *Armature* is selected and extrude it again. Next, align it, as shown in Figure 9-17.

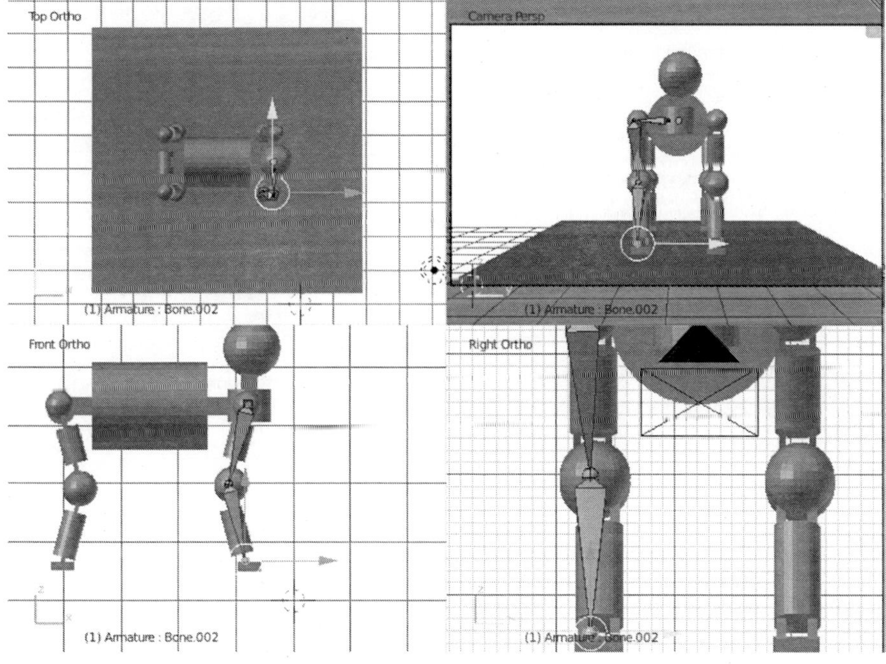

Figure 9-17 *Extruded Armature aligned*

6. Press SHIFT+A; a bone with the name *Bone.003* is created at the position of cursor. Make sure the tip of *Bone.003* is selected. Next, rotate it and align it, as shown in Figure 9-18. Note that you may need to reduce the length of *Bone.003* to match with *foot*.

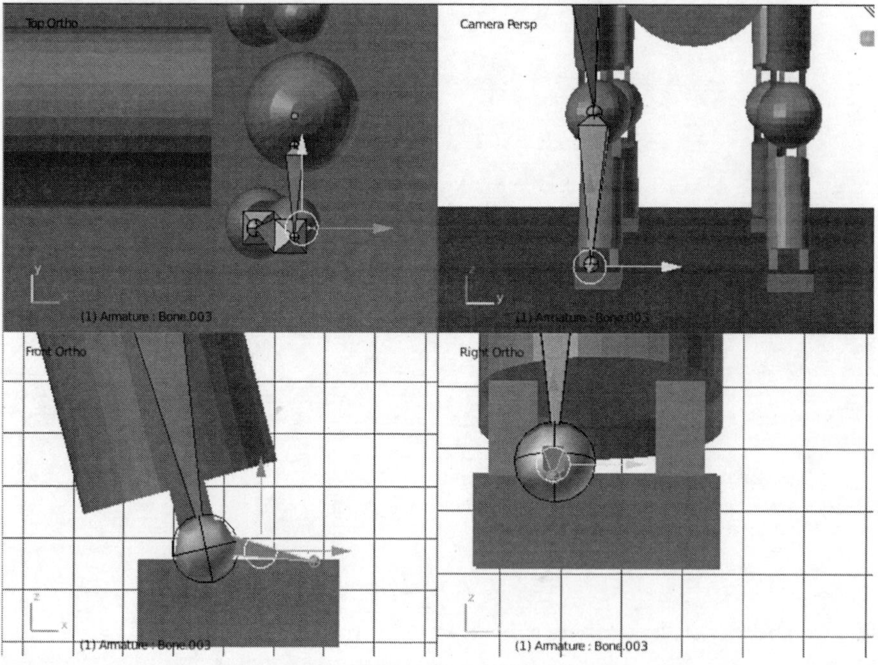

Figure 9-18 *Bone.003 aligned*

7. Choose the **Bone** button from **Properties Editor**. Next, rename *Bone.003* in the topmost edit box as *footbone*.

8. Press SHIFT+A; a bone with the name *Bone.004* is created. Rename it as *bodybone* and align it as shown in Figure 9-19.

9. Select bone that is located at *shoulder*. Next, press SHIFT and then select *bodybone*. Now, press CTRL+P; the **Make Parent** menu is displayed. Choose **Keep Offset** from the menu; *bodybone* is parent of the selected bone.

10. Choose **Pose Mode** from the **Mode** drop-down in **3D View Editor**. Next, move and rotate *bodybone*. You will notice that *Armature* also moves along with *bodybone*.

    Now, you need to reset position of all the bones in the scene.

11. Press A twice; all the bones in the scene are selected. Choose **Clear Transform > All** from the **Pose** menu of **3D View Editor**.

    Now, you need to connect *footbone* with *Armature* using the bone constraint.

12. Choose *Bone.002* located near *lowerleg*. Choose the **Bone Constraints** button from **Properties Editor**. Choose **Inverse Kinematics** from the **Tracking** category of the **Add Bone Constraint** drop-down. 

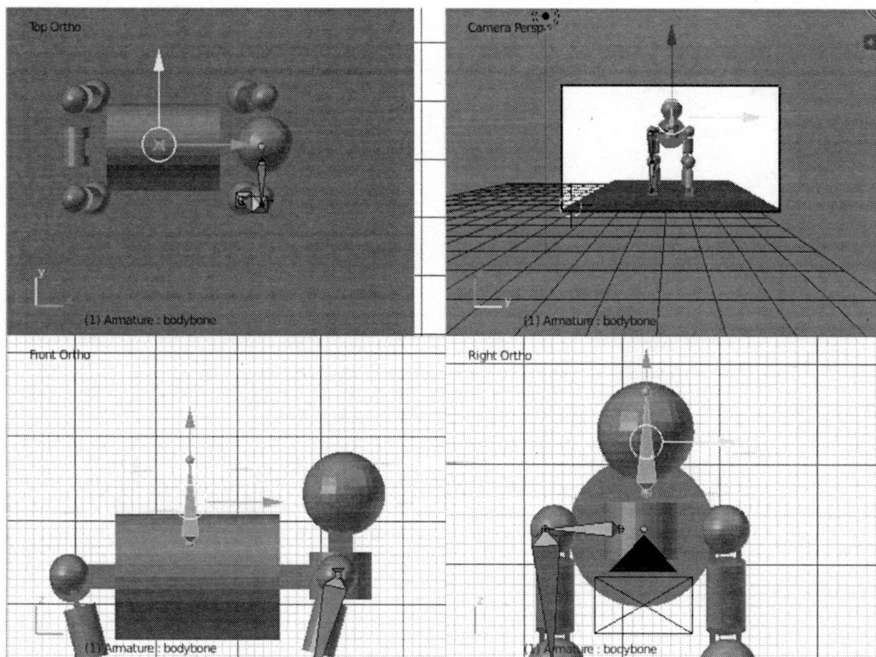

***Figure 9-19** The bodybone aligned*

13. Click on the **Target** edit box and select **Armature** from the list displayed. Similarly, click on the **Bone** edit box and select **footbone** from the list displayed. Also, enter **3** in the **Chain Length** slider.

    Value in the **Chain Length** slider specifies the number of bones connected with the lowermost bone using the **Inverse Kinematics** constraint.

Copying Front Leg Rig to Other legs

1. Switch to **Edit Mode**. Select *footbone, Bone.002, Bone.001*, and *Bone* in a sequence and then press SHIFT + D; copy of bone chain is created. Next, move it to back leg in the Front ortho view, refer to Figure 9-20.

2. Select the joint between *Bone.004* and *Bone.005* and move it to align with back leg, as shown in Figure 9-20.

3. Create two more copies of bone chain and align them to other legs, refer to Figure 9-21.

4. Switch to **Pose Mode**. Next, move *bodybone*. You will notice that all the bones except foot bones move with it. Now, move each foot bone one by one and check if the movement is correct for each leg.

    Now, you will create head bone that controls the whole body.

5. Switch to **Edit Mode**. Next, press SHIFT + A; a bone is created. Rename it as *headbone*.

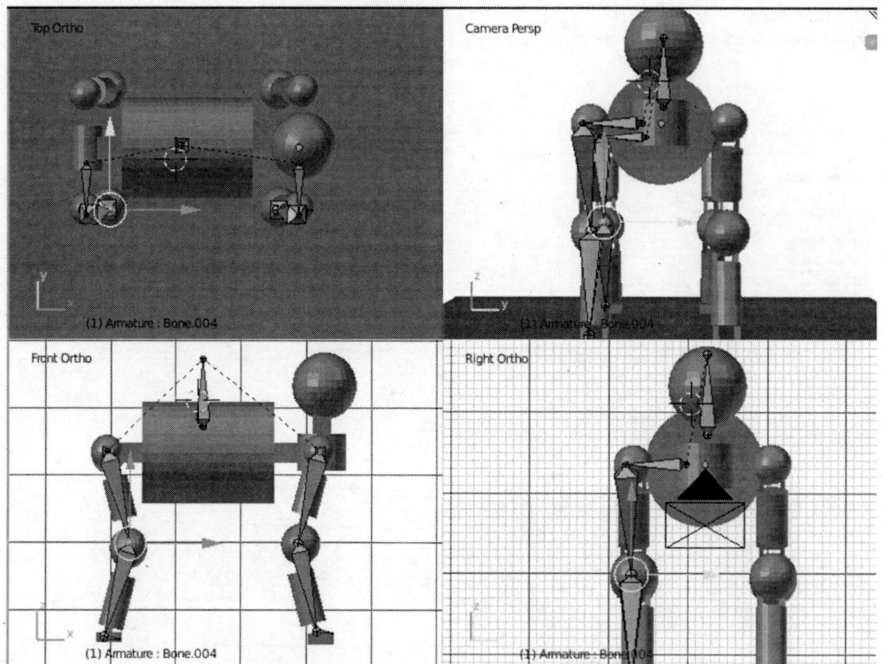

Figure 9-20 Copy of bone chain aligned

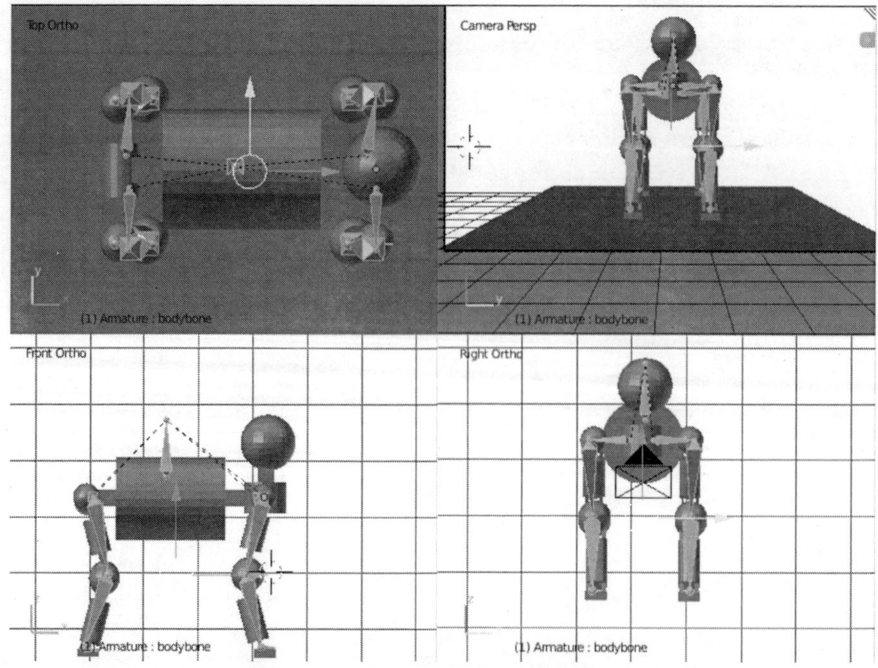

Figure 9-21 All bone chains aligned

6. Align it on the top of *head* in all the views. Select *Bodybone*. Press and hold SHIFT and then select *footbone, footbone.001, footbone.002, footbone.003*, and then *headbone*. Next, press CTRL+ P; the **Make Parent** menu is displayed. Choose **Keep Offset** from it; *headbone* becomes parent of *bodybone* and all foot bones, refer to Figure 9-22.

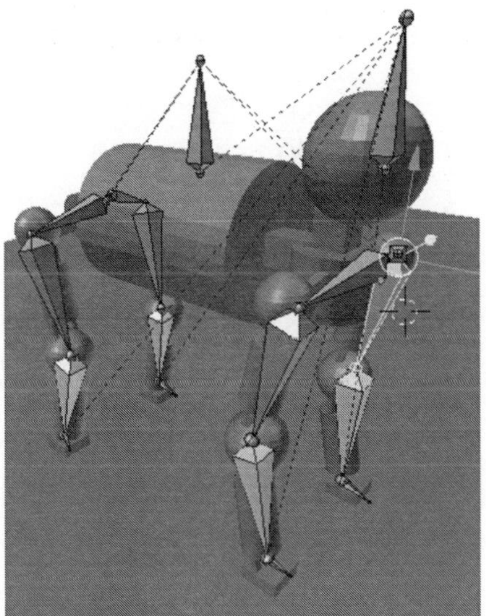

Figure 9-22 *All interconnected bones*

7. Switch to **Pose Mode**. Next, move *headbone*. You will notice that all the bones including foot bones move with it.

Binding the Rig

1. Make sure **Pose Mode** is chosen. Select *foot*. Next, press SHIFT and select *footbone*. Now, press CTRL+P; the **Set Parent To** menu is displayed. Choose **Bone** from the menu; *foot* becomes parent of *footbone*.

2. Select *lowerleg* from **Outliner**. Next, press SHIFT and select *Bone.002*. Now, press CTRL+P; the **Set Parent To** menu is displayed. Choose **Bone** from the menu; *Bone.002* becomes parent of *lowerleg*.

3. Select *upperleg* from **Outliner**. Next, press SHIFT and select *Bone.001*. Now, press CTRL+P; the **Set Parent To** menu is displayed. Choose **Bone** from the menu; *Bone.001* becomes parent of *upperleg*.

4. Select *shoulder* from **Outliner**. Next, press SHIFT and select *Bone*. Now, press CTRL+P; the **Set Parent To** menu is displayed. Choose **Bone** from the menu; *Bone* becomes parent of *shoulder*.

5. Similarly, bind all other legs as described in Step 1 through 4.

6. Select *body* from **Outliner**. Next, press SHIFT and select *bodybone*. Now, press CTRL+P; the **Set Parent To** menu is displayed. Choose **Bone** from the menu; *bodybone* becomes parent of *body*.

7. Select *head* from **Outliner**. Next, press SHIFT and select *headbone*. Now, press CTRL+P; the **Set Parent To** menu is displayed. Choose **Bone** from the menu; *headbone* becomes parent of *head*.

8. Switch to **Pose Mode**. Next, move *headbone*. You will notice that the whole body moves with it. Similarly, move *headbone*. The whole body (except all the foots) moves with it.

Saving the Scene

In this section, you will save the scene that you have created.

1. Choose **File > Save** from the **Info Editor** menu bar.

Tutorial 2

In this tutorial, you will create text animation and path animation. Figure 9-23 shows the text and cart at frame 55. **(Expected time: 20 min)**

Figure 9-23 *The text and cart at frame 55*

The following steps are required to complete this tutorial:

a. Open and save the file.
b. Animate the text.
c. Animate the cart.
d. Save and render the animation.

Opening and Saving the File

1. Choose **File > Open** from **Info Editor**; **File Browser** is displayed.

2. In **File Browser**, browse to *\Documents\blender2.79\c09\c09_tut2_start.blend* and choose the **Open Blender File** button; the *c09_tut2_start.blend* file is displayed in 3D view, as shown in Figure 9-24.

Figure 9-24 *The c09_tut2_start file*

3. Navigate to *\Documents\blender2.79\c09* and create a new folder with the name *c09_tut2.*

4. Choose **File > Save As** from the **Info Editor** menu bar; **File Browser** is displayed.

5. Navigate to *\Documents\blender2.79\c09\c09_tut2* and enter **text and path animation** in the **File Name** edit box. Next, choose the **Save Blender File** button to save the file at the specified location.

Animating the Text

1. Select **CADCIM** from **Outliner**. Make sure the time cursor is at frame 0. If not, enter **0** in the **Current Frame** edit box. Next, hover the cursor in Camera Persp view and press I; the **Insert Keyframe** menu is displayed.

2. Choose **Location** from the menu; a keyframe is inserted at frame 0 for location coordinates. and is indicated by yellow vertical line at frame 0 in **Timeline**.

3. Again, hover the cursor in Camera Persp view and press I. Next, choose **Scaling** from the **Insert Keyframe** menu displayed; a keyframe is inserted at frame 0 for scaling coordinates.

4. Choose the **Object** button from **Properties Editor**. You will notice that **X**, **Y**, and **Z** sliders in the **Location** and **Scale** areas of the **Transform** panel turns yellow as the keyframe is created for them.

Note

*You can also right-click on the parameters in **Properties Editor** and choose **Insert Keyframe** from the menu displayed to insert a keyframe.*

5. Move the time cursor at frame 25 manually or enter **25** in the **Current Frame** edit box. Next, enter **1.08** in the **X** slider of the **Scale** areas of the **Transform** panel and right-click on it; the **X** menu is displayed. Choose **Insert Keyframes** from it; a keyframe is inserted at frame 25 for x coordinate and indicated by yellow vertical line.

6. Move the time cursor at frame 50. Next, enter **8.41246** in the **Z** slider of the **Location** area of the **Transform** panel and right-click on it; the **Z** menu is displayed. Choose **Insert Keyframes** from it; a keyframe is inserted at frame 50 for z coordinate and is indicated by a yellow vertical line.

7. Move the time cursor at frame 75. Next, enter **6.43485** in the **Z** slider of the **Location** area of the **Transform** panel and right-click on it; the **Z** menu is displayed. Choose **Insert Keyframes** from it; a keyframe is inserted at frame 75 for z coordinate and is indicated by a yellow vertical line.

   Next, you need to copy location and scaling keyframes at frame 0 to frame 100. To do so, you need to switch to the Animation layout.

8. Choose **Animation** from the **Screen Layout** drop-down in **Info Editor**. Move the time cursor to frame 0. Press B and select all the location and scaling keyframes for *CADCIM* from **Dope Sheet**, as shown in Figure 9-25. Move the time cursor to frame 100. Next, press CTRL+V; all the keyframes at frame 0 are copied to frame 100.

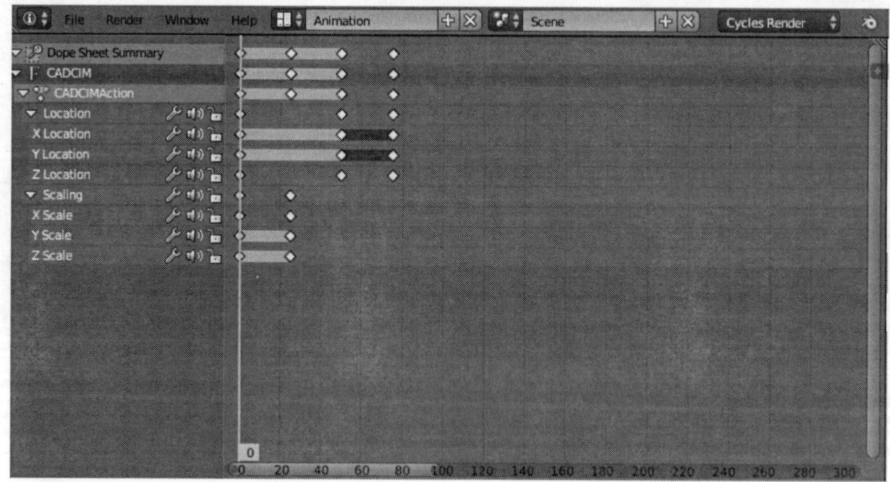

Figure 9-25 *Selected keyframes at frame 0*

9. Press ALT+ A to play the animation of *CADCIM Technologies*.

Animating the Cart

1. Switch to Default layout. Select **Cart** from **Outliner**. Next, choose the **Object Constraints** button from **Properties Editor**. Now, choose **Follow Path** from the **Relationship** category in the **Add Object Constraint** drop-down and then, refer to Figure 9-26. Also, select the **Follow Path** and **Curve Radius** check boxes.

2. Select *Path* from **Outliner**. Next, choose the **Object Data** button from **Properties Editor**. 

3. Move the time cursor to frame 0 and expand the **Path Animation** panel. Right-click on the **Evaluation Time** slider; the **Evaluation Time** menu is displayed. Choose **Insert Keyframe** from the menu; a keyframe is inserted for *path* at frame 0 and the **Evaluation Time** slider turns green as keyframe is set for it.

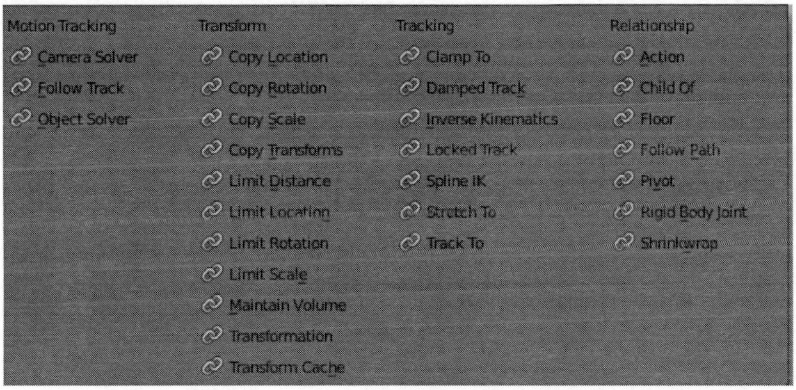

***Figure 9-26** The **Add Object Constraint** drop-down*

4. Move the time cursor to frame 101. Enter **100** in the **Evaluation Time** slider and right-click on it; Next, choose **Insert Keyframe** from the **Evaluation Time** menu displayed; a keyframe is inserted for *path* at frame 101.

5. Press ALT+ A to play the animation.

   You will notice that *cart* is not moving exactly on *path*. To move it on *path*, follow the steps given next.

6. Select *cart* from **Outliner**. Move to frame 0. Next, choose the **Object Data** button from **Properties Editor**.

7. Enter **0** in the **X**, **Y**, and **Z** sliders of the **Location** area in the **Transform** panel. Also, enter **0** in the **Z** slider of the **Rotation** area in the **Transform** panel.

8. Press ALT+ A to play the animation. You will notice that *cart* is following *path* exactly.

Rotating the Wheels of the Cart

In this section, you will separate the parts of *cart* and set keyframes for wheels to rotate them individually.

1. Select *cart* from **Outliner**. Next, switch to **Edit Mode**. Press P; the **Separate** menu is displayed. Choose **By loose parts** from the menu; all the wheels and upper part of *cart* are separated.

2. Switch to **Object Mode**. Next, select all the wheels one by one and rename them as *wheel01* to *wheel04* sequentially in **Outliner**. Also select the upper part and rename it as *upper body*.

3. Select *wheel01*. Choose the **Tools** tab from **Toolshelf**. Next, choose **Origin to Geometry** from the **Set Origin** drop-down in the **Edit** panel; the pivot of *wheel01* is set at the center of *wheel01*. Now, move the time cursor to frame 0.

4. Choose the **Object Data** button from **Properties Editor**. Right-click on the **X** slider of the **Rotation** area in the **Transform** panel and choose **Insert Keyframes** from the **X** menu displayed; a keyframe is inserted at frame 0.

5. Similarly, move the time cursor to the frames mentioned in Table 9-1 and add keyframes by setting the rotation values in the **X** slider as given in Table 9-1.

Table 9-1 *Rotation values for wheel01*

Frame to be selected	X
5	-90
10	-180
15	-270
20	-360
21	0

You will notice that one round of rotation of *wheel01* is completed by setting the keyframes mentioned above. Next, you need to copy these keyframes to repeat the rotation of *wheel01*. To copy the keyframes, you will use **Dope Sheet** from the Animation layout.

6. Choose **Animation** from the **Screen Layout** drop-down in **Info Editor**; the Animation layout is displayed, as shown in Figure 9-27.

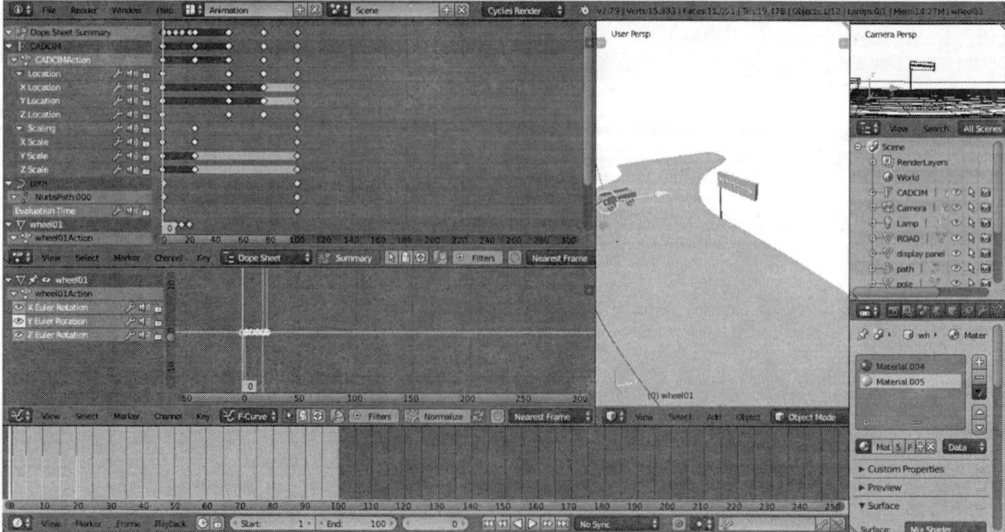

Figure 9-27 *The Animation layout*

7. In the Animation layout, enlarge **Dopesheet**. In **Dopesheet**, right-click to deselect any of the keyframes. Next, press B and select five keyframes (excluding the keyframe at frame 0) of *wheel01*, as shown in Figure 9-28.

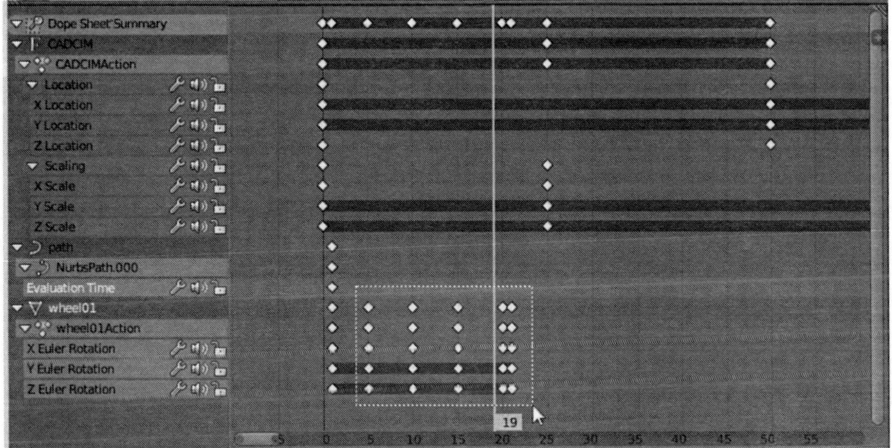

Figure 9-28** Selected keyframes in **Dopesheet

8. Press CTRL+C; the selected keyframes are copied. Now, move the time cursor to frame 25 and press CTRL+V; the copied keyframes are pasted on frame 25.

9. Move the time cursor to frame 45 and press CTRL+V; the copied keyframes are pasted on frame 45.

10. Move the time cursor to frame 65 and press CTRL+V; the copied keyframes are pasted on frame 65.

11. Move the time cursor to frame 85 and press CTRL+V; the copied keyframes are pasted on frame 85.

12. Select *wheel02*. Choose the **Tools** tab from **Toolshelf**. Next, choose **Origin to Geometry** from the **Set Origin** drop-down in the **Edit** panel; the pivot of *wheel02* is set to its center. Now, move the time cursor to frame 0.

13. Choose the **Object Data** button from **Properties Editor**. Right-click on the **X** slider of the **Rotation** area in the **Transform** panel; the **X** menu is displayed. Choose **Insert Keyframes** from the **X** menu; a keyframe is inserted at frame 0.

14. Select *wheel01*. Right-click in **Dopesheet** to deselect any of the keyframes. Next, from **Dopesheet**, select all the keyframes except the keyframes at frame 0 and press CTRL+C.

15. Select *wheel02*. Move the time cursor to frame 5. Next, press CTRL+V; all the keyframes are pasted.

16. Repeat the process followed in step 12 through step 15 to set keyframes for *wheel03* and *wheel04*.

Saving and Rendering the Animation

1. Choose **File > Save** from the **Info Editor** menu bar.

2. Choose the **Render** button from **Properties Editor**. Expand the **Output** panel. Choose the Open Folder button located next to the edit box; **File Browser** is displayed. Browse to *\Documents\blender2.79\c09 folder* and enter **c09_tut2_rndr** in the **File Name** edit box and choose **Accept**.

3. Choose **AVI JPEG** from the drop-down in the **Output** panel.

   After the completion of the rendering process, the final output of the animation is saved at the specified location in the **.AVI* format. You can view the final output of the animation by opening the corresponding **.AVI* file.

Self-Evaluation Test

Answer the following questions and then compare them to those given at the end of this chapter:

1. Which of the following modes is used to set up a bone structure?

   (a) **Edit Mode** (b) **Object Mode**
   (c) **Pose Mode** (d) **Weight Paint**

2. __________ are small triangles at the bottom of keyframes.

3. The playback range is specified in __________ color in **Timeline**.

4. The keyframe is set at the current position of the time cursor. (T/F)

5. **Dope Sheet** is used to modify an animation using F-curves. (T/F)

Review Questions

Answer the following questions.

1. Which of the following modes is used to set up poses for an object?

   (a) **Edit Mode** (b) **Object Mode**
   (c) **Pose Mode** (d) **Weight Paint**

2. Which of the following combinations of shortcut keys is used to play animation?

   (a) SHIFT+A (b) **ALT+A**
   (c) **CTRL+SHIFT+A** (d) **ALT+SHIFT+A**

3. The __________ edit box is used to set/specify the current frame.

4. The __________ button is used to add a keyframe automatically at the position of the time cursor when you transform the object in 3D View.

5. The keying sets in the **Keying Set** drop-down are the groups of properties of the object. (T/F)

EXERCISE

Exercise 1

Create a table lamp, as shown in Figure 9-29 and create a rig for it, refer to Figure 9-30.

(Expected time: 15 min)

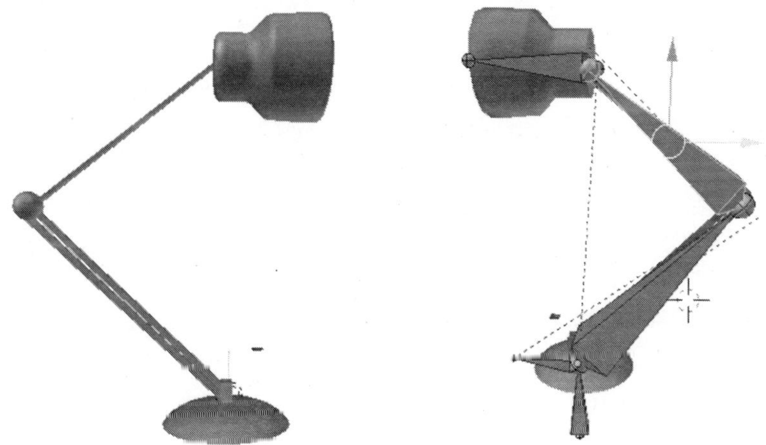

Figure 9-29 *The model of a table lamp* ***Figure 9-30*** *The rig of a table lamp*

Answers to Self-Evaluation Test

1. a, **2.** Markers, **3.** grey, **4.** T, **5.** F

Chapter 10

Rigid Body Dynamics

Learning Objectives

After completing this chapter, you will be able to:

- *Create active and passive rigid bodies*
- *Simulate various physical effects*
- *Understand rigid body constraints*

INTRODUCTION

A rigid body is an object which does not deform on colliding with another object. In Blender, you can convert objects in a scene into rigid bodies to simulate various physical effects in real world. To simulate these effects, you may also need to use the rigid body constraints. In this chapter, you will learn about the types of rigid bodies and their use. Additionally, you will learn about rigid body constraints that help to create smoke, fluid, wind, cloth simulation, and so on.

TYPES OF RIGID BODY

In Blender, there are two types of rigid bodies: Active and Passive. These types are discussed next.

Active Rigid Body

An active rigid body represents an object in the real world. It means that it falls with gravity, can collide with other objects, and can also be pushed by other objects. The motion of an active rigid body can be controlled by simulation. It can also be animated by using standard animation methods. To convert an object into an active rigid body, select the object and choose the **Physics** button from **Properties Editor**; various buttons will be displayed in the **Enable physics for** area, as shown in Figure 10-1. Choose the **Rigid Body** button; the selected object will be converted into an active rigid body and a green border will be displayed around the object. Also, **Rigid Body**, **Rigid Body Collisions**, and **Rigid Body Dynamics** panels will be displayed in **Properties Editor**, as shown in Figure 10-2. These panels are discussed next.

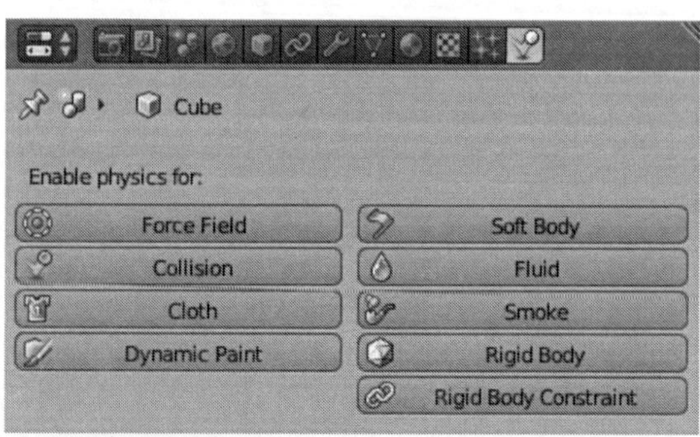

Figure 10-1 *Various buttons in the* ***Enable physics for*** *area*

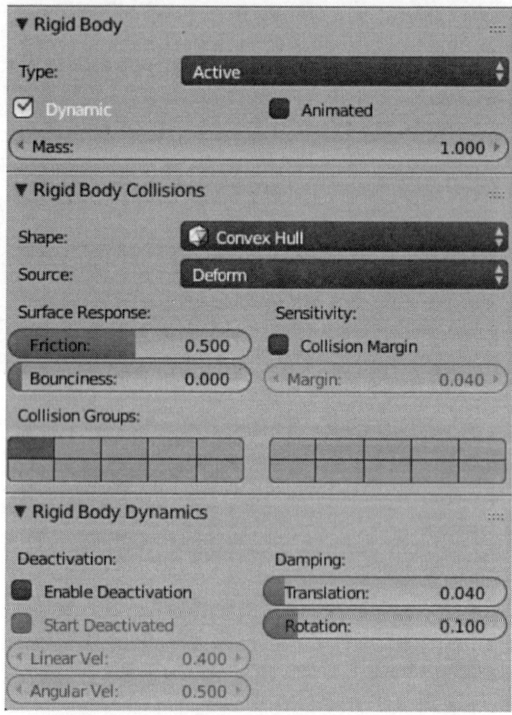

Figure 10-2 *Various panels in* ***Properties Editor***

Rigid Body

The **Type** drop-down is used to change the rigid body type. The **Mass** edit box is used to specify the mass of the rigid body. By default, the **Dynamic** check box is selected that enables simulation of the rigid body. If the **Animated** check box is selected, you can animate the object as well.

Rigid Body Collisions

The **Shape** drop-down is used to specify the collision shape of the object, refer to Figure 10-3. The options in the **Source** drop-down specify whether the modifiers applied to the object will be taken into consideration, refer to Figure 10-4. If the **Base** option is chosen, applied modifiers, if any, will not be considered at the time of collision. The **Friction** edit box is used to specify the opposing force offered to the object in simulation. The **Bounciness** edit box is used to define bounciness of an object on collision with another object.

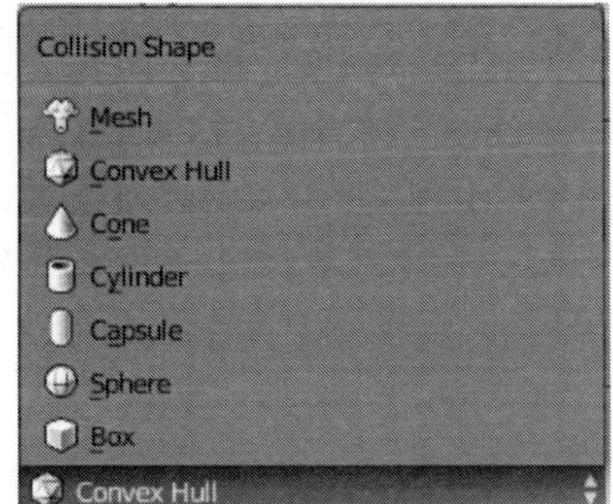

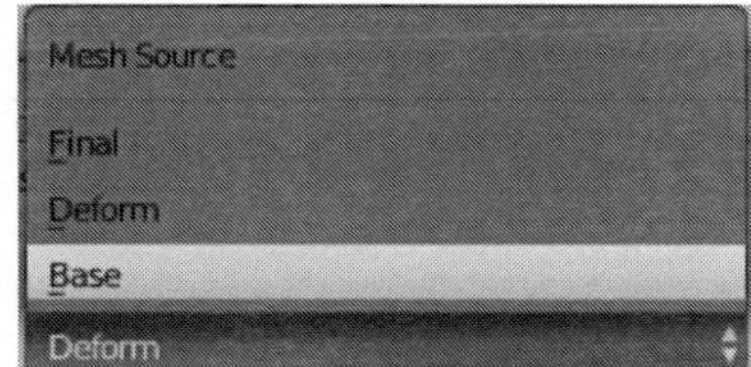

***Figure 10-3** The **Shape** drop-down* ***Figure 10-4** The **Source** drop-down*

Rigid Body Dynamics

This panel is available only when an active rigid body is selected. The parameters in this panel are used to deactivate the rigid body during the simulation process, specify linear and angular velocities below which deactivation is enabled, and also specify the damping of the angular and linear velocities of the object over time.

Note

*You can also use the options in the **Physics** tab of **Toolshelf** to convert the objects into rigid bodies, change properties of the rigid bodies, and so on.*

Passive Rigid Body

A passive rigid body remains static throughout the simulation. An active rigid body can collide with it and may bounce after colliding, but the passive rigid body will not be affected. A static rigid body is used to simulate wall, container, floor and so on. To convert an object into a passive rigid body, select the object and choose the **Physics** button from **Properties Editor**; various buttons will be displayed in the **Enable physics for** area, as shown in Figure 10-1. Choose the **Rigid Body** button. Next, choose **Passive** from the **Type** drop-down in the **Rigid Body** panel; the selected object will be converted into passive rigid body and a green border will be displayed around the object.

TYPES OF EFFECTS

There are various physical effects that can be simulated in Blender using the rigid body. Some of these effects are discussed next.

Force

Various types of forces such as wind, magnetic, Boid, and turbulence can be simulated. To enable a force field from an object, select the object. Choose the **Physics** button from **Properties Editor** and the **Force Field** button from the **Enable physics for** area. Next, choose desired option from the **Type** drop-down and then set rest of the parameters in the **Force Fields** panel. You can enable a force field from an empty object. To do so, select the empty object and choose **Add > Force Field** from the **Add** menu. Next, choose desired force field.

Collision

You can use a mesh object in the scene as a collision object to which the particles, soft bodies, and the objects converted as cloth object can collide. To simulate an object as a collision object, select the object and then choose the **Physics** button from **Properties Editor**. Next, choose the **Collision** button from the **Enable physics for** area. The **Collision** panel will be displayed in **Properties Editor** to set the desired parameters.

Cloth

To simulate an object as a cloth, select the object and then choose the **Physics** button from **Properties Editor**. Next, choose the **Cloth** button from the **Enable physics for** area; the **Cloth** button will be modified with two icons on it. First icon is used to display the simulation at the time of rendering and the second icon is used to show the simulation in viewport.

You need to choose an option from the **Preset** drop-down in the **Cloth** area to specify the type of cloth to be simulated, refer to Figure 10-5. Also, there are variety of options available in the **Cloth** area to specify mass, velocity, bending ability, and so on of a cloth. The options in the **Cloth Collision** panel are used to specify the parameters related to collision of cloth such as repulsion force, distance between the cloth and the collision object at the time of collision, friction, and so on. The options in the **Cloth Stiffness Scaling**, **Cloth Sewing Springs**, and **Cloth Field Weights** are used to set the advanced parameters of the cloth.

***Figure 10-5** The **Cloth Preset** drop-down*

Soft Body

Soft bodies are the rigid bodies that get deformed on collision. You can convert an object into a soft body to simulate elastic objects, flags, jelly, clay, and so on. To convert an object into a soft body, select the object and then choose the **Physics** button from **Properties Editor**. Next, choose the **Soft Body** button from the **Enable physics for** area; the **Soft Body** button will be modified with two icons on it as discussed earlier. Also, various panels are displayed in **Properties Editor** to control the properties of the soft body. Note that all the mesh primitive objects, curves, surfaces, and lattice objects can be converted into a soft body.

Fluid

To simulate an object as a fluid, select the object and then choose the **Physics** button from **Properties Editor**. Next, choose the **Fluid** button from the **Enable physics for** area; the **Fluid** button will be modified with two icons on it as discussed earlier. Also, the **Fluid** panel will be displayed in **Properties Editor**. Apart from the object that simulates the fluid, you need to simulate other objects that control the whole fluid simulation process such as domain in which the fluid will be restricted, the objects to control the volume of fluid, obstacles in the fluid flow, and so on. Figure 10-6 shows the options in the **Type** drop-down.

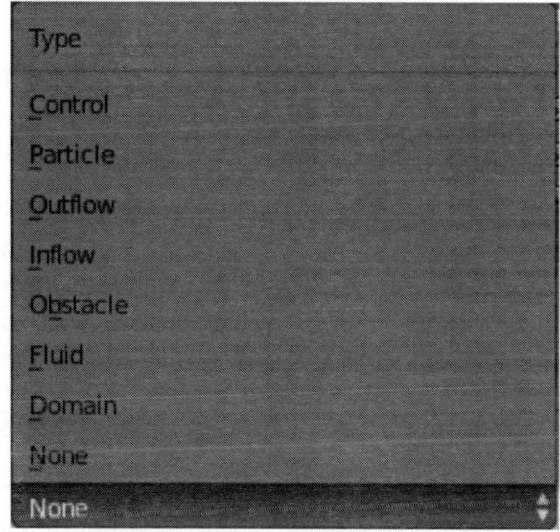

***Figure 10-6** The **Type** drop-down*

Smoke

To simulate an object as smoke, select the object and then choose the **Physics** button from **Properties Editor**. Next, choose the **Smoke** button from the **Enable physics for** area; the **Smoke** button will be modified with two icons on it as discussed earlier. Also, the **None**, **Domain**, **Flow**, and **Collision** buttons will be displayed in **Properties Editor**. Apart from the object that simulates the smoke, you need to create a domain in which the smoke will be restricted. The **Domain** button is used to create the domain. The **Collision** button is used to simulate the object that will act as a collision object. When you choose one of these buttons, corresponding panels will be displayed in **Properties Editor** to set desired parameters.

RIGID BODY CONSTRAINTS

Rigid body constraints are used to restrict the movement of rigid bodies in simulation. Various types of constraints are available in Blender such as fixed constraint, hinge constraint, and motor constraint. These constraints make two rigid bodies work together. A constraint links two rigid bodies together or links a single rigid body to a fixed point in global space. The constraints develop a hierarchical relationship in which the child object must be an active rigid body, while the parent object can be an active or passive rigid body, or can be a point in the global space. Most commonly used constraints are discussed next.

Fixed Constraint

Fixed constraint is used to connect two objects together so that both move as a single object in simulation. To apply a fixed rigid body constraint to the objects, convert them into active rigid bodies as discussed earlier. Make sure one of the object is selected and the **Physics** button is chosen in **Properties Editor**. Next, choose the **Rigid Body Constraint** button from the **Enable physics for** area. Scroll down in **Properties Editor** and choose **Fixed** from the **Type** drop-down in the **Rigid Body Constraint** panel, refer to Figure 10-7. Now, click on the **Object 1** edit box and choose one of the objects from the menu displayed. Also, click on the **Object 2** edit box and choose the second object.

Hinge Constraint

As the name suggests, hinge constraint works like a hinge in between two connected objects. To apply a fixed rigid body constraint to the objects, convert the objects into active rigid bodies. Clear the **Dynamic** check box in the **Rigid Body** panel for the object that would act as a static object. Make sure one of the objects is selected and the **Physics** button is chosen in **Properties Editor**. Next, choose the **Rigid Body Constraint** button from the **Enable physics for** area. Scroll down in **Properties Editor** and choose **Hinge** from the **Type** drop-down in the **Rigid Body Constraint** panel. Now, click on the **Object 1** edit box and choose one of the objects from the menu displayed. Similarly, click on the **Object 2** edit box to choose another object.

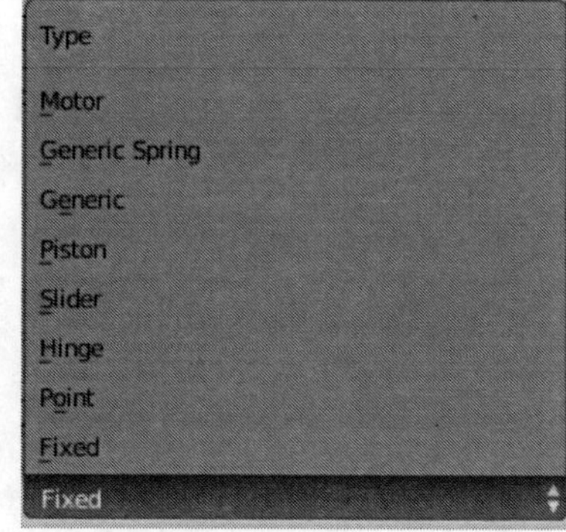

Figure 10-7 *The **Type** drop-down*

Motor Constraint

The motor constraint allows translation and/or rotation around the x axis between the two objects. You also need to use hinge constraint so that motor constraint yields the desired result. To apply a motor rigid body constraint to the objects, convert them into suitable rigid bodies and apply the constraint as discussed earlier.

Slider Constraint

Slider constraint is used to restrict translation of the constraint object in x axis only. In other words, it does not allow translation in other axes and rotation in any of the axes of the object. To apply a slider rigid body constraint to the objects, convert them into suitable rigid bodies and apply the constraint as discussed earlier.

Point Constraint

The point constraint is similar to the hinge constraint with the difference that the object on which this constraint is applied can rotate in all the three axes. To apply a point rigid body constraint to the objects, convert one of the objects into a passive rigid body. This object will remain static throughout the simulation. Convert the other object into an active rigid body. This object will rotate around a point in the scene. This point can be the center of the two objects, center of the active object, or center of the selected object. Next, apply the constraint as discussed earlier.

Piston Constraint

Piston constraint is used to allow translation and rotation of the constraint object along x axis. You can set the lower and upper limits for translation and rotation of the object. To apply piston rigid body constraint to the objects, convert them into active rigid bodies as discussed earlier. You need to clear the **Dynamic** check box in the **Rigid Body** panel for the object that would act as a static object. Next, apply the constraint as discussed earlier.

TUTORIALS

Before you start tutorials of this chapter, you need to download *c10_blender_2.79_tut.zip* file from *www.cadcim.com*. The path of the file is as follows: *Textbooks > Animation and Visual Effects > Blender > Blender 2.79 for Digital Artists*

Browse to *\Documents\blender2.79* and create a folder with the name *c10*. Next, extract the content of the zip file in this folder.

Tutorial 1

In this tutorial, you will create a scene showing the simulation of falling balls from a bowl connected with a hinge constraint, refer to Figure 10-8. **(Expected time: 20 min)**

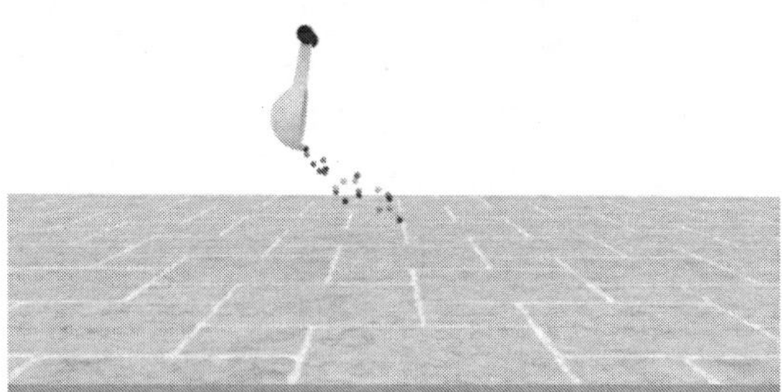

Figure 10-8 *Balls falling from bowl at frame 55*

The following steps are required to complete this tutorial:

a. Open and save the file.
b. Convert objects into rigid bodies.
c. Apply the hinge constraint.
d. Play and bake simulation.
e. Save and render the animation.

Opening and Saving the File

1. Choose **File > Open** from **Info Editor**; **File Browser** is displayed.

2. In **File Browser**, browse to *\Documents\blender2.79\c10\c10_tut1_start.blend* and choose the **Open Blender File** button; the *c10_tut1_start.blend* file is displayed in Camera Persp view, as shown in Figure 10-9.

3. Navigate to *\Documents\blender2.79\c10* and create a new folder with the name *c10_tut1*.

4. Choose **File > Save As** from the **Info Editor** menu bar; **File Browser** is displayed.

5. Navigate to *\Documents\blender2.79\c10\c10_tut1* and enter **Falling ball simulation** in the **File Name** edit box. Next, choose the **Save Blender File** button to save the file at the specified location.

Figure 10-9 The c10_tut1_start file

Converting Objects into Rigid Bodies

1. Select *floor.* Choose the **Physics** button from **Properties Editor**. Next, choose the **Rigid Body** button from the **Enable physics for** area; *floor* is converted into an active rigid body. Notice that green border is displayed around *floor* in 3D view.

2. Choose **Passive** from the **Type** drop-down in the **Rigid Body** panel; *floor* becomes passive rigid body.

3. Select *ball01*. Choose the **Physics** button from **Properties Editor**. Next, choose the **Rigid Body** button from the **Enable physics for** area; *ball01* is converted into an active rigid body.

4. Make sure **Convex Hull** is chosen in the **Shape** drop-down of the **Rigid Body Collisions** area.

5. Select all the other balls from the scene. (*ball02* through *ball25*) Choose the **Physics** tab from **Toolshelf**. Next, choose **Copy From Active** from the **Object Tools** panel in **Toolshelf**; all the selected balls are converted into active rigid bodies.

6. Select *bowl*. Choose the **Physics** button from **Properties Editor**. Next, choose the **Rigid Body** button from the **Enable physics for** area; *bowl* is converted into an active rigid body.

7. Choose **Mesh** from the **Shape** drop-down in the **Rigid Body Collisions** panel.

8. Select *rod*. Choose the **Physics** button from **Properties Editor**. Next, choose the **Rigid Body** button from the **Enable physics for** area; *bowl* is converted into an active rigid body.

9. Clear the **Dynamic** check box from the **Rigid Body** panel.

Applying the Hinge Constraint

1. Select *rod*. Choose the **Physics** button from **Properties Editor**. Next, choose the **Rigid Body Constraint** button from the **Enable physics for** area.

2. Scroll down in **Properties Editor** and choose **Hinge** from the **Type** drop-down in the **Rigid Body Constraint** panel.

3. Click on the **Object 1** edit box and choose **rod** from the menu displayed. Also, click on the **Object 2** edit box and choose **bowl** from the menu displayed.

Playing and Baking the Simulation

1. Press ALT+A; the simulation starts in the Camera Persp view.

2. Press ALT+A to stop the simulation.

3. Select all the balls in the scene. Next, choose **Bake to Keyframes** from the **Object Tools** panel in **Toolshelf**.

Saving and Rendering the Animation

1. Choose **File > Save** from the **Info Editor** menu bar.

2. Choose the **Render** button from **Properties Editor**. Expand the **Output** panel. Choose the Open Folder button located next to the edit box; **File Browser** is displayed. Browse to *\Documents\blender2.79\c10* and enter **c10_tut1_rndr** in the **File Name** edit box and choose **Accept**.

3. Choose **AVI JPEG** from the drop-down in the **Output** panel.

   After the completion of the rendering process, the final output of the animation is saved at the specified location in the *.AVI format. You can view the final output of the animation by opening the corresponding *.AVI file.

Tutorial 2

In this tutorial, you will create cloth simulation, as shown in Figures 10-10 and 10-11.

(Expected time: 20 min)

Figure 10-10 *Cloth simulation at frame 35*

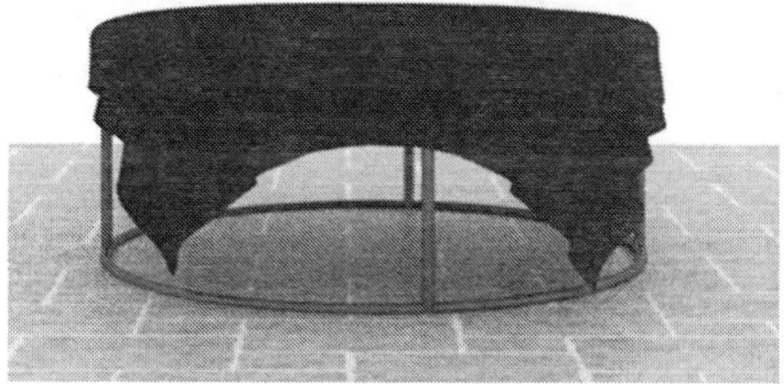

Figure 10-11 *Cloth simulation at frame 100*

The following steps are required to complete this tutorial:

a. Open and save the file.
b. Simulate the cloth.
c. Play and bake the Simulation.
d. Save and render the animation.

Opening and Saving the File

1. Choose **File > Open** from **Info Editor**; **File Browser** is displayed.

2. In **File Browser**, browse to the *\Documents\blender2.79\c10\c10_tut2_start.blend* and choose the **Open Blender File** button; the *c10_tut2_start.blend* file is displayed in Camera Persp view, as shown in Figure 10-12.

Figure 10-12 *The c10_tut2_start file*

3. Navigate to *\Documents\blender2.79\c10* and create a new folder with the name *c10_tut2.*

4. Choose **File > Save As** from the **Info Editor** menu bar; **File Browser** is displayed.

5. Navigate to *\Documents\blender2.79\c10\c10_tut2* and enter **Cloth simulation** in the **File Name** edit box. Next, choose the **Save Blender File** button to save the file at the specified location.

Simulating the Cloth

1. Select *tablecloth*. Next, choose the **Physics** button from **Properties Editor**.

2. Choose **Cloth** from the **Enable physics for** area. Next, choose **Silk** from the **Presets** drop-down in the **Cloth** area.

3. Expand the **Cloth Collision** panel. Next, select the **Self Collision** check box to enable self collision of *tablecloth*. Also, enter **0.75** in the **Distance** slider to avoid tearing of cloth on collision with *table*.

4. Select *table*. Next, choose **Collision** from the **Enable physics for** area.

Playing and Baking the Simulation

1. Press ALT+A; the simulation starts in the Camera Persp view.

2. Press ALT+A to stop the simulation.

3. Select *tablecloth* in the scene. Next, choose **Bake to Keyframes** from the **Object Tools** panel in **Toolshelf**.

Saving and Rendering the Animation

1. Choose **File > Save** from the **Info Editor** menu bar.

2. Choose the **Render** button from **Properties Editor**. Expand the **Output** panel. Choose the Open Folder button located next to the edit box; **File Browser** is displayed. Browse to *\Documents\blender2.79\c10,* enter **c10_tut2_rndr** in the **File Name** edit box, and choose **Accept**.

3. Choose **AVI JPEG** from the drop-down in the **Output** panel.

   After the completion of the rendering process, the final output of the animation is saved at the specified location in the *.AVI format. You can view the final output of the animation by opening the corresponding *.AVI file.

Self-Evaluation Test

Answer the following questions and then compare them to those given at the end of this chapter:

1. Which of the following objects does not deform when it collides with another object?

   (a) Active rigid body (b) Passive rigid body
   (c) both a and b (d) soft body

2. The __________ rigid body can be animated by using the standard animation methods.

3. __________ are used to restrict the movement of rigid bodies in simulation.

4. In the __________ effect, an object can simulate as a paint brush that is used to paint on the other objects in the scene.

5. Soft bodies are the rigid bodies that get deformed on collision. (T/F)

Review Questions

Answer the following questions:

1. Which of the following rigid bodies remains static throughout simulation?

   (a) Active rigid body (b) Passive rigid body
   (c) both a and b (d) soft body

2. A __________ links two rigid bodies together or links a single rigid body to a fixed point in global space.

3. The **Shape** drop-down in the **Rigid Body Collisions** area is used to specify the _________ of the object.

4. A passive rigid body can fall with gravity, collide with other objects, and can also be pushed by other objects. (T/F)

5. The mesh primitive objects, curves, surfaces, and lattice objects can be converted into soft bodies. (T/F)

EXERCISES

Exercise 1

Create a scene as shown in Figure 10-13 and simulate a ball falling on sliders. Figure 10-14 shows the falling ball at frame 504. **(Expected time: 15 min)**

Hint: Increase the playback range so that ball touches the ground at the end of the simulation. Also, set the same value in the **End** edit box of the **Rigid Body Cache** area to enable simulation for the whole playback range.

Exercise 2

Create a scene as shown in Figure 10-15 and simulate balls falling in a bowl, refer to Figures 10-16 and 10-17. **(Expected time: 15 min)**

Hint:
Use hinge constraint for the upper assembly and piston constraint for the lower assembly.

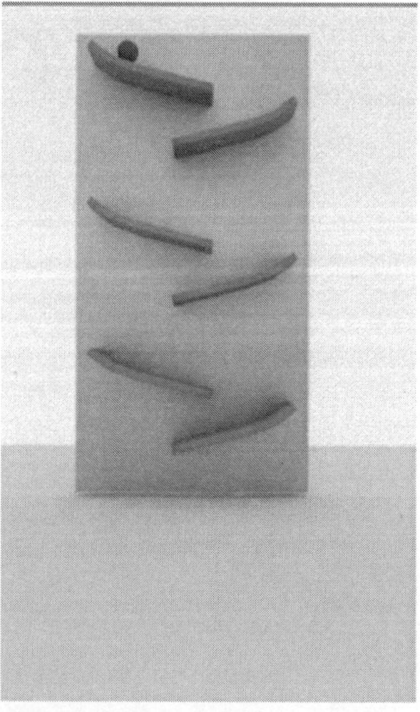

Figure 10-13 *The scene with sliders and a ball*

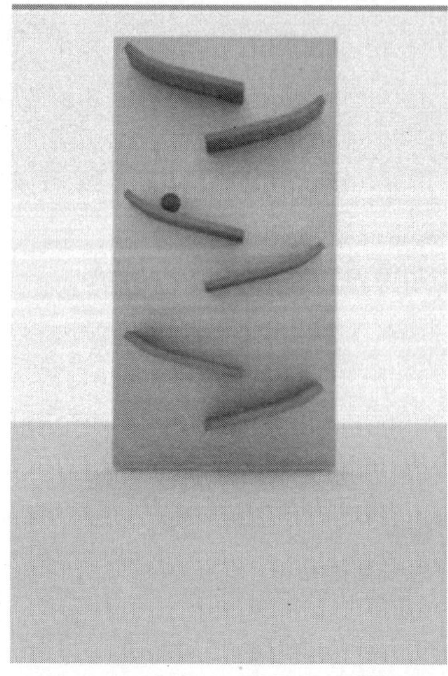

Figure 10-14 *Ball at frame 504*

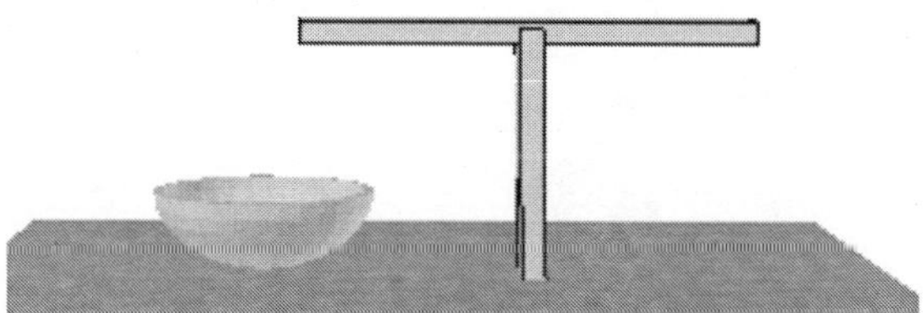

Figure 10-15 *The scene with two assemblies, balls, and a bowl*

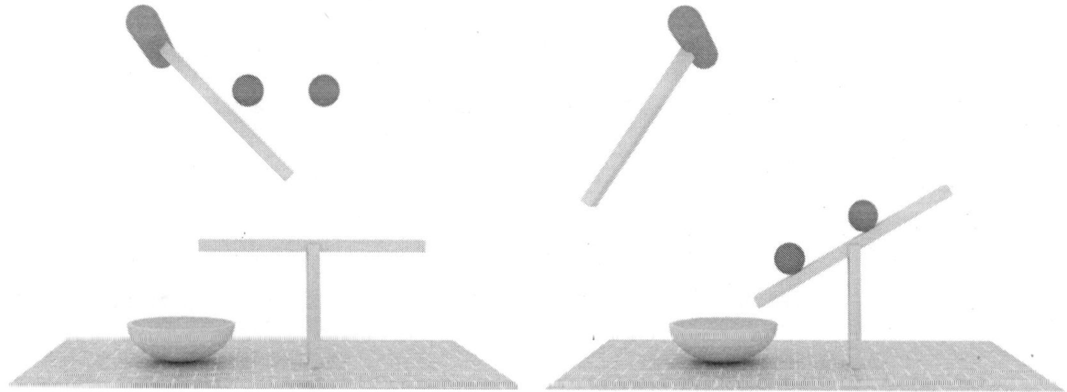

Figure 10-16 *Simulation at frame 25*

Figure 10-17 *Simulation at frame 45*

Answers to Self-Evaluation Test

1. c, **2.** active, **3.** Rigid body constraints, **4.** Dynamic Paint, **5.** T

Chapter 11

Working with Particles

Learning Objectives

After completing this chapter, you will be able to:

- *Understand particle system*
- *Understand various simulation techniques*

INTRODUCTION

In Blender, you can use an object as particle system. Particle system is used to emit particles that are used to simulate snow, dust, rain, fluid, and so on. In this chapter, you will learn to create particle system and use various simulation techniques.

PARTICLE SYSTEM

To create a particle system, choose the **Particle** button from **Properties Editor**; **Properties Editor** will be displayed, as shown in Figure 11-1. Select the object that is to be used as a particle system and then choose **New** from **Properties Editor**; the selected object will be converted into a new particle system. Also, various panels and options at the top will be displayed in **Properties Editor**, as shown in Figure 11-2.

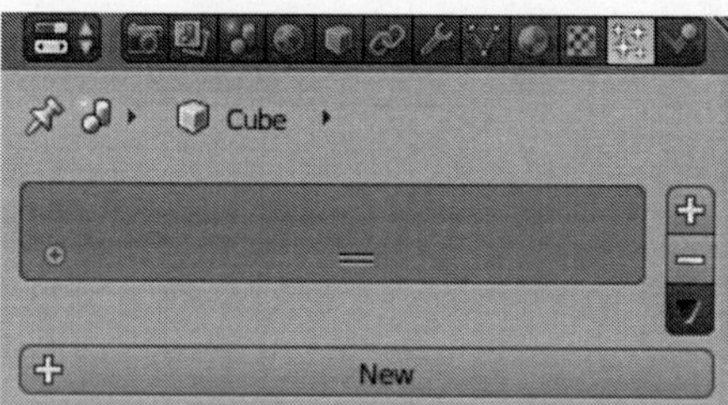

*Figure 11-1 The **Properties Editor** on choosing the **Particles** button*

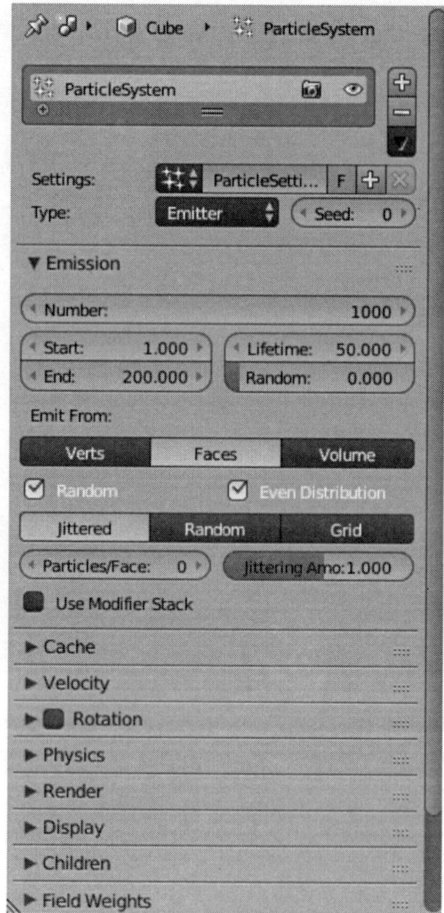

*Figure 11-2 **Properties Editor** on choosing the **New** button*

Particle Stack

Particle Stack is located at the top in **Properties Editor**. As you add a new particle system to the object, it gets added to the stack. To rename a particle system, double-click on its name in

Particle Stack. To add or remove a particle system, choose **+** and **-** buttons, respectively, on the right side of **Particle Stack**.

Settings

As you create a particle system, you need to set parameters in various panels of **Properties Editor**. To save the settings, type a name in the **Settings** text box located below **Particle Stack** and press ENTER. The name of the settings saved will be added to the **Settings** drop-down. You can choose settings from the **Settings** drop-down whenever required. The **+** button on the right of the **Settings** text box is used to add a new particle settings. The **F** button is used to create a fake user. This saves the settings for future use.

Type

The **Type** drop-down has two options: **Emitter** and **Hair**. By default, the **Emitter** option is chosen. As a result, particles are emitted from the object. If you choose the **Hair** option, particles come out as strands from the object. Also, some panels and parameters in some of the panels in Properties Editor differ for these two options.

Most commonly used parameters in the panels that are displayed when **Emitter** is chosen in the **Type** drop-down are discussed next.

Emission

The **Number** slider is used to specify the number of particles emitted from the object. The **Start** slider is used to specify the frame at which the object starts emitting the particles and the **End** slider is used to specify the frame at which the object stops emitting the particles.

The **Lifetime** slider is used to specify the lifespan of the particles in frames. The **Random** slider is used to specify the value that determines the randomness in lifespan of the particles. The formula for the randomness in lifespan is **Lifetime** X (1- **Random**). It means that if **Lifetime** = **200** and **Random** = **0.5** then the lifespan of particles varies from 100 to 200.

If you choose the **Verts** button from the **Emit From** area, particles will be emitted from the vertices of the object, refer to Figure 11-3. The **Random** check box located below this button is used to add randomness in the emission of particles from the selected elements of the object.

If you choose the **Faces** button from the **Emit From** area, particles will be emitted from all the faces of the object, refer to Figure 11-4.

If you choose the **Volume** button from the **Emit From** area, particles will be emitted from the volume that is formed by the enclosed mesh of the object, refer to Figure 11-5.

On choosing the **Faces** and **Volume** buttons from the **Emit From** area, some additional parameters will be displayed. These parameters are discussed next.

If the **Even Distribution** check box is selected, distribution of particles is directly proportional to the surface area of the object.

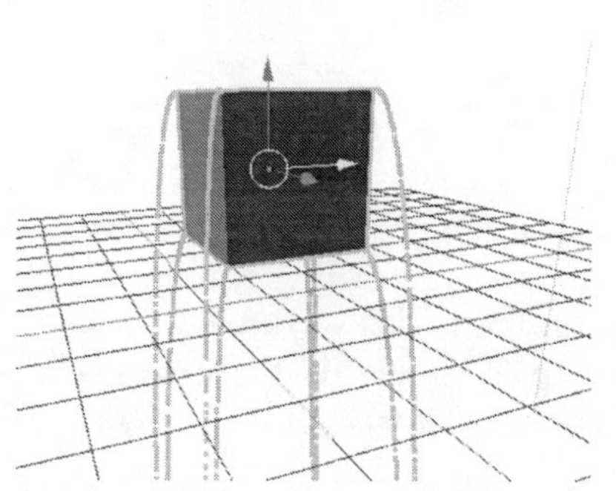

***Figure 11-3** Particles emitted from the cube on choosing the **Verts** button*

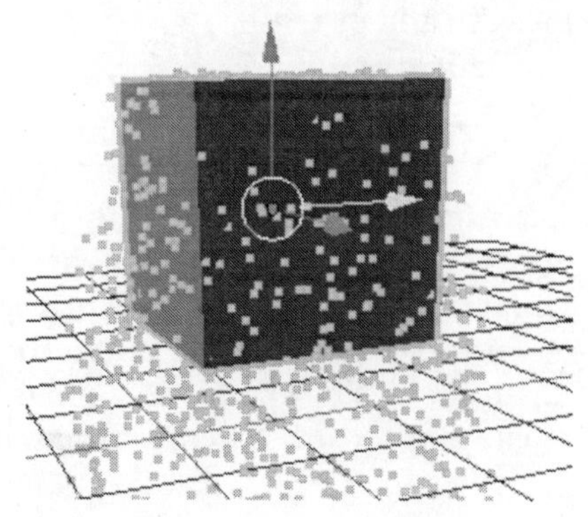

***Figure 11-4** Particles emitted from the cube on choosing the **Faces** button*

If the **Jittered** button is chosen, placing of the particles will be at jittered intervals. Similarly, if the **Random** button is chosen, particles are emitted from random places on the surface area of the object and if the **Grid** button is chosen, particles are set and emitted in grid, refer to Figure 11-6.

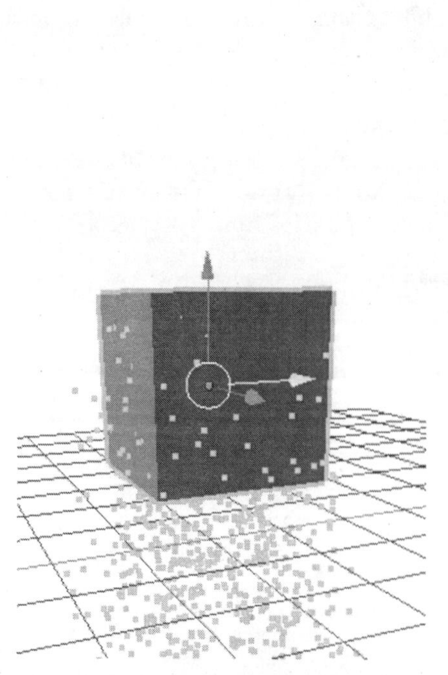

***Figure 11-5** Particles emitted from the cube on choosing the **Volume** button*

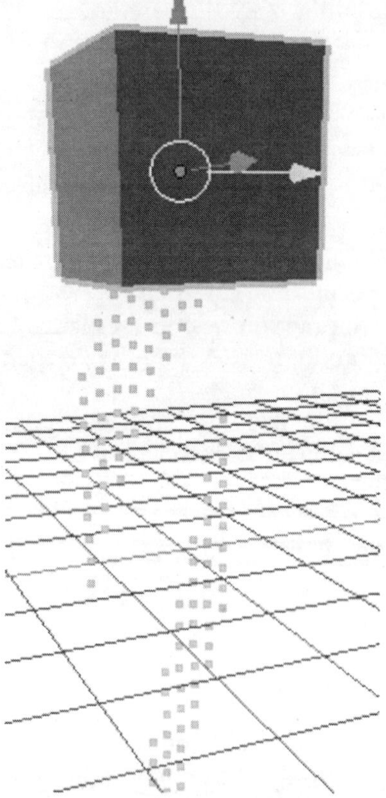

***Figure 11-6** Particles emitted from the cube on choosing the **Grid** button*

If the **Use Modifier Stack** check box is selected, all the modifiers applied to the object will be taken into account at the time of emission.

Cache

Parameters in this panel are used to cache the emission data to avoid calculation of particles again and again. This panel also includes parameters to bake the data.

Velocity

The starting velocity of the particles can be changed by changing the value in the **Normal** and **Tangent** sliders. The **Rot** slider is used to rotate the surface tangent of the object.

The **X**, **Y**, and **Z** sliders are used to emit the particles with an initial velocity in x, y, and z directions, respectively. The **Random** slider provides variation in starting velocity of the particles.

Rotation

You need to select the **Rotation** check box to enable the parameters in this panel. The **Initial Orientation** and **Angular Velocity** drop-downs are used to specify orientation of initial and angular velocity of the particles, refer to Figures 11-7 and Figure 11-8. You can also add variation to these velocities by specifying desired value in the **Random** slider.

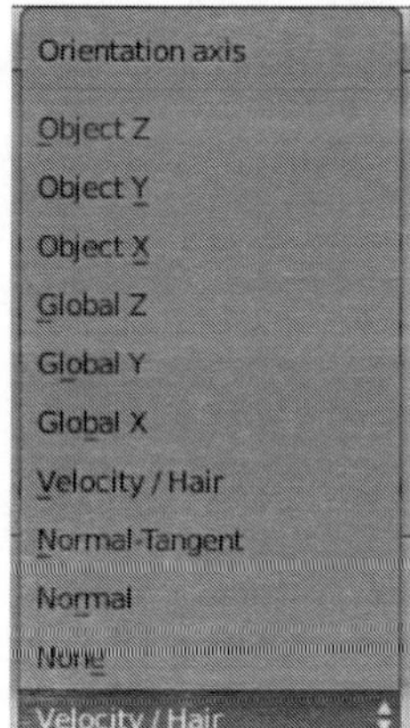

*Figure 11-7 The **Orientation** drop-down*

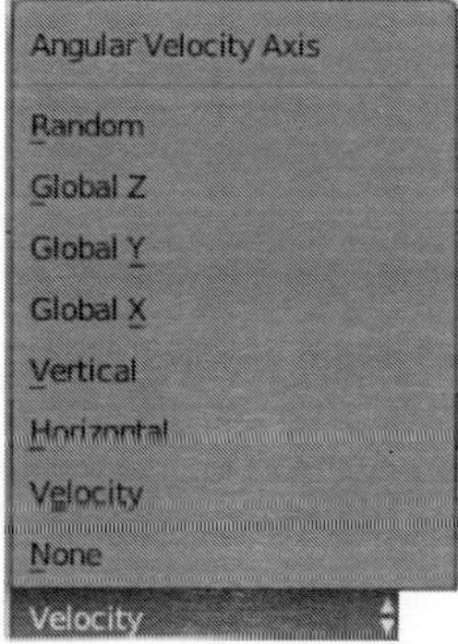

*Figure 11-8 The **Angular Velocity** drop-down*

If the **Dynamic** check box is selected, particle retains its specified initial and angular velocities till the physical simulation changes it.

Physics

Buttons at the top in this panel are used to specify the type of particles to be emitted. Other parameters displayed in this panel depend on the button chosen. Some of the parameters are common for all the types of particles to be emitted and are discussed next.

The **Size** and **Mass** sliders specify the size and mass of the particle, respectively. The **Random** slider specifies variation in the size of the particle.

If the **Multiply mass with size** check box is selected, the mass of the particle depends on the size of the particle. If the value in the **Random** slider is more than zero, size of the particles will vary.

Performance of the emitted particles in simulation largely depends on the button chosen at the top in this panel and is discussed next.

No

If you choose this button, particles emitted will be motionless and therefore, particles will remain at the surface of the emitter for their total lifespan, refer to Figure 11-9.

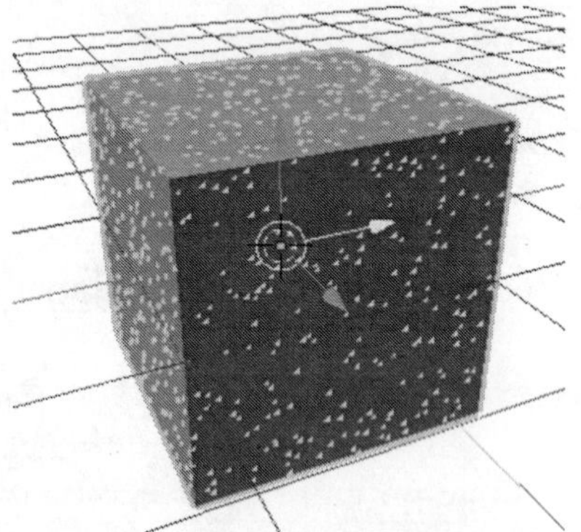

***Figure 11-9** Particles emitted from the cube on choosing the **No** button*

Newtonion

By default, this button is chosen in the **Physics** panel. As a result, the movement of particles is based on Newtonion mechanics. The Newtonion mechanics is the system of mechanics which relies on Newton's laws of motion regarding the relations between forces acting and motions occurring. You need to set the strength of the forces by setting the values in the **Brownion**, **Drag**, and **Damp** sliders. Figure 11-10 shows the parameters displayed in the **Physics** panel on choosing the **Newtonion** button.

Keyed

You need at least two particle systems for keyed type of particles. Path of the keyed particles is from the emitter of the first particle system to the particles of another particle system. As a result, chains of particle systems can be created. These type of particle chains are useful in making long strands, long attractive moving particle chains, and so on.

Figure 11-11 shows the parameters displayed in the **Physics** panel on choosing the **Keyed** button. The **Keys Stack** is used to add or remove a particle system from the chain of particle system. First particle system has to be a keyed particle system whereas the second particle system need not be keyed particle system.

Boids

The boids particle system has limited artificial intelligence. Performance of this particle system depends on the location of the particles in the scene. Figure 11-12 shows the parameters displayed in the **Physics** panel on choosing the **Boids** button.

By default, the **Allow Flight** check box is selected. As a result, particles will move in air. You can set the parameters listed below the check box to specify particle speed in the air, angular velocity, acceleration in air, and so on.

If you select the **Allow Land** check box, particles are allowed to move on land. Also, you can set the parameters such as speed of particles on land, acceleration on land, jumping speed, and so on.

If the **Allow Climbing** check box is selected, particles are allowed to climb the object that has positive spherical field.

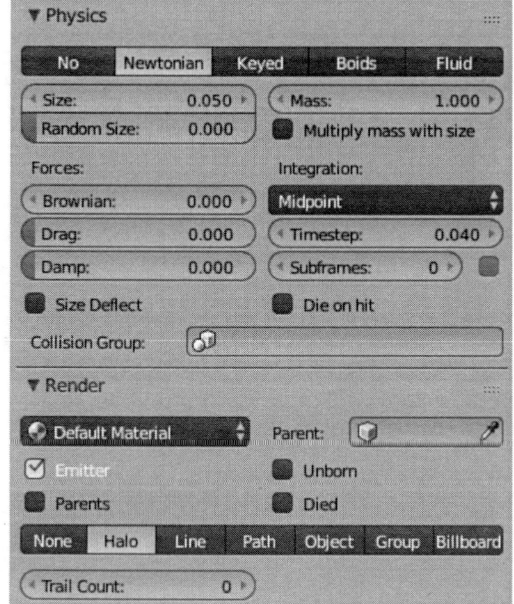

*Figure 11-10 Parameters in the **Physics** panel on choosing the **Newtonion** button*

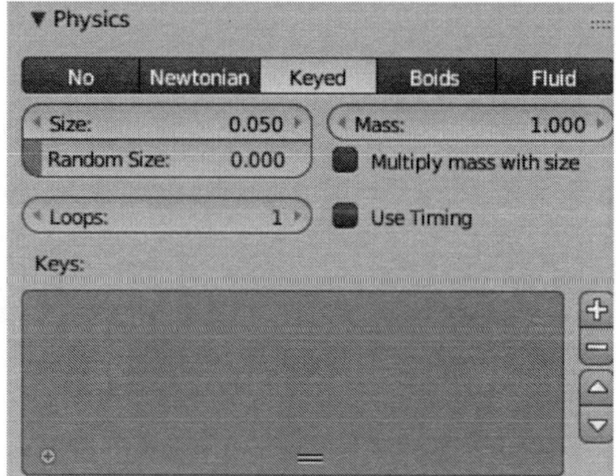

*Figure 11-11 Parameters in the **Physics** panel on choosing the **Keyed** button*

There are some more parameters in the **Battle** area that determine strength, health, distance, and accuracy of boids particles when they attack each other.

The **Relations Stack** is used to add or remove the particle system that will react with the boids particle system.

The **Boid Brain** panel is also available in **Properties Editor**. The parameters in this panel are used to control how the particles will react with each other.

Fluid

Fluid particle system is used to simulate liquid, smoke, slime, and so on. Figure 11-13 shows the parameters displayed in the **Physics** panel on choosing the **Fluid** button. Blender uses the smoothed particle hydrodynamics (SPH) method for fluid simulation.

Depending on the type of fluid to be simulated, you need to set the parameters in the **Fluid Properties**, **Advanced**, and **Springs** areas.

Render

Parameters in the **Render** panel are used to specify the render settings of the particle system, refer to Figure 11-14. Choose the desired material for the particles to be emitted from the **Material** drop-down.

If you select the **Emitter** check box, object that is used as an emitter will be rendered. To render the parent particles, you need to select the **Parent** check box.

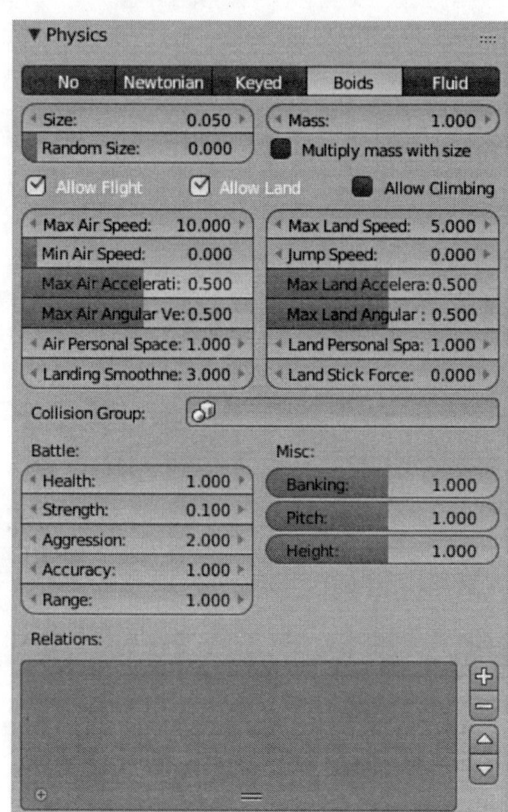

*Figure 11-12 Parameters in the **Physics** panel on choosing the **Boids** button*

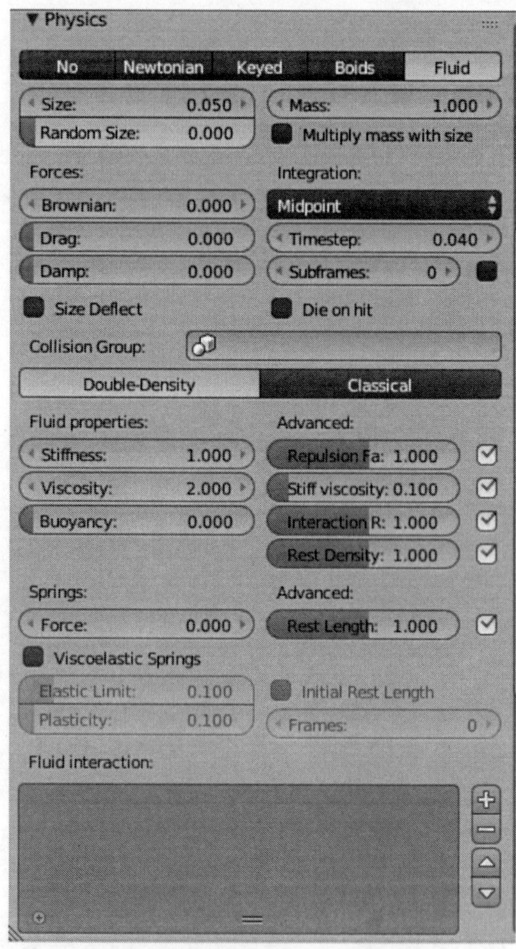

*Figure 11-13 Parameters in the **Physics** panel on choosing the **Fluid** button*

The **Unborn** check box, if selected, displays particles in render before they are born. Similarly, the **Died** check box, if selected, displays the particles in render after they are dead.

If you choose the **None** button, the particles are not rendered.

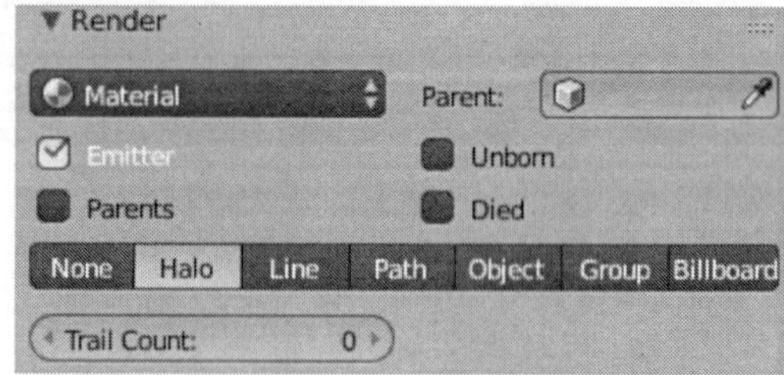

*Figure 11-14 The parameters in the **Render** panel*

If you choose the **Halo** button, particles are rendered as halo particles. Halo particles are the glowing dots with no substance. However, they do not cast light in the scene. Figure 11-15 shows particles rendered as halo particles being emitted from a cube with **Trail Count** = **2**. As the value in the **Trail Count** slider is set to more than one, the **Length** and **Random** sliders are the parameters that are available to set the trail length and randomness in it.

Figure 11-15 Rendered halo particles

As the name suggests, the **Line** button is used to render the particles as lines. Figure 11-16 shows the particles rendered as lines with the parameters set as shown in Figure 11-17.

If you choose the **Object** button, the **Dupli Object** drop-down along with an edit box will be displayed below it. You need to choose the object from this drop-down or enter the name of the object in the edit box. This object will be used as a particle at the time of emission.

Figure 11-16 The particles emitted as lines

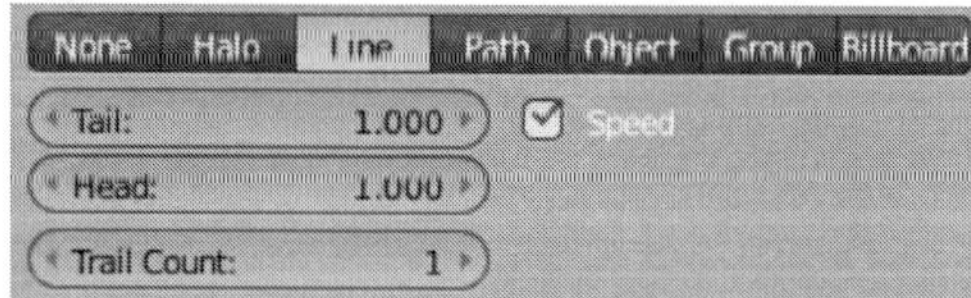

*Figure 11-17 The parameters in the **Render** panel*

If you choose the **Group** button, the **Dupli Group** drop-down along with an edit box will be displayed below it. You need to choose the group from this drop-down or enter the name of the group in the edit box. The objects in this group will be used depending on the options chosen below the drop-down.

If you choose the **Billboard** button, the particles emitted will be the square planes. By default, the orientation of these planes is aligned to the camera. However, you can change the orientation by using other options in the panel.

Display

The options in this panel are used to specify how the particles will be displayed in the viewport. Note that the display of particles in the viewport does not affect their display on rendering.

TUTORIALS

Before you start tutorials of this chapter, you need to download *c11_blender_2.79_tut.zip* file from *www.cadcim.com*. The path of the file is as follows: *Textbooks > Animation and Visual Effects > Blender > Blender 2.79 for Digital Artists*

Browse to *\Documents\blender2.79* and create a folder with the name *c11*. Next, extract the content of the zip file in this folder.

Tutorial 1

In this tutorial, you will simulate smoke emerging from smokestack, as shown in Figure 11-18.

(Expected time: 20 min)

Figure 11-18 *Smoke simualtion at frame 80*

The following steps are required to complete this tutorial:

a. Open and save the file.
b. Add force field.
c. Create particles.
d. Create smoke material.
e. Simulate smoke.
f. Play and bake the Simulation.
g. Save and render the animation.

Opening and Saving the File

1. Choose **File > Open** from **Info Editor**; **File Browser** is displayed.

2. In **File Browser**, browse to *\Documents\blender2.79\c11\c11_tut1_start.blend* and choose the **Open Blender File** button; the *c11_tut1_start.blend* file is displayed in Camera Persp view, as shown in Figure 11-19.

   Note that the Cycles Render engine is used in the *c11_tut1_start.blend* file.

3. Navigate to *\Documents\blender2.79\c11* and create a new folder with the name *c11_tut1*.

4. Choose **File > Save As** from the **Info Editor** menu bar; **File Browser** is displayed.

5. Navigate to *\Documents\blender2.79\c11\c11_tut1* and enter **Smoke simulation** in the **File Name** edit box. Next, choose the **Save Blender File** button to save the file at the specified location.

***Figure 11-19** The c11_tut1_start file*

Adding Force Field

In this section, you will add force field that will act as wind in the scene.

1. Create a plane. Rename it as *force1*. Choose the **Object** button from **Properties Editor**. Enter the values as shown in Figure 11-20 in the **Transform** panel of **Properties Editor**; *force1* is aligned.

2. Choose the **Physics** button from **Properties Editor**. Next, choose the **Force Field** button from the **Enable physics for** area; the **Force Field** panel is displayed in **Properties Editor**.

3. In the **Force Field** panel, choose **Wind** from the **Type** drop-down and **Point** from the **Shape** drop-down. Also, enter **25** and **5.4** in the **Strength** and **Flow** sliders, respectively.

4. Create one more plane. Rename it as *force2*. Choose the **Object** button from **Properties Editor**. Enter the values as shown in Figure 11-21 in the **Transform** panel of **Properties Editor**; *force2* is aligned. Figure 11-22 shows *force1* and *force2* aligned in the scene.

▼ Transform

Location:	Rotation:	Scale:
: -39.43000	X: 97.8°	X: 1.000
Y: 2.36000	Y: -5.86°	Y: 1.000
: 23.18000	Z: 82.4°	Z: 1.000

Figure 11-20 *Values in the* ***Transform*** *panel*

▼ Transform

Location:	Rotation:	Scale:
X: -2.46000	X: 37.2°	X: 1.000
Y: -8.08000	Y: -26.3°	Y: 1.000
: 17.76000	Z: -99.1°	Z: 1.000

Figure 11-21 *Values in the* ***Transform*** *panel*

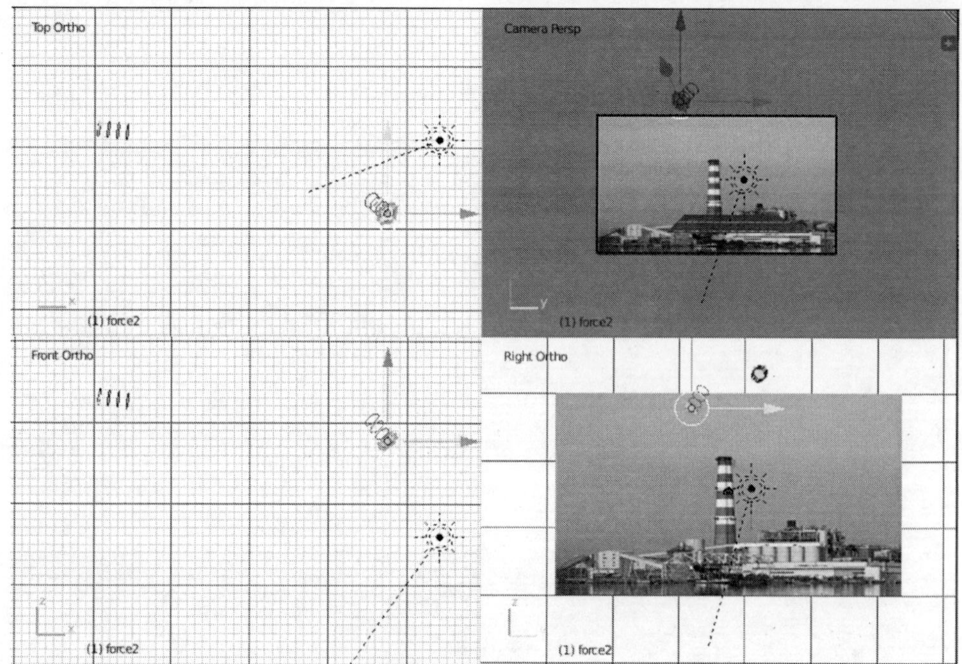

Figure 11-22 *The force1 and force2 aligned*

Creating Particles

The current scene consists of a background scene, sun lamp, force field, and a camera. In this section, you will add a small plane that will act as an emitter to simulate smoke.

1. Create a plane. Rename it as emitter. Choose the **Object** button from **Properties Editor**. Enter the values as shown in Figure 11-23 in the **Transform** panel of **Properties Editor**; *emitter* is aligned, as shown in Figure 11-24.

2. Make sure *emitter* is selected. Choose the **Particle** button from **Properties Editor**. Next, choose **New**; **Properties Editor** is modified.

Location:	Rotation:	Scale:
: -21.63420	X: 0°	X: 1.600
Y: -3.16302	Y: 30°	Y: 1.600
: 10.01614	Z: 0°	Z: 0.000

Figure 11-23 *Values in the* ***Transform*** *panel*

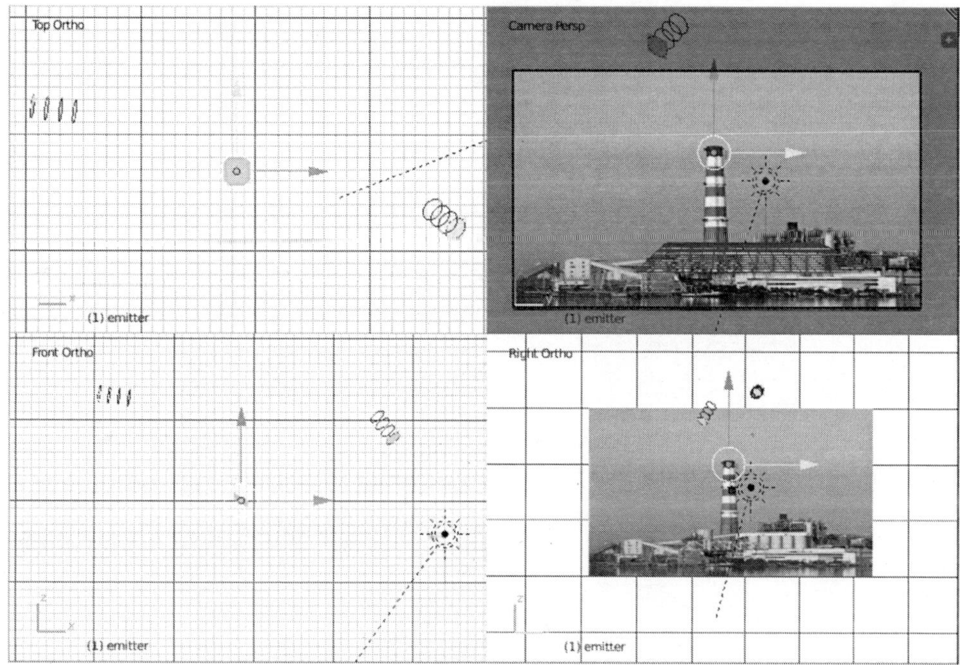

Figure 11-24 *The emitter aligned*

3. Press ALT+A to play the animation; particles are emitted from the emitter, refer to Figure 11-25.

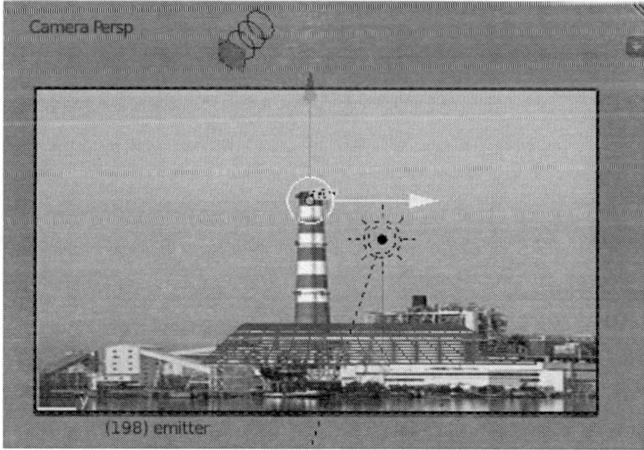

Figure 11-25 *Particles emitted from emitter*

With the default settings, particles are emitted but they are not going upward due to gravity.

4. Scroll down in **Properties Editor**. Expand the **Field Weights** panel. Next, enter **-1** in the **Gravity** slider.

5. Expand the **Velocity** panel and enter **10** in the **Z** slider as starting velocity. Play the animation again. Notice that particles are emitting upwards now.

   Next, you need to increase number of particles and their lifetime.

6. In the **Emission** panel, enter **5000** in the **Number** slider. Also, enter **250** and **100** in the **End** and **Lifetime** sliders, respectively.

7. Press ALT+ A. Notice the change in the number of particles and lifetime of the particles, refer to Figure 11-26.

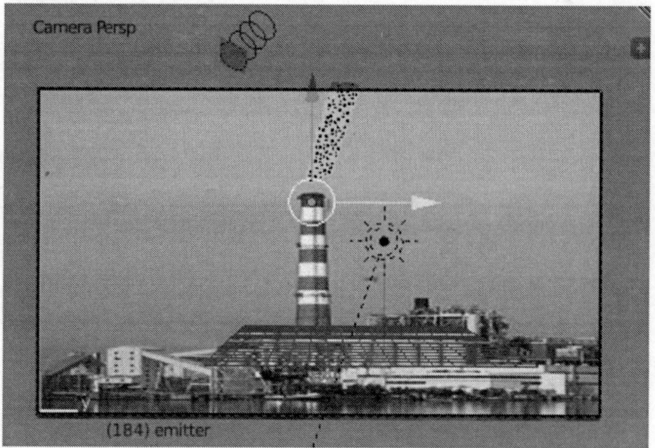

***Figure 11-26** Change in number and lifetime of particles*

Creating Smoke Material

In this section, you will create a group that consists of spheres of different sizes. These spheres will be used as particles. You will also create a smoke material for these spheres.

1. Create a sphere. Apply the **Subdivision Surface** modifier to the sphere to make it smooth.

Note

*You may increase the subdivisions in the **Subdivisions** area of **Properties Editor** by changing the values in the **View** and **Render** sliders.*

2. Create three more copies of it. Scale the copies of spheres to get different sizes, refer to Figure 11-27.

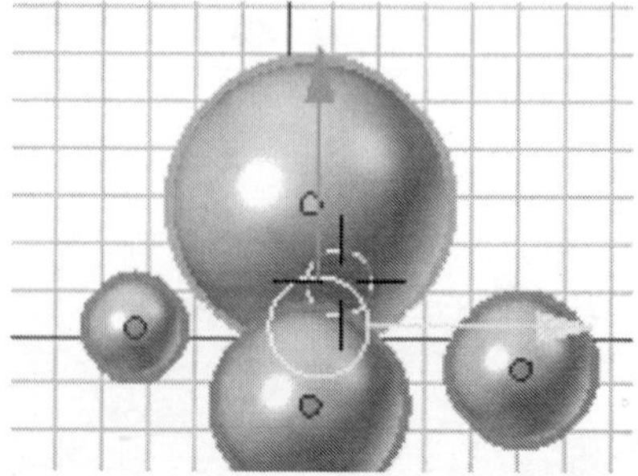

***Figure 11-27** Spheres of different sizes*

Next, you need to create smoke material for the spheres.

3. Make sure one of the spheres is selected. Next, choose **Compositing** from the **Screen layout** drop-down. Choose the **Shader nodes** button in **Node Editor**.

4. Choose **New** from **Node Editor**; a new material is created and the **Diffuse BSDF** and **Material Output** nodes are displayed in **Node Editor**. Remove connection between these two nodes. Enter **smoke material** in the text box located on the left of the **Material** drop-down in **Node Editor**.

5. Click on the color swatch in the **Diffuse BSDF** node. Enter **0.313** in the **R**, **G**, and **B** sliders of the Color Picker window displayed; grey color is displayed in the color swatch.

6. Hover the cursor in **Node Editor** and press SHIFT+A; the **Add** menu is displayed. Choose **Texture > Image Texture** from the menu; the **Image Texture** node is attached to the cursor. Place this node on the left of the **Diffuse BSDF** node.

7. Choose **Open** from the **Image Texture** node; **File Browser** is displayed. Navigate to *\Documents\blender2.79\c11\c11_tut1* and select **smoke.png** from it and then choose **Open Image** button from **File Browser**; the **Open** button in the **Image Texture** node is replaced by *smoke.png*.

8. Set the parameters in the **Image Texture** node, as shown in Figure 11-28.

9. Hover the cursor in **Node Editor** and press SHIFT+A; the **Add** menu is displayed. Choose **Vector > Mapping** from the menu; the **Mapping** node is attached to the cursor. Place this node in between the **Image Texture** node and the **Diffuse BSDF** node such that the **Vector** input of the **Mapping** node is connected to the **Color** output of the **Image Texture** node and the **Vector** output of the **Mapping** node is connected to the **Color** input of the node. Also, choose **Texture** in the **Mapping** node, refer to Figure 11-29.

***Figure 11-28** Parameters in the **Image Texture** node*

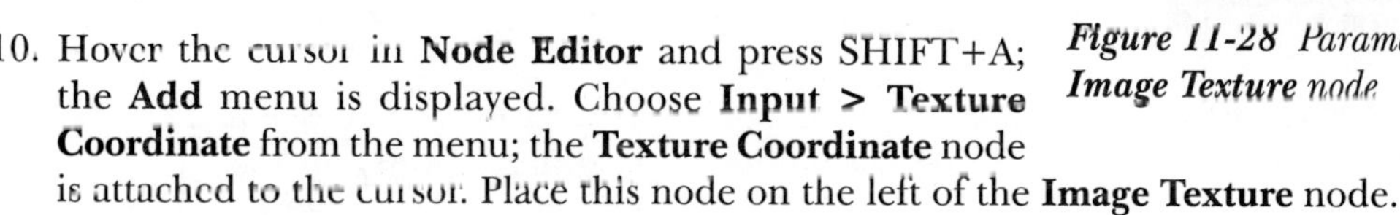

10. Hover the cursor in **Node Editor** and press SHIFT+A; the **Add** menu is displayed. Choose **Input > Texture Coordinate** from the menu; the **Texture Coordinate** node is attached to the cursor. Place this node on the left of the **Image Texture** node.

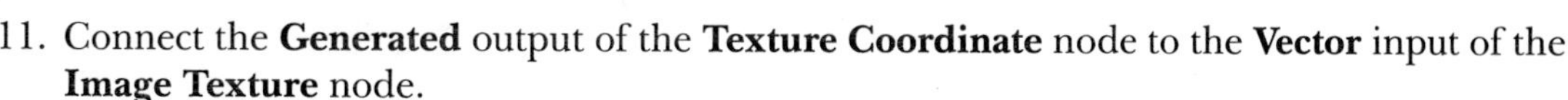

11. Connect the **Generated** output of the **Texture Coordinate** node to the **Vector** input of the **Image Texture** node.

12. Add the **Mix Shader** and **Transparent BSDF** nodes in **Node Editor** and make the connections to create the node network, as shown in Figure 11-29.

13. Select other spheres in the scene one by one and apply smoke material to them.

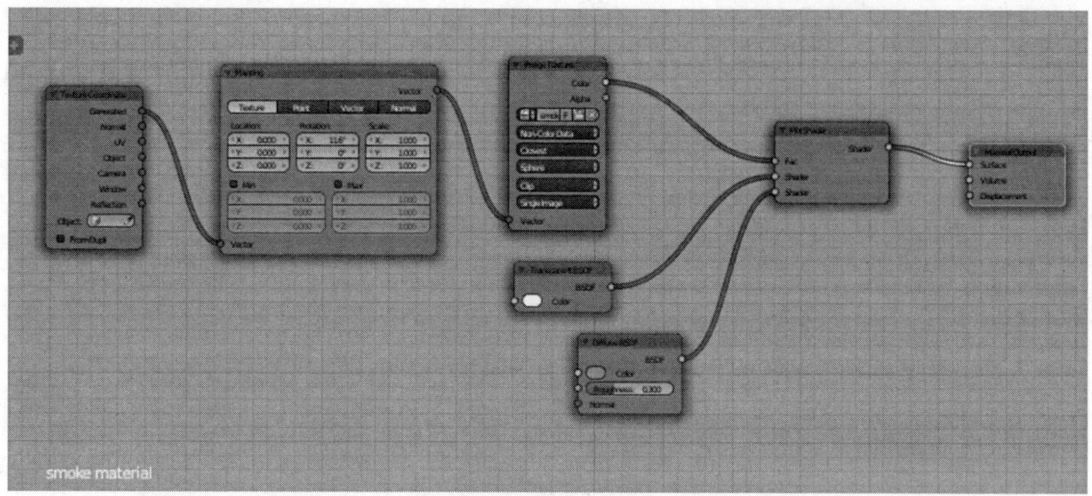

***Figure 11-29** Node network for smoke material*

14. Select all the spheres and press CTRL+G; a new group is created that consists of all spheres.

    Notice that green border is displayed around all the spheres.

15. Make sure the **Object** button is chosen in **Properties Editor**. In the **Groups** panel, enter **smoke objects** in the edit box; group is renamed as *smoke objects*.

Simulating Smoke

1. Select **emitter** from **Outliner**. Make sure the **Particles** button is chosen in **Properties Editor**. Next, scroll down and expand the **Render** panel. In this panel, choose the **Group** button.

2. Click on the **Dupli Group** edit box and choose **smoke objects** from the menu displayed; all the emitted particles get converted into spheres in the *smoke objects* group with smoke texture on it. Select the **Pick Random** check box. Also, enter **1** in the **Size** and **Random Size** sliders.

   Next, you need to rotate these planes randomly and also increase their size.

3. Select the **Rotation** check box in the title bar of the **Rotation** panel. Select the **Dynamic** check box and enter **1** in the **Velocity** slider of the **Angular Velocity** area.

4. Press ALT+A. Pause the animation at approximately frame 80. Now, press F12.

   Notice the change in size, type, and velocity of the particles emitted in the rendered image, refer to Figure 11-30.

5. Select *lamp* in **Outliner**. Choose the **Object data** button in **Properties Editor**. Enter **5** in the **Strength** slider of the **Nodes** area.

Figure 11-30 *Smoke simulation at frame 80*

6. Repeat step 4. Notice the change in the intensity of the light.

Playing and Baking the Simulation

1. Press ALT+A; simulation starts in the Camera Persp view.

2. Press ALT+A again to stop the simulation.

3. Select *emitter* from **outliner**. Make sure the **Particles** button is chosen in **Properties Editor**. Expand the **Cache** panel in **Properties Editor**. Next, choose the **Bake** button.

Saving and Rendering the Animation

1. Choose **File > Save** from the **Info Editor** menu bar.

2. Choose the **Render** button from **Properties Editor**. Expand the **Output** panel. Choose the **Open Folder** button located next to the edit box; **File Browser** is displayed. Browse to *\Documents\blender2.79\c11* folder and enter *c11_tut1_rndr* in the **File Name** edit box and choose **Accept**.

3. Choose **AVI JPEG** from the drop-down in the **Output** panel.

   After the completion of the rendering process, the final output of the animation is saved at the specified location in the *.AVI format. You can view the final output of the animation by opening the corresponding *.AVI file.

Tutorial 2

In this tutorial, you will simulate snow fall, as shown in Figure 11-31.

(Expected time: 20 min)

The following steps are required to complete this tutorial:

a. Set up the scene.
b. Create particles.

c. Create snow material.
d. Simulate snow fall.
e. Play and bake the simulation.
f. Save and render the animation.

Figure 11-31 *Snow simulation at frame 100*

Setting Up the Scene

1. Navigate to *\Documents\blender2.79\c11* and create a new folder with the name *c11_tut2*.

2. Press CTRL+N or choose **File > New** from the **Info Editor** menu bar; a menu is displayed. Choose **Reload Start-Up File** from the menu; the startup file gets loaded.

3. Choose **File > Save** from the **Info Editor** menu bar; **File Browser** is displayed

4. Navigate to *\Documents\blender2.79\c11\c11_tut2* and enter **snow simulation** in the **File Name** edit box. Next, choose the **Save Blender File** button to save the file at the specified location.

5. Delete *cube* from the scene. Also, choose Cycles Render from the **Engine** drop-down in **Info Editor**.

6. Choose **File > User Preferences** from the **Info Editor** menu bar. Next, choose the **Add-ons** tab from the **Blender User Preferences** dialog box displayed.

7. Select the **Import-Export: Import Images as Planes** check box and then choose **Save User Settings** from the **Blender User Preferences** dialog box. Next, close the dialog box.

8 Hover the cursor in 3D view and press SHIFT+A; the **Add** menu is displayed. Choose **Add > Mesh > Images as Planes** from the menu; **File Browser** is displayed. Navigate to *\Documents*

blender2.79\c11 and select **snow scene** from the list displayed. Next, choose **Import Images as Planes** to close **File Browser**. Notice that a plane is added with the name *snow scene*.

9. Increase the size of *snow scene* approximately 3 times. Next, choose **Texture** from the **Viewport Shading** drop-down. Adjust the view in User Persp view so that front of *snow scene* is visible, refer to Figure 11-32.

Figure 11-32 *Adjusting the view*

10. Select *camera* from **Outliner**. Next, choose **View > Align View > Align Active Camera to View** from the **3D View Editor** menu bar. Also, align camera manually so that it covers maximum portion of *snow scene.* Press 0; Camera Persp view is displayed, refer to Figure 11-33.

Figure 11-33 *Camera Persp view displayed*

11. Create a plane. Rename it as *emitter*. Resize and place *emitter* at the top of *snow scene*, as shown in Figure 11-34.

Creating Particles

1. Select *Emitter*. Choose the **Particles** button from **Properties Editor**. Next, choose **New** from **Properties Editor**; various panels are displayed.

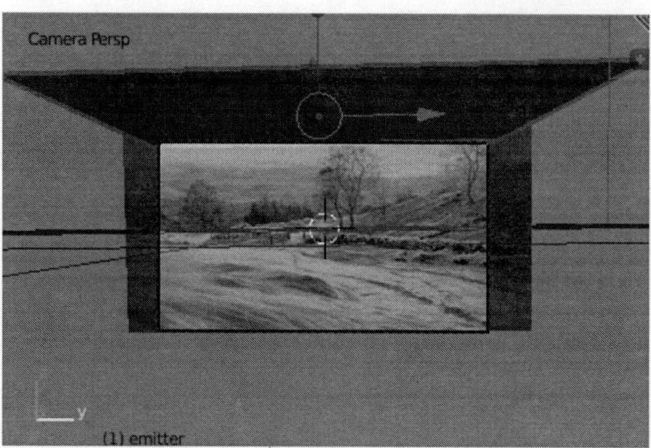

Figure 11-34 Emitter aligned

2. In the **Emission** panel, enter **10000** in the **Number** slider. Next, enter **-50** and **300** in the **Start** and **Lifetime** sliders, respectively. Also, enter **250** in the **End** slider.

Note

*Negative value in the **Start** slider ensures emission of particles from the first frame itself.*

3. Press F12; particles are emitted from first frame and continues till the end frame as a result of the parameters set above.

4. Press F12 again to stop the emission. Next, create an icosphere and place it outside the camera range. Apply the **Subdivision Surface** modifier to icosphere.

5. Select *emitter*. Make sure the **Particles** button is chosen in **Properties Editor**. In the **Render** panel of **Properties Editor**, choose the **Object** button. Next, click on the **Dupli Object** edit box and choose **Icosphere** from the list displayed.

6. In the **Render** panel, enter **0.02** in the **Size** slider.

7. Press F12. Notice that icospheres are emitted from *emitter*.

Creating Snow Material

In this section. you will assign snow material to the icosphere and split it into smaller parts to simulate as snow flakes.

1. Select *icosphere*. Next, choose **Compositing** from the **Screen Layout** drop-down. Choose the **Shader nodes** button in **Node Editor**.

2. Choose **New** from **Node Editor**; a new material is created and the **Diffuse BSDF** and **Material Output** nodes are displayed in **Node Editor**. Enter **snow material** in the text box located on the left of the **Material** drop-down in **Node Editor**.

3. Hover the cursor in **Node Editor** and Press SHIFT+A. Next, choose **Texture > Voronoi** texture from the **Add** menu displayed.

4. Delete the **Diffuse BSDF** node. Next, add and connect the nodes and set their parameters, as shown in Figure 11-35.

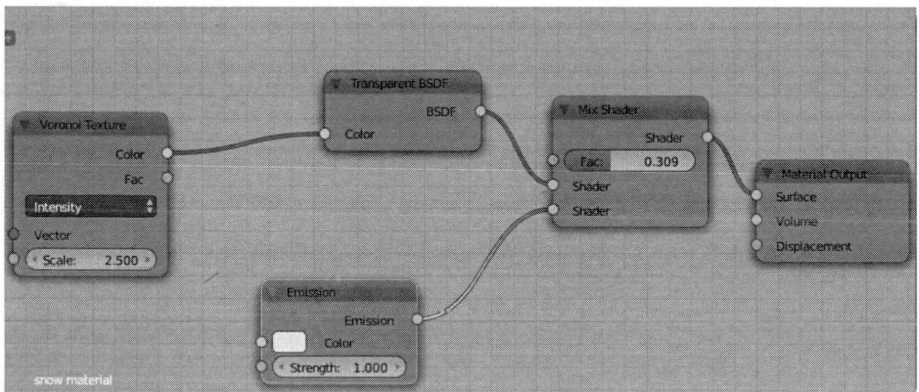

Figure 11-35 *Node network for snow material*

5. Choose **File > User Preferences** from the **Info Editor** menu bar; the **Blender User Preferences** dialog box is displayed. Make sure the **Add-ons** tab is chosen. Next, select the **Object: Cell Fracture** check box and choose the **Save User settings** and close the dialog box.

6. Make sure *icosphere* is selected. Next, choose the **Tools** tab from **Toolshelf**.

7. Choose the **Cell Fracture** from the **Edit** panel; the **Cell Fracture selected mesh objects** dialog box is displayed.

8. In this dialog box, enter **16** in the **Source Limit** slider and **1** in the **Recursion** slider. Next, choose **OK** to close the dialog box.

   Notice the splitting process of *icosphere* in 3D view. Also, notice that one more layer is created with the parts of *icosphere*. In default layer, *icosphere* acts as a single object whereas in layer 2, parts of *icosphere* are available.

9. Select layer 2. Make sure *icosphere* is not selected. Next, select all the parts of *icosphere* and press CTRL+G; a new group is created that consists of all the parts. Notice that a green border is displayed around all the parts. Also, the **Create New Group** is added to **Toolshelf**. Enter **snow objects** in the edit box; group is renamed as *snow objects*.

Simulating Snow Fall

1. Select layer 1. Next, select *emitter*. Make sure the **Particles** button is chosen in **Properties Editor**. In the **Render** panel, choose the **Group** button and click on the **Dupli Group** edit box and choose **snow objects** from the menu displayed; the split icospheres in the *snow objects* group start getting emitted.

Next, you need to rotate these parts randomly and also provide angular velocity to them.

2.. Select the **Rotation** check box in the title bar of the **Rotation** panel. Choose **Object Z** from the drop-down in the **Initial Rotation** area and enter **0.344** in the **Random** slider below it. Also, enter **0.390** and **0.790** in the **Phase** and **Random** sliders, respectively. Next, select the **Dynamic** check box and enter **1** in the **Velocity** slider of the **Angular Velocity** area. Choose **Random** from the drop-down in the **Angular Velocity** area.

Next, you need to apply various forces to *snow objects* and change the mass of these objects.

3. In the **Physics** panel, enter **0.26** in the **Random Size** slider and enter **1.25** in the **Mass** slider. In the **Forces** area, enter **1.5, 0.65,** and **0.5** in the **Brownian, Drag,** and the **Damp** sliders, respectively.

4. Press F12. Notice effect of applied forces and change in the speed as well as rotation of particles.

Next, you need to add wind and turbulance to *snow objects.*

5. Press SHIFT+A. Next, choose **Force Field > Wind** from the **Add** menu displayed; **Field** is added to the scene. Rename it as *wind.*

6. Make sure *wind* is selected and the **Physics** button is chosen in **Properties Editor**. In the **Force Fields** panel of **Properties Editor**, enter **5** and **0.2** in the **Strength** and **Noise** sliders, respectively. Next, align *wind,* as shown in Figure 11-36.

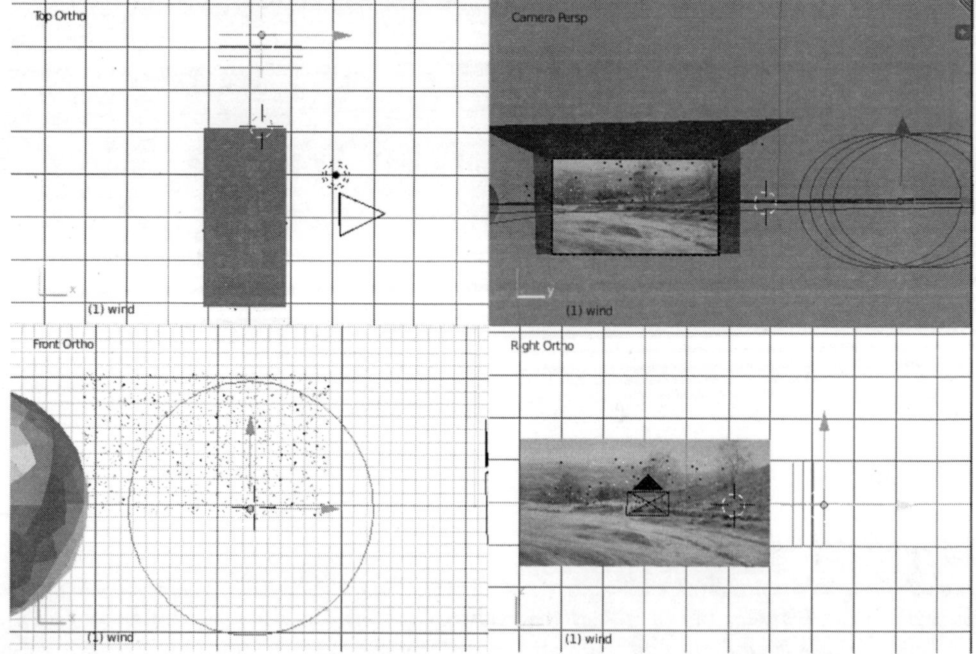

Figure 11-36 *wind aligned*

7. Press SHIFT+A. Next, choose **Force Field > Turbulance** from the **Add** menu displayed; **Field** is added to the scene. Rename it as *turbulance.*

8. Make sure *turbulance* is selected. In the **Force Fields** panel of **Properties Editor**, enter **7** and **3.5** in the **Strength** and **Size** sliders, respectively. Next, align *turbulance* at the center of *snow objects*.

   Next, you need to add motion blur to the scene.

9. Choose the **Render** button from **Properties Editor**. Select the **Motion Blur** check box and expand the **Motion Blur** panel. Enter **0.65** in the **Shutter** slider.

   Next, you need to change the parameters of *lamp* in the scene.

10. Select *lamp*. Choose the **Object data** button from **Properties Editor**. In the **Lamp** panel, choose **Sun**. Next, choose the **Use Nodes** button and set light blue color in the **Color** swatch to simulate night scene.

Playing and Baking the Simulation

1. Press ALT+A; simulation starts in the Camera Persp view.

2. Press ALT+A again to stop the simulation.

3. Select *emitter* from **outliner**. Make sure the **Particles** button is chosen in **Properties Editor**. Expand the **Cache** panel in **Properties Editor**. Next, choose the **Bake** button.

Saving and Rendering the Animation

1. Choose **File > Save** from the **Info Editor** menu bar.

2. Choose the **Render** button from **Properties Editor**. Expand the **Output** panel. Choose the **Open Folder** button located next to the edit box; **File Browser** is displayed. Browse to *\Documents\blender2.79\c11* and enter *c11_tut2_rndr* in the **File Name** edit box and choose **Accept**.

3. Choose **AVI JPEG** from the drop-down in the **Output** panel.

   After the completion of the rendering process, the final output of the animation is saved at the specified location in the *.AVI format. You can view the final output of the animation by opening the corresponding *.AVI file.

Self-Evaluation Test

Answer the following questions and then compare them to those given at the end of this chapter:

1. Which of the following buttons from the **Physics** panel is used to retain the particles at the surface of emitter for their total lifespan?

   (a) **Newtonion** (b) **No**
   (c) **Keyed** (d) **Boid**

2. The __________ particle system has limited artificial intelligence.

3. Parameters in the __________ panel are used to cache the emission data to avoid repetitive calculation of particles.

4. The __________ slider in the **Emission** panel is used to specify the lifespan of the particles in frames.

5. If you choose the **Volume** button from the **Emit From** area, particles will be emitted from the surface of all the faces of the object. (T/F)

Review Questions

Answer the following questions:

1. Which of the following panels includes parameters to bake the data?

   (a) **Physics** (b) **Render**
   (c) **Display** (d) **Cache**

2. The __________ slider in the **Emission** panel is used to specify the number of particles emitted from the object.

3. The __________ button is used to create fake user for the particle settings created.

4. If you choose the **Verts** button from the **Emit From** area, particles will be emitted from the vertices of the object. (T/F)

5. The **Catche** panel also includes parameters to bake the data. (T/F)

EXERCISE

Exercise 1

Simulate a rainy scene using particles, refer to Figure 11-37.

(Expected time: 15 min)

Figure 11-37 Rain simulation

Answers to Self-Evaluation Test

1. b, **2.** Boids, **3. Cache, 4. Lifetime, 5.** F

Index

Symbols

A

B

C

D

T

U

V

W

X

Z

CAD/CAM/CIM/GIS/ANIMATION/CIVIL BOOKS

by **Prof. Sham Tickoo** (Purdue University, USA and Autodesk Authorised Author)

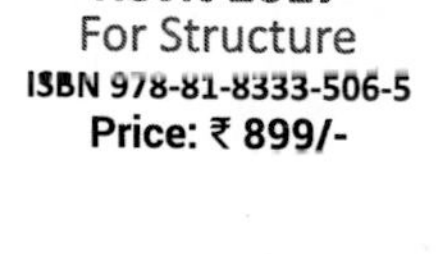

Exploring Autodesk
Revit 2017
For Structure
ISBN 978-81-8333-506-5
Price: ₹ 899/-

Exploring Autodesk
Revit 2018
For Architecture
ISBN 978-93-8655-172-6
Price: ₹ 999/-

Exploring Autodesk
Revit 2018
For MEP
ISBN 978-93-8655-173-3
Price: ₹ 799/-

Exploring Autodesk
Revit 2018
For Structure
ISBN 978-93-8655-174-0
Price: ₹ 799/-

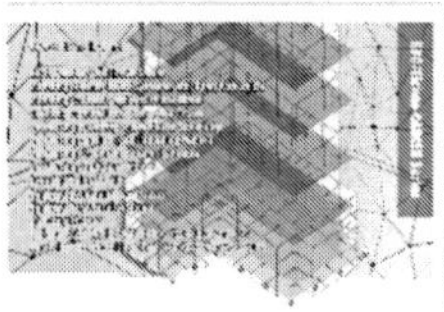

Exploring Autodesk
Revit 2019
For Architecture
ISBN 978-93-8817-633-0
Price: ₹ 1199/-

Exploring Autodesk
Revit 2019
For MEP
ISBN 978-93-8817-635-4
Price: ₹ 899/-

Exploring Autodesk
Revit 2019
For Structure
ISBN 978-93-8817-634-7
Price: ₹ 899/-

Exploring
RISA-3D 14.0
ISBN 978-93-8655-108-5
Price: ₹ 499/-

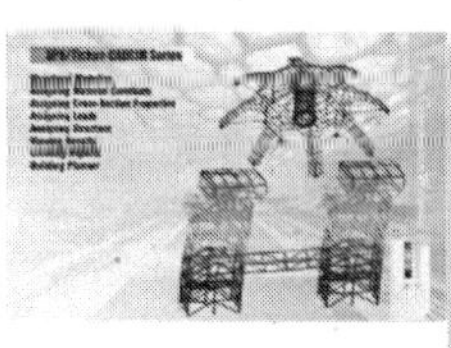

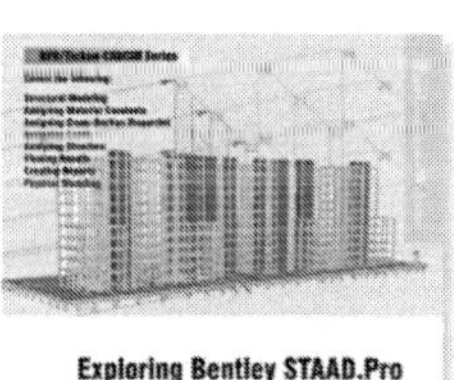

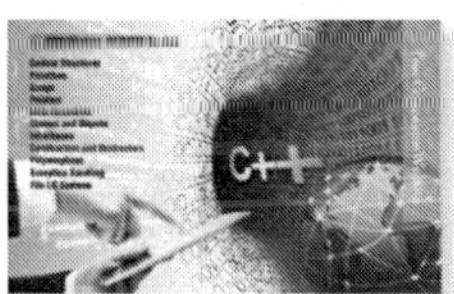

Exploring AutoCAD Raster Design 2017
ISBN 978-93-8655-109-2
Price: ₹ 499/-

Exploring Bentley STAAD.Pro (Select Series 6)
ISBN 978-93-8655-110-8
Price: ₹ 599/-

Exploring Bentley STAAD.Pro (Connect Edition)
ISBN 978-93-8728-414-2
Price: ₹ 499/-

Introduction to C++ Programming
ISBN 978-93-8655-116-0
Price: ₹ 699/-

Available on **www.bpbonline.com** and all leading book stores.

#1 Publisher of Computer Books | 62 Years of Excellence | OVER 90 Million Books Sold Worldwide